OLIVER CROMWELL
SOLDIER

OLIVER CROMWELL SOLDIER

The Military Life
of a Revolutionary at War

❧❧❧❧❧❧

ALAN MARSHALL

BRASSEY'S

First published in 2004 by Brassey's

An imprint of **Chrysalis** Books Group plc

Brassey's
The Chrysalis Building, Bramley Road, London W10 6SP
www.chrysalisbooks.co.uk

Distributed in North America by Casemate Publishing,
2114 Darby Road, Havertown, PA 19083, USA

Alan Marshall has asserted his moral right to be identified
as the author of this work.

Library of Congress Cataloging-in-Publication Data available

British Library Cataloguing-in-Publication Data:
a catalogue record for this book is available
from the British Library

ISBN 1 85753 343 7

Illustrations
Portraits of Cromwell, Essex, Manchester,
Fairfax, Ormonde and Lambert are reproduced by
courtesy of the National Portrait Gallery, London. All
other images are from the author's collection

Edited and designed by DAG Publications Ltd
Designed by David Gibbons
Edited by Michael Boxall. Layout by Meredith MacArdle
Cartography by Anthony A. Evans

Printed in Great Britain

CONTENTS

LIST OF MAPS

INTRODUCTION

'If you wage war, do it energetically and with severity. This is the
only way to make it shorter and consequently less inhuman.'
– Napoleon Bonaparte

'There have been few persons,' wrote an early biographer of Oliver
Cromwell in 1698, 'upon whose actions so many different sentiments have
passed, as upon those of Oliver Cromwell; some advancing his Courage &
Reputation to the height, others on the contrary, depressing them as low,
and not allowing that he had any thing praiseworthy in his Conduct
attributing all to Hypocrisie and ambition, asserting that he had hopes and
expeditions of raising himself to that Grandeur where unto he after
arrived, many years before he had attained it.'[1]

Few men in the past have attracted more enthusiasts and detractors
than Oliver Cromwell, and there have naturally been countless biographies
and studies of Cromwell written since his death in September 1658. As
Burton noted, some of these writers have taken great care to praise openly
his many virtues as a hero, whilst others have plainly sought to put weight
on his numerous faults and vices as a villain. The present reader may
therefore enquire: why add yet another volume to this accumulation of
books? There is a simple enough answer.

In the first place Cromwell's career, like history itself, has always been
(and doubtless always will be) subject to fresh interpretation. In the end,
Cromwell remains a figure who will be subject to endless debate by successive generations of scholars, even though the essential outlines of his military and political career are well known. Whether he was one of history's
great captains is a debatable point, as we shall see, but his role as the
greatest Englishman of his era is probably unquestioned. There is, it
seems, no end to Cromwell, and the career of this colossus of the seventeenth century continues to both fascinate and trouble us.

Secondly, the focus of this particular book is Oliver Cromwell's military
career. Surprisingly enough, there have been very few studies of Cromwell
that have concentrated solely on his generalship. Indeed Lt-Col. T. S.
Baldock wrote one of the most detailed studies of Cromwell as a general in

1899. Since then, few historians have analysed the depth or degree of this Englishman's so-called 'genius' for war.[2] For Cromwell the soldier, unlike Cromwell the politician, we are generally left with the traditional portrait of the blunt and naive man, who without any real background in soldiering and military affairs suddenly discovered, in the course of civil war, an intuitive flair for managing men and a natural talent for warfare. Indeed, as one recent biographer has noted, Cromwell's soldiering, on the surface at least, seems to be the 'least controversial aspect of his reputation' – a reputation that, even at the best of times, remains studded with controversy.[3]

It is, perhaps, time to re-open the question of Cromwell as a military leader. If his military career as a heroic general in his day needs some context, and in itself justifies an examination, then, arguably, much of Cromwell's success (or notoriety) as a public figure in the 1640s and 1650s cannot be really understood without realising that it was built upon his ostensible military accomplishments. Whether Cromwell really was a great captain of war, as some historians have claimed, or merely, as one contemporary statesman called him, a 'lucky fool' (and lucky generals tend to be successful), triumph in war undoubtedly made his name. There is also little doubt that his soldiering became as prominent as it did because of the popular Press and the art of the day: in parts of the contemporary Press, news of Cromwell as a soldier sold very well indeed.[4] As a result, Cromwell's apparent military significance was not doubted in his day. But was this success exaggerated? As we shall see, in order to answer this question, this volume has at its core an attempt to reconsider Cromwell's qualities and defects as a soldier and commander in the fields of war from 1642 to 1651, as well as his role in the battles and strategies of the British Civil Wars.

Oddly enough, however, we begin Oliver Cromwell's military story where he began himself – in obscurity. For the Cromwell who embarked on the Civil Wars in 1642 began his military life as a plain and rather anonymous captain of horse, who saw little, if any, action in the course of the first great battle of the war at Edgehill. Only with his transformation into a colonel of cavalry, as he shaped his own regiment of horse in 1643 (they later acquired the nickname of 'Ironsides'), did Cromwell's military career really begin to get underway. As the regiment and their colonel fought their way through numerous local campaigns, skirmishes and battles, their reputation grew steadily. Cromwell's rise to become a lieutenant-general of the cavalry in the Army of the Eastern Association was the next phase in this process. In this army, and under the command of the Earl of Manchester, Cromwell organised the cavalry, fought in some of the major battles of the Civil War, and was eventually to become one of the most prominent supporters of the establishment of a successful strategy through the creation of the New Model Army. He was afterwards to become a significant member of that force in its campaigns of 1645–46. In the later stages of his military career, he became a full general who fought (and won) four controversial campaigns, and was victorious in three major battles of his own. His military success as Captain-General of the English Republic finally enabled him to reach the dizzy heights of Head of State from 1653 until his death in 1658, although he claimed (at least, publicly) that he took up the latter role most unwillingly.

Militarily, as we shall see, Cromwell was ever, by inclination, a cavalry soldier, and although his greater strategic sense is often debatable (arguably, he made many errors of grand strategy), his tactical use of cavalry in particular was remarkable – all the more so for its seemingly intuitive nature. The factors that made Cromwell such a good leader of men were his authority over his troops, his charisma, and his soldier's zeal for training and battle. Ultimately, he was only given three real opportunities to command more than 10,000 men in battle, but he did achieve success on all three occasions. These were at Preston (1648), Dunbar (1650) and Worcester (1651). He certainly showed superior generalship in these battles, and his eagerness to engage in wars of annihilation marks him out from contemporaries. The controversial Irish campaign of 1649 illustrates Cromwell's other, darker side. In the course of this campaign, Cromwell seems to have lost control not only of himself but also of his men, who, at the sieges of Drogheda and Wexford, perpetrated massacres that have led to his moral condemnation in some circles ever since. Although, in a contemporary Irish military context, these actions were merely part of the cycle of violence that struck that country from 1641, Cromwell did his reputation no good at all by inflicting them on his enemies. Cromwell's other role – that of the military politician – is arguably as significant as any of his actions on the field of battle. It has its dark side, but will only be briefly touched upon here. In politics, his position as a soldier gave him authority in the chaotic political world of his day, and he frequently used his military power to intervene in the political life of the country.

Oliver Cromwell was unquestionably the phenomenon of his age. He has remained a controversial figure ever since his death in September 1658, and not merely for his military actions. He has been seen as a political and religious visionary, regicide, Lord Protector, military politician, proto-fascist, and New Model Soldier. All of these versions of Cromwell have passed under the eye of historical scholarship. The popular and academic work on Cromwell's career is legion and continues to grow every year. Each age, it has been said, gets the Cromwell it wants. Here, it is Cromwell the soldier and commander that we will explore. We will begin by investigating his origins, and his family and personal background, then we will briefly examine the causes of the war that broke out in 1642 and investigate the nature of warfare as it appeared to the soldiers on the ground. Only then may we begin to examine Cromwell's early battles, and his generalship in the major battles in which he had a part – Marston Moor, Second Newbury, Naseby, Preston, the Irish campaign, Dunbar, and the 'crowning mercy' of Worcester in 1651 that ended his military career in the field.

My thanks are given to the following for their assistance in this work: Rod Dymott, John Lee and David Gibbons. Catherine Robinson, Elaine Chalus, John Newsinger, Fiona Montgomery, Anne Dowle and Margaret Collins were of great help, as were the staff at numerous libraries and archives. Lastly, my special thanks go to Claire Tyler for her patience.

A. M.

CHAPTER I

ORIGINS

'... he smelleth the battle afar off, the thunder of the captains,
and the shouting.' – *Job* 39:25

FOUNDATIONS

Oliver Cromwell was born in Huntingdon on 25 April 1599 and was the only
surviving son of Robert Cromwell (1560–1617), himself a younger son of Sir
Henry Cromwell of Hinchingbrooke, and Elizabeth Steward (1579–1654).
The origins and social status of the Cromwell family in the Early Modern
England of the day began with the rise of Morgan ap Williams and of his rela-
tive Thomas Cromwell, Earl of Essex. Although the details of the family's
earlier rise are too familiar to be more than sketched here, suffice to say that
the future soldier was a descendant of the enterprising Williams who had
hitched his star, so to speak, to one of the more notorious ministers of Henry
VIII – Thomas Cromwell, the architect, in many ways, of the English Reformation. He had also changed his name to Cromwell.[1]

Whatever his ancestors might have been, Robert and Elizabeth
Cromwell's son proved to be English to the core. He was a member of a
family that had raised itself through the Tudor, Elizabethan and Stuart
courts with great aplomb, and he was, unsurprisingly, to become a person
of some significance in his community. The family had continued to rise
mainly through the activities of Richard Cromwell (at the court of Henry
VIII) and his son, and Oliver Cromwell's grandfather, Sir Henry Cromwell.
Social advance had brought in its wake money and, in the latter's case, a
knighthood from Queen Elizabeth in 1563 and enough wealth to be given
the nickname 'The Golden Knight'. It was his riches that created the lavish
surroundings of Hinchingbrooke House in Cambridgeshire. His second son
was Robert Cromwell, Oliver's father, who would have had to be content
with what was passed to him by his father and his elder brother. Despite this,
the branch of the family established by Robert had a plentiful supply of
cousins and other relations to provide the fluid of patronage and marriage
upon which much local and national politics ran. More often than not it was
whom one knew, or the people to whom one was related, that produced the
greatest benefits to any young man's career at this time.

Oliver Cromwell's own social status was undoubtedly significant to him in his military life. In a speech in September 1654 he noted, 'I was by birth a gentleman, living neither in any considerable height, nor yet in obscurity.'[2] Yet the fact that he began life as the son of the younger son of a knight meant that he had already acquired that gentlemanly status that meant so much to the society surrounding him. He would naturally enter the war as an officer, yet his social status had been under some threat in the 1620s and 1630s – and, as we will see, this was a fact of great importance for the later soldier.

His father, Robert Cromwell, remained throughout his adult life an unexceptional urban gentleman with a town house and an income of around £300 per annum. He had been educated at Cambridge, although like many of his contemporaries he took no degree, and finished his education at the Inns of Court. On returning home, he had undertaken most of the gentlemanly pursuits of the day to no great effect, although he occupied the position of Justice of the Peace and other local offices, and retained just enough family influence to become a one-term Member of Parliament for Huntingdon in 1593. He was in the end a very minor figure, a sober man of religious duty and a good neighbour, so that truly, as he himself pointed out in his will, 'man's life in his sound and perfect health is like a bubble of water', and we hear very little ill of him.[3] His death, on 24 June 1617, left only a small inheritance for his wife, his only surviving son and his seven daughters – which, in this large family, with most of them female and in need of dowries, would have caused his heir considerable problems. The relationship between father and son remains suitably obscure, as one might expect, illuminated only by the fact that it was Robert Cromwell who had placed Oliver under Dr Thomas Beard; as will be seen below, the latter's educating hand may well have had some effect on his pupil.

Relations between mother and son may perhaps have been more significant. Elizabeth Cromwell, née Steward, not only was well connected, but also lived to a mature old age. She was, according to some sources, a woman of good judgement and good sense.[4] Certainly, she appears to have had a close and loving relationship with her son, and Oliver paid her much attention in the course of his life.

In the fullness of time, the heir of Robert Cromwell began to show every sign of becoming one of the declining Early Modern gentry of which historians were once so fond. Nevertheless, the failing influence of the Cromwell family in the county lasted just long enough to launch Oliver into a political career – albeit an initially abortive one – as MP for Huntingdon. He could also count on numerous relatives who were able to help at a later date in this career, but over the next few years he faced several problems, not the least of which were financial. Indeed, the 1620s and 1630s have been discovered by Cromwell's biographers to have been a time of trial that brought his problems of social status into acute focus. A change in the form of government in the Borough of Huntingdon in 1630 left him out in the cold, and his 'disgraceful and unseemly speeches' landed him in trouble with the Privy Council.[5] This affair managed to damage not only his local standing, but also his honour and whatever friendships he had in the town, so much so that, seeing no way forward, he decided to sell up and move on. By 1631 he had sold much of his inheritance from his father for a lump sum and had taken up residence in St Ives, where he effectively became a yeoman farmer, whatever his later claims of self-importance. The unsettled Oliver subsequently moved on a few times thereafter.

In social terms, this gradual decline in status and the near-loss of gentlemanly rank was of some significance for Cromwell. It was partly resolved in 1636 with the death of his mother's brother and his coming into this inheritance, which at least gave him an income of some £300 per annum. By 1640 he was enjoying an annual income of some £500 – which made him somewhat better off than his father but still placed him at the lower end of the gentleman's scale.

Why would Cromwell's being a gentleman be so important to him? The contemporary publication *The Gentleman's Calling* (1660) listed four characteristics of the gentleman – wealth and authority, 'an ingenious and refined education', 'reputation and esteem', and 'time' or leisure.[6] These characteristics, and the general culture surrounding gentlemen in Early Modern England, gave such men their moral authority in society and established their moral worth to others. It was something that Cromwell would need in his military career. A decline in social status such as Cromwell experienced, while it could happen even in the best-established gentry families, was undoubtedly a difficult burden and was to leave him, as John Morrill has noted, with, at best, a somewhat forced and 'brittle' social standing. Alongside Cromwell's political failures in Huntingdon in 1630, this seems even to have aggravated a personal religious crisis in these years.[7] Yet this period of apparent social failure would also give him a good understanding of the men he was later to recruit and lead into battle, first in his troop and then in his regiment, as for a good few years at least he had been one of them. While he remained always willing to stress his gentlemanly status on many occasions thereafter, he was nonetheless also willing to defend such men as 'plain' Captain Margery in 1643. In the war, Cromwell was to prove one of the few who were prepared to see beyond the social status of an individual in favour of his relationship to the cause, and to use those who were eager to fight, whatever their background. As he noted:

'It may be it provokes some spirits to see such plain men made captains of horse. It had been well that men of honour and birth had entered into these employments, but why do they not appear? Who would have hindered them? But seeing it was necessary the work must go on, better plain men than none, but best to have men patient of wants, faithful and conscientious in the employment.'[8]

It was an image, more or less, of himself. Moreover, in his famous conversation with John Hampden after Edgehill, he also claimed to have said:

'Your troopers, said I, are most of them old decayed serving men and tapsters, and such like fellows, and, said I, their troopers are gentleman's sons, younger sons, persons of quality: do you think that the spirits of such base and mean fellows will ever be able to encounter gentlemen that have honour, courage and resolution in them? Truly I pressed him in this manner conscientiously, and truly I did tell him, You must get men of a spirit ... of a spirit that is like to go as far as a gentleman will go, or else I am sure you will be beaten still ... He was a wise and worthy person, and he did think that I talked a good notion but an impracticable one ... [but] I raised such men as had the fear of God before them, and made some conscience of what they did ... [and] wherever they engaged the enemy they beat them continually.'[9]

As the head of a household in these formative years, what sort of man was Oliver Cromwell? Later tales of the wildness and follies of youth seem to have been somewhat exaggerated, mainly by Royalist propagandists intent upon making merry with the facts to suit their politics. Yet there may have been some truth in such rumours. No man is ever free of the follies and sins of youth. Even Cromwell admitted to some such sins – although, as with most of those who had undergone the experience of Calvinistic conversion (which we shall shortly explore), he retained a heightened sense of what to us would seem like minor follies: 'Oh, I lived in and loved darkness,' he said, 'and hated the light. I was a chief, the chief of sinners. This is true; I hated godliness, yet God had mercy on me.'[10] Afterwards, noted one of his earliest biographers, 'he became more solid and considerate, so that in a while he was as remarkable for his Sobriety, as before for his Rudeness and Vaniety.'[11]

There are very few clues to the future soldier in Cromwell's early life. Certainly, his personal humour and grim charm always seem to have been of the basic rough-and-ready sort, and were to appeal to the men he led. One of them, Captain Hodgson, noted on the Scottish campaign of 1650 that 'Oliver loved an innocent jest',[12] and there was always a certain penchant for horseplay, particularly at times of tension in his life. Burton tells the story – and it may be no more than this – of Cromwell's love of diverting 'The robust and sturdy soldiers … by making them sometimes throw a burning coal into each others Boots, or to fling cushions at one another's heads.'[13] This somewhat grim humour reappears in the tales of Cromwell and Henry Ireton inking each other's faces with pens after they signed the death warrant of Charles I. What is clear is that Cromwell certainly lacked the witty repartee and fashionable clothes of the noble courtier of the day. Sir Philip Warwick, who claimed to have observed him in the Parliament of 1640, condescendingly noted a man who was

'… very ordinary apparelled … a plain cloth-sute, which seemed to have bin made by an ill country taylor; his linen was plain, and not very clean; and I remember of a speck or two of blood upon his little band … his stature was of good size … his countenance swoln and reddich, his voice sharp and untunable, and his eloquence full of fervor.'[14]

Cromwell apparently enjoyed the rough-and-tumble of physical games, notably at Cambridge, where he allegedly neglected his studies for such pursuits. Again, this should not be dismissed entirely as Royalist propaganda, for throughout his life he remained a man with a keen eye for horseflesh and hunting, and when Lord Protector was the recipient of many gifts of hawks and horses. Indeed, hunting became one of his major passions, and no doubt provided useful knowledge for the future cavalry commander, who needed to know horses as well as the lie of the land.

His marriage to Elisabeth Bouchier, the daughter of a substantial London fur trader and leather dresser, on 22 August 1620 seems to have

provided that family stability and love which was also one of the foundations of his complex character, as well as helping to establish him further in
the Essex gentry. In personal terms, she was never very far away from his
thoughts. In the end, we can say that his education and family background
were probably no worse than many another of his day, and in his years of
obscurity he remained – at least, on the surface – an apparently plain man:
with his rustic clothes and careless manner, he was a fairly typical 'honest
Englishman', with all the simple, gentlemanly attributes of the Old School.

As to physique, aside from Warwick's description we may also cite that
by John Maidstone, one of his servants when Cromwell was Lord
Protector, who noted that

> 'His body was wel[l] compact and strong, his stature under 6 foot
> (I believe about two inches); his head so shaped, as you might see it
> a storehouse and a shop of both a vast treasury of natural parts. His
> temper exceedingly fiery, as I have known, but the flame of it kept
> downe, for the most part, or soon all ayed with thos[e] moral
> endowments he had. He was naturally compassionate towards
> objects in distress, even to an effeminate measure; though God had
> made him a heart, wherein was left very little roome for any fear,
> but what was due to himselfe, of which there was a large propor-
> tion; yet did he exceed in tendernesse toward sufferers. A larger
> soul, I thinke, hath seldome dwelt in a house of clay, than his was.'[15]

The Reverend James Fraser, a Scot visiting London in the 1650s, also
noted of Cromwell that

> 'His stature is tall & statly and pretty lusty ... his constitution
> Sanguin a reed in his face a high Roman nose & a fierce Sparking
> eye and agil active body & a strong temprament his posture in
> walkeing was stout a long step ... [with] his hand upon his sword,
> the other often upon his breast, his diet temperat being an enemy to
> ease & excess his head not great Chestnut haire & short his beard
> also reedish.'[16]

As to his 'habit & Cloaths, he was no friend to fashiones, nor the prodigall
vaingloriouenes of Garbs, he went plain, and grave, in his habit more like
a Senatour that a Souldior ... I never saw him alter one Cullour of Cloath
it was darke nearest black and commonly called the Protectors collor.'[17]

The satirists were quick to pick on Cromwell's complexion once his fame had begun to spread, and his nose was often a subject of ridicule, being in truth both fiery and large. Satirists linked this to the alleged previous occupation of his family as brewers and his own (alleged) drinking habits, so that 'Copper Nose' was to keep Royalist jesters in business throughout the later Civil War. Ironically, as one historian has noted, this mockery also gave Cromwell 'a greater role in print than he had in political reality', thereby raising his profile in the process.[18] Underneath this appearance, however, as both Maidstone and Fraser hint, lurked a strange and turbulently passionate man. While outwardly 'he seemd to have little of vainglory in him turning his darke Lanthorn to himself, his closeness being allwayes such that this great Politician walkt invisible, others stood in the light to him, but he in ye dark to all.'[19] It was this darkness of character that made Cromwell's motivations for his actions in the world obscure, not to mention his soldiering. These difficulties revolve around the all-important question of his religion.

RELIGION

If the young Cromwell was not decidedly Puritan in his youth, he came to be seen as such. The meaning of the term 'Puritan' remains the subject of complex argument amongst historians. David Underdown neatly defined it as relating to 'religious idealists who strained towards the godly Reformation that had been so nearly accomplished in the reign of the much admired ... Queen Elizabeth.'[20] This sums up Cromwell's position very well: he was a seeker after reformation, not just in the institutional sense, but the spiritual reformation of souls – and English souls in particular. Indeed, it is very difficult – though perhaps not surprisingly so, with our modern-day penchant for arranging people in categories – to place Cromwell in denominational terms. Richard Baxter was to note that 'he [did] not openly profess what opinion he was of himself, but the most that he said for any was for Anabaptism and Antinomianism, which he usually seemed to own.' More importantly, we do know that Cromwell was also for 'liberty of conscience, which was the common interest in which they [the men in his regiment] did unite.'[21] Cromwell vigorously defended his officers and men when many accused them of being too extreme in their religious beliefs, being regarded by many as Anabaptists or worse, although he was also capable of punishing those who went too far. In any case, as Christopher Hill has pointed out, denominational labels in the period are all too obscure, and more often than not were labels foisted on religious groupings by persecution or dislike: '"sects" … would have resisted any sectarian labelling … Such labelling was done by enemies,' so that in the end the descriptive terms used by contemporaries remain clumsy ones.[22] More important, perhaps, were the more subtle 'lines of division' – those theological distinctions between Protestants.[23]

Seventeenth-century Protestantism had its origins in the Elizabethan settlement of the Church in 1559. This had, under Elizabeth's moderate hand, created a broadly consensual Church of England with a Calvinist background, although therein lay some complex theological variations. The primacy of the Bible, as well as the search for God through piety and discipline, were just two of its distinguishing characteristics, although, with a Church structure inextricably linked with the State's intent on order and conformity, any dissent from the Church's official teachings could have political implications. Other difficulties occurred over the place of the epis-copacy and of religious ceremony in the Church structure. A belief that these could be too 'popish' in outlook came to feed a myth that the Protes-tant religion could be all too easily undermined from within by 'popish forms'. Ultimately, a minority of believers whispered that this settlement and all its subsequent creeds remained a botched reformation, and that a more purified Church was needed if the nation were to reach godly perfec-tion. If this were not to be achieved within the established 'Church of confusion' then separation, both spiritual and physical, was the answer. The moderates, of course, wanted reform from within, and looked to the King, as Head of the Church, to achieve this.[24] In the end, 'Puritanism' became to the establishment a contemporary term of abuse; the separatists themselves were more inclined to employ the word 'godly'. Of course, these questions and divisions were not just matters of form, of theology, or even of politics, but were essential to the fate of the individual immortal soul and an inherent part of a system of belief that dominated the minds of the men and women of the day.

Amongst the more radical elements, there was some continued theo-logical disputation that came to be of primary importance to men such as Oliver Cromwell – differences over the nature of the questions of election and salvation, problems over the use of ceremony in church services, and a varied dislike of the unfortunately more popular habits of the English, such as plays, bear-baiting, and other sports. These, indeed, seemed to constitute obvious evidence to the godly that spiritual reformation had not gone far enough. Their ideal came to be an attempt to create a New Jerusalem, a godly commonwealth upon earth, filled with a pious and morally sober people, a godly nation, aware of its special nature as the new chosen people, with the 'saints' – God's 'chosen' – in the vanguard.

In theological terms, there was also increasing conflict between ideas of predestination and free will in order to reach salvation. The idea of predestination in particular was as significant to Cromwell as it was to many others at the time. Indeed, it was central to Calvinist doctrine. In effect, predestination expressed the view that some individuals were, from the very beginning of time, predestined to be saved (the saints), whilst others (the majority) were predestined to be damned. The catechism lodged in the Genevan Bible printed in England (and undoubtedly closely read by men such as Cromwell) made this essential theological point clear:

'Question: Are not all ordained unto eternal life?

'Answer: Some are vessels of wrath ordained unto destruction, as others are vessels of mercy prepared to glory … all men have in themselves sin which deserveth no less, and therefore the mercy of God is wonderful in that he vouchsafeth to save some of that sinful race and to bring them the knowledge of the truth.'[25]

Faith and good works, therefore, had little to do with the eventual destination or salvation of the individual in this seemingly harshest of all theological doctrines, although it was beholden upon the godly to do good as such activities were the 'markes and effects infallible of our predestination.'[26] The real means of becoming aware of being one of the 'chosen' was through that spiritual crisis that each of the saints had to undergo. Cromwell's own spiritual trial was to have consequences not only for himself, but also for many of those who were to come into contact with him. Indeed, it was arguably the most formative period in his life and psychology, the foundation of his later success as a soldier. Yet it would be fraught with doubt.

CONVERSION

In general, the Calvinist conversion experience had some common characteristics: a growing sense of despair and dissatisfaction with the form of life the individual was leading, the inspiration or fear being drawn from the words of preachers and others; a round of endless prayer; and a 'seeking for the Lord'. Taken together, these would almost always lead to a psychological crisis that would precipitate a new beginning for the soul, a new doctrine of assurance, albeit with a continued belief that one still needed to secure salvation via a searching of the inner soul and the scriptures, as well as by following religious duties closely, and by being active in the world. For to be active in the world, and to carry out a reforming nature by rooting out sin and creating the New Jerusalem, was part of the pattern of this experience. In the end, the conversion experience remained a 'dark night of the soul' – a gradual conviction of the sinful nature of the individual that through much internal hardship would result in the conviction that the individual was one of the blessed.

Oliver Cromwell had been treated for what in modern parlance would be called 'depression' in London in 1628, having consulted Dr Theodore Mayerne, who described his condition as 'valde melancholicus'.[27] A somewhat dubious later source also claimed that Cromwell's own doctor, Simcott, stated that he had frequently been called out to Cromwell at 'such unseasonable hours, very many times, upon a strong fancy, which made him believe he was then dying.'[28] In any case, he noted that his patient was always a 'most splenetic man, and had fancies about the cross' in Huntingdon, even telling people that he would be 'the greatest man (not mentioning the word King) in this kingdom.'[29] Whether believable or not, such fanciful visions are evidence that Cromwell was undergoing some sort of spiritual crisis in the years 1628–1630. Looking back in 1638, he was able to see his experience thus:

'Yet to honour God by declaring what He hath done for my soul ... Truly, then, this I find: That he giveth springs in a dry and barren wilderness where no water is. I live (you know where) in Mesheck, which they say signifies *Prolonging*; in Kedar, which signifies *Blackness*: yet the Lord forsaketh me not. Though He do prolong, yet He will (I trust) bring me to His tabernacle, to His resting place. My soul is with the congregation of the first born, my body rests in hope, and if here I may honour my God either by doing or by suffering, I shall be most glad.

'Truly no poor creature hath more cause to put himself in the cause of his God than I. I have had plentiful wages beforehand, and I am sure I shall never earn the least mite. The Lord accept me in His Son, and give me to walk in the light, and give us to walk in the light, as He is the light. He it is that enlighteneth our blackness, our darkness. I dare not say, He hideth His face from me. He giveth me to see light in His light. One beam in a dark place hath exceeding much refreshment in it. Blessed be His name for shining upon such a dark a heart as mine! You know what my manner of life hath been. Oh, I lived in and loved darkness, and hated the light. I was a chief, the chief of sinners. This is true; I hated godliness, yet God had mercy on me. O the riches of His mercy! Praise Him for me, pray for me, that He who hath begun a good work would perfect it to the day of Christ.'[30]

It is difficult to overstate the importance of this most revealing of all Cromwellian documents, for it leads us into the heart of the Cromwellian mystery. It influenced much that occurred in later years, not least in Cromwell's military career. In fact, it was a conversion that was ultimately to be the greatest experience of his life, as it gave him a profound understanding of his place in the world in relation to God. It was a conversion he thought undeserved; yet he was saved none the less, to enjoy a 'unilateral covenant in which God undertakes all, and the poor soul nothing.'[31] He was to refer to it time and again as a comfort: 'I bless God I have been inured to difficulties, and I never found God failing when I trusted in him; I can laugh and sing in my heart when I speak of these things.'[32] Cromwell became not only a religious man through this experience, but also a man to whom religion was everything.

His education may well have had some role to play in this. Cromwell's university education at Sidney Sussex, Cambridge, in 1616 was soon cut short by the death of his father on 24 June 1617, but his early education under the Huntingdon schoolmaster Thomas Beard has come in for some exploration by historians. While, as John Morrill has shown, the influence of Beard may well have been exaggerated, he was the author of a best-selling book that clarified the role of Providence in daily life. At the grammar school at Huntington, this doctrine would have been widely preached to the pupils, and Cromwell, like many others, seems to have taken it on board. In *The Theatre of God's Judgements*, Beard reviewed the means by which Christians could be responsive to the will of God. True knowledge could be gained by the constant reading of ideas on moral responsibility. Although the actions of God were nearly always unfathomable to man, many examples of His Providence existed. Life itself was an educative theatre, a process of continuous revelation, where the wicked were punished and the good naturally received God's just reward.[33] Oliver Cromwell was never what one could term an intellectual, and he left no final testament to 'those strange windings and turnings of providence' that were the main basis of his thought, but, although these remained often cloudy and obscure, he was willing to believe that what Providence disposed he could only accept.[34]

In a letter to Robert Hammond on 25 November 1648, Cromwell revealed further significant aspects of his ideological or theological view of the world. He noted his previous experiences as 'having a body of sin and death, but I thank God, through Jesus Christ our Lord there is no condemnation, though much infirmity, and I wait for the redemption. And in this poor condition I obtain mercy, and sweet consolation though the Spirit.' He also charged Hammond to note outward dispensations, in particular 'remarkable providences, and appearances of the Lord. His presence hath been amongst us, and by the light of His countenance we have prevailed.' Even so, the nature and trials of daily life were not to be thought of as heavy, even if they felt so at the time, for

> 'If your Father laid it upon you, He intended neither. He is the Father of lights, from whom comes every good and perfect gift, who of His own will begot us, and bade us count it all joy when such things befall us; they being for an exercise of faith and patience, where by in the end we shall be made perfect.'[35]

Above all there was the working of God in the world:

> 'If thou wilt seek to know the mind of God in all that chain of Providence, where by God bought thee thither, and that person [the King] to thee; how, before and since, God has ordered him, and affairs concerning him; and then tell me, whether there be not some glorious and high meaning in all this, above what thou hast yet attained? And, laying aside thy fleshly reason, seek of the Lord to teach thee what that is; and He will do it … My dear friend, let us look into providences; surely they mean somewhat. They hang so together; have been so constant, so clear and unclouded. Malice, swoln malice against God's people, now called Saints, to root out their name; and yet they, by Providence, having arms, and therein blessed with defence and more.'

To Cromwell, prayer was yet another safe measure by which God's will could be known. Keith Thomas has outlined three forms of prayer in this period. The first was petitionary prayer – asking for material things. The second was non-petitionary prayer – worshipping and giving thanks that made strength of the Christian's 'own piety and devotion in the process'.[36] Thirdly, there was 'the type of prayer which helped men take decisions in difficult situations'.[37] Such prayer gave a focus to problems and so brought solutions in its wake.

Prayer thus became almost a part of a divination process, enabling men to seek supernatural guidance in their choice of actions.

Finally, but not least important to Cromwell, was the Bible. This was as much a book of revelation of the workings of God in the world as it was a fundamental part of his everyday life and speech. The Bible was the foundation for him, as well as others, of nearly all of his thinking, for it was the Word of God. He naturally read the Scriptures with diligence, his letters and speeches were saturated with its words, and the Bible was seen in revelatory terms that provided, to some degree at least, answers to those who wished to understand the daily motivation for their actions. It gave Cromwell absolute confidence that God would never neglect his creation.

The Bible was also possibly the most significant of all of the military texts from which Cromwell may have learnt. The battles fought by the children of Israel gave him access not only to metaphorical tactics, but also to some greater strategic sense, in that God's working in the world could be literally seen if one looked. If God provided in the heat of battle, as He had done for His people in Biblical texts, He could do it now – and who was Cromwell to gainsay it? Others were also aware of this. Richard Bernard in 1629 had written a book that he called *The Bible-Battells: or the Sacred Art Military*. In this, Bernard argued that real Christian soldiers should eschew tales of 'heathen commanders', such as Alexander or Caesar, and instead choose to read the 'right art militarie indeed' to be found in the Bible.[38] In his exposition on the military aspects of the Old Testament, he claimed that such studies would 'make your Armies strong and yourselves victorious'.[39] Thus the Bible was a military as well as a sacred text, and full of general advice to soldiers. This was a matter even taken up in the Civil War with the publication in 1643 of the *Souldier's Pocket Bible*, plainly showing the usefulness of the texts to warfare. While John Morrill has pointed out Cromwell's ruminations on the matter of Gideon in 1648, there are many other hints that the Israelite heroes also provided some practical guidance to Cromwell in his military career.[40] If they did nothing else, they provided him with heroic role models, who showed him how to act in battle.

Furthermore, the Psalms, ostensibly written by King David (with whom we know Oliver did later identify), provided a great comfort. One contemporary noted that, towards the end of his life, Cromwell

'… caused one of his Gentlemen often to read the tenth Chapter of Matthew's Gospel; and twice a day himself rehearsed the 71 Psalm of David, which hath so near a relation to his Fortune and to his

Affairs, as one would believe it had been a Prophesie purposely dictated by the holy Ghost for him; or else that this great Personage was the Mortal Figure of that great Favourite of God, who had done so many marvellous things.'[41]

As Paul notes, the parallels between the Israelite hero-king as the servant of the Lord and Cromwell's own conception of himself as divinely commissioned became a key to his sense of vocation: 'I am as a wonder unto many; but thou art my strong refuge.'[42] The Psalms themselves provide much insight into Cromwell's thought throughout his career. They were, for example, frequently quoted and ruminated upon by Cromwell in times of danger. Psalm 110 was of some significance to him, while he noted that Psalm 46 was 'a rare Psalm for a Christian' and, one might add, for a soldier:

'He maketh wars to cease unto the end of the earth; he breaketh the bow, and cutteth the spear in sunder; he burneth the chariot in the fire.

'Be still, and know that I am God: I will be exalted among the heathen. I will be exalted in the earth.

'The Lord of hosts is with us; the God of Jacob is our refuge.'[43]

At Dunbar in 1650 it was to be Psalm 68 that he quoted at the height of the battle:[44]

'Let God arise, let his enemies be scattered: let them also that hate him flee before him.'[45]

There were numerous other Biblical verses that were cited by Cromwell in this form of militant Christianity.

The Bible, Providence, prayer and divine guidance can be seen as the essential elements in any explanation of Cromwell's character, as well as his subsequent actions and career as a soldier and politician. If this might be thought an unusual basis for a practical soldier's thought – and many great captains have been religious men – then it was not so for Oliver Cromwell. Indeed, in his military career, the key to understanding his actions nearly always lies in his relationship with God. Cromwell the soldier was also Cromwell the godly warrior. This is why, to the end, he remained very self-effacing in his attitude to military success. For, in all of his reports and letters, when he writes of victory, it is God alone who has the sole claim to it: Cromwell became merely the instrument of His hand. As Carlyle once noted, 'what good could it do him to be "noticed" by noisy crowds of people? God his maker already noticed him. He, Cromwell, was already there; no notice would make *him* other than he already was.'[46] God in Cromwell's speeches and actions was raised at every opportunity; for he was a God-besotted man. This should not be seen, as it once was, as an example of the Machiavellian schemer able to use the language of the godly for his own particular ends (although there is little doubt that it proved to be very useful on occasion): it was, rather, a genuine and consistent part of his being. Cromwell was never the master philosopher or politician, but a man led by the spirit. It was the spiritual side that made the calculations in battle; it was the spiritual side that caused him to agonise over political decisions; and it was the spiritual side that created the active Cromwell we see in the historical record. In consequence, he learnt to create his armies, and to win his battles, in his Bible and at prayer as much as in the field, and where there were gaps in his strategy God's Providence would fill them. It was his role as an actor to make use of them. His personal fearlessness arose from an absolute confidence in his cause, and 'in his God ... Every letter he wrote from the battlefield, unquestioningly attributes the action and the result to God.'[47]

This was natural enough. Others, although they themselves never fought, expressed similar views from the sidelines. The many Puritan divines filled their sermons and pamphlets with notions that God had a real part to play in the Holy Wars of the 1640s. Invariably it was the Old-Testament God – He who ruthlessly destroyed His enemies – who was invoked. John Arrowsmith had God mustering men and ordering ammunition like some divine quartermaster. Stephen Marshall was even blunter, telling the Royalist enemy that they would fail because 'it is Emmanuel's cause ... it is Emmanuel who is the leader, the generall of that Army.' God possessed the strategic skill to 'out-wit you, and out-plot you, and out-fight you.'[48] Consequently Cromwell's final authority was the understanding of the Holy Spirit on his conscience, his gathered fellowship with others in congregation, and through his reading of the Bible. This was not unusual, and it could, and would, be used in battle. It would, naturally, give him great latitude in day-to-day decisions, and could be one reason why he has been frequently seen as inconsistent or hypocritical in his actions. As S. R. Gardiner long ago noted, 'The very vividness of his apprehension of the supernatural enabled him to pass rapidly without any sense of incongruity from religious exhortations to the practical satisfaction of the demands of the material world' – or, to put it another way, he lived in a spiritual world whose very essence could be found in practical action.[49] It also brought him into a very close relationship with God, and the idea of Cromwell being part of the Divine Will was reinforced by his successes as a commander in the field; the one fed upon the other, and became self-sustaining. It was part of the Calvinist doctrine and concept of Providence – a means of seeing patterns in the chaos of everyday life. It would have been eminently suitable for the military life, for what can be more chaotic than battle? To feel that God was present at all times in battle was doubtless the most comforting of thoughts. Battle, like life itself, therefore became not a lottery, but a winnowing of the good and bad amongst humanity – a phrase that Cromwell himself used of the great changes in 1644–45:[50] submit to God and thus draw consolation. The belief that no harm could come to those whom God favoured also had a self-confirming quality: to survive uninjured meant that God was looking after the survivor. The individual also needed continually to search his inner soul for the righteousness of the decisions occurring around him.

To us, Providentialism often seems to be an inherently subjective system of belief, but it gave power and a moral certainty in the chaos of the world. As J. F. C. Fuller once noted, 'It is in this moral sphere of war that the decisive battle is waged.'[51] Naturally, Cromwell's protestations about the hand of God being of guidance in all aspects of his life brought with it accusations of mere opportunism and hypocrisy. He himself was aware of this, and angrily sought to disassociate himself from such a possibility. In his speech to Parliament on 22 January 1655, he said:

> 'But if any man shall object … It is an easy thing to talk of necessities, when men create necessities, would not the Lord Protector make himself and his family great? Doth not he make these necessities … ? This were something hard indeed, but I have not yet known what it is to make necessities, whatsoever the judgements or thoughts of men are. And I say this, not only to this assembly, but to the world, that the man liveth not, that can come to me and charge me that I have in these great revolutions made necessities … let men take heed and be twice advised how they call His revolutions, the things of God, and His working of things from one period to another, how I say, they call them necessities of men's

creation. For by so doing they do vilify and lessen the works of God, and rob Him of His glory.'[52]

MILITARY EDUCATION

Little enough is known of Cromwell's life in the 1630s; almost the only evidence we have comes from later hostile witnesses. Heath, the author of the hostile early biography *Flagellum,* claimed that the farm at Ely was neglected in that 'every morning before they stirred out, the Family was called together to prayers, at which Exercise very often they continued so long, that it was nine of the Clock in the morning before they began their work', with further religious devotions in the afternoon.[53] It is clear that Cromwell was still concerned with his religious prayer and devotion in these years, otherwise there is no evidence of his opposing either Ship Money or the forced loans of the King. No doubt he was frustrated by his place in society and by the doings of the government, particularly in its foreign and religious policy, but on the whole this seems to have been a time of hard work, farming and the inevitable reflection. The death of his uncle enabled him to move to Ely in 1636 to begin a period of comparative prosperity as a man of property, and he may well have thanked God that, after he had spent so many years in the wilderness, his fortunes were beginning to rise once more, for great things were happening in the country and in Europe, where a great war in Germany was taking place.

On the question of his military education we are left asking whether Cromwell had some vicarious experience of war through a reading of Europe's conflicts, soldiers and their battles, their strategies and tactics. We have seen how he could have used the Bible, but did he have access to contemporary military tracts such as *The Swedish Intelligencer* and other pamphlets that were commonly sought for reading of the deeds of the 'Protestant hero' Gustavus Adolphus of Sweden? And if he did read such literature, how far did this influence him? It seems that Cromwell did read such journals, for in June 1655 he was to tell the Swedish Ambassador of his admiration for Gustavus, and that when

'... a private person, he nevertheless had always followed his great campaigns with the greatest pleasure, had many times thanked God, with tears of joy in his eyes, for His gracious mercies, and when the tidings came of his death, had so mourned it that he could scarcely believe that any Swede could mourn it more bitterly.'[54]

Otherwise, Cromwell rarely recommended reading material beyond the Bible and, most famously, Sir Walter Raleigh's *History of the World*. However, he noted that one should

'... mind and understand business, read a little history, study the mathematics and cosmography: – these are good with subordination to the things of God. Better than idleness, or mere outward worldly contents. These fit for public services, for which a man is born.'[55]

Others had used the burgeoning literature of war prior to 1642 to train themselves for the potential conflict. The narratives 'formed expectations as to the character of war, and strengthened resolve, once it came to England.'[56] The numerous technical manuals printed prior to 1642 illuminated both strategy and tactics, and claimed to teach their readers the art of war and of manoeuvring men. Hence civilians such as Cromwell, while still armchair theorists, could at least be mentally prepared for some form of command. In the end, we do not know what exact access Cromwell had to such material, but, as we have seen, he certainly claimed an interest in the campaigns of the Swedish King, and what he learned there may well have assisted him in his later career.

Even so, he was clearly not too hidebound by the rules of war in 1642. A natural instinct for tactics in the field was already grounded in his love of hunting and horses. It would have given him an eye for the capabilities of cavalry and the ground on which they acted. Biblical and other reading would have illuminated the wars of the Israelites and the King of Sweden. His ability to control others in combat was to be achieved by training and by the sheer force of a dominant personality as much as by his own energy, order and discipline. For, above all, in these years he came to control himself through his religion and was also similarly to come to know his men, what they were capable of and how to control them. Taken together, the result was to be victory. Matched with an innate puritan belief in himself and the part played by God in his life, it was to make him into a soldier.

CHAPTER 2

THE ROAD TO WAR

'… the greatest evil that can happen in this life.'
– Thomas Hobbes, *Leviathan*, 1651.

THE ORIGINS OF THE CIVIL WARS

The King under whom Oliver Cromwell spent most of his adult life was Charles I, who ruled his kingdoms from 1625 to 1649. His was a reign increasingly punctuated by crises, and these would eventually end in disaster for himself, his house and the peoples he governed. Some of these crises were subject to closure, whilst others were left to fester and rankle beneath the skin of the body politic. While the long-term dysfunctional problems of kingdoms ruled by Charles I ultimately contributed to the disorder that allowed the actual system to break down, it is arguable that political crisis in general in the period – and that of 1638–42 in particular – tended to be subject to more immediate short-term problems and foci. Indeed, however we examine the period 1638–1642, whether as a whole, merely taking the winter of 1641/42, or considering only the summer of 1642, there was something at fault in the Stuart kingdoms, and historians have spent many years, and engaged in numerous and quite often heated arguments, in their attempts to discern what these problems really were and whether they could have been resolved without civil war and violence. For this was a state which, as Thomas Hobbes noted, 'is the greatest evil that can happen in this life.'[1]

That the societies of the seventeenth century had a latent fear of disorder and its consequences there is no doubt. Indeed, the need for order and hierarchy are central to an understanding of the seventeenth-century psyche. There was a passionate need for stability in a period of political, religious and occasional social turmoil. Given this fact, many were puzzled at the time – and have continued to be puzzled – as to how the societies in the British Isles broke down sufficiently to fall into civil war. However, the causes of the Civil War are numerous and well-argued; each generation has laid its particular stamp upon them. The breakdown of any political system, much less the breakdown of a system that spread across four nations and many millions of people into civil war, invariably has multiple causes. Contemporaries themselves were confused as to how they had found themselves in such a cruel situation, so perhaps we should not look for any simplistic answers. Such answers as seem to surface, however, revolve around difficulties as to the nature of the Stuart kingship; the troubles of the British Isles, itself a multiple state with major problems; a court-versus-country debate; and – possibly the most significant of all – the religious dilemmas faced by an Early Modern state.

Perhaps we should really ask what it was that Charles I was trying to achieve. A general turn towards some form of centralisation in Church and State under the Stuart dynasty was almost inevitable, especially in light of the activities and moves towards 'absolutism' in the monarchies of Europe. In addition, the nature of personal monarchy in this era was significant: kings ruled as well as reigned, and this meant that the personality of the monarch was crucial to the politics of the day. Certainly, the personality of Charles I had a role to play in the emergence of civil war.[2] Aged twenty-five on his accession, at first Charles I seemed to promise well: a conservative man, as a monarch he would prove active and vigorous. He was noble and graceful in his attitudes and dignified in his private life, with little hint of any sexual scandals or the rather loose ways at court held by his father. Charles I was sincerely religious. He had a taste for fine arts and literature, and he spoke and wrote correctly with a plain and open hand. Conversely, he was a reserved man. He 'is usually a prince of few words, and even on this great and extraordinary occasion he was as reserved as usual,' noted the Venetian envoy in 1630.[3] In addition, Charles also had little enough sense of humour and arguably just as little enough insight into the ways of men or his people. On some matters, he proved all too inflexible. As Sharpe points out, he saw the 'royal word as the end not the beginning of the processes of command and obedience.'[4] Upon his rights and his status as King, Charles I tended to see matters in black or white, not the usual shades of grey that exist in the real world. In essence, Charles was not a politician, seeing the art of the possible; he always lacked imagination, and in general he disliked argument. More significantly, he could neither charm nor flatter, and he found it difficult to persuade. In the end, Charles I was not a man willing to accept the realities of life. Above all, he was a staunch believer in the moral absolutism of his reign and in his own relationship with God and his people. This was, to his mind, fixed, and it was not the business of the governed to interfere with government, but to accept what was given. Given that he also had the tendency to choose poor advisors (Buckingham, Laud, Strafford, his wife), troubles came not in ones and twos, but in scores during the reign. Charles's worst moral failing, as it emerged during these years, was that he dissembled far too often, and there was also, within his character, the element of the martyr.

If the war of 1642 had a primary cause other than the King (and it is difficult in retrospect to see it occurring without him), then perhaps it lay in religion. Fractious personalities, problems with Parliament and foreign affairs, a 'British' problem, court-versus-country, questions of patriarchy, hierarchy and the nature of society, the 'great chain of being' from God to the lowliest peasant, the class system – all had their part to play, but all in the end bow down to the religious view of life. For religion in post-Reformation Britain, as we have seen with Oliver Cromwell, lay at the centre of people's lives. Any attempt to change it was bound to have repercussions.

The idea that a general consensus in religious matters was the order of the day in England until it all broke down in the 1620s and 1630s has become something of new orthodoxy in the history of the period. In this we find not a Puritan revolution forcing the pace, but rather a Caroline/Arminian religious revolution, led by the King and his Archbishop William Laud, working to establish a new Caroline Church. It has been argued that their imposed form of anglicised Arminian theology (labelled 'Laudianism') ultimately threatened to overturn the consensual Calvinist theological certainty with ideas of the non-absolute nature of Predestination, allowing for the suggestion of free will and good works to bring salvation. These were already controversial topics. Furthermore, given that the new royal orthodoxy also imparted a particular stress to ritual and ceremony in church, and gave prominence to the position of the clergy – particularly bishops – as intermediaries between the congregation and God, some Puritans regarded this as indistinguishable from a return to outright popery. Laud and the new orthodoxy were also obsessed with conformity, and therefore with a lack of tolerance (not that either side was very capable of this); and conformity brought with it the persecution of those who refused to obey the rules of the Church's theology. It naturally led to great difficulties and fear. As we know today, religious fear in itself is more than sufficient to bring war in its wake. In the seventeenth century, with fear came the demonisation of opponents, and with this the inevitable closing of minds. Indeed, some have argued that this religious quarrel eventually so poisoned the political atmosphere that some form of civil war was in the end almost inevitable.

A further element in this religious conflict was the concentration laid upon the problem of Roman Catholicism in the 1630s and 1640s. This generally revolved around beliefs in a 'popish plot' working to undermine Protestant England and her institutions, whether monarchical or parliamentary. A belief in a popish plot in the seventeenth century was almost self-evident to many politicians of the era and was frequently to be found at the heart of the political debates of the day. It is difficult to convey the depth of hatred towards Roman Catholicism in seventeenth-century England. The nation's view of the 'bogeyman' – the Pope – and all he stood for was based upon a long tradition of myth, bigotry, plain stupidity and, just occasionally, a little reality. Originating in the sixteenth century, anti-Catholic rhetoric was omnipresent in many a commemoration of victory over the popish Church that was still celebrated in the English calendar, and such yearly events kept the evils of Catholicism firmly in the Protestant eye. Nor did these former victories provide total consolation, for while plots and conspiracies against Protestant England had resulted in, for example, the defeat of the Armada (1588) and the discovery of the Gunpowder Plot (1605), in the English national consciousness, undermining the Protestant citadel continued apace. Moreover, with a small minority of Catholics still present in English society, the danger was apparently ever-present. This number also appeared to be growing, especially at the centre of political life and society – the King's court. One naturally could not blame the King, only his 'evil advisors'; so Laud and his ideas seemed to be only one example of what might happen if such wickedness took hold. To a true believer of the popish plot, such designs would inevitably lead to the widespread slaughter of Protestant men, women and children in a manner already to be seen in the frightful accounts of the religious wars in Germany. It could, so it was thought, happen here.

The late 1620s and the 1630s typify such growing problems in the Caroline state, although there were many others. In practical political terms, such discord represented a continual background noise that explains much of the fractiousness of these decades. There was also a more immediate reaction to the problematic foreign policy of the King, as well as hostility to Charles's favourite, the Duke of Buckingham. All this meant that the third Parliament of the reign in 1628–29 was a troubled one, and it led to the Petition of Right and further attacks on Buckingham's position. Fortunately, the Duke was removed from the equation by assassination in August 1628, whilst at Portsmouth and about to embark on yet another foreign adventure. Yet, even after Buckingham's removal, animosity between the King and his Parliament over issues of taxation and religion, as well as a growing awareness of deeper constitutional strains, continued, and further Parliamentary complaints about innovations in Church and

State finally led to the dissolution of the Parliament amidst angry scenes. It was at this point that the King made it clear that he would not summon another Parliament in the foreseeable future, and for the time being he sought to rule without one. At the same time, the King was unceasing in his introduction of innovations in the nation's religious life, and he also went ahead with modifications in government, taxation and foreign policy.

The 1630s turned into a period of so-called personal rule, with national politics dominated by advisors such as Archbishop William Laud and Thomas Wentworth. With the ecclesiastical changes initiated by Laud and backed by the King as the greatest bones of contention, especially to those with a puritanical turn of mind, a policy of 'Thorough' to try to obtain unity in the state ended up being equally disruptive. Ideas of extraparliamentary taxation such as Ship Money to raise funds for the royal schemes only inflamed the political elite and raised growing distrust in the nation, yet in places such as Ireland a man like Wentworth, with his strong-minded views and the support of the King, was also to succeed for a time. The problems came when such policies were eventually tried in Scotland. In his attempt to impose a religious solution on this part of his kingdom that he found acceptable, Charles I not only challenged the Scottish nation's self-worth, he also provoked resistance, and eventually the King drove the Scots into taking arms against him.

It was the action taken to impose an anglicised prayer book in Scotland's religious life that in 1637 led to riots in Edinburgh. To the aristocracy and gentry leaders of Scotland – a Presbyterian nation – this action against their Kirk fuelled the already incipient fears amongst them over Charles's plans for their land and estates. Theological ideas were always controversial in Scottish life, and theological ideas with a touch of English arrogance built into them could only lead to conflict. Together they raised Scottish national feeling to a new pitch, and it resulted in the signing of the National Covenant. Charles I's own stubbornness when faced with any resistance easily explains what happened next. Although the King attempted some negotiation, his honour and authority as a monarch were now at stake, and Scotland would eventually have to be brought to heel by force. To do so, the King would need an army – and an army, moreover, created without money from an English Parliament that would ask far too many awkward questions. At the outset, voluntary contributions from both the clergy and laity and non-parliamentary taxes would have to suffice to fund this force. In the interim, the Scots themselves had not merely relied on paper bullets to protect the nation, but had begun to raise a formidable army, drawn in part from many of that nation's professional soldiers who had long served in Continental wars. By June 1638, they had some 20,000 men in arms. Charles in turn managed to raise some 21,000 English troops, but the conflict that followed was brief and inconclusive. A truce signed at Berwick in June 1639 did not promise any real resolution, and left the King humiliated, as well as in need of more funds which were really only obtainable from the English Parliament. So it was that in April 1640 the King finally sought financial help from his English Parliament to raise a new army to settle the Scottish question.

When the Parliament arrived at Westminster in April 1640, it was soon clear that its view was that the King should first redress its own grievances before he received any supply to deal with the Scots. Almost immediately it asked for what the King saw as too many concessions, and as a result ended up being swiftly dissolved on 5 May 1640. Yet, even in its brief life, the Short Parliament had begun to set out three trends in policy that would have implications for the future: firstly, Parliament had its own rights, and government, where it had transgressed, must be held to account; secondly, there must be some dismantling of innovations imposed on the Caroline Church; and thirdly, Parliament alone controlled the taxes of the nation. Worse was to follow for the King: while Charles was once more planning an invasion of Scotland, the Scots pre-empted his scheme and trounced his forces at Newburn-on-Tyne on 28 August 1640. The Scots Army subsequently occupied the northern counties and the city of Newcastle with its vital north-east coalfields. A council of peers called to York by the King recommended that the only real solution was a new Parliament. Moreover, the Scots also made it clear that they would not leave the north until the English Parliament ratified any settlement.

On 3 November 1640, what was to become known as the Long Parliament finally met. Now Charles I's demand for supply was tied by the Parliament not only to changes in government personnel, but also to the permanent removal of some of the King's most hated advisors, such as Strafford and Laud. It was the crafty politician John Pym who led the chase after Strafford. The earl was first imprisoned in December, later put on trial, and, when that failed to pin him down, executed by attainder. Laud was just imprisoned and left to rot until someone remembered him in 1645 and he was executed. Parliament then took steps to ensure it could not be dissolved, and what many saw as the root of the problem – popery and its influence around the King – became a major point of debate. Changes were thought necessary in both Church and State.

Cromwell's part in all of this has been well documented.[5] He was a man on the periphery of the political faction that eventually opposed the King in 1640. His main interest was in godly reformation, but he was noted for his impulsive and hasty actions and was not that reliable nor much of a force of importance in these early years. Naive is perhaps the kindest way to describe his part in the great events in which he was now becoming involved, although some might rather say he was impetuous, blustering and self-righteous. At the least he seems to have grown ever fearful that the cause of religious reformation that he now held so dear would be lost unless real action were taken, and he became the almost archetypical angry middle-aged man in the process. One of his greatest interests in these heady days was in Ireland: while the King and Parliament squabbled, a still more serious issue had emerged across the Irish Sea, for in October 1641 a full-scale rebellion broke out there.[6]

On one level, the rising of 1641 was a conspiracy, led in part by Rory O'More, who was of an Irish family which had lost its wealth and most of its property. The plan was to seize Dublin Castle, the seat of royal authority in Ireland, while a wider rising took place in Ulster. The conspirators were foiled in their plans, but this did not prevent a serious rebellion beginning in Ulster which soon spread rapidly throughout the island. The heavy hand of Wentworth and the early Stuart plantation polices that had caused such underlying resentment amongst the native Irish exploded in 1641. Many of the plantation strongholds soon fell to the rebels in the north-eastern part of Ireland, and, as a result, massacres on both sides took place. While the hideousness and savagery of these killings were clearly exaggerated, they were bad enough. Although the numbers of those actually killed in the rising are a continuing topic for discussion amongst historians, the impact of the slaughter on the English nation was a profound one. The number of deaths is estimated to be in the region of 4,000, and perhaps more than this, and many more thousands of people died of privation in the winter that followed. The figures were certainly nowhere near the 154,000 (four times the number of settlers actually inhabiting Ulster during this period) often alleged.[7] Propagandists were ever eager to make English flesh creep with their stories of atrocities, and no one's flesh crept more than Oliver Cromwell's. Indeed, the reports permanently twisted his views on that country. The fact was, however, that large numbers of people did die, and still more came over to England with their tales of atrocity and barbarity. Whether these were true or not, the stories, related both in print and by word of mouth, led many to the belief that a widespread massacre of Protestants had taken place in Ireland. Such matters made a 'wonderful impression upon the minds of men', and also raised fears that the Irish would invade England.[8] The 1641 rising should also be seen in light of Europe's wars of religion. With Catholics apparently in command in Ireland, the back door to Protestant England was now wide open and religious conflict lay on her borders. In what was to follow, the effects of the rising of 1641 are not to be underestimated, for the rising not only generated a miserable series of wars in that country in which little quarter was given or received, but created an intense crisis in the neighbouring kingdoms.

Clearly, an army had now to be sent to restore order in Ireland, but the government of Charles I was found to be largely powerless to intervene in this situation. Indeed, the Irish state of affairs swiftly entangled England in searching questions of trust between King and Parliament, which would lead that country itself into civil war. As King and Parliament argued over whether Charles I could be trusted with an army to quell the Irish rebels – and Cromwell, for one, contributed some of his newly acquired wealth to the expedition planned to take the country back – propaganda on both sides exploited the situation. John Pym acted to tie the King down via the Grand Remonstrance, a document that had fears of a popish plot at its heart – a plot obviously proved at least in part by the recent events in Ireland. On the other hand, the King's mistimed attempt at a *coup* on 4 January 1642 (he tried to seize the five Members of Parliament he thought most hostile to him) was condemned outright by Parliament as a breach of privilege. The MPs now swiftly withdrew to the Guildhall in the City of London, citing fears for their safety. With popular pressure growing in the streets of London, Charles also feared for his own and his family's safety and finally withdrew from the city. The Parliamentarians then came back to Westminster in some pomp and a war of words followed, while both sides, including Oliver Cromwell, began to eye the country's military assets in order to protect themselves from the other.

Even at this stage, war was not inevitable. In February 1642, Charles made what for him were considerable concessions by offering to remove the Bishops from the Lords and stating that he was willing to lead the Army to Ireland in person if Parliament wished it. However, suspicions of the King's motives were now considerable, and the arguments over who would control the militia in the country grew. It was to prove an ill-disciplined and ill-equipped force for the task, and their protestations of immunity from service outside their own counties made the soldiers reluctant warriors at the best of times, even though, because there was no standing national army, in any military conflict both sides would be initially forced to rely on local militias.

The major question is why it took so long in 1642 to come to blows. In fact, both sides tried to place blame upon the other. Parliament's drawing up of the Militia Ordinance in January 1642 was certainly an attempt to put the nation in a state of readiness for war and to seize all forts, magazines and *matériel* essential for prosecuting it. In turn, Charles's attempt to seize the military magazine at Hull, still replete with equipment from the Bishops' Wars, clearly demonstrated *his* intent. He was surprised to be denied access to Hull, and arguments over the militia continued. A Parliamentary delegation to the King at Newmarket on 9 March merely asked Charles to surrender control of the militia for 'a time'. He refused point blank. That being so, the Militia Ordinance was passed in Parliament, and the King's Navy also fell under Parliamentary control.

Meanwhile the war continued in Ireland. The Scots sought to intervene in April 1642, further confusing the issue. The summer of 1642 passed with a 'paper war' raging in England over fundamentals, while the King sought loans from loyal members of his aristocracy and anyone else who was willing to lend him money to raise troops. He also took to chiding those who would not serve him. In truth, most of the population sought to retain as much of a neutral status for as long as possible. The Nineteen Propositions, sent to Charles in June by Parliament, in effect called for the King to surrender: they removed the royal veto, and required him to give up the militia and concede to Parliament the means of government. Distrust oozed into the documents of these days, and by July 1642 the country had staggered to the precipice of civil conflict. It seemed that the fortunes of both sides in England would have to be settled by violence – involving all the nations of the three kingdoms.[9]

Parliament's choice as its defender in the field fell upon the portly figure of Robert Devereux, 3rd Earl of Essex (1591–1646), a man nicely summed up by S. R. Gardiner as 'steady, honourable, sober minded ... without a spark of genius ... [and] hardly ... likely to know what to do with a victory even if he got one.'[10] As Lord General, Essex was now empowered to issue commissions to officers, who in turn would raise men. Of course, he faced immediate problems: in an essentially peaceful society, he had to raise and train troops to undertake a civil war in which he, as well as others, was reluctant to engage in the first place. That Essex ever overcame the major problems of logistics, finance and morale, enabling Parliament to field any sort of army at all, was in itself perhaps his greatest achievement. Like

Charles's, Essex's strategic sense as a general was never very sophisticated; similarly again, he was both overcautious and frequently unrealistic in his aims. Equally, Essex was often reluctant to act forcefully – he had few dynamic attributes – yet his background at first made him seem eminently suited to high command. One of the richest men in England, he was the son of that Earl of Essex famously executed for rebellion against Elizabeth I. While this in itself gave him some reputation, his personal life had been an unhappy one, and this had pushed him into a peripatetic career of soldiering. In the 1620s he had seen service in Europe in command of a regiment under Sir Horace Vere. He was in the Netherlands in 1623 and 1624. In 1625 he was offered high command in the Cadiz expedition, but was then demoted by Buckingham to regimental commander. A similar thing occurred in 1626, and again in 1639, when he was initially appointed lieutenant-general of horse in the campaign against the Scots, only to be discarded in favour of the Earl of Holland. It seems that Essex was to be as unlucky a soldier as a husband. In political terms he did become Lord Lieutenant of Staffordshire, entering the House of Lords in 1614. There, in general, he had begun to side with the 'opposition', led to them as much by his hostility to Strafford and the persistent refusal by Charles I to use him wisely as any political conviction. Ultimately, circumstances led to his open opposition in 1642, although how well he would perform on the field remained to be seen.

By the time the King raised his own standard at Nottingham on 22 August 1642, fighting had broken out. The MP for Cambridge, Oliver Cromwell, had already begun his war. He had, alongside his brother-in-law, Valentine Walton, apprehended arms and ammunition laid in Cambridge, and also prevented the University's plate from leaving for the King's coffers. He soon acquired a commission to raise a troop of horse that was to begin to bring him towards the centre of a war that would now provide him with great opportunities. Finally, he was to be part of God's plan; the battles and mêlées ahead were merely punctuation points in the great text of godly history. He could shake off his previous troubles and now follow a vision. If this vision were to leave his strategy and tactics difficult to comprehend at times, then it also gave him some advantages, as we shall see.

CHAPTER 3

THE FACE OF WAR, 1642

'To your tents, O Israel' – *I Kings* 12:16.

OCTOBER 1642

A misty morning on 23 October 1642 found the inexperienced armies of both King and Parliament in the damp fields around Edgehill in Vale of the Red Horse in Warwickshire. Several of the soldiers on opposing sides on that autumn day now hoped that one big battle would resolve the political stalemate that had ensnared the country for so many months. However, many of the military men who were to be involved in the first battle of the Civil War, including Oliver Cromwell, were amateurs in a new world. For them the war began in the context of an English nation that had mostly been at peace for many a long year and had only reluctantly taken up the tools of warfare. What would they find on the field of battle? What did the face of war look like in 1642?

EARLY MODERN WARFARE

Whilst most of England had been unaffected by war on her soil until 1642, for a good number of Europeans – and for many in the Celtic nations ruled by Charles I – warfare had become something of a way of life. It may be that, for some at this time, war remained a cloud on the horizon, seeking only their money through taxation, but for others it had a more profound and visible impact on their lives. For Early Modern war took their sons to serve in the armies of Europe, or, worse, it visited their own hearths and homes. Early modern warfare also brought not just deaths from combat and other casualties, but maimed lives, rapine, pillage, disease and economic crisis in the wake of the armies who serviced it.

It is arguable whether warfare was actually endemic in Early Modern Europe, but it often seemed to have been unavoidable. War was, after all, one of the two pastimes in which most Early Modern monarchs were obliged to succeed (the other being ostentatious display). Thus in many senses war was the monarchy's real profession, and the use of military violence was the ultimate exercise of power to settle the political and religious disputes of the day. Although it was disliked by many contemporary humanists and religious men, war also brought with it honourable ideas of princely glory and marks of distinction. Many were the theoretical publications that proclaimed the virtues of war. Yet it was self-evidently a destabilising element in society, especially for those who suffered from it, and even its defenders regarded civil war as the most dreadful form of all: 'nothing under Heaven [is] more ghastly and dreadful ... nothing so nearly resembles hell' as civil war, noted one contemporary.[1]

In many ways, medieval warfare had been an integral part of life, though it was limited, as is all war, by the available technology of arms and equipment, as well as the size of the forces involved, its duration, and the occasion of its use. Two overriding doctrines emerged that were to affect war in the Early Modern period: the evasion of the pitched battle; and a 'siege mentality', that is, a need to control territory by the use of garrisons in castles, and the capture of these fortifications.[2] Present-day experts in this field are currently dispelling many of the myths of medieval warfare. They now seek to stress that, although limited in its aims, the warfare of the day, being largely geared to the capture of fortresses, did stimulate the advance of many new military methods. Indeed, if we are in search of a motive force to account for military change between the years 1400 and 1600, then it surely lies in the rise of ever more complex fortifications and the enhancement of the necessary methods of capturing such defences. Where large-scale campaigning did take place in the medieval period rather than battles, success was often measured in the number of fortifications taken. While tactical battles occurred, they were often reluctantly undertaken, often hurried and unplanned, with the individual heroic element being most prominently displayed.[3] For a time it was cavalry, in the shape of the heavily armoured knight, situated alongside a feudal array, that became the standard expression of military skill in Western Europe. The knight was able to use his armour, mass and impact to cause damage both to other knights and to foot soldiers. Only when the old feudal hordes began to be gradually displaced by more professional forces did a reformation of the tactics of war begin to take place. Mercenary infantry soldiers now emerged, mostly alongside native levies, bringing with them specialists and innovation.

In this sense, the rise of the longbow and pike were developments in the art of war. Indeed, so significant was the myth of the longbow in bringing about English victories in the Hundred Years' War that even under the Tudors and Stuarts it was still being advocated as a useful long-distance weapon to place alongside the pike and musket. This myth even caused one commentator in 1625 to advocate the use of the pike and longbow by one and the same soldier, and he offered up numerous impractical looking illustrations to demonstrate his point.[4] On the other hand, the development of the Swiss tradition in the use of the pike also gave infantry another role in the world of battle. The Swiss became redoubtable mercenary soldiers and experts in the use of an eighteen-foot long pike. Their courage, training and ferocity in action made them for a time Europe's most feared and sought-after soldiers. They also had a strong commercial attitude to war ('*Point d'argent, point de Suisse*' – 'No Money, no Swiss') that made them exceptionally mercenary in the way they conducted themselves. Their tactics were deceptively simple. Three large columns of pikemen were the most common formation, of a size that usually depended on the circumstances. They moved forward at speed *en echelon*, and sought to 'steamroll' the opposition into submission. The greatest success of the Swiss was in the battles of the fourteenth century, but they finally met their match at Marignano (1515) and Bicocca (1522), for the reason that there was a new innovation on the scene – the handgun.[5]

It was the evolution of a practical form of handgun in the Renaissance period that really began to signal changes in the art of war. We should perhaps see this as part of a continuing 'military reformation' (to use J. R. Hale's phrase), as it gradually changed the face of tactics and was linked to even deeper changes in society, as well as to the creation of larger armies requiring more money.[6] At first, of course, the hand weapons available to soldiers were crude and inaccurate, whilst their bigger brothers, the artillery pieces, were also immobile, but both weapons were subject to swift development. It was in the sixteenth century that firearms really began to come into their own and an apparent military revolution took place.

A MILITARY REVOLUTION?

The idea of the military revolution originated with a lecture in 1956 by Michael Roberts and has been debated, fine-tuned and disputed almost to the point of extinction ever since. Roberts originally claimed that the revolution he was describing was 'the great divide separating medieval society from the modern world'. Military reforms, principally led by men such as Maurice of Nassau and Gustavus Adolphus of Sweden, had so changed the nature of warfare in sixteenth- and seventeenth-century Europe that the old medieval style of warfare was swept away in favour of something new and much more innovative. Bigger, more permanent armies were now to become the norm. They were mostly to be under state control, and they to be were used as tools to build up the centralised power of the state. There was to be far less emphasis on the individual and much more on the effectiveness of the military unit, while more unit training and a stricter discipline in the new technologies of pike and musket had a subsidiary effect on tactics and even strategy. Much of the latter was in any case derived from a re-reading of the classical authors, and new translations and editions of these works by Renaissance scholars now became essential reading for any ambitious prince.

A subsequent critique of Roberts' ideas, mostly by Geoffrey Parker, extended the period of discussion somewhat, from 1560–1660 to 1530–1710. It also cast doubt on the explanation of a 'revolution', and even on the idea itself. Even so, later critics have generally recognized that there were some significant changes in Early Modern warfare: the growth in size of armies is one factor, and remains possibly the most significant of all the changes from the medieval period. Another was an increased professionalism in soldiering: the nature of the troops began to change from temporary militias to standing armies, resulting in better discipline and more uniformity in terms of weapons, drill and dress. Increased discipline was essential in order to cope with technological advances in weaponry, and this could only come through ceaseless training. These new methods led in turn to changes in tactics and strategy, which became more complex, while generalship became more of a professional pursuit. In fact, military life became for some a career. Perhaps most importantly of all, these activities could only be achieved by means of a vital growth in the state's bureaucracy, for only through this could enough finances be gathered and the state intervene in the economy of the society it purported to manage, in order to maintain the tools of war. The arrival of ideas of credit in the financial world also enabled states sometimes to find the necessary finance (or simply go into debt) in order to maintain ever-greater numbers of troops and larger navies. If the finances and energies of the state could be harnessed, then the extent of war would logically transform itself; further, all princes wished to engage in war and thereby win honour and prestige, so they were all eager to adopt the latest innovations.

Nevertheless, there were, of course, still very many constraints on Early Modern warfare, and even the best armies of the day remained limited in what they could do. Early Modern warfare tended to be a seasonal occupation, mainly because of the appalling state of the roads. As a result, winter campaigns were technically difficult undertakings, so war tended to come with the spring and leave in the autumn. Moreover, logistically the need to feed, clothe and maintain increasingly large numbers of troops and horses, as well as the thousands of others who made up an army, soon became possible only as part of the state's business. The dawn of the military-fiscal state had arrived.

In any event a crude logistical base still meant that, as the armies grew in size, the difficulties grew likewise. In fact, there were three main methods of feeding an army of the day – trade between the troops and the local population, the creation of a commissariat to organise resources, and abandoning the troops to live on free quarter or plunder. Problems existed with all of these – not least that of keeping large bodies of armed and potentially violent men under control, and that of financing of the whole system – and, taken collectively, more often than not they combined to prevent innovative and inspired generalship.

The geography of the areas fought over could also have a limiting effect on what was achievable in land warfare. Armies naturally tended to funnel themselves into logistically fertile areas, or into areas dominated by towns and garrisons, merely in order to survive. The cost in men, and the attitude to war itself, also meant that few generals were willing (or able) to risk everything on the big 'encounter battle'; they and their masters still much preferred wars of manoeuvre and siege, in which objectives could be limited and not everything would be gambled (or wasted) on one throw of the dice. Despite this, soldierly skills soon became a valuable marketable commodity, and specialisation in arms meant that those princes whose subjects did not possess the right skills were forced to use foreign merce-naries. These men were, naturally enough, reluctant to put their lives on the line merely for money, and instead favoured sometimes aimless manoeuvring to actual combat. Here the great Italian states of the fifteenth and sixteenth centuries provided role models. Rich and turbulent in their political life, their rulers often flinched from arming their own populations, and were forced to seek out paid professionals to fight for them and relieve their citizens of what was in any case an unpopular duty. Thus the rise of military contractors, mercenary generals and engineers able to supply soldiers, train troops or protect and build fortresses in the latest style was yet another innovation.

In the seventeenth century, the soldier of fortune became a somewhat representative figure of his time. The unremitting conflict and the increasing scale of war meant almost continuous employment for such a man. In addition, adventure, excitement and the spoils of war, not to mention the possible honour and advancement war could bring with it for those with little possibility of such matters at home, were important incentives in recruitment. Regions naturally poor in resources tended to be fertile areas for recruitment. This was especially true of the fringes of the European world, for example in Ireland and Scotland. In addition, the period also saw the arrival of the phenomenon of the gentleman soldier, keen to trail his pike in foreign wars. Young men of high birth often undertook a short spell of active service abroad as part of their education and became a common sight in Europe's wars.

As to generalship, what were the difficulties now to be confronted by Charles I and Essex facing their first real battle? Over the previous centuries, generalship as an art had changed very little from that described by the ancient commentators, one of whom had declared that 'The duty of a general is to ride by the ranks on horseback, show himself to those in danger, praise the brave, threaten the cowardly, encourage the lazy, fill up gaps, transpose a unit if necessary, bring aid to the wearied, anticipate the crisis, the hour and the outcome.'[7] In the field, the ability of the average seventeenth-century general to command and control was generally limited. Orders were issued by word of mouth, or by a handwritten note, and subordinates could accidentally, or deliberately, misunderstand either. The general would move forward himself to see, to encourage, and to threaten. He would engage in action and more often than not in hand-to-hand fighting. His role was that of a hero. Unfortunately, as formations became increasingly difficult to control, the general became ever more reliant on his subordinate officers. The development of the divisions of the army and of large units (that is, the regiment and battalion) often left actual generalship at a loss. In reality, the run-of-the-mill general was much more pleased to be able to sit down to a siege than to look for a decisive result on the battlefield, and at times warfare became something akin to a stately dance, with both sides seeking the advantage that would bring short-term victory.

Battles in Early Modern warfare were mainly actions of encounter, with the two sides finding themselves in close proximity, taking care to choose their ground where they could and then engaging in attrition. As has been noted, most generals were inbred with some offensive spirit, for that way lay glory and honour, if they could be sure of winning. Then again, the world of Early Modern military engineering had seen perceptible changes. Increasingly, stress was laid upon the sophistication of fortifications to defeat the enemy. Bastion-traced areas strengthened urban defences so much that, despite developments in artillery, laying siege to towns became a time-consuming business – although, as John Childs has pointed out, we scarcely ever hear 'of an unsuccessful siege ... all these marvellous and expensive works ... fell when subjected to sustained pressure.'[8] Indeed, although much of the combat in the Civil War involving the three kingdoms was to comprise siege warfare, modern fortifications were relatively rare: both sides were generally forced back upon the old medieval castles, which may have been modernised where feasible. With the localised strategy in existence after 1642, most battles or sieges were a gamble, as they could lead to the loss of many trained troops (a valuable commodity in a war largely made up of amateur soldiers). To some, the avoidance of engagement in favour of endless manoeuvring and sieges was to become increasingly restricting, although in the political situation of 1642 these methods of conducting warfare initially suited both Essex and Charles I.

STUART WARFARE

The idea that the Stuarts were militarily impotent in the pre-Civil War period of expanding and developing European warfare is a fixed point with most historians.[9] The fact that the common currency of the Stuart government's military prowess seems to have been the many far-flung (and failed) expeditions of the 1620s has strengthened this view. Expeditions to Cadiz in 1625 and the Isle of Ré in 1627 did nothing to assist the image of English military prowess either at home or abroad. Indeed, the nature of the armies haphazardly flung towards Europe, apparently on the whim of the King's favourite, naturally dictated the results achieved. The rounding-up of various rogues and vagabonds to serve in the ranks of the Stuart forces also resulted in drunkenness and dissolution when these armies finally arrived at their destinations. If amateurs pretending to be professionals invariably formulated Stuart strategy, it was inevitably badly carried out. Moreover, the cost of warfare to the monarchy proved enormous. In Stuart military culture, most Englishmen had little enough military responsibility to the state of their birth, but more than enough to their locality in which they lived. Even then, becoming a soldier had a bad reputation, and the pacifist policies of James I, blithely and impotently searching for peaceful solutions to Europe's political problems, had led to a decline in the nature of home soldiering, as well as in training and military skills that could have been valuable to the state. It was safer by far to sit by the fire and read of others' exploits.

Yet although inertia and poverty in the arts military seemed, on the surface, to have become standard under the Stuarts, this was not the whole picture. The case of the well-trained London bands is one point of interest prior to 1642, and the many professional English, Scottish, and Irish mercenary soldiers who were to be found serving abroad in Europe, and who returned home with decent reputations in 1642, was yet another. As we have seen, there was also a large amount of military literature available to the average gentleman if he wished to read of such matters. Mostly, a gentlemen's motivation for serving abroad, as opposed to staying at home and reading about military exploits, was either educative or negative. Hardships at home because of too high prices, religious and political disturbances, a second son with no inheritance to speak of – all these were good recruiters. For those at the lower end of the social scale there was always coercion: men could be, and often were, press-ganged into Europe's armies with very little choice. Nevertheless, some inevitably sought the benefits of pay and plunder: warfare was, after all, an attractive alternative to the harsh civilian existence of work, poverty and taxes. Excitement, adventure, danger, honour and glory (particularly for the officer class), and opportunities for travel abroad, were also powerful motivations. If all this meant that, as Mark Fissel has rightly pointed out, the 'English art of war was learnt abroad', then in 1642 it came home to try its hand at Edgehill.[10]

1642: STRATEGY

In 1642, once its relationship with the King had broken down, the first need for Parliament, as we have seen, was to find a general and to create an army for its defence against the monarchy. With no standing army in the nation, each side initially sought to rely on the militia as the basis for its army, but this was often to prove an ill-disciplined and ill-equipped force. Moreover, cries of immunity of service outside their home counties made men reluctant to cross boundaries, so that the King's Commission of Array and the Parliament's Militia Ordinance of March 1642 led both sides to try raise men, and to secure *matériel* to equip them, in other ways.

As to the strategies, on both sides the plans were cumbersome. Cut off from supplies and foreign troops by elements of his navy, Charles I was forced to take the initiative in raising troops from the counties. The summer of 1642 may well have been spent in abortive political negotiations, but it also saw King Charles trying to raise men. Once a field army was available, the main strategy of the Royalists would presumably be to march on the capital. Even though Charles I's strategic vision was never very clear, eventually it would be necessary to break into London, since here was the heart of the Parliamentary resistance. Yet Charles often squandered his advantages as King. He was naturally loath to prosecute the war on his own people too vigorously, and in his council of war he was often too hesitant in co-ordinating the efforts of the Royal forces being raised across the country. While seeking a decision at Edgehill would prove the worth of one facet of his strategy – outright battle – the hesitancy shown at Turnham Green would confound the Royalist plans of 1642.

PARLIAMENT'S ARMY

In June 1642, on the other hand, Essex had worked hard to find sufficient men able enough to be officers in his army. The King had the simple appeal of loyalty; Essex was working under the ideas of Parliament. In the end, an appeal was sent out for men who were able to maintain a horse and horsemen. They were to be paid 2s. 6d. per day, and many eager volunteers subsequently proceeded to the Guildhall. Once forty to sixty men were enrolled, an officer would be appointed for the troop, and about seventy-five troops of horse and five of dragoons were soon raised by this means. While the cavalry raised by Essex were to be of a higher social class than infantry, as yet they were not regimented. Control of the London armouries should also have given Essex's men access to much useful equipment, but, as in any war, *matériel* was often scarce, and no doubt the joke used by soldiers since time immemorial was heard at this time: there were only two sizes of equipment in stock – either too big or too small.

In the event, the higher-status cavalry were usually better equipped. It was normally the responsibility of officers to equip their men, although some of the latter would have brought their gear, tack and a horse (often of dubious quality) with them. Otherwise the troopers would have been given a shirt, stockings, boots, hats, breeches and coats; a saddle, metal headpiece, sword, cuirass or buff coat and leather belts for equipment and a pistol or carbine were also part of the gear of a cavalryman. The dragoons Essex raised were cheaper to subsidise, as they were not expected to fight on horseback but act as mounted infantry. They would also generally receive horses and saddles of poorer quality, with uniform coats, muskets and other equipment.

Essex gave out the colonels' commissions needed raise the infantry regiments. These generally went to gentlemen of rank, who were also given money to levy foot soldiers into regiments. They in turn issued commissions

to captains, who levied the men into companies. The nominal strength of
an infantry regiment in the war was to be 1,200 (200 in the colonel's
company, 140 in the lieutenant-colonel's company and 700 in the five
captains' companies, not including subordinate officers). Infantrymen
were more often than not also issued with a uniform coat and breeches in
an attempt at co-ordination in the ranks. They would be given a 'snapsack'
– a bag of linen or leather – in which to carry their possessions and rations,
and, most importantly, a musket or pike. If he were a pikeman, the soldier
would also be given a short, poor-quality sword called a 'tuck'. While both
infantry and cavalry officers equipped themselves, they dressed as befitted
their rank and wealth. An orange sash (Essex's own colour) usually distinguished them from their men. For the common troops, there were more
matter-of-fact signs to differentiate them from the enemy in the field, such
as a white handkerchief, or a piece of paper in the hat, or a shirt tail
hanging out. Regiments would be known by their colonel's name, and
carry a regimental flag or banner inscribed with some phrase or suitable
illustration as a rallying point.

Parliament's first army was a force of some 24,000 infantry, plus officers,
and, on paper, some 5,000 cavalry, together with dragoons. Absenteeism
and pluralism, as well as an inability to recruit and a lack of pay, were to be
its main problems before it entered the field. In the case of the officers,
nepotism also had a place. Local influences rather than skill often gave many
officers their position. This need not have been such a terrible thing to
contemporaries, as most government posts at local and national level were
filled in this way, but inexperienced officers could cause problems. However,
most of the newly formed regiments had at least one professional soldier in
their ranks somewhere, often hired by the colonel as his deputy to train the
men while he retained the honour of the rank.

Infantry, once placed in regiments, had in theory ten companies per
regiment; three were commanded by field officers and the remainder by
captains. The Company Commander had one lieutenant and an ensign,
two sergeants, three corporals and two drummers, and also a surgeon,
with a surgeon's mate under him. A chaplain was provided for each of the
regiments. One infantry regiment may serve as an example at this point.
Denzil Holles' foot regiment was raised in London; most of the recruits
parading in their new redcoats in the late summer of 1642 had been
London apprentices. They were rather undisciplined. Sergeant Nehemiah
Wharton was a non-commissioned officer in their ranks.[11] A former
apprentice to a London merchant, Wharton found himself with many

another London apprentice in the sixth company of the regiment. At first, to some of his company the war was a huge lark, a chance of adventure, with a little illicit plundering thrown in. Some of his fellow soldiers were fired with religious hostility, particularly to altar rails and churches, enough to despoil them at the least opportunity. They also had a dislike for those whom they believed to be papists. Like most Londoners outside their home ground, everything was compared to London and nothing much came up to standard. Wharton and his men spent most of their spare time training. They disliked their first lieutenant-colonel, Henry Billingsley, as 'a Godamme blade, and doubtlesse hatche[d] in Hell', and hoped that the authorities would remove him, or that God would convert him – or, failing these, that the devil would take him away in the first action.[12] Aside from this, they were unsophisticated fellows, firing off their weapons and on occasion accidentally killing not only companions but also civilians. Added to this was their fondness for looting, stealing venison ('venison is almost as common with us as beefe with you'), and generally being undisciplined. They were, in short, a handful.[13] Moreover, they frequently refused orders. In Northampton, they demanded 'five shillings a man, which they say, was promised them monthly by the Committee, or they would surrender their armes.'[14] Colonel John Hampden came in to try to persuade them of their duties, and failed. There were also tensions between the infantry and the cavalry: the latter frequently took a high hand, and some cavalry troopers pillaged Wharton himself. He complained that 'they tooke from me about the worth of three pounds.'[15] Otherwise, his soldiers complained most of the time, for both Wharton and the sixth company of Denzil Holles' Foot were still learning their trade, and the regiment spent not a few mornings 'skirmishing'. He also noted that his office was troublesome, and that an infantryman's war was drill, boredom and just occasionally, as we shall see, fear.[16]

PIKES

In theory, Essex's army allowed for the usual infantry ratio of two-thirds musketeers to one-third pikemen, since, in respect of all the military tools available to the general, the pike was still regarded as the 'queen of the battlefield' and the noblest of all weapons. In a pre-bayonet era, the pike retained its usefulness as a defensive battlefield tool. At eighteen feet (later cut down to sixteen, or even thirteen, by the men themselves), the steel-tipped, ashwood pike, with langets of metal at the top (to prevent the head from being lopped off) and wielded in large, tightly packed bodies of pikemen, provided a formidable defensive screen; it was said that one could hear the bullets 'chattering' as they passed though the hedge of pikes. In close ranks and facing the enemy, pikemen would push their weapons into the faces and bodies of their opponents while trying to prevent the latter from doing likewise. This meant that unit discipline, drill and training were essential, while manoeuvring, as a unit, needed a good command organisation. It was said that veterans could guess a unit's morale merely by the steadiness with which they held their pikes.[17]

Usually the strongest and tallest men were chosen for duty as pikemen as originally they were meant to have been heavily armoured, with metal corselet, helmet or 'pot' and their tuck. The armour restricted mobility (its natural weight lying upon the shoulders), and so it gradually began to be discarded, or was restricted to the front and rear ranks of the pikes, the most vulnerable parts of the unit. Even with their armour in place, the pikemen were at risk from musket fire, and the lighter nature of un-armoured pikemen at least gave them more manoeuvrability. In addition, given that the commands to use the pike *en masse* were technically complex and that the soldiers in the first engagements were raw troops akin to Sergeant Nehemiah Wharton's apprentices, in the field this complexity would have been seen as ultimately impractical. The commands used at Edgehill, and for some time beyond, would have almost certainly been reduced to the basics: 'Stand to your arms' (holding the pike upright in right hand, with left hand on hip); 'Advance your pikes' (with the pike supported upright on the right shoulder); 'Charge your pike' (with the pike held horizontally at shoulder level, a move mostly used for advancing on the enemy); and 'Charge to horse' (with the pikemen crouched, the butt of weapon resting on right instep and the pike angled upward to meet the enemy at the breast height of the horse).

The bodies of pikemen in any Early Modern army were now there as much to defend the musketeers as to be used aggressively. They continued to confront enemy pikemen in a 'push of pike' – when opposing blocks of troops (invariably shouting) advanced on each other holding their weapons shoulder high, jabbing and swinging at the enemy's face, until one or the other gave way either through casualties or fear – but of more significance to the military art of the day was the musket.

MUSKETS

The use of the hand-held gunpowder weapon had begun in the Middle Ages. The harquebus was one of the first practical infantry weapons, although still cumbersome at some four to five feet long, with a weight of some twelve pounds and firing a lead ball of one and a half ounces by a matchlock lowered into the priming pan by a trigger. From the 1560s, the appearance of the musket gave infantry a more valuable weapon to use. It was initially much longer – 6 feet, with a forked wooden pole, or rest, to support the gun – and gave a greater range, with a heavier ball. Its other advantages were that it was easily repaired and relatively cheap to produce (the matchlock cost some 10s. to 11s. 6d. in 1645, compared to the flintlock's 14s. 6d. to 15s. 6d.). The disadvantages were its awkward nature in loading, unreliability in ignition, and harsh recoil as it was fired from the shoulder. It was also noisy, and there was a large amount of smoke, so visibility was impaired. Moreover, the firing mechanism was usually a matchlock. In this, a lighted match discharged the already loaded gun by its application to the pan filled with gunpowder, which ignited in the touchhole and caused the gun to fire. This could lead to difficulties in inclement weather and a great use of the slow-burning match, and to make sure the musket was always ready the match had to be kept alight. Troops who let their matches go out, or were even ordered to do so by incompetent officers, could be at a disadvantage, as was to occur in the Scots army at Dunbar in September 1650. The invention of the wheellock as a firing mechanism was of some help. Its importance lay in combining firepower with mobility, but its complexity meant that it was expensive and difficult to manufacture. Finally, the flintlock showed the way forward. In this, a piece of flint held in a metal 'cock' provided the ignition. It struck a metal plate, pushing it forward and thus creating the spark that ignited the piece.

Over the next 100 years, tactical innovations in musketry were to be found in the actual use made of the men in formation rather than in any fundamental changes in the weapons. While Cromwell as a commander had little to add to the science of infantry warfare, there was an increasing reversion to linear tactics in Early Modern warfare, increasing firepower with a second and third line to prevent penetration or outflanking. Nevertheless, changes in the ability to fire exactly by rotation and countermarch were just two of the means by which infantry officers tried to bring weapons to bear. Volley fire was more appropriate. Maurice of Nassau had first used the battalion, a shallow formation of some ten ranks, to deliver fire. Gustavus Adolphus had reduced this still further to six ranks. The older style of firing by countermarch was in the end to prove both too complex and too unwieldy for the reality of war.

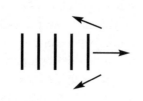

First rank fires at front then retires left and right to rear, there to reload, while second rank takes its place, and so on. This began to be replaced by salvo firing. Allowing for the fact that one rank needed to be firing whilst another was ready to fire and the third was reloading, this would enable a continuous fire to be kept up.

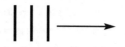

Front rank kneeling, second rank standing, and third rank behind them. All fire at once or by rank.

Musket drill remained a series of complex manoeuvres, and although (as with the pike) the choice in the field would have been to simplify as much as possible, the musketeer's drill could be made up of as many as thirty or more 'motions'. Slow and deliberate fire, it is estimated, could well take one man up to two minutes per round to effect. In the field, however, a well-trained musketeer would simply drop many of the recommended motions and merely listen to three orders – 'Make ready', 'Present' and 'Give fire'. Thus he could loose off a shot every 35–45 seconds, until he ran out of the limited amounts of ammunition he usually carried.[18] The gun would then be reversed and wielded as a primitive club.

There was also some debate about the Dutch-versus-Swedish style of infantry fire and tactics. In the Dutch style, infantry regiments fought as a unit, with pikes in the centre and musketeers on the wings, or 'sleeves', 8–10 ranks deep. Fire could be by introduction, where the front rank fired and the rear rank marched forward between files and fired, the next rank advanced, and so on. Alternatively, there was fire by extraduction, a process that was the reverse of the actions described. The following is the process of the countermarch, as described in a drill manual of 1638:

'When yee are commanded *Files to the right hand counter march*, then all the file leaders together at one instant steppe forward with the right legge, and bringing about their left legge, turn their bodie to the right hand, and so marche down thorow the files, till they come to the place of the bringers-up or last ranke, all that follow the file-leader, must not offer to turn, before they have come up to the

place of the file leaders, and every follower must remarke and keep
that distance with his leader which hee had before they began to
counter-march: *As you were*: step forward with the righte legge and,
cast about the left legge to the right hand, and so march back to
your place.'[19]

Such elements of the military doctrine as were found in the contemporary
drill books were much simplified once men were beyond training and in
the field, and, in the end, it was the Swedish style of infantry training that
was adopted. Here the musketeers would be massed in blocks three to six
ranks deep (50 men) and would fire *en masse*, or by one rank at a time. This
enabled firing in salvo, giving a greater weight of shot against a target. The
pikes remained embodied together, ready to defend the musketeers from
cavalry. Such tactics now gave infantry more flexibility, but training and
experience were also necessary.

The musket's accuracy in this period has been the subject of some
debate. The weapon's effective range was about 100 yards, but this was in
volley firing rather than sharpshooting. W. P. Guthrie makes the important
point that 'all weapons were essentially handmade and varied to a greater
or lesser degree' in accuracy.[20] In general, musket accuracy seems to have
been tolerable. It must be remembered that these were smoothbore
weapons propelling a spherical bullet of lead by means of a gunpowder
charge. Accuracy was in any case difficult without rifling, so mass formations were essential. The handgun was a short-range weapon, but most of
the targets were very large, so most musketeers had a chance of hitting
something. Hughes gives the following table of statistics from 1800, for
trained soldiers against a target measuring 1.75 x 3.00 metres:[21]

Range (metres)	Percentage of shots hitting target
75	60
150	40
225	25
300	20

These percentages may have been much smaller in conditions of combat,
but the musket was still an effective enough tool of war and one not to be
underestimated: men would not, as in modern warfare, inhabit an empty
battlefield, but be trained to stand in tight formations, generally in full
sight of each other.

In battle, the average infantry regiment would be drawn up into various divisions:

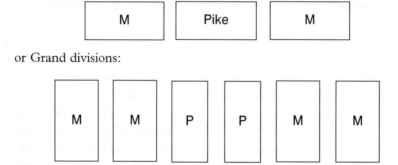

or Grand divisions:

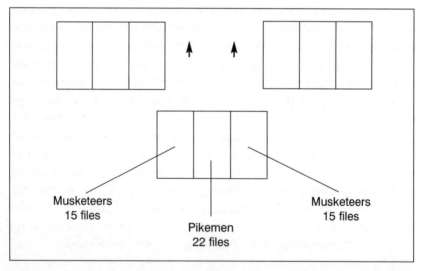

Other formations in use included the Swedish brigade, where three or four battalions were combined into a wedge-shaped formation with one battalion in reserve and even light cannon between the units.

The use of a 'forlorn' was also a common occurrence. This was a group of musketeers pushed out in front of the army as a screen in order to break up the enemy's attack. The contemporary theorist Robert Ward noted that the forlorn was intended to 'see if they can disorder any of their Divisions, or gain some Prisoners whereby the Generall may learn how they are imbattled, and what Stratagems they intend to use.'[22] The armed infantry would generally advance to give fire, and then push forward with pike; the musketeers would then fall back and re-load, and thus begin firing again. Faced with cavalry, the troops may well have formed a circle or square, with the pikemen protecting the musketeers, or one of the many elegant but sometimes impractical manoeuvres the military theorists of the day seemed inclined to impose on their men.

ARTILLERY

In this era there were generally two types of artillery, field and siege. The widest use of this weapon was in light field guns; anything heavier was simply too difficult to manoeuvre in battle. Most artillery pieces remained crude and inaccurate, and had a slow rate of fire. Their primary ammunition was a round metal ball. Case shot – hundreds of musket balls in a canvas bag – was for use against mass formations. In general, ten rounds an hour was a high rate of fire for an artillery piece. After about forty rounds, the barrel would also grow too hot and need cooling. All artillery shots tended to take time, and both loading and sighting the weapon, as well as the weight of the heavier pieces, tended to restrict their use in battle. They were far more practicable in the much more static conditions of siege warfare, where they were, more often than not, decisive in creating a breach in walls that could be exploited by infantry.

In reality the need for the general of the day was to form an adequate train of artillery that could function in either battle or siege, and use as many specialists as possible to control its use in action. On the whole, the use of artillery by generals was not particularly innovative, and after some initial pounding the gun was of little use. In siege warfare there was much more scope for the gunner's technical skills. Here the military engineer could place his cannon and mortars scientifically, the aim being to create a breach in the walls large enough to enable a storming party to enter the town or city. It was usually to be hoped that the citadel would surrender long before this occurred, thus saving casualties on both sides, but, as we shall see, towns sometimes proved to be resistant to the principles of war.

The effect of artillery fire on the human body could, of course, be horrific. Round shot could break walls, so its effect on men was nothing less than devastating, and the heavier the shot the greater its velocity at target. There had been little uniformity in cannon design prior to 1642. All guns were individually made, and standardisation only came with the war. There were three principal field pieces – 3-, 6- and 12-pounders. The weight of the shot governed the type of gun. In combat, the weapons usually had to be set up in smaller batteries between the infantry in the centre of the line of battle, their task being to soften up the opposition by sending round shot carving through the enemy ranks and thus killing men as well as breaking their comrades' morale. However, since artillery was not very mobile, it was left to the infantry and, above all, the cavalry to win the battle.

CAVALRY

In the military textbooks of the day, it was the meetings of large bodies of horse against each other that were the ultimate ambition of any general in land warfare. Indeed, it could be argued that the Civil Wars were in many senses essentially cavalry wars.[23] Psychologically, the horseman still regarded himself as the superior and noblest force in battle, and it was the charge that remained his *métier*. As the theorist John Cruso noted, 'to know rightly how to charge the enemy, is a matter of great consequence.'[24] The horseman needed level ground and an unhindered countryside to ply his trade to the full. In reality, charges at high speed, such as are often depicted in art or the cinema, would result in carnage among both horses and men, 'growing bigger as succeeding ranks [were] carried on to the leading ones by their own impetus.'[25] This was well known amongst devotees of the cavalry at the time and afterwards; as one nineteenth century expert commented, 'Cavalry seldom meet each other in a charge executed at speed; the one party generally turns before joining issue with the enemy, and this often happens when their line is still unbroken and no obstacles of any sort intervene.'[26]

This basic fact meant that the mass cavalry charge would actually occur at much lower speeds, even almost stopping dead at the point of impact, allowing one side to open its ranks and the other to penetrate them, or for the opponent to turn away. Cavalry action was the classic case of the moral over the physical, for it was seeing the oncoming cavalry approaching that should theoretically lead to the disintegration of the troops facing them. As the theorist du Picq later wrote, 'Cavalry action … is an affair of morale.'[27] It was also recommended that some men be held in reserve for 'the meer sight of a reserve gives a terrour' to the enemy.[28]

If the evolution of the pike in war had at first left the cavalry bereft of a role on the battlefield, the much more defensive idea of the caracole was born as a result: cavalry now resorted to using shot from pistol or carbine in order to blast their way through the infantry ranks. Generally the horsemen would ride up in ranks, each firing and then wheeling left or right to return to the rear in order to reload. They would continue the process until an opening sufficiently large to penetrate appeared in the enemy ranks or they were shot off their horses by musket fire.

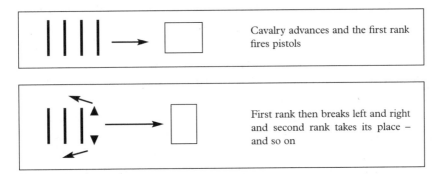

Cavalry advances and the first rank fires pistols

First rank then breaks left and right and second rank takes its place – and so on

Gradually, this idea was dropped in favour of employing cavalrymen in their true role as shock troops, using their weight, mass and cold steel in an aggressive manner. Here, a heavy mass formation of six (or three) ranks, three abreast in close order (knee to knee) or open order six feet apart, who would reserve their fire for as long as possible, moved forward at a reasonable rate towards the enemy. Each man was armed with a long sword, which had a three-foot, double-edged blade and a basket hilt (now given the modern name 'mortuary sword'). While useful for cut and thrust, another type, the backsword, only had one cutting edge to it.

It was Gustavus Adolphus of Sweden who had first favoured this more dominant role for his cavalry. Sometimes musketeers were attached to cavalry troops to give them covering fire and disrupt the opposition. In terms of other cavalry weapons, the lance had generally fallen out of favour, but it still remained effective when wielded on the field of battle by, for example, Scots and Border moss-troopers or irregular cavalry. On the other hand, the use of dragoons – in effect, mounted infantry – was becoming much more widespread in the armies of the day. They would carry swords, but they lacked armour, and their mounts were normally much cheaper than the normal cavalry horses (and often little more than flea-bitten nags). As mounted infantry, dragoons were used to advance before the rest of the army and hold a defensible post, and to retire behind the army to give harassing fire to the enemy. They usually dismounted before they opened fire, and one in ten of the dragoons would be left as a horse-handler behind the firing line. William Barriffe applauded their use, for they were, he said, 'intended for special service, to assist the Cavalry as Infantry, there being many exploits which cannot be effected by the Cavalry alone.'[29]

Despite attempts to keep the standard cavalry troops together in battle, there would have been some natural dispersal in action: some men would be more eager to reach the fray than others, and horses were prone to acting in an unruly manner and could disrupt the lines. Raimondo Montecuccoli, a military commentator on the battles in the Thirty Years' War, noted of cavalry warfare that 'over a distance of 200 paces one sees this long rank [of horse] thin out and dissolve. Great breaches appear within it … On many occasions only twenty or twenty-five of a hundred horse actually charge.'[30] The actual fight would then degenerate into a series of individual actions. Some would be more harmless than others as helmets, body armour or buff coats deflected the blades of the swords. In these combats, 'the next Man can hardly make a true relation of the Actions of him that is next to him; for in such a Hurry and Smoke as in a set Field, a Man takes notice of nothing but what relates to his own safety.'[31]

The Royalist Richard Bulstrode was to serve in Northampton's troop in the Prince of Wales's Regiment of Horse, and he found himself in the thick of the action at Edgehill. He noted that 'I was wounded in the Head by a Person who turned upon me, and struck me with his Pole-axe, and was seconding his blow, when Sir Thomas Byron being near, he shot him dead with his pistol.'[32] In his previous action at Powick Bridge, Bulstrode's 'unruly horse … ran away with me amongst the enemy', and he is unlikely to have been the only one to suffer in this respect in battle.[33] Officers also faced real difficulties in keeping the men in close order in such bedlam, while actually rallying them after any success was a major achievement. The successful charge in Early Modern warfare seems to have automatically engendered a race across hill and dale in an often bloody pursuit. This, naturally, led to confusion, blown horses and disorganised men.

WARRIORS

Essex's army was the first in which Captain Oliver Cromwell was to serve. Like other gentlemen captains, Cromwell had been commissioned to raise a troop of horse in August 1642. This troop was to be the sixty-seventh in Essex's army, and for the privilege he was paid the sum of £1,104. His particular choices of subordinate officers were Lieutenant Cuthbert Baildon, Cornet John Waterhouse and Quartermaster John Desborough. About the first two men little is known, but Desborough was Cromwell's brother-in-law. In the event, Cromwell was soon active as a captain, and for his men, of course, nothing was too much trouble; indeed, he thought that he had 'a lovely company'. The men themselves were all hand-picked volunteers from his own areas of Huntingdon and Cambridge – active soldiers of conviction and with a spiritual side, as well as friends, neighbours and kinsmen. The sum of the troop was completed in August 1642 and it was generally ready for the field in September, although it still lacked some saddles. Cromwell also hoped to be able to subject his men to an 'iron discipline', and they were men whom he hoped would draw their sword for the Lord's cause.[34] Eventually this troop became the core of the regiment that later emerged as the 'Ironsides'. In these early days, both the men and their commander practised and then rode off to join the army of Essex. They were placed in the Lord General's own regiment under the command of Sir Philip Stapleton, and it was intended that they would fight under him in battle.

All sorts of novice soldiers joined Essex's army in 1642. Most, like Sergeant Wharton, were young, and they became involved in the war for a variety of reasons. The majority were volunteers who had attended the grand raising of the army at the Artillery Ground. Later, men were to be pressed when sufficient volunteers were not forthcoming, and this resulted in a more reluctant soldiery. The London-trained bands themselves were supposed to recruit 'none of the meaner sort', who were left to the auxiliaries, but some of the men dragged into the infantry proved to be the sweepings of the gaols and the marginal in society.[35] The contemporary view was that the effectiveness of these troops depended on the initiative and skill of the colonels, as well as their training and the experience of the subordinate officers. It was a common belief amongst the generals of the day that men would not fight without good officers to lead them, and, as we have seen, most of the men in Essex's army were raw soldiers, unaccustomed to military discipline or soldiering in the field. Still, Essex as Lord General was a popular choice, and the 'darling of the swordsmen'. At his first appearance in the Artillery Ground, where the volunteers were to be listed, 'there came in no less than four thousand of them in one day; who declared their resolutions to live and die with the Earl of Essex.'[36]

One of the men who joined Essex in this new venture was Edmund Ludlow. Aged twenty-eight in 1642, Ludlow was a gentleman living in London and attending the Inns of Court, when he

'... thought it my duty, upon consideration of my age and vigorous constitution, as an English-man, and an invitation to that purpose from my father, to enter into the service of my country ... I thought the justice of that cause I had engaged in to be so evident, that I could not imagine it to be attended with much difficulty.'[37]

This being so, he, and others of a like mind from the Inns of Court, got together for some instruction of arms under an old soldier they recruited for the purpose, and were soon to be met frequently at exercise on the Artillery Ground. Being gentlemen all, they were in a good position in August 1642 to enter into the Earl of Essex's own Life Guard under the command of Sir Philip Stapleton. Ludlow's fellow troopers were fifty gentlemen, who were paid 8s. a day; fifty other troopers received 3s. a day. Many of these gentlemen proved to be very notable figures in the years ahead. Along with Ludlow himself, Charles Fleetwood, Thomas Harrison and others were to dominate the war and politics of the 1650s, and were to become closely associated with Cromwell. As young troopers, they rode cheerfully off to war, already convinced of the justice of their cause and dubiously aware of some of the problems to be faced.

Essex himself had set off to war in a melancholy mood. Parliament had wished him well, although it had refused to give him powers to negotiate with the King. Despite this, he had left London to general cheers, and with his coffin, shroud and family escutcheon in his baggage in case of any mishaps. Most of his army had preceded him, cheerily looting the countryside as they went forward. Essex's force finally managed to converge on Northampton, and by the beginning of August 1642 the Parliamentary army had marched up and down the Midlands, for the most part training as they did so. Many of the new recruits were soon found to be incapable of the elaborate actions needed for Early Modern warfare, so these activities, alongside the endless marching, would have been important for them as they bedded into military life.

In the meantime, the King, steadily gathering forces, had moved down from York, loudly claiming to his men that 'You shall meet no enemy but traitors and most of them Brownists, Anabaptists and Atheists, such as desire to destroy both Church and State.'[38] Charles I had first raised his standard at Nottingham and was then foiled at Hull, and, apparently at a loss as to what to do next, manoeuvred rather aimlessly round the Midlands recruiting troops to his cause. His eventual strategy was to advance and capture London. Essex, meanwhile, moved north via Nottingham and Coventry, manoeuvring in the best traditions of the seventeenth-century general. Eventually he headed towards Worcester, which was garrisoned by the Royalist Sir John Byron.

POWICK BRIDGE

The first clash between the two armies came on 23 September 1642 south of the city of Worcester. It did little to raise the morale or the confidence of the Parliamentarians. The dashing and aggressive Prince Rupert met Colonel Nathaniel Fiennes' cavalry near Worcester and swiftly routed them; even Essex's own bodyguard was caught up in the débâcle and performed badly. The Royalist Lord Falkland was now openly contemptuous of his opponents, crowing that most of the prisoners were raw soldiers and 'tailors or embroiderers, or the like.'[39] Richard Baxter, who had 'a great mind to go see [an army] never having seen any part' of such a thing, was marching with the army of Essex. He was equally unimpressed. To him, the flight from the Powick Bridge was a 'sight quickly told me of the vanity of armies, and how little confidence is to be placed in them.'[40] Despite this, Essex still occupied Worcester and then took Hereford and lesser places, while Rupert and Byron retired towards King Charles and his main army, located at Shrewsbury. The Royalists were now confident that whatever Essex could throw at them they would be able to handle with ease.

THE APPROACH TO BATTLE

In fact the Royal army was undergoing a reorganisation at Shrewsbury when Rupert and Byron arrived. The new troops were being placed 'into several Regiments of Horse, Foot, and Dragoons … The Horse were put into several Brigades, the Foot into Tertia's (as they were then called) and we had Three or Four Regiments of Dragoons.'[41] Conversely, Charles was still short of supplies, men and money – and, above all, arms. The capture of London would bring all of these and, he hoped, an end to the rebellion. Thus on 12 October the King began his march towards London, having first refused Essex's pleas for an armistice by proudly declaring he would receive nothing from the hand of a traitor. By 20 October he had skirted past Warwick and Coventry and on towards Banbury, his immediate objective, and London began to look anxiously northwards for its defenders.

Essex eventually lumbered after the enemy, having first, in a review at Worcester, attempted to instil some discipline and understanding into his army as to what they were about. By 22 October 1642 Essex found himself at Kineton seeking rest, for the next day was a Sunday. He intended to move on the following day to Banbury. He was unaware of the proximity of the King's forces, and took the chance of a halt to allow the straggling elements of his army to catch up. In the meantime, the

King's army lay at Edgecott, seven miles away. Neither side was initially very aware of the other's presence, although on 22 October Richard Bulstrode recounted that after dark 'we saw several Fires not far from us, and sending out a Party to see, we were soon informed, that the Earl of Essex was there with his whole army.'[42] Bulstrode's regiment was swiftly drawn up into the fields and placed on guard all night. There was much discussion in the ranks. Would the King now strike for London or turn and attack Essex? To avoid Essex and instead advance on London would be to leave a powerful army at his back. Eventually advised by his eager nephew Rupert, Charles decided to offer battle. On 23 October his army occupied the most conspicuous point around, the ridge at Edgehill. Three miles across and facing to the north-west, it was a steep slope with some hedges on the plain below.

EDGEHILL: 23 OCTOBER 1642

Essex finally discovered the whereabouts of the Royal army at about eight o'clock on the Sunday morning, but delayed occupying the ridge and found himself not only faced with the King's army but also cut off from his supply base in London. He had, moreover, been forced, or had thought it wise, to leave behind men in garrisons on his march, depleting his army as a result. In addition, John Hampden and two infantry regiments, with most of the artillery, was a day behind him, still labouring to catch up to the main army. Most of the artillery had also been left behind, mainly 'through want of Draught-Horses, and through other Omissions of Monsieur Du-Boys.'[43] Some scattered elements of horse, including Cromwell and his troop, also seem to have been misplaced, and were quartered some distance away from the field. This lack of concentration of force might well have placed Essex at a disadvantage, and at the least it reveals that he had not intended to fight that day. Nevertheless, having discovered the King's forces, he intended now to order his own troops, wait on events and hope that some of his missing army could catch up. Essex sent out orders for his forces to draw up a short distance from the foot of Edgehill on a small rise, and there he stood his ground. According to the Parliamentary account, 'the Wind was much for their Advantage, and they endeavoured to get it more; which to prevent we were inforced to draw out our Left Wing to a great breadth, and by that means, before the Battel was done, gained it wholly from them.'[44] Here was to be fought the first real large-scale battle of the Civil War, and it was to show the inadequacies of the military system on both sides.

Essex drew up his battalions in the usual formation – cavalry on the wings and infantry in the centre, at the bottom of the hill in two lines. On his left wing were the cavalry of Sir James Ramsey, behind which, in the second line, lay the regiment of Denzil Holles and, to the right, Thomas Ballard's infantry brigade. To Ramsey's right, in the centre and the front line, was the four-regiment infantry brigade of Charles Essex, and to their right was Sir John Meldrum's three-regiment infantry brigade, with the infantry of Sir William Fairfax behind. The cavalry regiments of Sir Philip Stapleton and Sir William Balfour also sat behind Meldrum. On the right wing was Lord Fielding's regiment of horse, with some 700 dragoons placed to protect his flank. The right wing was the weakest, some of the cavalry having not yet arrived; amongst the latecomers were Oliver Cromwell and his troop, whose whereabouts at this time are unknown. In order to strengthen the position the bushes were lined with dragoons 'to make a shew'.[45]

While the marshalling of the army was taking place, the Parliamentarians, having observed that the notorious Prince Rupert was now facing their left wing, and already fearing his reputation as a notable warrior, sought to place their greatest strength in cavalry there. As it turned out, they need not have bothered. Nonetheless, Ramsey had taken care to position his cavalry in a 'Posture defensive, and offensive, interlining the squadrons with a convenient number of Musqueteers'.[46] He had also protected his left flank with two or three hundred musketeers drawn from Ballard's brigade and Holles' regiment, and made them line the hedges there.

Some 13,000 men were now with Essex, and the Earl placed what artillery he had between the infantry regiments, although most of the Parliamentarian artillery, as has been noted, was still some distance away. As such, he had some forty-two troops of horse, between 700 and 1,000 dragoons and twelve infantry regiments, and around 2,000 horse and 11,000 foot, allowing for desertions and the sick left on the roads behind him. Some other regiments had been left to garrison certain places en route or were guarding the laggard artillery train as it moved forward.

As they stood in formation on a slight rise, the bright morning sun rose. Most of the men were tired and hungry. Ludlow later noted that he and his men had had little rest, and less food, over the last two days. The chaplains began to pass busily through the ranks, offering spiritual comfort where they could, but there was little else to distract the soldiers. Noon came and went. Essex proved to be cautious enough not to wish to manoeuvre uphill and launch an offensive on such a strong position. He did seek some advantage by forcing the Royal army to change its position,

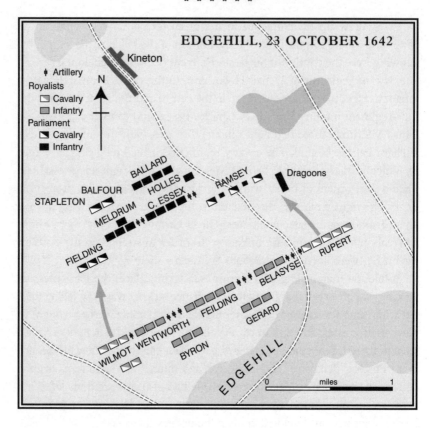

and in due course Charles and his men took the hint and began to move slowly down the hill and on to the plain below, under cover of some of their artillery. Despite their difficulties (Edgehill is on a 1 in 4 incline), no attempt was made by Essex to disrupt the Royal army's columns while they descended. The enemy army manoeuvred down the fairly steep slope and was left alone to get on with it. Essex, in the end, was a conventional general, and in the first great battle of the war convention was everything.

By one o'clock in the afternoon the King's forces had reached the plain below Edgehill. The King, naturally, now sought to order his battalions. As a general, Charles was to prove largely ineffective in these wars. His reluctance to give a clear lead – a trait perceptible in his whole reign – and then often a mistaken lead when he did finally make up his mind, was to cause frequent difficulties. While the King was brave enough on the field of battle, he was arguably no commander. As a strategist he was flawed, and tactically he was inexperienced (except at Lostwithiel in 1644). His qualities of leadership consisted of attempts at an 'affability' to all men, as Clarendon put it, and this 'not only hampered him on the field of battle, but added to the dissension and jealously on it.'[47] On this day, he ordered Lord Ruthven, an experienced Scots officer who had formerly served under Gustavus Adolphus, to draw up his line of battle. In the process, he much offended his actual general (the Earl of Lindsay), who, already angry following a quarrel with Rupert concerning the merits of the Dutch method of war over the Swedish, finally stormed off in a huff, the angry Scot loudly claiming that if the King thought him unfit to perform as commander-in-chief then he would serve him as a colonel. Lindsay subsequently placed himself at the head of his own regiment of foot; here he was to be wounded, be captured in the battle, and later die of his wounds. The Royal army, in the meantime, was drawn up in Swedish fashion. On the right wing lay the Royal cavalry in two lines (three deep), commanded by that dashing and headstrong Prince of the Rhine, Rupert, the King's nephew, and on the left the cavalry was commanded by Lord Wilmot, his lieutenant-general. Dragoons protected the flanks. In the centre, the Royal infantry (six deep) was commanded by Ruthven, and under him was Sir Jacob Astley. In all, there were some 14,300 men in the force now facing Essex.

Despite his youth, Prince Rupert was one of the most able Royal generals on the field that day. He had already made something of a reputation before Powick Bridge – enough, at any rate, for Wharton to describe him as 'Prince Robert, that diabolical Cavaleere', and he was to emerge from the war as the most celebrated of all cavalry generals next to Cromwell and Fairfax.[48] Unfortunately, his character had a degree of impetuosity and tactlessness that was to make him a number of enemies around the King. Decisive in his opinions and hot-tempered in war, Rupert was often hasty and impractical in his ambitions. He was popular with the soldiers, but more often than not he was unable to control them in battle or willing to do so out of it, bringing a touch of the German wars into English life.

Once their forces had been drawn up, the senior Royalist generals went to the King and persuaded him to retire to some rising ground close by, so that he would be out of danger. Charles, dressed in a black velvet coat lined with ermine and a steel cap covered with velvet, and with his two eldest sons nearby, did so unwillingly. At least none could doubt the King's bravery. Both sides continued to stare at each other warily as Essex's artillery now began a desultory preliminary bombardment. The guns on the right wing opened a slow but steady fire, particularly on that part of the field where the King was conspicuous, surrounded by his entourage, moving along his lines and encouraging his men. Shooting at the opposing general was not unknown in the day, but shooting at the King himself suggests a certain seriousness of disposition in Essex's, or his subordinates', attitude to the business at hand. Edmund Ludlow claimed that the barrage went on for about an hour, but his estimate may well be awry. Few of the officers in the armies involved possessed accurate watches, and, in what was to follow, timings could never be certain. We do know that some damage was caused to the Royalist side by the barrage, and that the first casualty of the battle was a Royalist officer. Finally, no doubt to the relief of the waiting troops, the battle proper got under way at about three o'clock in the afternoon.[49]

Beyond the embattlement of the troops, there seems to have been little overall control of the combat on either side. Indeed, it is arguable that, like many early seventeenth-century battles, Edgehill became merely a series of relatively clumsy actions. In the event, the first real exploit of the day was to be a cavalry charge by Rupert and his men. This swiftly got out of hand, although Rupert seems to have taken pains prior to setting off to give his men as many positive commands as possible about keeping in close order and refraining from fire until they had actually closed with the enemy.

Some Parliamentary musketeers and dragoons, who would have flanked any movement, were chased off before the action, and the Royalist cavalry under Rupert now advanced, slowly at first, and leaving no reserve, but moving at a steady pace, slightly outflanking the Parliamentarian horse who sat and waited for them. On their extreme right, some of the Royalist cavalry found the hedges and ditches, causing some disorder. While some of the Parliamentary cannon fire opened fire upon them, it seems to have overshot and it did little to slow the advance. The Parliamentary left wing was already nervous and unsteady, and it fired its carbines while their enemy was still a long way off, some of the men shooting into the air. It then began to panic.

Sir Faithful Fortescue's Irish troops in the Parliamentary lines chose at this point to switch sides, and suddenly joined in the Royalist assault. Most of the Parliamentarian horse almost immediately lost their heads, shot into the air, wheeled and ran off, leaving their musketeers behind to face the onslaught of the cavalry. Some of the Parliamentary horse crashed into its own infantry as it fled and scattered four regiments of foot. The Royalist cavalry now followed in. Richard Wiseman graphically revealed what this actually meant in his book *Chirurgicall Treatises*:

'When horsemen fall in amongst the Infantry [they] cruelly hack them; the poor Souldiers the while sheltring their Heads with their

Arms, sometime with the one, then the other, untill they be both cruelly mangled: and yet the Head fareth little better the while for their Defence, many of them not escaping with lesse then two or three Wounds through the Scull ... And if the man fly, and the Enemy pursue, his hinder parts meet with great Wounds, as over the Thighs, Back, and Shoulders and Neck.'[50]

Fleeing cavalry also shattered the regiment of Denzil Holles, and somewhere in this mêlée Sergeant Wharton was killed or mortally wounded, although Holles himself stood firm and attempted to rally the cavalry. In the end he managed to hold on to three troops of horse. In fleeing, the Parliamentarian cavalry exhibited the normal behaviour of inexperienced troops, but they opened themselves up to a five- to six-mile killing zone as Rupert's men eagerly followed them. Unfortunately, Rupert's excited troops rode off the field in a wild pursuit and did not return, for they found the Parliamentary baggage in Kineton and were soon excitedly helping themselves to its contents. Others rode still further, up to two miles from the field, and were only checked by an encounter with Hampden's two regiments hurriedly coming up to join the battle. Even the King's own bodyguard, discouraged by being mocked by many in his army as a 'Troop of shew', joined in, thus leaving the Royal army bereft of most of its cavalry.[51]

On the Royalist left wing, the ground was more tangled with hedges and ditches. The cavalry here was forced to pass through hedges lined with scattered groups of musketeers. The Royalist Sir Arthur Aston, whom we shall meet again, was sent in with his dragoons to disperse them, and once this had been achieved the left wing moved steadily forward. Again the Royalists easily routed and dispersed the Parliamentarian horse, and then almost all began an uncontrolled pursuit, leaving the field behind. Essex, however, still had two regiments of cavalry, those of Stapleton and Balfour, neglected and undiscovered 'in a corner of the field',[52] although Sir William Fairfax's regiment of foot ran off, leaving its officers standing. The remnants of the Parliamentarian cavalry and infantry now sought to hold on as the King's infantry moved forward to complete the victory. In a dramatic fashion beloved of generals of the day, Essex dismounted and snatched a pike from a soldier, resolving to die in the field.

Some, at least, knew that this would still be a day of business rather than romantic gestures. The old soldier Sir Jacob Astley, commanding the Royal infantry, was said to have spoken the following soldier's prayer: 'O Lord! Thou knowest, how busy I must be this day. If I forget Thee, do not thou forget me', and with that he rose up, crying 'March on, boys!'[53] At a steady pace, the infantry advanced, the mud from the autumn rains making the ground heavy under foot. They were formed up six deep, in 'nine great bodies'. Some of the Welsh foot involved did not even possess a pike or musket, being armed only with 'pitchforks, and such like tools, and many only with good cudgels.'[54] Clarendon claimed that there 'was in the whole body ... not one pikeman who had a corselet, and very few musketeers who had swords.'[55] Drums would also have been beating. As one commentator noted, the drum was 'the voice of the commander, the spurre of the valiant, and the heart of the Coward ... when the roaring cannon, the clashing of armes, the neighing of horses, and other confused noise causeth ... neither Captain, nor other officer can bee heard.'[56] Crossing a small brook and marching up the slope, they all too soon found themselves facing the Parliamentary infantry. The Duke of York, writing much later, claimed that the infantry let loose a volley of shot as they marched forward and then engaged in a 'push of pike'. Although the Parliamentary commanders tried to hold their men in check, they failed. Despite Mandeville's men being belaboured and cudgelled into ranks, some of them now took to their heels. An infantry mêlée now began with those still left, and both sides engaged in 'push of pike', using their musketry to blast gaps in their opponents' lines. The crudeness of seventeenth-century warfare began to show itself.

Infantry still represented the only force in the era 'by which ground could (and can) be held'.[57] Elements such as discipline and leadership, as well as the ability to hold in check the men's natural instinct for flight in such circumstances, now determined this grisly meeting of mass bodies of men. Commanders tended to place their most inexperienced soldiers in the middle of the ranks and files and the more experienced on the outside, and this explains, in part, the formations most infantry soldiers were locked into – for defence, but also literally to keep them in line. The distances at which the threat they faced was offered, as well as the 'will to combat', determined their critical reaction. Qualities such as honour, friendship, fear of a loss of face, bullying, rage and the possibility of loot and drink sustained their will to combat. In this period, we can also add God to the mix. Chaplain Bifield sought to bring courage from God to the Parliamentarians as he passed 'from Regiment to Regiment, and Troop to Troop to encourage them at the latter end of the fight, not knowing what the issue of things might be, in the darksome evening.'[58]

Marshalling the regimental or troop ethos around a standard formed, it was hoped, even more group solidarity. The standards of the day, most emblazoned with symbols of some significance to their captains, were points of honour for the soldiers. Aside from their practical function as rallying points, they raised the morale and self-worth of the men who stood under them. Officers could exploit this relationship with their men. Wharton related how, early in the campaign, his men had been alarmed by rumours of approaching cavaliers: 'in half an hour all our soldiers, though dispersed, were cannibals in arms, ready to encounter the enemy, crying out for a dish of Cavaliers for supper.'[59] This was the sort of morale that any officer would be looking for, although it seems not to have done Wharton much good.

The face of battle in 1642 would have been unnatural and obscure to most of those involved, cloudy with smoke, with waves of noise, and often deadly to the common soldier. As Jonathan Shay points out, 'Danger of death and mutilation is the pervading medium of combat. It is a viscous liquid in which everything looks strangely refracted and moves about in odd ways, a powerful corrosive that breaks down many fixed contours of perception and utterly dissolves others.'[60] Most would have had a restricted view of the action; inside the unit formation, the view would have been blurred by another man's head and body, and only the heightened senses would have made men aware of the carnage around them – the deafening crash of the big guns; the crack of the muskets near the ear; the sweat of fellow soldiers in their heavy woollen clothes, helmets or body armour; the stink of men whose fear got the better of them and made them lose control of their bowels; the acrid smell of clouds of gunpowder, smoke and blood; the clatter, crunch and splintering of pikes; the screams and cries of the dying and wounded. There would have been little awareness of the time or the action on a broader scale, even, one suspects, for some of the officers and generals, as vision was fragmented to only a few feet as the combat became less one of units and more one of bunches of men fighting for their lives. Armies of the era still tried to manoeuvre to catch the wind and blow the smoke into their opponents' faces. Thus what appear to us to be simple movements on nicely drawn maps were in practice rather more difficult for those involved.

The cumbersome nature of the weapons meant that the length of time needed to load muskets would have slowed even further amidst the confusion, fear, noise, gunfire, smoke, officers' cries of 'Make ready' and 'Give fire' and general pandemonium. The absence of tactical flexibility meant that both sides could do little but face each other in an attritional struggle. Charging forward, skirmishing, firing muskets so that one could literally in some cases see the whites of the enemy's eyes (muskets were good at fifty yards and worse the further away one stood), the infantry fired for as long as it had ammunition, and then retired a few feet. Men were pushed and beaten into keeping their ranks in this scrum of bodies. The need was to keep up the momentum in the scrum, for the natural inclination from the rear ranks would have been to slip away, and then to run. Formations, if they broke, tended to break from the rear, as individuals or groups of men could see what was happening and then make the choice not to go forward into the mêlée. While the officers tried to push men into the gaps as they occurred and the wounded, if they were able to, crawled away to seek the limited medical help, the unit as whole would begin to break down as fear spread.

In Early Modern warfare, wounds from the lead musket balls could be horrific. The soft lead sometimes flattened out on impact and at a relatively slow speed punctured armour, coat and skin. Possessing low energy, the ball would rarely exit the body and carried infection into the wound with it. Bones were shattered, muscle tissue and vital organs disintegrated, and death could rapidly follow. Even if one survived, infection could take hold as attempts were made to remove the ball. Shattered bones meant amputation; wounds that penetrated the body could lead to peritonitis. The wounded were treated as quickly as possible, but many had to endure a long wait for a doctor or a surgeon and the loss of limbs – if they were lucky.[61]

It was also expected that one side would flee at some point, but at Edgehill, as James, Duke of York, observed, 'as if by mutuall consent [each] side retired some few paces, and they struck down their colours, contin-uing to fire at one another even till night.'[62] Some form of obedience kept the two armies together in the chaos, and, like exhausted heavyweight boxers, they clung to one another, bloody and bruised, even while trying to find the mortal blow. Hand-to-hand fighting quickly exhausted the combatants involved, and only the factors of morale and comradeship, and the leadership shown by the men, the officers and the non-commissioned officers, kept them together. The German novelist Grimmelhausen described such a battlefield in his novel *Simplicissimus*:

'In the battle itself each one tried to prevent his own death by slaugh-tering his nearest enemy. The horrible shooting, the rattling of harness, the crashing of pikes, and the shouts of the wounded and aggressors made with trumpets, drums and pipes a gruesome music. One could see nothing but thick smoke and dust, which seemed to veil the fearful view of the wounded and dead, and in it one heard the lamentations of the dying ... Mutilated soldiers begged for the *coup de grâce*, although certain death was close enough and others prayed for pardon and the sparing of their lives. In short, there was nothing else but a miserable and pitiful spectacle.'[63]

In the chaos, Balfour's cavalry troopers were still in order, and he decided to throw both them and Stapleton's forces into the fray. These two regiments, as we have seen, had been missed by Wilmot's charge. Edmund Ludlow in Stapleton's forces found himself involved in action for the first time:

> 'By this time the foot began to engage, and a party of the enemy being sent to line some hedges on our right wing, thereby to beat us from our ground, were repulsed ... The enemy's body of foot, wherein the King's standard was, came on within a musket-shot of us; upon which we observing no horse to encounter withal, changed them with some loss from their pikes, tho very little from their shot; but not being able to break them, we retreated to our former station.'[64]

On their return, they discovered that the men deputed to guard the artillery had run off, and so they sought to defend the Parliamentary guns, even managing to get one loaded – only to fire it accidentally at Balfour's returning cavalry.

Balfour's men, in their charge, had more success. They managed to rout two Royalist infantry regiments, the first on their own – possibly the regiment of ill-armed and ill-disciplined Welsh foot – and the second in conjunction with some of their own foot. They broke through to reach the Royalist cannon, now behind their infantry. Unfortunately, they now found themselves without any nails to spike the guns. However, they did kill the gunners cowering under the gun carriages, and broke the traces of the guns, thus immobilising them. Some of them also came close to capturing the Prince of Wales, but most returned to the mêlée.

Bryon's brigade was now exposed on the flank as it moved forward to attack Meldrum's, but it fought off a charge from Stapleton's troopers and a further struggle at pike followed, first with the regiment of Roberts and Constable and then with Essex's own regiment and Lord Brooke's men. Bryon's men now found themselves beset on both flank and rear by the returning Parliamentary horse. Initially mistaking Balfour's men as their own cavalry, the Royalist centre began to give way. Lindsay's regiment also crumbled, and he himself was wounded in the leg. His son, Lord Willoughby, moved to rescue him, but, unable to move him, 'he stood undauntedly with his pike in his hand bestriding his father, and in that posture wounded one of their Captains in the face, and almost push'd him off his horse; but his own men at the same time giving back, he was left ingaged in the midst of the Enemies', and he was captured.[65] Others were also wounded. Lieutenant William Holles, of Captain John Smith's company in Sir Lewis Dyve's regiment, was wounded in the face but refused to leave the field, and 'he exprest a great deale of courage and resolution.'[66] In a fierce 'push of pike', the King's own standard was captured and the standard-bearer, Sir Edmund Verney, was cut down as the Royal Foot Guards crumbled under attacks from the Parliamentarian cavalry and infantry and began to retire. Belasyse's regiment was also struck, and many of his officers were killed or captured. The remnants of the regiment retired to join the left wing across the other end of the field. Fortunately for the Royalists, the two regiments remaining on the right stood firm and prevented the retreat from becoming a rout. Furthermore, the Parliamentarians began to run short of powder and ammunition. The Royalist cavalry eventually returned to the field, but were so disorganised and blown that they could do little to resolve the combat

As night closed in, the battle staggered to a halt, and a cold north-easterly wind got up. Edmund Ludlow, hungry and unable to find either his servant or his cloak, and 'having nothing to keep me warm but a suit of iron … was obliged to walk about all night, which proved very cold by reason of a sharp frost.'[67] Another Parliamentary soldier said that 'we were almost starved with cold that bitter night, our Army being in extreme want of victuals.'[68] As the shocked and exhausted men on both sides lay amidst the bloodied bodies, few were ready to re-engage in combat. This reluctance partly explains why a traumatised Essex, despite being reinforced with 4,000 men, disengaged the next morning and moved off towards Warwick, somewhat reluctantly harassed by Rupert's cavalry. While both sides claimed success after Edgehill, both may have been equally alarmed at what had actually occurred. On 27 October Charles took Banbury and on 29 October 1642 he entered Oxford to joyous acclamation. Essex in the meanwhile marched to London in order to bar the King's way to the capital.

There is good evidence that Captain Oliver Cromwell and his men either were not in the battle or turned up only towards the end. The troop found itself caught up in the sheer clumsiness of the distribution and manoeuvring of that day, which placed them out of touch with the battlefield. Captain Nathaniel Fiennes' account of the battle noted that Cromwell and his troop, in conjunction with Captain Edward Knightley's thirty-five troop, finally joined up with some rallied Parliamentarian soldiers beyond Kineton, before then joining Hampden's brigade as it marched towards the sound of the guns. Knightley was quartered some five miles from the battlefield with his men, and only the sound of the guns around one o'clock roused him. He hastened toward the field with the thirty-eighth troop, commanded by 'Sergeant Major [Alex] Douglas ... and over tooke one other troope.'[69] As they were nearing the field, some 200 horse came past 'with all the speed they could out from the battell, saying the King had the victory, and that every man cried for God and King Charles.'[70] The officers tried to rally them, but to no avail, and the panic now struck their own men. Of the 'three troopes, two of them were runne away and of my troope I had not six and thirtie men left.'[71] They waited nearby and took some prisoners, but then moved off to join up with Captain John Fiennes and Cromwell.

We can dismiss the tales that Cromwell deliberately avoided the battle through cowardice; these canards only emerged later and seem to have no basis in fact. What were to be important, as we shall see, were the lessons he might have learned from his first real encounter with the face of war. His observations are to be found in his conversation with John Hampden after Edgehill. Cromwell later claimed to have said,

'At my first going out to the engagement I saw these men were beaten, and at every hand ... And I desired him too, that he would make some addition to my Lord of Essex's army of some new regiments, and I told him I would be serviceable to him in bringing such men in as I thought had a spirit that would do something in the work ... Your troopers, said I, as most of them [were] old decayed serving men and tapsters, and such like fellows, and, said I, their troopers are gentleman's sons, younger sons, persons of quality: do you think that the spirits of such base and mean fellows will ever be able to encounter gentlemen that have honour, courage and resolution in them? Truly I pressed him in this manner conscientiously, and truly I did tell him, You must get men of a spirit ... of a spirit that is like to go as far as a gentleman will go, or else I am sure you will be beaten still ... He was a wise and worthy person, and he did think that I talked a good notion but an impracticable one. Truly I told him I could do somewhat in it. I did so ... I raised such men as had the fear of God before them, and made some conscience of what they did ... wherever they engaged the enemy they beat them continually.'[72]

The result of this conversation was to have profound effects on the future of the war.

CHAPTER 4

THE LOCAL WAR, 1643

'Thus like a Deluge War came roaring forth,
The bending West orewhelm'd, and riseing North.
A Deluge there; and high red Tides the while
Oreflowd all parts of Albions bleeding Ile.'
– Abraham Cowley, *The Civil War*, 1643

BEYOND TURNHAM GREEN

The events at Turnham Green made certain that the Civil War in England would not end in a Parliamentary defeat. On 13 November 1642, faced once again by elements of Essex's army, which had been supplemented by the London Trained Bands, Charles I turned away from London and withdrew to make his wartime base in the city of Oxford. In the stalemate that followed, each side was willing to attempt some negotiations as the war closed down for the winter, but each also roundly accused the other of a lack of trust. For Captain Cromwell, there would now be a return to his home ground in what was to become the Eastern Association and the establishment of a formidable regimental command. With hindsight, we can also see that 1643 for Cromwell was to be a year of minor skirmishes at Grantham, Gainsborough, and Winceby. These lesser victories would allow him to sharpen his skills and experience as soldier and to train his men in the form of warfare that he now so desired to practise.

GRAND STRATEGIES

In the year 1643 we can also see, for the first time, the development of a wider strategy for the war. In the spring the King chose to renew the war from his Oxford base, but the conflict had also widened across the country, and now other Royalist forces had entered the fray. The second, post-Edgehill phase of the Civil War often had a regional face to it. It tended to be a decentralised and a strategically unambitious affair, made up of local politics, garrison warfare and petty skirmishes. From the first, King Charles and his advisors seem to have realised that London should be their most important objective, and they had some vague notions of co-ordinating all the Royal forces to that end, but they were also hampered by the realisation that the

Royalist cause itself needed to retain control of territory and raise men and money, merely in order to survive as a power in the land. Ireland also would eventually become part of the key to the King's strategy: if its war could be settled and a compact made with the Confederates there, then Irish troops could be released to bolster the Royal armies.

Parliament's strategic approach in 1643 was to prove just as defensive in outlook, and equally regional. The control of interior lines and the economic and strategic hub of London meant that, in theory, they could strike against the King at Oxford, but John Pym's desperate struggles to hold together the political factions of the war and Lord General Essex's sluggish approach to campaigning following Edgehill meant that, rather than grasping the nettle of the wider strategy needed to win the war, for the Parliamentarians 1643 was also lost in the fog of local politics, skirmishes and petty sieges.

PARLIAMENTARY POLITICS

Ironically, part of the reason for seemingly endless local disputes in the war lay in the factional nature of central politics. In Parliament, the dominant figure of John Pym, motivated by his fear of 'popery', proved to be a shrewd and daring politician. Royalists now hated Pym as the 'promoter of the present rebellion', but to many others he became the spirited leader of the Parliamentary cause.[1] After Edgehill and Turnham Green, Pym was forced to work hard to bond a unified group in Parliament. Parliament itself became divided, with loose amalgams of extremist 'hawks' (a war party), 'doves' (a peace party), and the majority of moderate groups. We should remember that the idea of solidified 'parties' in this period was something of a misnomer, and all these factions, and not a few individuals, had views on how the war should be run, and what might be the processes by which it could be ended, given a King who now openly considered them as rebels. The peace group, led by men such as Denzil Holles, who had seen the face of war and disliked it intensely, advocated defensive strategies. They hoped that conciliatory negotiations would bring about a peaceful conclusion to the war. They were also fearful of the social and religious problems that the war was now beginning to bring to the surface.

To some extent, Essex and his subordinates in the field shared these views. The 'hawks' – MPs such as Sir Henry Vane, Arthur Haselrige and Henry Marten – varied in their aims. Marten, if not an outright republican, at least had notions of such a solution to the country's ills, but all these men were clear that the King must be defeated before negotiations could take place. This would mean the adoption of an offensive strategy, and if Essex was not up to the task (and there were already doubts about his attitude), a more vigorous general must be found to carry it out. In the middle sat the majority of MPs. Their moderate solutions had generally been expressed in the Grand Remonstrance and the Nineteen Propositions. As a majority, they were men whom John Pym now tried to lead as the balance of forces in Parliament. While most of them wished to keep the war going for fear of worse horrors, some did share a number of the war group's aims as regards strategy. On the other hand, many still craved a constitutional settlement that could bring the nation together.

In order to win the war, Pym and his allies would also need to manage other elements at Westminster, and on the local level; a form of central control, finances, military reorganisation, allies, and any negotiations with the King were some of these. Such a form of central control eventually emerged with the establishment of the Committee of Public Safety, replaced, on the conclusion of the alliance with the Scots, by the Committee of Both Kingdoms. In theory, this body had strategic control over Parliament's war, but in practice wilful generals sometimes ignored it. The finances for war were ultimately found in a series of fiscal measures that involved taxation, sequestration and loans. The establishment of local county committees and various sub-committees in the counties also provided an essential way of gathering funds and working with the military, and they eventually enabled Parliament to put its military arm on a reasonable financial footing. Allies would also be found, after considerable negotiation, in the Scots Covenanters – so far neutral, but able to bring to the dispute their considerable military power as a counterbalance to any Continental and Irish dabbling by the King. While both politicians and generals needed subtle management, military reorganisation would take more time and, to be really successful, would need to overcome local interests and prejudices. In theory, Essex had control over the volunteers and the general commissioned officers appointed to marshal the counties or later associations, while the county committees naturally took a keen interest in the doings of their local militia. These, they thought, were better used to protect the interests of their own county than as part of any greater strategy that might take them over the border. Nevertheless, some attempt at co-operation would emerge with the establishment of country associations such as the Eastern Association on 20 December 1642, in which Oliver Cromwell, for example, would become heavily involved; much more would be achieved with yet another ordinance authorising impressments of men into Parliament's scattered forces. Yet much was also problematic in this year, not least the round of negotiations with the King insisted on by the peace group and members of the City, and the fear of local officials regarding the civil discord that was now bubbling up in their communities.

In November 1642 fresh peace proposals had originated from the growing Parliamentarian peace party, but it was soon clear that Charles would not accept them. Further peace negotiations actually began on 1 February 1643, and a Parliamentary deputation was sent to Oxford. The negotiations meandered on until April. Their collapse left both sides politically deadlocked, and by that stage the spring campaigning season had begun.

CAMPAIGNS OF 1643

Militarily, the year 1643 saw a series of local clashes in the south, the north and the Midlands of England. The great Royalist strategic plan, where it can be discerned at all, was, it seemed, only randomly pursued. There were, of course, some suggestions at Oxford that all the Royal forces should at the first opportunity move on London, thereby connecting the loyal Earl of Newcastle's army in the north and Sir Ralph Hopton's forces in the south-west with the main Royal army under Charles around Oxford. On the other side, Essex, with his forces based to cover London, were meant to be the great hope, but it was Sir William Waller, the Lord General's new rival, who soon emerged as the general most likely to create an opening for Parliament's war in the south.

Aged only forty-five at the outbreak of the war, Waller, a soldier MP, drew his military experience from his former service in Germany and Italy.[2] Commissioned to raise a regiment of cavalry in 1642, he soon demonstrated tactical skill and proved to be a good 'chooser of ground'. Waller had achieved enough victories by December 1642 to be nicknamed 'William the Conqueror' by Parliamentary news sheets desperate for a hero. As a result, he became one of the great hopes of the Parliamentarian side. So Parliament, through Essex, made him general of the forces in the West Country. There he was to engage his rival and friend Sir Ralph Hopton in battle. Hopton also had expertise from the German wars and was a sound commander, although with a tendency to hesitate in the field. Nevertheless, Hopton had been able to consolidate the Royalist hold on Cornwall, and when Waller, following a series of skirmishes, eventually moved to capture Hereford on 25 April 1643 and then moved on the south-west to confront Hopton, he was ready.

Hopton scored a victory at Stratton on 16 May 1643, and by the end of the month he found himself in control of most of Devon and part of Dorset. Meanwhile Essex finally stirred himself sufficiently to move on Reading on 26 April, only to have his advance grind to a halt. While Essex still remained inactive, Hopton and Prince Maurice, in the south-west, took on Waller, who had by now positioned his forces around Bath. Their manoeuvres were eventually to lead to the Battle of Lansdown on 5 July 1643. Waller was now forced back into Bath, but a bloodied Hopton moved off to Devizes, hoping to pick up supplies coming from Oxford. Having regrouped, Waller then set off in pursuit of his foe, only to be badly beaten on 13 July at Roundway Down outside Devizes. This action, as well as the fall of Bristol that same month, left most of the south-west in Royalist hands.

Yet again, the Royalist forces seemed to have the advantage in the war, but the King was still unable to co-ordinate any real strategy. Defeat in the field and continued calls for negotiation with the King had left Pym hanging in the air, fearful of yet another Parliamentary reverse. Most of the criticism at Westminster now began to be directed at Essex. Open doubts were being expressed in London over his generalship, his religion and his politics. That he was an easy target, having disappointed with a less than dynamic display of the military arts, did not help his cause. Few took into account his force's logistical constraints, its irregular pay, its desertions and the sickness now raging in the ranks of the army. The loss of confidence in Essex by his political masters was a gradual one. Pym had shrewdly acted as nursemaid to the Lord General at first, and had often calmed his ruffled temper by using his associate John Hampden as his intermediary. Unfortunately, Hampden's death at Chalgrove Field on 18 June 1643 removed one of Parliament's most brilliant politicians. Essex's subsequent noisy claims, in the face of increasing criticism, that he already knew how to 'do his duty' only raised further voices against the Earl. Parliament's war seemed hopeless.[3]

THE WAR IN THE NORTH AND MIDLANDS

Meanwhile, in the north of England, command of the Royalist forces had fallen upon a fifty-year-old aristocratic gentleman (and expert horseman), William Cavendish, the Earl (later Marquis) of Newcastle.[4] Despite his lack of experience of soldiering – Newcastle's wealth had really bought him his command – he remained sensible enough to surround himself with professional soldiers such as the Scot James King, later made Lord Eythin. Newcastle's task in the north was twofold. First he had to seize control of

Yorkshire and the northern counties for the King, and secondly he would eventually have to turn south to join in an assault on London. This would bring him into the debatable lands of Nottinghamshire and Lincolnshire that both the King and Parliament claimed as their own, and within the orbit of Colonel Cromwell. Newcastle and his 16,000 men struggled to control Yorkshire against those who fought for the Parliamentary cause there. Their leaders were the elderly Ferdinando, Lord Fairfax and his energetic, soldierly son Sir Thomas Fairfax.[5] At this stage Sir Thomas was still only thirty, but, with the experience of continental armies as well as service in the Bishops' Wars behind him, Fairfax was to prove to be one of the most dynamic soldiers of his day and popular with his men. He was a placid man off the field of battle, but on it he showed all of his passion and vigour for war. He could be decisive in action and was able to encourage much devotion among his troops.

In December 1642 Newcastle had marched south from the Tyne to take York, the northern capital, as his base. He then routed Lord Fairfax and his forces at Tadcaster on 6 December 1642 and moved on Pontefract. This enabled Newcastle to cut off Hull, still under the Parliamentarian governorship of the scheming Sir John Hotham, from the West Riding clothing towns that were largely Parliamentarian in inclination. Newcastle now despatched Sir John Henderson southwards to support the Royalist forces under Sir John Digby holding Newark. Newark was to be a major strategic focus for the next year's campaigns. The town not only commanded the main road south, but also an important bridge over the Trent. It was the link route to the King's forces further south and acted as a rallying point for Royalists in Nottinghamshire; moreover, control of Newark gave the Northern Royalists *entrée* into Lincolnshire. On his arrival, Henderson began to fortify the place and position some smaller garrisons as protective outposts for the town; the manor house at Wilden, for example, threatened Parliamentary forces in both Derbyshire and Nottingham. Belvoir, the home of the Earl of Rutland, was garrisoned for the King, while the mansions at Shelford and, north of the Trent, at Thurgarton also had their garrisons. Efforts were made to unify the Royal forces located in Leicestershire, Derbyshire, Nottingham, Lincolnshire and Rutland. Partly as a response to this, a new Parliamentarian association of Buckinghamshire, Bedfordshire, Northampton, Huntingdon, Rutland, Leicestershire, Derbyshire and Nottingham was created. Thomas, Lord Grey of Groby was made the association's major-general. The town of Nottingham was strengthened and now became the main opponent to the garrison at Newark. The area between and around the two towns became a war zone of petty skirmishes, minor garrison warfare and raids, while both sides awaited the coming of Newcastle's army.

Newcastle continued to struggle in Yorkshire, necessitating the withdrawal of some of his men from around Newark in January 1643. With the easing of pressure on Nottingham, the local commanders now sensed an opportunity. Parliamentary troops began to gather at Nottingham from Lincolnshire, Nottinghamshire and Derbyshire, for a push forward towards Newark. However, Sir John Ballard, placed in command of the Lincolnshire troops, seems to have deliberately prevaricated: he was already divided in his sympathies, and eventually he flatly refused to go to the rendezvous near Newark. Delay followed delay, and Henderson took the opportunity to strengthen the Newark defences. When Ballard finally moved, it was much too late and the Parliamentarian forces were repulsed in an attack on 28 February. While this action was occurring, Newcastle remained at York. There Queen Henrietta Maria, who with some difficulty had brought supplies of arms and money from the Continent for the King's cause, joined him. The Parliamentary governor of Hull, Sir John Hotham, had already opened secret negotiations to surrender the garrison there, and Lord Fairfax found himself besieged in Leeds.

Newcastle began his next offensive in March. First he occupied Wakefield, and then, after he had fortified his family seat at Welbeck, Rotherham fell to his troops in April, as did Sheffield. Newcastle was now poised for an invasion of Lincolnshire or Nottinghamshire. He had already sent his cousin Charles Cavendish to reinforce Newark, and on 23 March 1643 both Cavendish and Henderson stormed Grantham. Lincolnshire was now in fear of being lost to the Royalists, so Colonel John Hutchinson was sent down to Parliament to ask for assistance. An appeal was also directed to Lord Fairfax for help, but he was far too occupied to assist. Essex, on the other hand, was ordered to send assistance from the Eastern Association troops and to concentrate other forces on Nottingham. The command was given to Lord Grey.

A combination of some 5,000–6,000 men began to assemble in May 1643. Lord Grey came up from Leicestershire and Lord Willoughby of Parham from Lincolnshire, while Sir John Gell brought in a Derbyshire contingent and Sir John Hotham's son, his father's treachery still unknown, brought some Yorkshire troops. Colonel Oliver Cromwell brought some of his troops from the Eastern Association, including his own regiment of cavalry. The other commanders already knew Cromwell and his men, as on the 13th of the month he had won a minor skirmish at Grantham. He had hoped subsequently to attack Newark, but local co-operation had unfortunately broken down. Now he was back and in the mood for a fight.

IRONSIDES

After Edgehill, Oliver Cromwell's troop of horse had retreated to Warwick, and by November 1642 it was located around London. In December they were described as being a 'troop of eightie arquebuziers', a lighter armed form of cavalry.[6] In less than a month, mainly because of the political needs in the eastern counties, Cromwell returned to East Anglia and his men went with him. In January 1643 they became part of his plan to raise his own regiment of cavalry. William, Lord Grey of Warke, had become commander of the forces of the newly formed Eastern Association, and he now commissioned Cromwell as a colonel in this army.

As we have seen, associations were to be formed of counties in close proximity to defend the cause of Parliament. The Eastern Association originally comprised Essex, Suffolk, Norfolk, Cambridgeshire and Hert-fordshire; Huntingdonshire joined later, and Lincolnshire was a member by 20 September 1643. The Midlands also had an association (of which Huntingdon was a part), and Cromwell now found himself politically prominent in both of these groupings. However, the Eastern Association, created by a Parliamentary ordinance of 20 December 1642, was the first real army where Cromwell could win his military spurs.

In the months and years that followed, the Army of the Eastern Association became a significant force on the Parliamentary side, and it was the appointment of the Earl of Manchester as commander in August 1643 that finally gave the army its particular flavour. While ineffective as general, Manchester had been drawn into opposition through his father-in-law Warwick. He had been one of the five members whom Charles I had sought to arrest, and in August 1642 he had raised a regiment and served under Essex. Manchester was an aristocrat and a gentleman, a mild-mannered Presbyterian, at first always willing to defer to the military experts, but a good organiser. Unfortunately, he was to face numerous difficulties with his more rigorous subordinates as the war progressed, for he came to have a grave dislike of the conflict. The forces that he came to control were both locally raised infantry and cavalry. The infantry had generally been raised by conscripting men from the associated counties; volunteers or transfers also came in, from other associations.

Two types of troops had been raised for the cavalry of the Eastern Association – those horse raised by individual initiative, and further troops raised by ordinance in 1643–45. Furthermore, over many months the regiments sought to recruit piecemeal, to make up for losses through combat, desertion and sickness. If most infantry recruits were generally in the ranks because they had little choice, the cavalry recruits were, more often than not, a little different. Men of a higher social rank – tenant farmers, copyholders, craftsmen and apprentices – were the norm, entering the war through social or religious conviction, or even family pressure. There were also some who were fascinated by the soldier's life of glory. Not all were from the fens; some had served in other armies and in other areas. Some were recruited while the army was on campaign, and others had joined for the reason that religious tolerance was beginning to be seen in Manchester's army but not in Essex's. As a whole, they had great potential.

The next few months were to find Oliver Cromwell engaged in keeping the peace in the counties around Cambridge, collecting monies for the cause and, once established in Cambridge, rapidly building his original troop of horse into a regiment. The type of man that Cromwell now began to recruit was naturally of great significance for the future of the conflict, and says much about his development as a soldier. Bulstrode Whitelocke was to describe his men as 'freeholders and freeholders' sons', engaged indeed, as was Cromwell himself, on 'a matter of Conscience'.[7] They were, it was claimed, for the most part religious and sober men – those whom Cromwell, at least, would have called 'godly precious men'. Richard Baxter, who was asked at one stage to became chaplain to the regiment, but refused, noted that Cromwell took 'a special care' to get religious men into his troop: 'These men were of greater understanding than common soldiers, and therefore were more apprehensive of the importance and consequence of the war.'[8] Baxter also noted that they were more interested in 'publick felicity' than in making money, and that Cromwell knew it, hoping thereby to avoid a regiment of soldiers responsible, as soldiers all too often were, for 'disorders, mutinies, plunderings, and grievances of the country'.[9] The Earl of Manchester and his friends were to be less sure about Cromwell's choice of men. They were later to accuse some of them of having a touch of the fanatic, and some indeed 'profess they have seen visions and had revelations'. The hostile Royalist Press was to label many of them as a 'barbarous breed of Brownists' who indulged in the wanton destruction of churches and in 'committing many outrages on the house of God'.[10] There seems little doubt that both the officers and men were chosen with great care, and later on with little enough regard for gentle-manly status, for some of them were described as 'common men, pore and of mean parentage'.[11] Cromwell did not care – or, if he did, he thought that their rallying to the cause and their godliness were a far more important measure of these 'russet-coated captains' than their social rank or wealth. To put it another way: 'Sir, the state, in choosing men to serve them, takes no notice of their opinions; if they be willing faithfully to serve them, that satisfies.'[12] Herein lie both his and their novelty.

One such recruit was Edward Sexby.[13] The historian C. H. Firth noted that there was 'no more remarkable career in the annals of the New Model army', and it was the renegade Sexby, author of one of the most famous pamphlets of the day on political murder, who became the driving force behind a scheme to kill Cromwell in the late 1650s. A gentleman's son and a London apprentice in his youth, Sexby may originally have had family connections with Cromwell, and in 1643 he joined Cromwell's regiment as a trooper. He was to eventually come under the influence of the emergent Leveller ideas, and made a name for himself as an agitator amongst the troops, becoming a conspicuous link between the Leveller leaders in London and the army. Sexby proved to be a man of action in other ways. He was involved in the seizure of Charles I at Holdenby House in 1647. He was also prominent at the Army debates in Putney Church that same year, where, as a representative of the ordinary soldier, he was, not for the last time, to cross swords verbally with Cromwell. His political views on Charles I were equally blunt: 'We have been by Providence put upon strange things ... We have laboured to please a king, and I think, except we go about to cut all our throats, we shall not please him.'[14] The turbulent years of civil war opened many eyes to the problems in society, and for a brief period we can hear the questioning voices of soldiers such as Sexby. Unfortunately for the Levellers, the events of 1647–49 meant that the movement itself lost whatever base it had in the Army, and the alternative political strategies it put forward were soon dissipated. Moreover, with Cromwell himself vowing (or so John Lilburne said) to break the Levellers, the unstable movement eventually collapsed. Sexby briefly left the Army at this point, only to resurface as a captain in 1649.

Cromwell used his own patronage for most of his officers, many of whom were related to him in some way. This was natural enough. His brother-in-law John Desborough was to become Captain of the Third Troop, while James Berry became the Captain-Lieutenant of the First (Colonel's) Troop. His own son, Oliver, became the Captain of the Fourth, while Valentine Walton, his nephew, took over the Fifth Troop. By March 1643, when Cromwell went into action at Lowestoft, he had some five troops with him, by September he had ten, and eventually there were some fourteen troops, making some 1,000 men in all.

The winter was mostly spent training and raising the funds to keep the force in being. From the first, Cromwell seems to have been a good admin-istrator, eager to pledge his own wealth as well as to make many appeals to reluctant local communities for the sustenance of particular troops and officers. The raising of the so-called 'Maiden Troop' (Troop number eleven) is a case in point. In this instance, Cromwell received the offer of supplying funds from a group of 'men and maids' to raise and partly equip a troop of horse. The offer was accepted with alacrity, the more so as Cromwell claimed that it would be of 'far more advantage to the cause that the two or three foot companies.'[15] What followed was his

> '... advice ... that you would employ your twelve-score horses; for 400 [sterling] more will not raise a troop of horse. As for the muskets that are bought, I think the country will take them of you. Pray raise honest godly men, and I will have them of my regiment. As for officers, I leave it as God shall or hath directed to choose.'[16]

Captain Swallow was given command of the eighty men and soon joined the regiment. In recompense, it must be said that Cromwell was equally concerned to hold his men in the strictest of discipline. When, in April, two of his troopers tried to desert in Huntingdon, he had them publicly whipped in the market-place on their recapture. Later punishments were equally severe. In June 1650 a man from Pride's regiment had his neck and feet tied behind his back and the regiment marched past him as a punish-ment. He was then expelled from the Army. His crime had been to steal a hen. Other crimes, such as blasphemy, saw one dragoon have his tongue bored through with a hot iron, while plunderers on campaign were simply hanged. The need to keep such wayward souls under control was upper-most in Cromwell's mind while on campaign, for their crimes were invari-ably directed against civilians and he was always conscious of sparing the local population where he could from the natural chaos caused by soldiery. It also damaged the morale of his own troops. A commentator later wrote:

> 'As for Cromwell, he hath 2,000 brave men, well disciplined: no man swears but he pays his twelve pence; if he be drunk he is set in

the stocks, or worse, if one calls the other 'Roundhead' he is cashiered; insomuch that the counties where they come leap for joy of them, and come in and join with them. How happy were it if all the forces were thus disciplined.'[17]

If the troops were not all the ideal, Psalm-singing, godly soldiers of myth, they were certainly better disciplined and more conscious of their cause than many other troops of the day. R. S. Paul speculated that the men in the first troop Cromwell recruited could even be seen in terms of a gathered church – united spiritually, as well as by their military tasks, 'a kind of militant congregation'.[18] Godly warriors or not, these soldiers were to become a formidable force, well-trained and led, and the basis of his military success. Cromwell thought very highly of them. In one of the many letters of these days wherein Cromwell pleaded for money to pay his men, he noted that:

'Those honest men under my command, who have been, who are in straits if want of clothes, boots, money to fix their arms, to shoe their horses be considerable, such are theirs not in an easy degree, truly above what is fit for the state to suffer. Sir, many may complain they are many weeks behind of pay, many who can plunder and pillage; they suffer no want. But truly mine (though some have stigmatised them with the name of Anabaptists), are honest men, such as fear God, I am confident the freest from unjust practices of any in England, seek the soldiers where you can. Such imputations are poor requitals to those who have ventured their blood for you. I hear there are such mists cast to darken their services. Take no care of me, I ask for your good acceptance, let me have your prayers, I will thank you ... but for my poor men, help them what you can, for they are faithful.'[19]

His instinct had told him that these were the type of soldier he should aim to recruit – sober, honest and godly. Having got them, he then wished to do well for them. There is a story of him actually weeping with frustration when he came to Boston at one time 'and found no moneys for him from Essex and other counties'.[20] Cromwell learnt to fear that without pay his men would disperse, and if they did then the cause would fail. It seems that, for the most part, the soldiers under Cromwell reciprocated in kind, and the conjunction of military success with the ideas of righteousness before the Lord inculcated into them was eventually to wield a splendid instrument for the Almighty.

Cromwell was not always content to let God provide his officers: many were the subsequent complaints about the type of men who could become officers under Colonel Cromwell. This element of social levelling was to dog his command. Cromwell rebuffed it all. Captain Margery was one case in point. Slighted by some as a man who was not a gentleman, Cromwell angrily lambasted the Suffolk Committee in his support, saying:

> '... it may be it provokes some spirits to see such plain men made captains of horse. It had been well that men of honour and birth had entered into these employments, but why do they not appear? Who would have hindered them? But seeing it was necessary the work must go on, better plain men than none, but best to have men patient of wants, faithful and conscientious in the employment, and such, I hope, these approve themselves to be.'[21]

Even Manchester agreed on this point; indeed, he set the trend by basing his selection of officers on men with some previous experience of war, godliness and devotion to the Parliamentary cause.

James Berry became Cromwell's own captain-lieutenant, and then commanded his own troop in the regiment. Berry proved to be the classic godly, conscientious soldier. Before the war he had been a clerk in an iron-works in Shropshire, although he may have had some military experience under his belt prior to joining the troop. His subsequent career was a lengthy one. An early letter (from 1638) reveals some of his personal motivation and is useful as guide for many of his fellow officers:

> 'I, who have had experience of man's weakenes and find by mine owne triall that if we doe not make God as it were the workman and sett him before us in all our works, we are no body able to doe nothing as we should but are sure to run into errors ... sett him continually before your eies doe all you doe as in his presence mistrust your own strength and implore the lords aide in every thinge.'[22]

In terms of pay, the average trooper in the regiment would have expected to receive 2s. 6d. per day, while a corporal or trumpeter was paid some 3s. Much was defrayed out of this sum – clothes, food, lodgings, iron shoes, and feed for the man's horse. Captains of a troop received £1 19s. 0d. per day, a lieutenant 18s. 6d., a cornet 13s. 6d. and the quartermaster 9s. 0d. The bodily and spiritual needs of the troops were also provided for. The employment of a chaplain at 8s. od. per day was meant to fulfil their religious needs. In fact, the nature of this regiment was such that many of the men were lay preachers, and prayer was reputedly commonplace in the ranks as well as amongst the officers. Some of the men were drawn from the left-wing tendency of the English Church. Accusations of Anabaptism in the ranks were rife, and in some cases were true, although Cromwell denied them. Yet the religious beliefs of some of the men – they often rode into battle singing psalms – were crucial to raising their morale and promoting unity.

In style they were 'harquebusiers', a lighter sort of cavalry than cuirassiers. They were each armed with an iron helmet or 'pot' and a cuirass of back and breastplate. Otherwise their body armour may have consisted of a buff leather coat. As cavalry, their weapons consisted of a sword and pair of pistols, and the average trooper was mounted on a horse worth between £5 and £10. Even though Cromwell made great play of ensuring that the men kept their horses in good condition, well fed and watered, the horses tended not to be the 'nags' foisted on the dragoons. Cromwell was above all a horseman, and well aware of the limits of horseflesh and the use to which it could be put. Obtaining good horses was difficult at the best of times, and this fact often brought the regiment into conflict with local owners, piqued to discover that their best horses had been pressed into service with little enough compensation – although Cromwell's ever-ready conscience prevented him from going as far as some in this matter.

John Vernon, in his contemporary work *The Young Horseman* (1644), gives some insight into the type of horse and training the cavalry required, and into the methods of training that Cromwell would have used. Horses should be, Vernon noted, 'nimble and able ... of a convenient stature, of 15 handfuls high, sad coloured, as black, brown, chestnut, dun, bay, sorell, Iron grey, Rone and the like.'[23] White horses Vernon rejected as being far too conspicuous in the field. Ideally, the horse needed to be at least four years of age. Training was vital, for the horse was always assumed 'to be full of malice', and the animal, as well as its rider, was to be trained in manoeuvres as frequently as possible.[24] Ideally, exercise at least twice a week when in camp or in garrison was necessary, so that both horse and rider would respond instantly to commands. This exercise would include riding in the 'Ring', and then in a figure eight, 'first in a greater compasse and afterwards in a lesser by degrees; first on his pace, then on his trot, and so to his gallop, and lastly, in full careere.'[25] A nineteenth century cavalry expert recommended that 'All [cavalry] evolutions should combine simplicity, directness and accuracy ... because confusion is fatal to the mounted arm, for depending as it does upon movement, the elements of disorder are latent in its every action.' Cromwell seems to have held similar views.[26] Vernon suggested a series of rewards to the animal for a job well done, and that the horse be inured to the noise of battle, introducing it to a gradual increase in the 'smell of gunpowder, a sight of fire and armour, hearing of drums and trumpets, and shouting of Guns but by degrees, when he is eating of his Oats.'[27] In other words, much the same techniques were called for as are used with police and cavalry horses today.

If the horse needed training, then so too did the rider. Most cavalrymen would have had some experience of riding prior to joining up, but, as one might expect, no experience of riding as a unit, nor, usually, in the use of weapons. Wielding the sword on horseback could often be an awkward and dangerous learning process, not only for the rider but also for his horse, and for his comrades. In the end, it was the horsemanship of the rider, as much as his weapons training, that made him effective in combat. There were essentially four methods for the Cromwellian cavalryman to fall upon an opponent with a sword – 'cut, reverse, downward blow, and thrust'.[28] The rider had to draw the weapon from the scabbard over his left arm, this being the hand that held the reins, and use a number of gestures to engage the enemy with cuts to the left or right, or extend the sword arm outwards or downwards while moving. Alternatively, one could try to kill the opponent's horse. The authorities were generally divided on the merits of this, the one real way of stopping any enemy dead in his tracks, but in practice it was doubtless a common enough tactic. Certainly infantry, with their proverbial antipathy to the arrogant cavalry, had no qualms about the matter.

Exercises and training in the martial arts were essential to a regiment's success. Combat was a different matter. In personal cavalry combat, Cruso noted that the rider should aim for the

> '... bellie of the adverse horse-man ... or at his arm pits, or his throat, where if it pierce not (as it is very like it will not fail, by slipping under the casque) yet meeting with a stay in that part of the bodie ... and having a sword of a very stiffe blade ... it will doubtlesse unhorse him. Being past his enemie, he is to make a back-blow at him.'[29]

Another writer noted that

'In the mêlée one must be aware of everything going on about you, in order to parry or strike to the right and to the left, and to make the sword come and go like a flash of lightning as opportunity and necessity arises without the slightest pause.'[30]

In organization, Cromwell's cavalry regiment remained a standard unit, but its size varied. In the end, the regiment became a double regiment, many of its officers men who were to be of great significance over the next few years. Parliamentarian cavalry units tended to have two field officers, a colonel and a major (who were also troop commanders). In theory, between 71 and 80 officers and men were in the individual troop. They normally fought in a formation three deep, only occasionally doubled to six deep in the early days of the war. The officers in the troop would usually have been located with the captain at the front, and with two trumpeters and a cornet behind him, right and left. The front rank would have the first corporal on the right, the second on the left and the third and fourth corporals correspondingly posted in the rear ranks. A lieutenant would bring up the rear of the troop. As already noted, there was a constant debate about the best tactical use of cavalry and their use of firearms. The use of the carbine or harquebus that gave these troops their name was not regular in the regiment. Indeed, it seems to have been phased out at an early stage, and tactically the decision was soon made by their colonel that these cavalry would be shock troops and used in that fashion. Here, the need for discipline in combat would be paramount.

In these years, the tactical foundations for Cromwell's warfare were laid mainly through discipline and training. 'Solidity and weight', and size and appearance, rather than outright pace, enabled him to use his cavalry as shock troops, enabling them to use 'cold steel' to break through the enemy lines. As du Picq noted, 'The charge at a trot exacts of leaders and men complete confidence and steadfastness ... the gallop is and should be ... the winning, intoxicating gait, for men and horses.'[31] Cohesion, unit organisation, discipline, confidence and enthusiasm, and, as we shall see, restraint and the ability to rally and charge again – if these could be blended together, then victory was certain. Their action was always geared towards the offensive, not the passive, for Cromwell realised that in cavalry warfare, 'defence lies in the offensive', and their use was as much moral and psychological as physical.[32] Their tactics were designed to break the resistance of the enemy, who would then be pursued across the countryside. The enemy's flanks were the most vulnerable part of his unit. If the cavalry could charge on the left or right flank while the front was occupied, then the enemy could be broken in the dynamics of combat. Only the cavalry could do this in Early Modern warfare: infantry generally proved too clumsy and static, and difficult to move either in advance or retreat. The real offensive in Early Modern warfare would be through cavalry action, and this gave the cavalry glory and honour.

In conjunction with his officers, Cromwell now began to find the emergent formula of a good tactician of cavalry. He was now ready to put this into practice by manoeuvre and in battle.

FIRST VICTORIES

Sunday 12 March 1643 found Colonel Cromwell and his troops, one thousand strong, marching to Norwich en route for Lowestoft. The latter port had gone over to the Royalist cause, and, picking up more men on the way from Norwich and Yarmouth, Cromwell arrived at the town and summoned it. He was affronted by their rejection, so he set about taking the town with the minimum of casualties, then retiring to Norwich a few days later. Much of his campaigning in East Anglia over the next month was akin to this. Seizing the 'malignant' element and rousting out the enemy from their home territory and taking control of potential strongholds were meat and drink to the Ironsides. There seems little doubt that intelligence-gathering would also have been part of this work, whether through spies or by means of patrols and outriders trotting through the countryside. The main headache for their colonel was money to finance the good work and to keep his troops in being.

Otherwise, the military significance of what may for the most part be termed 'police actions' is clear: they cleansed the area of Royalists – and doubtless they also helped Cromwell discover the worth of his officers and men and train them hard for the greater conflicts to come. There were later rumours that he set tests for his men – ambushes and so forth – to see how they would react. These apart, in this period of his career Cromwell was acting in a manner little differently from most of the country as it began to adjust to wartime conditions.

A brigade of men from the Eastern Association army had been sent off under the latter's major-general, Lord Grey of Warke, to join Essex's main field army in the Thames valley. The forces left behind were to defend the northern and north-western borders of the Association from the threats of the northern Royalist army under Newcastle. With the Royalists gathering in force near Newark, raids into Lincolnshire were now becoming commonplace. The Lincolnshire Royalists and elements of Newcastle's army under Charles Cavendish achieved a notable victory on 11 April at the Battle of Ancaster Heath. In April 1643 Oliver Cromwell was at Huntingdon still collecting troops. Around 12,000 men were finally located there by the end of the month. He then moved forward to Peterborough, where he established his headquarters. The danger from the Royalist stronghold of Newark was increasing. In that same month, he and some other officers undertook the siege of Crowland.

The first attempt on this place had been beaten back between 13 and 16 April 1643. In the course of the siege, the Royalist garrison had tied the vicar of Spalding, Robert Ram, and some other Parliamentary sympathisers before the breastworks while the guns played on them. Cromwell and three other colonels came with their troops to view the situation on 25 April. It was to be Cromwell's first real siege of the war. They decided to assault the place from the west, south and north, but bad weather (it rained heavily) led to their hasty withdrawal. Two days later they tried again, causing the garrison to surrender the next day. The casualties were five dead and eighteen or nineteen men wounded. It was, in the end, a minor affair, although Cromwell received some praise in the Press for his actions. In siege warfare, however, we can already distinguish Cromwell's embryonic tactics. Blunt and to the point, he offered quarter if the garrison surrendered swiftly; otherwise it was up to the will of God and the swords and muskets of his soldiers to decide the affair.

Cromwell then moved his force forward as part of an advance by Essex, who was finally shaking off his lethargy and approaching Reading. Cromwell's regiment spent most of this period in drill, and in destroying the religious trappings in Peterborough Cathedral, where, according to the Royalist Press, 'they broke down the organs, and destroy[ed] the glass windows, committing many outrages on the house of God, which were not acted by the Goths on the sack of Rome.'[33] Other 'barbarous outrages' apparently followed.[34] As the threat to the Eastern Association grew, Cromwell and his troops moved ever further into Lincolnshire. The initial intention was to scatter the enemy and carry Newark by assault in company with other Parliamentary forces. Lord Grey, however, failed to rendezvous at Stamford: he was afraid that any movement would lose Leicester for the Parliamentarian cause. Delay followed delay, until Cromwell finally decided to move forward with only the Lincoln forces.

On 9 May 1643, Oliver Cromwell, Lord Willoughby of Parham and John Hotham assembled at Sleaford on the road to Lincoln. Preparations

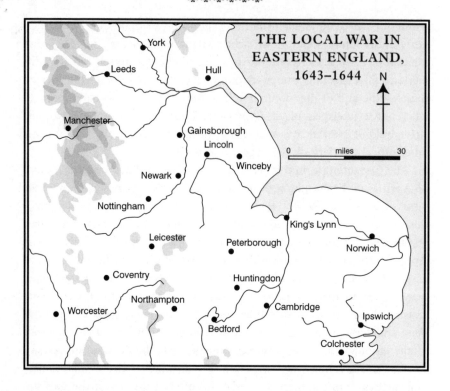

now began for an attack on Royalists at Newark, and by 11 May the force
had moved forward to encamp at Grantham. On 13 May a series of movements took place. As Grantham was considered to be too exposed a position, a move towards Nottingham or Melton was decided upon, and a
reconnaissance force under Captains Wray and Hull was posted in the
villages of Barkston and Honington to guard the roads towards Newark. It
was there that Colonel Charles Cavendish's troops, out of Newark,
surprised them after nine o'clock in the evening. Some of the troopers
escaped and soon brought news to Cromwell at Grantham. He now made
haste to draw out his eleven troops and some dragoons. The 'glorious
victory' that followed was in fact a minor cavalry skirmish, though it illustrates some of the developing cavalry officer's budding tactical sense.

Cavendish had already sent some of his prisoners back towards
Newark, and now planned to surprise Cromwell's forces as he had Wray's.
Late in the evening of 13 May, Cromwell drew out his troops within two
miles of the town on the Newark road and the Royalists faced them in a
level space. There, in the gathering gloom, both parties sat and watched
each other for about half an hour. Shots were fired by Cavendish's

dragoons, and in the twilight Cromwell seems to have drawn his cavalry up in the Dutch fashion. After some discussion, and in spite of the fact that it was getting very late for any action at all, the Parliamentary commanders finally agreed to charge. This they did at a 'pretty round trot', loosing some shot as they went, the Royalists standing firm to receive them. Then they 'durst not stand the charge, but immediately betook themselves to a confused flight.'[35] The Royalists were more numerous, but less well armed and drawn up three deep, and could not face the Cromwellian charge: they panicked, wheeled and fled. They were subsequently routed, and 'we had the execution of them two or three miles'. Cromwell's soldiers, or so he claimed, took the lives of two or three of the enemy each – the total losses were about 100 dead, but only two of them on the Parliamentary side – and also took 45 prisoners, as well as horses and arms, and four to five colours. The darkness closed in and the breathless Parliamentarian horse returned to the field of battle. 'God hath given us this evening a glorious victory over our enemies,' trumpeted an exuberant Cromwell in his official despatch,[36] after which his men marched away towards Lincoln, then skirted Newark and established themselves at Nottingham. While much has been made of this initial victory, it was, in the end, only a skirmish. There were, however, some signs of the emergent soldier, and the action set the scene for what was to come.

NOTTINGHAM

The army gathered around Nottingham that Cromwell joined in May 1643 was now selected to defend that town from any Royalist advance, except that on 21 May Sir Thomas Fairfax fashioned a victory at Wakefield that now compelled Newcastle to retire once more into Yorkshire. Opportunities were now in the hands of the Nottingham force. The Parliamentarians could either advance on Newark or move into Yorkshire in support of Fairfax. In the end, little was achieved, resentment and localism preventing any real movement. Grey proved to be a vacillating commander, and the younger Hotham did everything he could to forestall an advance, quarrelling with Lord Grey and even threatening to turn his guns on Cromwell. Like his father, he had been in secret communication with the Royalists. Cromwell and Colonel Hutchinson now took action to make sure that this situation could not continue by despatching a report to London. Hotham was arrested on 18 June. He eventually managed to escape, but was recaptured ten days later in Hull. Sir John Meldrum, a professional Scottish soldier who had fought at Edgehill, arrived in the area to take charge. All the same, nothing much went right in the field. Indeed, the Newarkers had become so bold as to brave the Parliamentarians in Nottingham under their very walls. By late June the Royalists even beat up the headquarters of the Parliamentarians, ostensibly as a cover for the Queen's move south to Oxford. With this drift in command, the Parliamentarian forces now began to go their separate ways, Gell to Derby and Lord Grey to Leicester. Cromwell eventually returned to the familiar territory of the Eastern Association, while Meldrum remained in Nottingham.

GAINSBOROUGH

In late June 1643 Newcastle began once more to move his forces. He defeated the Fairfaxes at Adwalton Moor on 30 June, thus clearing the West Riding of Yorkshire and opening up another potential move towards Lincolnshire and the south. However, an attempt to take Hull through the designs of the disloyal Hotham family failed, and Lord Fairfax managed to secure the city. Newcastle's next move was indecisive. He could either swing south or try to besiege Hull. He dithered, but then lurched south towards Lincolnshire.

This bitter little local war now swung towards Gainsborough and its passage into Lincolnshire. The strategic significance of Gainsborough lay in the fact that it stood on the Trent, blocking the northern and southern routes that were needed in any advance by Newcastle to support Newark, or to attack Lincoln. At first the town had attempted to remain neutral. Having said this, the inhabitants were keenly aware of its potential strategic significance, and had decided to invest in some earthworks and banks for its protection. In March 1643 it had surrendered to a Royalist force from Newark and was held by the Earl of Kingston. The town was then used as a position to harry Parliamentarian forces in Lincolnshire. Nevertheless, on 20 July Lord Willoughby of Parham had taken the place by storm, but that same day this action had provoked a counter-offensive, and the Royalists sent out another relief force under Charles Cavendish to recapture the town.

Burghley House seems to have been the victim of Cromwell's next real action after leaving Nottingham, but, again, it was minor affair. Cromwell, alongside Colonel's Hobert and Palgrave, arrived outside the house in July. Within its environs were two Royalist colonels, six captains and 200 horse and foot. A summons was sent in by a trumpeter to order the House to surrender on terms, quarter being promised if the occupants would leave the buildings and their arms behind them. This was refused, the defenders raucously claiming that they would rather fight to the death. Cromwell then ordered up the limited ordnance that he possessed, and in the early morning of 24 July allowed this to pound away for a good few hours, albeit achieving very little in the process. Frustrated, the Parliamentarians then drew up their musketeers in three 'squadrons' and made ready for a frontal assault. This was met with severe Royalist fire, and the assault fell back. By now it was afternoon, and the defenders, thinking better of their morning's defiance, finally called for a parley. This was granted, notwithstanding their initial refusal to surrender, and they yielded on terms. No more than six men had been killed in the affair. At the same time, a covering force had been sent out under Captains Dodson, Wauton and Desborough, and this saw off a relieving force of cavaliers of some 400 men. Dodson was wounded and unhorsed during the action, but Wauton soon rescued him. Some fifty of the enemy were slain, while the rest were dispersed. Once more, we can begin to detect the aggressive nature of early Cromwellian siege operations. While they may have been minor affairs, Cromwell was already showing that he would have little to do with the subtle methods of siege warfare: for him, this was too slow a process. It may of course be that he did not know any other way to go about matters at this stage, yet, as we shall see, these brusque tactics were to reappear continually in his later career.

Learning of the affair at Gainsborough on Wednesday 26 July, Cromwell now moved north with some six or seven troops of horse and 100 dragoons for a general rendezvous, about ten miles from the town, in order to bring succour to it. Lord Willoughby of Parham was being hard pressed by Lord Cavendish. In the late evening of 27 July, Cromwell made contact with the troops from Lincolnshire and Nottingham. Meldrum had brought about 300 of the Nottingham cavalry, while some Lincolnshire troops also joined them. Together they made up a force of some nineteen to twenty troops of horse. On Friday the 28th, at around two in the morning, some 1,200 men began their advance towards Gainsborough. Later that same morning the Parliamentarians arrived at a point about a mile and a half from Gainsborough, where they finally came into contact with the enemy. These men, a 'forlorn hope' placed there for just such a purpose, were soon beaten back, although the Parliamentary dragoons 'laboured' in the task. Indeed, the dragoons lost some four or five men in the skirmish, and only when the main body of the Parliamentary horse came up was the enemy finally beaten back. With the mêlée dying down, the Parliamentary forces then continued their advance towards the town.

Coney Warren (now known as Foxby Hill) was a hill overlooking Gainsborough, and it was here that many of the Cavaliers now posted themselves.

As the Parliamentarians approached, the Lincoln troops took the vanguard, with two of the Northampton, and three small troops of Nottingham horse were placed in the centre (or 'battle', as contemporary theorists termed it), while Cromwell and his troops brought up the rear. The Lincoln troops were unconcerned by the steepness of the approach uphill and advanced along some tracks. Despite being occasionally hindered by the Cavaliers, they soon pressed the enemy back and the whole body of Parliamentary horse followed in. There they found the enemy with three regiments of horse and a reserve of Colonel Cavendish's own regiment awaiting them. They were now placed so that a 'fair body' of horse was to the front, while the reserve stood behind them. Due to the many rabbit holes, the Parliamentarians had great difficulty in dressing their lines, but the forces began to advance within musket shot. Cromwell was situated on the right wing with his forces as both sides surged forward, 'horse to horse' and with swords drawn.[37] With clash of steel and shot they now attacked one another in close order, such that, as Cromwell later noted,

'... it was disputed very strongly who should break the other; but our men pressing a little heavily upon them, they began to give back, which our men perceiving, instantly forced them; brake the whole body, some of them flying on this side, some on the other side, of the reserve.'[38]

The Royalists then fled, carrying off some of the reserve on either side in the process.

A pursuit was now ordered of the tangled Cavaliers that lasted up to six miles. However, Cavendish's regiment held firm under their colonel. Cromwell had also held back some of his own men (two troops and one other under Major Whalley), aware that the Cavalier reserve was still in being. He now took care to re-dress his lines, as the Cavendish forces chose to engage with some of the Lincolnshire men in front of them and pushed them back. Seeing this, Cromwell unleashed the men under his control and hit Cavendish's forces in the rear, 'which did so astonish him, that he gave over the chase, and would fain have delivered himself from me.'[39] The enemy cavalry reeled and were swiftly driven down and forced into a muddy area at the bottom of the hill (later called Candish Bog). It was here that Cavendish was first unhorsed with a cut on the head and then given a thrust in the ribs by James Berry, Cromwell's captain-lieutenant. Cavendish was captured, but he died two hours later. The rest of his forces fled and were chased off the field, and the Parliamentarian forces began to converge on Gainsborough with ammunition and powder for the town's relief.

Beyond Gainsborough, however, lay advancing elements of Newcastle's northern army. Word having been brought to them that on the other side of Gainsborough, about a mile off, were six troops of horse and 300 foot, the Parliamentary commanders consulted as to their next move, and then sent out some 400 of Willoughby's foot and as many cavalry. Cromwell's men drove out some troops of horse at a nearby mill, and then discovered the presence of Newcastle's main army. On hearing this news, Willoughby and Cromwell, who was still in the town, agreed that their forces must withdraw, and Cromwell rode off to bring the Parliamentarians back. As he approached, the Royalist horse were continuing their advance, and the badly cut-up Parliamentary foot were scurrying back in a somewhat disorderly fashion into the town, a quarter of a mile away. The Parliamentary cavalry, also disorganised, now began to withdraw. With some difficulty, Cromwell, Whalley and Captain Ayscogh managed to halt some of them, and drew them up in a nearby field so as to order their lines. There, although weary, they now faced the enemy, and they began to check them in a number of clashes. Four of the Lincoln troops under Edward Whalley and four of Cromwell's regiment under Ayscogh were delegated to stand firm and then retire alternately and in order, so that they might cover Cromwell's main force.

In this smart little action, Cromwell was generous with praise for his officers, and particularly noted his cousin: 'Major Whalley did ... carry himself with all gallantry becoming a gentleman and a Christian.'[40] In this fighting retreat, eight or nine clashes occurred until the cavalry retired without the loss of one man. As the Parliamentary forces sent to relieve it withdrew towards Lincoln, Gainsborough was again besieged. While Cromwell hastily wrote letters calling for more troops to relieve it, the town fell once more on 30–31 July. Cromwell and his men now retired back to Huntingdon. Newcastle's advance could continue into the heart of the Eastern Association if he so chose, but he was soon forced to retire, mainly at the insistence of his own men, who were fearful of the presence of a large Parliamentary force at Hull.

WINCEBY

Following the defeat at Adwalton Moor, Lord Fairfax had retreated into Hull, where he was appointed Governor on 22 July 1643. He now had about 1,500 foot and 700 horses. His son, Sir Thomas Fairfax, positioned

himself at Beverley with the cavalry and about 600 infantry to avoid over-
crowding the city, but he was forced back by the advance of Newcastle's
army of 12,000 foot and 4,000 horse. By Saturday 2 September Hull was
under siege. While it was a strong defensive position, Lord Fairfax also cut
the banks and flooded the area so that both he and the Royalists were
forced to work in the wet ground. Clearly, however, Hull had to be
relieved, and so Lord Willoughby of Parnham and Cromwell, who was
back in Lincolnshire, crossed into the city on 26 September in order to
consult how best to assist the defenders. The result of this conference was
that Sir Thomas Fairfax and his cavalry were transported over the
Humber, while Lord Fairfax continued his defence against assault and
made various sallies. In much rain, the country flooded once more on 3
October. By 5 October the Earl of Manchester, now in command of the
Eastern Association forces, had sent 500 more foot into Hull under Sir
John Meldrum in order to secure the garrison. Four days later, Newcastle's
men finally undertook a grand assault to try to take the place, but were
beaten back with heavy losses. On 11 October Fairfax and Meldrum
returned the compliment by launching a major sally against the besiegers;
at first they were beaten back, but when they renewed their attack the
Royalists broke off and retreated. The siege was raised, and the Royalist
outworks and many of their guns were captured.

In Lincolnshire, meanwhile, Sir Thomas Fairfax had not been idle.
Manchester, who had been besieging Lynn, had begun his advance by way
of Boston to meet up with Willoughby, Fairfax and Cromwell at Kirby,
near Bolingbroke Castle. His infantry had occupied Bolingbroke village by
11 October and soon laid siege to the castle. Major Knight cautiously
approached the castle and called upon it to surrender, but was ignored. A
mortar fire now began to liven things up. The feisty garrison resorted to
taking pot shots at the besiegers. Knight was shot at, and Colonel
Bartholomew Vermuyden, a Dutch officer serving Parliament, was
wounded in the ankle. While the cavalry was sent out on difficult scouting
missions, the Parliamentary commanders consulted. Sir Thomas
Henderson, the Governor of Newark, had already begun to gather
numbers of troops from their garrisons, and the Parliamentarians quickly
learned that Henderson had begun an advance towards them with a force
of some 1,500–2,000 cavalry and 800 dragoons. He was now under orders
from Newcastle to relieve the castle at Bolingbroke. It seems that
Cromwell, at least, was unhappy in the conclusion that some action should
take place to stop this, for he thought 'our horse being extreme wearied

with hard duty two or three dayes together' would be incapable of doing themselves justice.[41] In the event, there was little choice in the matter. On 11 October 1643 the Parliamentarians met the Royalist cavalry coming in the other direction on the misty southern edges of the Lincolnshire Wolds in a place called Lushy Walk, close to the small hamlet of Winceby. It was open ground enclosed by two ridges, with only a boundary hedge to hamper the cavalry action.

The Royalist horse were made up of three divisions – Sir William Saville's on the left, Henderson's on the right, and Widdrington's in reserve. Widdrington later claimed that the 'ground they had chosen would not admit of above three divisions of Horse to charge at once.'[42] The Royalist dragoons were placed at the front. By noon the two sides could see one another. Colonel Bartholomew Vermuyden led the Parliamentarian forlorn hope of five troops, while Cromwell had the van and Fairfax the rear. The infantry were still some distance to the rear of the action, and, indeed, would play no part in it. After ordering the cavalry forward, Manchester retired to hurry along his infantry regiments. On spotting the Royalists, the Parliamentarian horse came on a brisk trot, 'full of joy and resolution, thinking it a great mercy that they should fight with them'; they were also singing psalms as they advanced.[43]

Vermuyden's dragoons were the first to clash with their counterparts on the Royalist side, who had dismounted and were giving a very sharp fire on their opponents. Seeing the Royalist cavalry also coming over the ridge, Cromwell's men now 'fell with resolution upon the enemy'.[44] As the Royalist dragoons gave them a volley, they charged. Cromwell had placed himself at the head of his men, and the Royalist dragoons managed to get in another shot before the Cromwellian cavalry caught them. As they fell beneath the hooves of the cavalry, one of these shots took down Cromwell's own horse and killed it. He crashed to the ground and then found himself in the midst of a dangerous mêlée. In the chaos of horses and clashing swords he got to his feet, but the passing Royalist Sir Ingram Hopton (who was subsequently killed), seeing his opponent stumbling around on foot, knocked Cromwell down again with a blow. Fortunately, at this moment of danger a soldier came up and gave Cromwell his own 'poor horse'. By the time the Colonel had ordered both himself and his unruly mount, the action had moved on, but, nothing daunted, Cromwell rode back into the fight.

In the sharp tussle that followed, the Royalist regiment of Saville was 'totally running disordered, and so put rout to our little Army';[45] the enemy front line actually fell back on the main body of their horse and disordered them. A sharp hand-to-hand struggle now followed, and the Royalist cavalry finally 'ran for it, leaving all their draggooneers which were now on foote behinde them.'[46] Fairfax had intervened, and his charge caught the Royalists heavily in their left flank. This was more than enough for them, and they scattered and fled, leaving their dragoons to their fate. The greatest part of the killing at Winceby took place over a five-mile stretch beyond the village, 'all the way being strewed with broken armes, dead men and horses'.[47] A hedge prevented many escaping, and the area known today as Slash Hollow conveys what happened to them. In all, the action was brief, lasting only some fifteen minutes to half an hour, and, according to Widdrington's report, the Royalists lost 'neer 800 horse, extremely dispersed, but no great number cut off'.[48] The Parliamentarians had lost far fewer wounded and killed, although one of the wounded was James Berry, Cromwell's captain-lieutenant. Fortunately, his wound was not serious. Manchester's infantry had by now moved into view, but found themselves too late to join the action. All in all, this was a successful day for the Parliamentarians, for the action at Winceby also took place on the same day as Lord Fairfax launched his sally from Hull that raised the siege. Indeed, it was said that Sir Thomas could hear the guns at Hull as he went into action.

This action at Winceby, alongside the raising of the siege of Hull, now freed up the greater part of Lincolnshire, and the Royalists abandoned both Gainsborough and Lincoln. Widdrington claimed that, 'Their horse are very good, and extraordinarily armed.'[49] Winceby was, if anyone's, Fairfax's victory. Manchester was too far off to control the action, although his initial dispositions were good ones, while Oliver Cromwell was all too soon unhorsed and seems to have been put into some confusion by the action. Certainly, the latter's very direct and incautious engagement with the enemy meant that he was unable to take a composed view of the action and make any cool decisions. Be that as it may, Cromwell had become a fighting soldier. The actions that year had seen him both win his spurs and institute training methods and discipline of a high order amongst his men. However, there had been little enough to distinguish him as yet as a great general. The most that can be said is that he was eager to lead from the front, and tactically was very ready to engage with the enemy – although on this occasion his concerns about the hard duties previously experienced by the Parliamentary horse gave him some qualms as to the immediate necessity of action. The honour of the day lay with his colleague

Thomas Fairfax. 'Meek and humble a carriage' in his personal life, he became 'highly transported' in battle and was beginning to reveal great tactical skills, as well as the essential qualities of leadership in combat. Having said that, it was his task as the reserve in the action to hold back until a crucial opportunity presented itself, while it was Cromwell's in the van to engage with the enemy. Even so, there were indications that a good working relationship was developing between the two men, and one that would bear fruit in time.

THE END OF 1643

If the continual uncertainty of Royalist strategy in 1643 had allowed Newcastle to try for Hull, it also allowed Prince Maurice, in the south-west, to besiege Exeter and then Plymouth. While they did so, Charles I and his main army had set off to capture Gloucester, whence Edward Massey and his men had been sending plaintive requests for help to London. Political opponents in Parliament had already been calling for Essex's head, and for a new army to be formed under Waller. Yet part of Pym's problem was that, although he had managed to get more men into Essex's army by raising money through sequestration and excise taxes and by conscription – or, at least, enough men for him to advance – Waller and Manchester's forces also benefited. Nevertheless, with Gloucester under threat, a fortified Essex set off on an expedition to relieve the place on 26 August 1643. He had reached the area by 5 September, and entered Gloucester on the 8th. The town was almost out of ammunition and supplies. The King, meanwhile, had broken off his siege and consolidated his forces at Painswick before moving on to Sudely Castle in order to intercept Essex on his return. The risk of being cut off finally led Essex to embark on a route that would take him south of Oxford. The King's forces missed his move and headed north, only realising their mistake when Essex reached Cirencester. With some rapidity, Charles now set off in pursuit, and he managed to get ahead of Essex's forces at Newbury. Thus cut off from London, Essex was forced to fight. In this first Battle of Newbury on 20 September, a brutal engagement only left both sides exhausted. Short of ammunition, rather than renew the conflict the King now withdrew his forces. So it was that the next day Essex found the battlefield abandoned and, thanking his luck, he quickly moved off towards Reading, arriving in London on 25 September. In reality, this significant campaign gave Pym time to build up his political forces and left both sides now seeking help from the other parts of the kingdoms – Pym from Scotland and the King from Ireland.

CROMWELL IN 1643

As a soldier, in 1643 Cromwell was beginning to show some of the elements that were to recur in his later career. He had emerged as an odd mixture of the practical and self-effacing. God was becoming the key to his role in all the battles and skirmishes in which he had been involved so far. He himself remained a godly man, and he employed godly men in victory. In 1645 he was to note: 'I hope you will pardon me if I say, God is not enough owned. We look too much to men and visible helps: this hath much hindered our success. But I hope God will direct all to acknowledge Him alone in all.'[50] Certainly, the reliance on the strengths of the godly gave him confidence in his actions and choices. As success followed, he became more than ever aware of God's apparent grace. God, in 1643, lay at the heart of his military life: God was the real captain; man was merely His instrument. He led from the front where he could fight, and in fighting there were few complexities. He was imbued with the certainty of salvation, and, as John Morrill puts it, 'victory revealed … God's purposes.'[51] In this sense, his early tactics remained impulsive. There was little of the cool leader in Cromwell at Gainsborough and Winceby, and, as yet, little strategic sense, but he had begun to show his basic qualities as a soldier at Gainsborough. Despite some hesitation before Winceby about his horse, Cromwell was now following certain rules: train your men, wait on the Lord, and the Lord will provide. Matched with a growing belief in himself and the part played by God in his life, these rules were now to make him one of the most able soldiers of his day.

CHAPTER 5

FROM MARSTON MOOR
TO NEWBURY, 1644

'... with shouting in the day of battle, with a tempest
in the day of the whirlwind.' – *Amos* 1:14

1644

The year 1643 had seen Oliver Cromwell take part in the wars of the
Eastern Association and increase his local reputation as soldier; 1644 was
to see him move further on to the national stage, often in a controversial
manner. The year saw Cromwell involved for the first time in two major
battles, his participation in them allowing partisans on either side to make
merry with his rising reputation. It was to end with a crucial political
victory that would sanction Cromwell's and his allies' plans to form the
necessary instrument, the New Model Army, which would allow Parliament to win its war in 1645.

The year was also to prove to be the high watermark of the King's war.
Charles I's three armies had scored some important tactical victories at
Lansdown and Roundway Down in July 1643, the capture of Bristol took
place in the same month, and Exeter fell on 4 September. Siege operations
against Plymouth and a move against Gloucester followed, but, with poor
co-ordination at the centre, the Royalists still could not land the final blow
necessary to give them victory. On the Parliamentary side, Essex's relief of
Gloucester had given the Parliamentarians some hope and a breathing
space, but equally poor centralised control also left them searching still for
a war-winning strategy. The solution for both sides now lay in the recruitment of allies, by bringing into the conflict both Scotland and Ireland in
order to tip the balance.

THE COMING OF THE SCOTS

Unsurprisingly, the Scottish Covenanters had viewed the slide to war and
subsequent events in England with some alarm, but attempts by them to
mediate in the conflict were snubbed by the King. Instead, Charles sought
to deflect their final entrance into the war through various schemes and
plots involving, amongst others, the Marquis of Hamilton, whilst carrying
on with his own Irish intrigues. Ultimately, these only led the worried

Scots, under the Marquis of Argyll, into urgent negotiations with John Pym, and these negotiations were to lead to the alliance of the Solemn League and Covenant.

In the short term, the Solemn League and Covenant was a defensive military pact that would allow the Scots to influence English affairs in return for an army of 21,000 men who would serve on Parliament's side. In the long term, the essential differences between the Parliamentarians and the Scots in questions of both politics and religion – particularly the latter – were to divide them severely. Sir Henry Vane, notorious as a favourer of sectaries, and the rising star of Parliamentary politics, led the English commissioners to the eventual treaty. The English were rather 'for a civil league' in these negotiations; it was the Scots who wanted a 'religious Covenant'.[1] A compromise was eventually cobbled together, with Vane cleverly making a loophole in the religious clause to allow sectarianism to survive. However, militarily the new strategies of 1644 would have a more profound effect, since the alliance allowed a Scots Covenanter army to operate in the north of England and this, to the Scots, was significant: a victory engineered by their army would naturally give them a dominating position in any post-war settlement.

THE YORKSHIRE PROBLEM

After Hull, Lincolnshire was cleared of Royalists, and on 20 December Gainsborough was recaptured. Sir Thomas Fairfax was then ordered into Cheshire, where Sir John Byron and his forces were threatening the Parliamentary garrisons. Bryon's army had been created to assist Newcastle's forces, to deflect the coming Scots and to capture Nantwich, the last Parliamentarian garrison in Cheshire. Instead, Fairfax's bold march caught Bryon at Nantwich on 25 January 1644 and his men decisively defeated him there. It was a victory that forced Charles to order Prince Rupert to reorganise his northern forces. Rupert arrived at Shrewsbury on 21 February. In London, in the meantime, a Committee of Both Kingdoms had been established in order to co-ordinate the new strategy between the Parliamentarians and the Scots, and in January the Scots army at long last entered England, although they were severely hampered in their marches by the bad weather.

At this time the Scots army had an impressive reputation, which dated from the Bishops' Wars. Modelled largely on the Swedish approach to warfare, it was to prove a formidable opponent. The backbone of the army lay in the infantry rank-and-file, dressed in their usual grey clothes and blue bonnets, and made up of young but fiercely motivated soldiers, for the most part professionally officered. They carried the standard weaponry of the day, musket and pike, in a ratio of two to one. While the infantry was good, the cavalry was poorer in quality and mounted on 'light, but weak nags'. It was the usual mix of men armed with pistol and sword of various troop strengths. At first, the cavalry tended to be placed with the foot, or as independent squadrons rather than regimented together. There were, however, squadrons of lancers in the Scots cavalry. They had already been used in Ireland, and were to prove an effective weapon in the English wars. On the other hand, artillery was plentiful, with a train of over sixty cannon, reflecting a strategy in which key northern English settlements – Carlisle, Newcastle, Durham and York – were to be taken and held where possible.

While the army's subordinate officers were generally veterans of various conflicts, there was also much military knowledge amongst the army's generals, who had seen many a long day's service on the Continent. It was Alexander Leslie, ever-prudent and a veteran of Dutch and Swedish armies, who was their general commander. Leslie, 'that old, little, crooked souldier' and 'Great Solyman', as Baillie called him, was a sixty-two-year-old professional soldier of great repute who had served in the army of Sweden since 1608.[2] By 1635 he had attained the rank of field marshal, as well as some celebrity as a fighting soldier. He had finally laid down his Swedish generalship in August 1638 and then returned home to Scotland, hoping for retirement. Two months later, Leslie had answered the call of Covenant, bringing his military expertise to the new army as its general in the First and Second Bishops' Wars. Following the treaty at Ripon, Charles I, hoping to placate him, had made him Earl of Leven. He had subsequently been recalled to take up this new command in late 1643. Leven was well versed in the strategy and tactics current in Europe. Under him were placed men such as David Leslie. Despite his name, Leslie was not related to Leven, but had also served, like many other Scots, in the Swedish forces under Gustavus, and he joined the Covenanters in 1643. If anything, he was a superior strategist to Leven, as Cromwell was to discover in 1650. The other commanders were all sound, experienced soldiers. They included Sir Alexander Hamilton, Lieutenant-General William Baillie and Major-General Lumsden.

Unfortunately, the Scots' advance that winter proved to be a slow one. In freezing weather, an army of some 18,000 foot, 3,000 horse and 500–600 dragoons tramped across the bridges of the Tweed on 19 January 1644. Their progress remained slow until they came to halt around

Newcastle-upon-Tyne. There they promptly laid siege to the city, but its inhabitants, familiar with Scots' pillaging in the recent past, defied them. Meanwhile, the Marquis of Newcastle had advanced his forces into Durham in order to succour the city. Both sides then skirted each other with the odd skirmish, especially after the Scots advanced to Sunderland on 4 March. More skirmishing, such as that at Boldon on 7–8 March, followed, and the marquis eventually withdrew to Durham. Logistical problems meant that the Scots 'were in great straits for want of victuall and provisions [as] The enemy hath wasted and spoyled all the Countrey and driven all away before them.'[3] The area being unable to sustain his troops, Leven was now forced to fall back, taking South Shields at the mouth of the Tyne in an action on 16 March. Newcastle then tried to offer battle at Hilton, but an indecisive contest led the marquis to retire once more towards Durham. There he learnt of the fall of Selby and was forced to turn south to protect York. Leven began to plod cautiously south after him.

While Newcastle had been defending the Tyne frontier, the Parliamentarian Sir John Meldrum, with 6,000, men, had besieged Newark and threatened Newcastle's southern communications. Charles and Rupert consulted as to what they could do to resolve the issue. They could turn their forces north, but this would leave Oxford uncovered and open to attack. However, without assistance, the Royalists in Yorkshire must surely fall. It was finally decided that Rupert should be sent north to relieve Newark, and on 21 March his forces caught up with Meldrum and forced his surrender. Once more, Royalists had control of western Lincolnshire – they even recaptured Gainsborough, Lincoln and Sleaford – but the Prince's forces were so thinly stretched that the victory proved to be a hollow one.

Fairfax's capture of Selby and the defeat of Colonel John Bellasis on 11 April now opened the route to York for the Parliamentarians. By this stage, Newcastle had retreated into York itself in order to protect that vital city. The Scots' movement across the Tees into North Yorkshire brought them into contact with Fairfax's army, and on 18 April they joined Sir Thomas Fairfax at Wetherby. On 22 April, Leven and Lord Fairfax's armies commenced the great siege of York. The Scots took post between Middlethorpe and Bishopsthorpe, while Fairfax's men crossed the Ouse and took their post from the Ouse to the Walmgate Bar. The north side of York was left open as the Allies still had too few troops to cover this area. Newcastle, inside the city with 5,000 foot, sent 800 of his horse into the countryside to free them from the perils of the siege, but if the siege were to be broken he still required assistance, without delay, from the King.

THE ARMIES OF THE NORTH

After conferring once more with the King, Rupert provided the solution. He picked up his forces at Shrewsbury and then moved into Lancashire. On 25 May Stockport fell to him, and on 28 May he 'impetuously' stormed Bolton in the rain. Two days later he linked up with Newcastle's cavalry under George Goring, and together they assaulted Liverpool with its 'mudd walls with barrs and gates' on 11 June.[4] While this manoeuvring was effective, it did little to help the Royalist forces in York, especially as Manchester and the army of the Eastern Association were now also on the move.

Under Cromwell, Manchester's cavalry first saw off a relief column attempting to relieve Belvoir Castle, and on 6 May Manchester's infantry stormed Lincoln and then Gainsborough. These preliminary manoeuvres allowed the army of the Eastern Association, some 6,000 strong, to march north to join their allies and complete the ring of the siege of York on 3 June 1644. The Allied force now numbered some 27,000 men. All the three commanders, Leven, Lord Fairfax and Manchester, continued to hold independent commands, but with Leven's obvious experience he was usually given precedence in any debates over the siege. The siege intensified, but was still prone to errors on the Allied side. Supplies grew scarce, and, thanks to Major-General Lawrence Crawford's errors, a botched attempt to blow a hole in York's defences cost many lives. Clearly, the situation at York was becoming critical, and the city's fall was almost inevitable without aid. Rupert now made his move to bring relief. His orders from the King at this point have often been seen as controversial, mainly because they led to his defeat, but in fact it was as necessary for Rupert to engage the enemy as it was for him to breathe: it was in his nature, and his aggressive strategy might well have given him an advantage over his lumbering opponents. Moreover, the implication in Charles's orders to his nephew and best general was that, if necessary, he was free to fight a battle in order to achieve his objective.

On 28 June 1644 the Allied commanders received news that Rupert, with 14,000 men, had finally crossed into Yorkshire; on 30 June he reached Knaresborough. At the Allied council of war, it was decided that the siege should be suspended, Scoutmaster-General Lionel Watson later noting, 'wee conceiving ourselves unable to keep the Siege, and fight with him with our whole strength.'[5] The Allied armies retreated to draw up on a position five miles west of the city at Long Marston in order to intercept the Prince. Later that day, when their sentinels outside York did not answer as they usually did when called for, Sir James Dudley sent out some men over the walls to examine the enemy camp. The camp had been abandoned, but, pressing forward, the Royalists engaged in a sharp skirmish a few miles further on and then retired back to the safety of the walls of York. In the meantime, Rupert, acting with characteristic speed and decisiveness, had outmanoeuvred his opponents and, throwing out a screen of cavalry, had crossed the Ouse on a bridge of boats constructed by his enemies at Poppleton. He then came down into York from the north-west and the siege was broken. Sir Thomas Fairfax later claimed that, on learning of this, the Scots were now for retiring 'to gain (as they alleged) both time and place of more advantage.'[6] The Allied generals decided to withdraw towards Tadcaster, and the unenthusiastic infantry began to trudge off in the early morning of 2 July, leaving a cavalry screen behind to cover their retreat.

At York, the impetuous Rupert now held sway. As usual, he was brimming with confidence – as well he might be, having just outmanoeuvred his opponents: he had some 18,000 men, and, with the necessary courage, he could now seek to engage his enemy. Newcastle was more wary, wishing instead to wait for the reinforcements of Colonel Robert Clavering and his 2,000 men, who were on their way. Newcastle's sensible argument was also based upon intelligence that, if left alone for a few days, the Allied forces would be compelled to divide for logistical reasons and could be dealt with piecemeal. Blithely ignoring Newcastle, and brandishing his letter from the King as his authority to command, Rupert sought his battle. With Newcastle's grudging agreement, he ordered out the army towards Marston Moor, pressing hard on the heels of the enemy.

There was now some delay, since Newcastle and his forces did not actually arrive on the field until around four o'clock in the afternoon. At first his friends had strived to persuade the marquis not to appear in the field himself, but Newcastle's loyalty to the Crown overrode any personal slights he may have felt and took him out to battle. First, however, he paid a visit to the enemy's camp and found there some abandoned *matériel*, boots and ammunition for his troops. More importantly, many of his troops were crying out for pay, and he had to use all of his persuasive powers to get them out of the city in the first place. As the Royalists began to deploy on the moor around ten o'clock that morning, some skirmishing broke out with the Allied rearguard. In the course of this action, Cromwell's nephew Valentine Walton was killed.[7] A cannon shot took off one of his legs below the knee and brought him down. Cromwell and his officers crowded around the popular young man, but could do nothing for him aside from supporting him so that he could see the Royalist cavalry retiring. Shortly after this he died. Fairfax, observing the developments on the moor, now urgently sent back for the infantry, and the Allies slowly turned and marched back to the field. It was now around two o'clock in the afternoon, and both sides began to prepare themselves for battle.

MARSTON MOOR: 2 JULY 1644

On their return, the Allies began to deploy south of the Tockwith–Long Marston road, on the slope of a low ridge which included the hill now known as Cromwell's Plump. In their front, down towards the road, lay fields of rye, by now rather sodden following rain showers. The road was more of a trackway, and north of this was cultivated land for about 400 yards or so, then a ditch of variable depth but mostly filled in at its west end. A hedge lay on the southern edge of this. Beyond was the moorland, mostly gorse bushes and rough patches of grass. Moor Lane was another trackway lying on the east and north of the road, flanked by a hedge and shallow ditch. Some boundary hedges were also to be found on the western end of the battlefield, although the ground was most difficult in the eastern part. Both armies were to rest their flanks on villages, Long Marston in the east and Tockwith in the west, but neither was to be fortified or to become scenes of action.

In terms of numbers of troops involved, most historians are agreed that this was the biggest battle of the war. For the Allies, Leven had some 2,000 cavalry and 13,500 infantry with him, while Fairfax's northern forces massed some 2,000 infantry and 2,000 cavalry. The Eastern Association forces possessed some 8,000 men, 3–4,000 of these being cavalry. In all, the Allies could mass some 20,000 infantry and 8,000 cavalry for the coming battle. On the Royalist side, Prince Rupert marshalled about 14,000 men.

The five hours before the action were spent jockeying the forces into position. Rupert was still impatiently waiting for Newcastle's infantry to arrive from York, and the Allies were returning to the battlefield. Rupert, leaving Goring's cavalry at Fox Covert in the east, now spread the remainder of the troops out westwards with the rest of the cavalry at the extreme edge of the line to form a right wing, opposite Bilton Bream. Some musketeers were also sensibly flung out as a forlorn in front of the line, so as to disrupt any attack. Rupert's marshalling of his line was held up by the late arrival of Newcastle's infantry, and in the end this rather disrupted his battle plan. Nevertheless, on the Royalist right wing lay a mixture of cavalry with some musketeers in the front line. The regiments

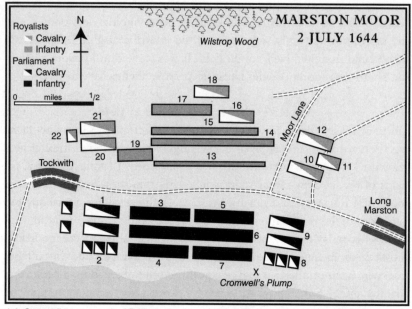

1. Cromwell	7. Fairfax	12. Dacre	18. Rupert
2. David Leslie	8. Scots Horse	13. Forlorn Hope	19. Napier
3. Crawford	9. Sir Thomas	14. Eythin	20. Byron
4. Manchester	Fairfax	15. White Coats	21. Molyneux
5. Baillie	10. Lucas/Goring	16. Blakiston	22. Tuke
6. Lumsden	11. Carnaby	17. Mackworth	

of Byron, Urry and Vaughan lay behind them, while Trevor lay on their extreme left behind Napier's infantry. In the second line, slightly disassociated and on the extreme right, stood the men of Samuel Tuke, behind whom, in a third line, were Molyneux's, Tyldesley's and Leven's troops. All in all, some 3,100 cavalry with 500 musketeers were drawn up. Slightly to their left stood Prince Rupert's regiment of horse. Many of the officers and men of these forces were veteran soldiers, and Cromwell, who would confront them in his first major battle, faced a formidable task.

The Allies' centre was broken into three lines. The Eastern Association infantry, under Crawford, had Lord Fairfax's infantry to his right and Baillie's Scots to their right (Rae, Hamilton, Maitland, Crawford-Lindsay); in the second line, behind Crawford's men, stood more Scots regiments (Yestre, Livingston, Cooper and Dunfermline), and behind Fairfax was Lumsden's command of Killead, Cassilles, Bucchleuch and Loudon; and in the third line stood Fairfax's foot on the left and Erskine and Dunhope in the centre, with some of Manchester's foot on the right. There were also two Scots regiments placed to the rear as a reserve. The

Scots, who had been in the van during the retreat to Tadcaster, were naturally the last to be placed on the field.

Cromwell was given command of the Allied left wing. He placed his Eastern Association troops in the front line, with some 800 Scots dragoons on his left. The solid Dutchman Vermuyden, a familiar face from Winceby, took the second line, and David Leslie's Scots cavalry occupied the third. Leslie, despite his experience, had demurred from commanding the wing and instead chose to serve under Cromwell. There were some 4,000 horse and 800 dragoons. On the right wing, Sir Thomas Fairfax was in command of 3,200 horse. He took the first line, while the second line was left to Colonel John Lambert, a native of Yorkshire, who had already shown some promise and enterprise as a soldier in the northern wars. The third line was made up of Scots horse under Eglinton.

Some desultory cannon fire now began to sputter across the field. It caused some damage, and the nervous, and thirsty, Allied infantry in 'Marston corn fields' fell 'to singing psalms' to pass the time and calm their fears amidst the sunshine and clouds. The latter periodically brought with them thunder and heavy downpours of rain, something of a blessing to men who had hardly any provisions and had been drinking from puddles that morning.[8] Spattered by the raindrops, by four to five o'clock that afternoon Rupert suddenly became convinced that there would be no action that day. Newcastle, who had finally turned up in his carriage, now mildly asked the Prince 'what service he would be pleased to command him; who returned this answer that he would begin no action upon the enemy till early in the morning.'[9] Rupert then sulkily rode off to have some dinner. General King had annoyed him, as when he had been shown the Prince's battle plan he had complained 'By God, sir, it is very fine on paper, but there is no such thing in the field.'[10] The puzzled Newcastle retired to his nearby carriage and phlegmatically lit his pipe. While they were thus engaged, the Allied commanders were having other ideas. A council of war was taking place. Leven, the experienced veteran of Gustavus Adolphus' wars, could see the Royalist formations from his position on a small hillock behind his developing lines. He saw not only the arrival of the rest of Newcastle's infantry, but also the Royalist army, seemingly settling down for the night. Following a brief consultation with his fellow generals, and ignoring the lateness of the day, orders to attack were now issued. The Allies had decided to seize the initiative.

The first the Marquis of Newcastle, quietly smoking his pipe in his carriage, heard of the Battle of Marston Moor was 'a great noise and thunder of shooting'.[11] To this was added a great storm of thunder and rain which crashed overhead, soaking both armies, as, at 7.30 in the evening, the Allied line surged forward at 'a running march', eager to hit the Royalist lines before they could respond and unleash any musket shot. This bold advance swiftly carried the position. The Allies seized some guns and chased off the skirmishers placed there by Rupert in the process. A worried Newcastle, in the meantime, hastened to put on his arms, only to see horsemen from the broken Royalist right wing already riding past him, fleeing the battlefield.

In the left centre of the field, Crawford's infantry had advanced to clash with the Royalist infantry at the same time. Indeed, Crawford 'over-winged' the enemy and fell on their flank. They then captured four of the Royalist cannon, allowing the Scottish foot to advance past the ditch. Further to their right, Lord Fairfax's infantry also marched up, but they soon hit the second line of the Royalist infantry and were pushed back in a rout. On the right wing lay Sir Thomas Fairfax. Before the battle, Fairfax had been suffering from ill health, but, as usual, he had risen to the occasion. Yet even he and his cavalry found it very difficult to debouch on the moor, and were hampered by 'whins and ditches'. When Fairfax finally managed to get some 400 of his men together, he attacked in an attempt to outflank the opposition. His target was Carnaby's horse, on the very left of the Royalist position. Fairfax pushed them back and then seems to have lost control of his men, who rode off in pursuit of their fleeing opponents. Behind him, and before they could get into order, George Goring had struck Fairfax's second line. There was some token resistance from the Scots, but the wing was soon broken. Goring then galloped on past the ridge into the Allied baggage train. With the Allied cavalry thrown into confusion and scattered in some disorder, Lord Fairfax's foot were now trampled in the rush and roughly handled. The two Scots brigades in the reserve also fled. As Goring's men pursued the escapees for some two miles, Leven and Lord Fairfax, believing that their gamble had failed and that the day was lost, fled the field. However, Lumsden managed to bring up the rest of the Scots infantry to hold the line. About five regiments now stood firm, and in hand-to-hand combat they fought off the Royalist cavalry of the second line with musket and pike.

Men were now streaming away on both sides in the drifting smoke, leaving Baillie's men in the centre exposed in their flanks. Some of these Scots now began to look to their own safety. Some way from the battlefield, Arthur Trevor met some Scots shouting out, 'Weys us, we are all undone' as they passed by.[12] Stragglers from both sides made for the nearest garrisons to hole up there rather than face the clash of arms. The

Scots infantry on the right also advanced into the first line of Royalist infantry, but when their flanks opened they saw Fairfax's men reeling back in disorder from an attack, and some of the Scots gave way.

Newcastle, in the meantime, had tried to rally some of the men who sped past him. He briefly succeeded, but they soon broke again, so he abandoned the idea and sought to discover how his own regiments were faring. On the way he came across a troop of horse made up of gentlemen of quality from York, whom he had promised to captain. They persuaded him to lead them into the battle, and so he joined the action in their company. They eagerly engaged with a Scots regiment of foot, which they routed. In his haste, Newcastle had forgotten his sword, and, borrowing his page's poor quality weapon, he bravely engaged the enemy. On the other hand, the Royalist Sir Philip Monkton 'had my horse shot under me as I caracoled at the head of the body.'[13] Dismounted, Monkton raced into the mêlée on foot and eventually found another mount, but he was unable to see what was happening because of the smoke and confusion. He was finally forced to retire from the fray. He later came across a group of horse from the Royalist right wing that had been broken and was milling about under the ridge that had been the original Allied start line. They would not rally, and Sir John Urry, the Prince's major-general, would not assist him. In the event, Monkton loitered on the field until late that night, and finally retired towards York.

After his charge, Sir Thomas Fairfax, blood now pouring from a heavy wound in his left cheek, had returned to the battlefield to find the rest of his horse in flight. The captain of his troop had been shot in the arm and his cornet severely cut about the hands; and, although he did not yet know it, his own brother had been mortally wounded. Seeing the turmoil in the Allied ranks, he now threw off his battlefield sign of a white handkerchief and warily moved through the Royalist lines. Some historians have claimed that Fairfax was trying to break clear of the field under the assumption the Allies had been defeated. Nevertheless, he came across Cromwell's troops, who he found had been undertaking daring feats of their own on the left wing.

In the plan, it had been Cromwell's part for his cavalry wing to smash through the enemy horse on the left and then join up with the cavalry wing of Fairfax doing likewise on the right, around the rear of the Royalist infantry, while the Allied infantry pinned the Royalist infantry in the centre. This was fairly standard battlefield practice. In reality, it hardly ever succeeded, for both sides tended to have the same strategy. Furthermore, planning, as is well known, rarely survives the first contact with the enemy; after that there is only improvisation. Despite this, Cromwell and his cavalry got under way,

Cromwell once more placing himself in the front line. Dragoons and pioneers had been already sent in to clear the hedges, and then he crossed in open order and went around the ditch. The dragoons soon chased off the musketeers Rupert had placed there as the cavalry quickly formed up on the other side and dressed their ranks. Scoutmaster-General Watson later gave an account of the attack by Cromwell's horse: 'We came down the hill in the bravest order … with the greatest resolution that was ever seen … Cromwell's division of 300, in which himself was in person, charged the first division of Prince Rupert's, in which himself was in person.'[14]

In the engagement that followed, Cromwell later noted that his men 'beat all the Prince's horse. God made them as stubble to our swords.'[15] In fact, the first division of the Eastern Association cavalry under Cromwell began to move left to the enemy's flank and engaged them by smashing into the extreme right of the Royalist horse, where stood the cavalry under Samuel Tuke, who was to become Cromwell's initial target. Tuke's men fell back, overwhelmed by this bold thrust in their flank, and then turned and

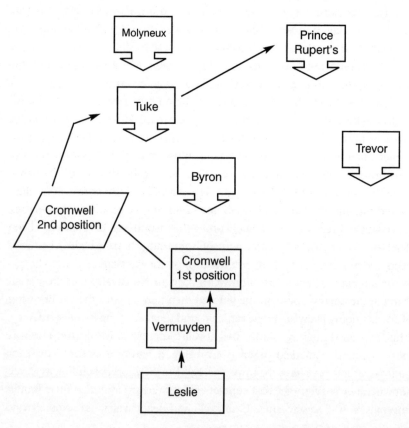

fled, only to collide with the unprepared Prince Rupert's regiment of cavalry, who also turned and scattered. This is a tactic that Cromwell was to return to at Dunbar. It is a common idea that occurs in the military manuals of the day, where the opponent's flank was noted as the most vulnerable point in any unit if it could be attacked at just the right time. The tactic seems to have succeeded, for the second line of the Allied cavalry now engaged Bryon's horse that had impetuously moved forward to attack.

Rupert had been sitting on the ground eating his supper when he heard the battle begin. He hastily abandoned his meal and mounted his horse to try to rescue the situation on his right wing. He managed to turn some of his cavalry about and led them in a charge, but their action proved fruitless, and, although some tough fighting lay ahead, it was soon obvious that the wing of the army had already been broken. Rupert led a charge which broke through some of Cromwell's troops, and he was then caught up in a fierce cavalry battle. He claimed to have killed some four or five of the enemy in order to break free. Rather less heroic claims later emerged that, on seeing the rout taking place, he had hidden in a nearby bean field. As his army began to crumble around him, Rupert abandoned it and came 'into Yorke alone about 11 o'clock at night'.[16]

While Cromwell had managed to hold his men in check after his charge, he now moved them back into the field to engage the infantry, but in turn he found himself attacked in the flank by Molyneux's cavalry and Trevor's troopers from the front. Scoutmaster Lionel Watson described what followed as a 'hard pull' as Cromwell's men were charged both in front and on the flank, and a mêlée ensued at sword point, the men 'hacking one another; but at last (it so pleased God) [Rupert, in the charge noted above,] ... brake through them, scattering them before him like a little dust.'[17] Leslie, with the reserve in the third line, now took his part and actually turned the tide, for by this time Cromwell had been given a nasty wound in the neck by sword point. This wound was later claimed as a cut from Marcus Trevor, writing after the Restoration of 1660,[18] but, whoever gave it, Cromwell was now forced from the field and retired to a small cottage not far away to have the wound dressed. He may also have had concussion, but his enemies were to make much of what they said was merely a minor wound and his absence from the fighting at the critical point. In fact, Watson, who was close by, calls his commander's wound 'a slight wound in the neck', which we may take to mean that it was a wound that was now 'slight' – that is, after the battle rather than at the time.[19] Denzil Holles, no friend of Cromwell's, claimed that Cromwell had 'neither part nor lot in the business', but this seems unlikely.[20] Holles gained this view from a conversation with Lawrence Crawford, another enemy of Cromwell's, who also related that he later came across Cromwell pleading, in a quavering voice, that he did not know what to do. Crawford then took command. Neither of these two sources is very satisfactory, as both writers were enemies. What we can say is that, at some point in the mêlée, Oliver Cromwell was injured severely enough for him to retire, and that he only returned for the second phase of the battle.

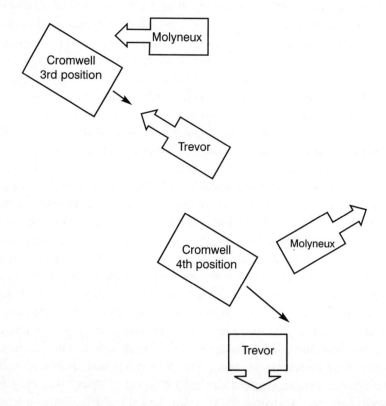

Both sides now stood at sword point, hacking at one another.[21] The Parliamentary cavalry now lost impetus, and Cromwell's hard-pressed troops were in danger of some disorder. Fortunately, as the cavalry began to fall back, David Leslie took his command up and caught the Royalist cavalry in the rear and right flank; then Cromwell's first line returned to the fray and the Royalist cavalry were 'roughly overpowered', either being cut down or turning in flight.[22] Rupert, as we have seen, now cut his way out at this point. Eventually the Royalist cavalry, somewhat disorganised, fled north, skirting Wilstop Wood. A few squadrons of Leslie's Scots were quickly sent off in pursuit, and the other Royalists fled to the dead ground behind the Allied lines, where, leaderless, they milled around. By this stage Cromwell had returned to the fray, and his and Leslie's firm hands now re-formed their horse and kept them together in close order. They then switched their front to the east.

It was after re-forming his troops well north of his original line, with Crawford's and Manchester's foot nearby, standing 'as a wall of brass', that Cromwell and Leslie received news through the drifting smoke of the left wing's disappearance and the blows to the Allied centre.[23] It may be that this news came from Sir Thomas Fairfax himself, who by now had crossed the field. At his order, the men under his command and Crawford and Manchester's foot now wheeled eastwards and moved off to the assistance of the Scots in the centre. Cromwell's and Crawford's cavalry and infantry attacked the infantry in the centre, and then Cromwell and Leslie moved further south and struck hard at Goring's returning Royalist cavalry on the other side of the battlefield, near where the Allied right wing had begun the day. With the co-operation of Crawford's infantry, they now routed the Royalist cavalry. The Royalist infantry, meanwhile, were only gradually driven from the field. Attacked from the rear by Cromwell's victorious cavalry, they began to collapse.

The last act of the day was left to Newcastle's valiant regiment of White-coats. The Eastern Association cavalry swept the fleeing Royalists off the field until they reached the Whitecoats, who courageously repelled one attack after another with pike and shot and then stood off dragoons and cavalry thrusts. However, they were trapped, and when their ammunition ran out they were bloodily cut down where they stood. Few survived. It was now around nine o'clock, and in the moonlight the bodies of hundreds of dead and dying men, on both sides, covered the moor. The dead and wounded now became prey to looters, searching for gold and other plunder, so that by morning many of the bodies were left exposed and naked.

Amongst the survivors of the battle there was little cheer. Manchester returned to ride about their ranks late that night. He found them very weary and thirsty, but was appalled by the scenes of carnage. In the end, he was unable to do more than promise food and drink for the next day.

Marston Moor was a Royalist disaster. Some 4,000–6,000 Royalists were casualties, and 1,500 of them became prisoners. The survivors managed to stagger back into York in great confusion, but the men at the gates only allowed in those who 'were of the town, so that the whole street was throng'd up to the barr with wound'd & lame people.'[24] Rupert now managed to rally 6,000 or so cavalry. He marched out northwards the next day, picked up Clavering's forces, and retired from the scene. Newcastle had also escaped from the battlefield, and he arrived at York late in the night. He seems to have felt only shame for the defeat, which was hardly his fault, and, despite Rupert's pleadings, he was completely disheartened, fearing the 'laughter of the Court and King'. As a result, he decided to abandon his command altogether and leave the country for exile on the Continent.[25] Together with James King, he now made for Scarborough, where he took ship. The rest of the troops left at York were soon besieged once more, and a fortnight later they capitulated. After this the Allied forces went their separate ways.

Amongst all the joy of victory, there was naturally some dissension as to who should get the credit for the success of this confused battle. The Scots were taken aback to learn that Cromwell's name was soon being trumpeted all around London as the architect of the victory. Robert Baillie indignantly noted in a letter that

> 'We were both grieved and angry that your Independents there should have sent up Major Harrison to trumpet over all the city their own praises to our prejudice, making all believe that Cromwell alone, with his unspeakably valorous regiments, had done all that service ... that the most of us [the Scots] fled.'[26]

As a result, stories of Cromwell's absence from the field were soon spread around, widening still further the breach between the Independents and the Scots. Despite this, Cromwell seems to have won the battle for public opinion, if not the historical arguments, though still more divisions were to follow.

Oliver Cromwell's part in this battle, like so much of his career, has always been contentious. While some were to give him credit for the victory that followed, others denied this and instead gave the palm to David Leslie, or even Fairfax. In reality, Cromwell's own expressed opinions on the encounter remain rather indistinct. From him, the main evidence concerning the battle lies not in any battlefield report, but in a personal communication to his brother-in-law Valentine Walton relating the death of Walton's son in the morning skirmish. Perhaps we should not be too surprised at this, as Cromwell was, after all, a subordinate commander, and he may have seen no need to write an account on his own behalf. Yet the disputes over his position in the battle that began almost immediately it was over may have led him to take refuge in silence. As usual, Cromwell's references to the combat, written three days afterwards, are filled with the inevitable paeans to the Lord for the actual triumph, and are less useful to explain what he actually did:

> 'We never charged but we routed the enemy. The left wing, which I commanded, being our own horse, saving a few Scots in our rear, beat all the Prince's horse. God made them as stubble to our swords, we charged their regiments of foot with our horse, routed all we charged ... I believe, of twenty-thousand the Prince hath not four-thousand left. Give glory, all the glory to God.'[27]

We can see that Cromwell divided his part of the action into two phases: the cavalry battle, then the cavalry-versus-infantry combat. He was less specific about the actual methods and events, does not mention his wound, and uncharitably relegates Leslie and the Scots to a 'few Scots' in the rear. Much has been made of this, but the fact that he was not writing for a wider audience but for a bereaved father – a situation in which he had also recently found himself – may explain much. It was also natural for him to give the glory to God, and while in this instance he was not obviously seeking any carnal glory for himself, he did not seem to want to give it to anyone else either. In this respect he was not alone, for none of the main Allied generals covered themselves with glory. As one contemporary put it on hearing of the precipitate flight of Leven, Fairfax and Manchester in the course of the action, 'God would not have a general in the army. He himself was general.'[28] Cromwell would doubtless have agreed that in the end it was God's victory; neither he nor any Scots could argue with that. Yet it is clear that, by this time, he and others were beginning to have reservations about the Scots, seeing them as much as potential political rivals as allies. For political reasons alone, some of the news sheets in London chose to emphasise Cromwell's part in the combat. They put a skilful 'spin' on his actions, for here at last was the emergence of a genuine Independent hero and a man who sought true liberty of conscience. As a consequence, Cromwell was to be hailed as the victor of the conflict, much to the distress and indignation of the others involved. Moreover, the visiting Henry Vane's persuasive arguments before the walls of York on the position of the King after the war, and Cromwell's already smouldering quarrels with the

Scottish Major-General Lawrence Crawford, over problems of religious dissent in the army of the Eastern Association, had begun to lead him to see the Scots as potentially dangerous for the godly cause.

For the most part, Cromwell's tactical role in the battle was generally smart and prompt in its actions. He had used his experience of the year before in his first major confrontation. His flanking move was successful, whereas the ground hampered Fairfax's gambit on the other side. More importantly, Cromwell was able to keep hold of his men in the mêlée that followed. Here the strict discipline and structure of his command paid off. These qualities had brought the Ironsides through the cavalry battle and broken their opponents' morale. They did not have it all their own way, and, but for Leslie's spirited and, at times, crucial support, events might have gone differently. Neither should the co-ordination of the pair with Crawford's foot be forgotten. It was the breaking of the Royalist right wing that led to the victorious conclusion. Nor should we neglect the real part played by the men themselves. If the part of their commander was obscure, then they at least had had a glorious day. Well might David Leslie later say that 'Europe, hath no better soldiers.'[29] On the other side, Rupert's mistakes in the battle were sufficient in themselves to cause the disaster. His belief that the Allies would stand and wait for his attack the next day was based on his previous experience and perhaps his reluctance to believe that they would ever have the necessary energy to attack. This arrogance had created the disaster – although it had not lost the war.

IN MANCHESTER'S ARMY

In the aftermath of Marston Moor, Manchester's army gradually moved further south seeking supply. Manchester's subsequent petulant actions, or inactions, now led to quarrels between himself and his general of horse. The two men began to argue continually. The victory at Marston Moor seems to have shocked Manchester as much as the Royalists. More than ever before, he was convinced that another such victory would totally destroy the King's cause. It would end the war by the sword instead of the compromise peace he wished to achieve, and in due course might only lead to complete social chaos. A somewhat reluctant participant in war, Manchester now sought to keep his army in check and prevent it from joining in the crushing blow that others, such as Oliver Cromwell, thought all too necessary to end the conflict. While Manchester wanted peace by accommodation, his lieutenant-general of horse, fired by his recent success, was now becoming publicly eager to end the war by military victory and was moreover entering into one of his most radical phases. Manchester's face must have grown even longer at the almost daily reckless comments of his lieutenant-general.

Cromwell's alleged defence of toleration, of changing the social structure of the state, as well as his barely suppressed dislike of the Scots, were shared by many of his men. Now his own commander's subsequent tardy actions began to infuriate him. Cromwell was already antagonistic to Crawford in the army owing to what he saw as the latter's persecution of Independent officers, whom he swiftly moved to defend in a blistering letter to the major-general. He now began to see both Crawford and Manchester as lapsed followers in the Lord's cause. Had not God and such men as he given them victory, and were they now to throw it all away?

Later that year Cromwell was to accuse Manchester of deliberately mismanaging the available forces and of squandering many opportunities that came the army's way following Marston Moor.[30] Newark might well have been blockaded, or taken, or Rupert attacked, or any number of other useful matters carried out. Instead, Manchester, according to Cromwell, now dithered and angrily criticised those who sought to challenge him. Cromwell's inability to use politic speech at this time widened the breach between them still further. Manchester and Crawford responded by attacking Cromwell's position in the army and openly condemning the types of men he had recruited and would always defend. Doubtless the feud was not made any better by the Press of the day and its paeans to its Independent hero.

As the feud between its commanders grew apace, the Eastern Association forces gradually drew southwards, and by 13 September all three men – Cromwell, Manchester and Crawford – had taken their case to the Committee of Both Kingdoms. Cromwell now argued that Crawford should be cashiered or else his colonels would lay down their commissions. The Committee tried to mollify, and failed, all the parties. In the field, however, uncertainty still reigned, and even Manchester could not prevent all three of them going to the aid of Essex and Waller.

THE NEWBURY CAMPAIGN

While the bells of victory had rung out for the battle in the north, in the south the strategic position was quite different. Here King Charles, still based at Oxford, saw his garrisons falling as Waller and Essex manoeuvred to try to cut him off from the south-west. By 3 June the King had feinted towards Abingdon, and when Waller retired to cover this move, he shifted off north-west towards Worcester. Essex and Waller had co-operated fitfully for some time, but, disliking each other's company, they eventually decided in June 1644 that, instead of following the King, they would separate their forces. While this flew against all the sensible strategies to bring as many forces to bear on the enemy as possible, Essex decided to draw his forces off to the West Country in order to raise the siege of Lyme. Waller, with his mostly London-based regiments, who were reluctant to leave their home ground in any case, agreed to ward off any strike by the King on the Lord General's rear.

A confident Essex marched off into the south-west of England and soon forced Prince Maurice to lift his siege of Lyme. He was then persuaded by his limited success to push still further into the Royalist territories, under the delusion that he would be welcomed as a liberator by entering the Royalist stronghold of Cornwall. In fact, Essex soon found himself in grave danger. In the meantime, Waller was in pursuit of the King, who had returned to Oxford and then moved off once more towards the north-east. On 29 June 1644 they finally clashed at Cropredy Bridge, where Waller was given a bloody nose. This now freed Charles and his army for a swift strike against the Earl of Essex. In August 1644, in what was to be his best campaign of the war, the King moved to cut off Essex and his forces at Lostwithiel in Cornwall. While the Lord General and his 10,000 troops plaintively called for help, none was forthcoming. Eventually Essex himself gave permission for his cavalry to break out. Seeing nothing but the awful spectre of a humiliating surrender before him, the Lord General chose rather to escape to Plymouth by boat, while the redoubtable Sir Philip Skippon was left behind to negotiate the surrender of the infantry.

By mid-October 1644 Charles and his army were returning from their victorious campaign at Lostwithiel and had marched into Salisbury. Their movements raised the fear that the King, having defeated both the southern commanders, would now advance upon London, but, in reality, Charles had much more mundane aims at this time, such as relieving the pressure on Oxford by sustaining his besieged garrisons at Basing House, Donnington Castle and Banbury.

By this stage, Parliament had three forces in the field. The remnants of Essex's re-formed army were now in Portsmouth, the King having rather foolishly let most of his infantry go. Also in the field was the squabbling army of the Earl of Manchester, based at Reading, and Sir William Waller's reluctant troops were falling back before the King towards Andover. An assembly point was now called at Basingstoke, where, together, the three armies would have some 19,000 men. On 18 October Waller was driven out of Andover, but the Parliamentary armies continued to converge: Manchester was at Basingstoke on 16 October and Essex had advanced his troops from Portsmouth to twelve miles south of that town on 17 October to join with Manchester's troops on 19 October. Sir William Waller reached them on 21 October.

The Parliamentarians' combination of the three armies now promised a 'Marston Moor of the south' if they were ably handled. The Parliamentary news sheets, in the best traditions of the writings of armchair generals everywhere, all situated safely behind the lines, were now screaming for an advance to battle. One such noted:

'Why not may we offer battle to the enemy, which yet we never did, they did to us at Edgehill, Newbury, Yorke, Horncastle, and other places, let us once, and if at any time at this time: we are a third in power more than they, which though victory be not allwayes to the greater number, yet it is the reason ground enough to charge through.'[31]

On 22 October Parliament even ordered a special day of prayer and humiliation in advance of the engagement. More practically, they ordered surgeons down to the combined army and also sent the Scot Archibald Johnston of Warriston and a colleague as their civilian advisors to the army from the Committee of Both Kingdoms sitting at Derby House. The politicians came down to try to create some form of unity in the generals, amongst whom, unfortunately, quarrels were now so deeply imbedded, particularly in the Eastern Association, that they would hamper subsequent operations.

No single commander-in-chief emerged from the conjunction of the three armies. Manchester, who had already ignored many messages from the central command in London to co-operate, would not agree to Essex's seniority and, opportunely, Essex withdrew sick to Reading (with the flux and piles caused by the cold and weakness, said some), so the command devolved on a council of war comprising Manchester, Waller and the other senior officers. It was the worst of all possible situations. While Cromwell and some of the junior men were angrily calling for an advance as swiftly as possible to strike against the King, Manchester, displaying a deliberate inertia, was for delay or even retreat.

Charles, in the meantime, had moved his forces forward to a point midway between Donnington Castle and Basing House at Kingsclere, a position he found too exposed, with the result that the army moved on to

Newbury. At this point, the relief of Basing House was beyond Charles, but Donnington Castle and Banbury were now realistic targets before the winter arrived to close the campaigning season down. He was sensibly not seeking battle with three armies – at least, not until Prince Rupert, once again in the south, arrived with 3,000 horse and dragoons from Bristol. On 22 October the King arrived in Newbury, and then sent the Earl of Northampton with some cavalry off to relieve Banbury Castle while he stood north of Newbury in a strong position with the remaining 9,000–10,000 troops.

The King's right flank rested upon the River Kennet and the already garrisoned town of Newbury. The Lambourne, a small tributary stream, and Donnington Castle protected his left, while his centre occupied Shaw House, the home of one Mr Dolman, which was soon converted into a Royalist stronghold and garrisoned by Sir George Lisle. The centre was largely made up of cavalry under Sir Humphrey Bennet, while the foot, under Lord Jacob Astley, lay between the Lambourne and Shaw House. Prince Maurice's forces – the Cornish foot, the Duke of York's regiment under Sir William St Ledger, and a brigade of Cornish horse with five field pieces – were detached to protect the rear of the Royal army around the village of Speen. The Earl of Cleveland, who was to be captured in the battle, later told his captors that the most reliable infantry was placed in the east, from where any Parliamentary advance would come, while 'the new ones, namely those whom they had driven along with them out of the Countries,' were in the west.[32] This was their weakest point.

The King now awaited the return of Northampton's men from the relief of Banbury, before deciding whether to strike towards Basing House. Soon news came in of the Parliamentary advance. If he had to fight, the King sensibly chose to remain in his strong defensive positions and await events. In any case, his military intelligence seems to have been limited. He later complained about the inhabitants of Newbury, pronouncing 'That they were most pestilent Roundheads, and that they were not so loyall as his Subjects of Cornwall, who would give him intelligence upon all occasions.'[33]

The news of the King's presence around Newbury was soon brought to the Parliamentary commanders, alongside erroneous tales of the Royal army's disorganisation. As a result, the commanders finally came to an agreement that they would attack, and they set out on 25 October. Some skirmishes and an artillery cannonade followed, and by the next day the Parliamentarian forces were on Clay Hill, a mile north-east of Newbury. There a council of war surveyed the whole scene, and then undertook a crucial debate in small cottage nearby. Cromwell later noted that in the council he had urged battle, and one observer noted his eagerness and 'joy that he had an opportunity to fight with the King's army'.[34]

Nevertheless, tempers were obviously frayed, and only after a struggle was it finally agreed that Manchester should try to pin down the King in the east while a substantial detachment of the army was sent on a wide arc to the right in order to outflank his position. If the manoeuvre proved successful, the King would be caught between two fires and his army completely crushed. Consequently, the Parliamentarians agreed to divide their forces, and a large part of the army was detached on a wide flanking march of some thirteen miles to reach Speen, west of the King's position, cutting off the Royal army from any relief from Rupert's forces. This was a risky strategy, and we do not know who suggested it – the signs are that it was the innovative Waller – but had the King been anything like an adventurous general it could have led to his opponents' defeat in detail. As it was, King Charles was to remain on the defensive throughout, and while he was to receive news of the flanking move, he did not choose to attack. Instead, he relied upon his move to shift some of his forces under Prince Maurice to a further position on rising ground, west of Speen. These forces would spend some of the morning of 27 October entrenching their position and bringing up some field pieces.

The Parliamentarian route march now lay three miles north-east, to Hermitage, then west via Chievely to North Heath, where it briefly halted, then south to Winterbourne, west to Boxford, south to Wickham Heath and south-east to Speen. It could, in theory, take nearly twenty-four hours to cover the ground, allowing for a halt. The outflanking forces were to consist of Essex's army under Skippon and Balfour, with Waller's and Cromwell's cavalry, Cromwell no doubt eager to be finally free from the dead hand of his commander. Skippon, Waller, and Balfour had joint command of the flanking force, and they set off around midnight. The agreed plan was that, once they had arrived in position at Speen, Skippon would fire four of his big artillery pieces simultaneously to give Manchester news of his attack, and Manchester would then launch his pinning assault in the east.

27 OCTOBER

In the early-morning haze of 27 October, in order to keep the Royalists occupied, Manchester began a diversionary attack on the Royal troops before him. His men moved swiftly over the Lambourne and marched towards the now fortified Shaw House. They assaulted the breastworks with great ferocity, but the attack soon got out of hand and the Parliamentary infantry were checked by a cavalry charge. The soldiers were only withdrawn with some difficulty, running into their own reserves on the way back. After this, Manchester once more lapsed into apathy with only the crackle of muskets and occasional artillery fire breaking the quietness of the day. He did, however, summon up enough energy to ride up and down the line encouraging his men.

Meanwhile Waller's forces were slowly making their way round the flank of the King's army, seizing some carts of supplies and taking some prisoners. Their presence was soon discovered, and the Royalists in Donnington Castle sallied out to fall on their rear and take some prisoners of their own. The advance nevertheless continued, encouraged by the arrival of news that Newcastle-upon-Tyne had finally fallen to the besieging Scots army. All the flanking force eventually arrived at their target at around two or three o'clock in the afternoon. Waller had the chief command, Sir William Balfour with his cavalry was placed on the right wing, while Cromwell took the left wing.

Waller later noted that their 'cannon played hard upon us … The hedges hindered our horse very much. Their cannon made the ground very hot. There was no way left but to fall on with horse and foot, and that without delay.'[35] Led by Lieutenant-Colonel Lloyd and Major Hurry, a forlorn of 800 musketeers was quickly flung out in the dying afternoon sun. Despite the enclosed fields and narrow lanes in their way, they sang psalms as they went forward, only to come under heavy fire from five artillery pieces west of the village of Speen. Skippon's infantry now followed them, and launched a desperate attack on the enemy trenches, at which point cannon fire from Donnington Castle also opened up on Waller's troops, the 'cannon and small shot on both sides firing with as quick a motion as was possible.'[36] Under heavy fire, Lloyd was almost immediately shot in the arm and fell, but Essex's infantry clambered up to the right hand of the position 'with great boldness'. The Red and Yellow regiments of the London trained bands also held the enemy on the right hand, and engaged them there. Colonel Aldridge's brigade (his own troops, and Davies's, Fortescue's and Ingoldsby's regiments) took the centre of the works as their target.

Lloyd having already fallen, Major Hurry took the infantry into a withering fire, only to stumble mortally wounded. There was now a very sharp struggle in the trenches as Essex's infantry, with 'lion-like spirit', finally overran Maurice's positions.[37] The infantry were delighted to find they had recaptured their own artillery, taken from them at Lostwithiel. They soon turned them on the backs of the retreating Royalists, shouting, 'We will shew them a Cornish hopp', while on the other side the Royalist infantry broke and fled, crying as they went, 'Devils, devils.'[38] Colonel Barclay and his brigade (Barclay's, Robert's and Skippon's) had resolutely repulsed three charges of Royalist horse, while the City's Blue regiment gave them support on their left. As the Royalists now fell back, Skippon's infantry pursued them into Speen, and a bloody, hour-long struggle in the gathering gloom and smoke drove the Royalists out of the hamlet. As Maurice's men staggered back along the Shaw road towards their cavalry and artillery placed in the fields behind Speen, much now depended on the Parliamentary cavalry, still struggling with the innumerable hedges and ditches, and upon Manchester's prompt response to the sound of the guns.

Both Balfour and Cromwell had been having considerable problems ordering their cavalry. The enclosed ground made keeping rank difficult, and as Balfour moved forward he cleared Speen church, skirting the marshy ground near the River Kennet and making his attack on the Royal guard. The brigade of horse shuddered and began to break. The King, near at hand, desperately tried to rally his horse, and the enemy briefly surrounded him. The Parliamentarians later claimed that they were even within pistol shot of the King, but Charles was finally rescued by two troops of the Queen's Regiment under Sir John Canfield and the life-guards, who returned to the fray and dispersed the enemy. It may have been at about this time that Sir William Waller was also nearly killed. He was, in the best traditions of the heroic general, 'mingled with the enemy, I had a great deliv'rance, for one of the adverse party coming behind me, and being ready to fire his pistol in my reines, in that instant one of my life-guard killed him, or otherwise in all probability he would have killed me.'[39] The Royalists charged forward again, Skippon's infantry caught them with musket and pike and a storm of fire forced them to retire.

Cromwell, on the left, found himself in toils. He was exposed to fire from the guns of Donnington Castle that played cheerfully upon his horse as he tried to marshal them into formation. Yet, for some puzzling reason, he was not at his best that day. Most of his biographers elide his actions on the day and pass swiftly on to the aftermath of the political conflict that followed the battle. There is no doubt that Manchester's continual unwillingness to act had left him fuming. The artillery fire from Donnington was over 1,000 yards away and an irritation, but the difficulties of the ground should not be underestimated. Indeed, one source claimed that 'some had not room, and so were much dejected that they could not get to the enemy'. The fact that Cromwell seems to have shown none of the eagerness for battle he had shown previously did not help.[40] Manchester's later comments that Cromwell 'did no service' on the day were motivated by political spite, but once again Cromwell's actions were obscure, and he may have been as blameworthy as his enemies were later to claim.[41] It may well be that, while engaged in the flank march, Cromwell had mused on the Providential nature of the test before him and the nature of the men in command. If so, he must have become severely depressed. His own comments on his actions in the battle are really rebuttals of the criticisms flung at him as Manchester responded to the accusations hurled at himself. There was even talk later that Cromwell was reluctant to give the Presbyterian a victory and may have deliberately stood aside, but this seems unlikely. In the end, it would seem that Cromwell's tactics and the nature of the ground had this time played him false. Whatever the true cause of the errors he made that day, for once he had been defeated, and his silence on the matter seems to reveal that he was well aware of it.

As far as we can trace their movements, Cromwell's troops appear to have first made for the cavalry of Sir Humphrey Bennet, located on the south-west of the Speen Fields. These troops fled, and Cromwell then advanced to the 'north side of the field', in the direction of Donnington, where Goring and Cleveland's brigade caught his men while crossing a ditch. At this point, God well and truly spoke against Oliver Cromwell: Goring and the elderly Lord Cleveland saw Cromwell's disorganisation and, bypassing some infantry embedded in ditches and enclosures, and ignoring their shot, they charged Cromwell's troops, bloodily striking the Parliamentarian horse and causing them to fall back. Cleveland and some other Royalists also tried to trick the Parliamentarian infantry they came across by making out they were their own cavalry, 'but being demanded the word, and not knowing of it, divers of them were knockt off their horses.'[42] Cleveland was captured after his horse was shot from under him in the confusion; nevertheless, Goring had halted his cavalry on the other side of the ditch after his first successful charge. Some re-grouped Parliamentary cavalry then courageously charged him, but he routed them once more. The Parliamentarian forces now fell back, especially when Sir John Cansfield and the King's lifeguard entered the fight, and, in the dusk, the grim combat came to a standstill. The Parliamentarian officers called a halt and drew their men in close to avoid further confusion.

Oliver Cromwell. (Samuel Cooper, 1649)

Above left: Oliver Cromwell. (Unknown artist, 1640s)

Above: Robert Devereux, 3rd Earl of Essex. (T. A. Dean, after Robert Walker, 1827)

Left: Edward Montagu, 2nd Earl of Manchester. (Wenceslaus Hollar, 1644)

Marston Moor, 1644

Top: View from the centre of the Allied lines.
Above: Another view from the centre of the Allied lines. The ground in the distance, towards Tockwith, is that over which Cromwell's cavalry wing attacked the Royalist position.
Right: Moor Lane on the right of the Allied lines.
Below: View from the Allied lines on the right-centre. The later monument to the battle is in the near distance.

Sir Thomas Fairfax. (William Marshall, after Edward Bower, 1647)

Above: Langport, 1645 – a view over the ford from the lines of the New Model Army.

Below: Siege artillery piece at Basing House, 1645.

James Butler, 1st Duke of Ormonde (after Sir Peter Lely, *c.* 1665)

John Lambert (after Robert Walker, *c.* 1650–1655)

Top: Modern Drogheda, viewed from the Millmount.

Above: Millmount, Drogheda – the Martello Tower is a later addition dating from 1808.

Right: Cromwell in battle – an idealised, mid-19th century engraving.

Above: Dunbar, 1650 – Doon Hill and the Scottish position are in the distance.

Left: Dunbar, 1650 – the Dunbar monument.

Below: Worcester, 1651 – Powick Bridge from the Scottish position.

At this point, about half an hour before sunset, no attack by Manchester to pin the enemy had yet occurred. Hearing the guns hammering away on the other side of the Lambourne, the junior officers around Manchester pleaded for him to strike, but instead he dithered. Eventually he was persuaded to launch an attack in two columns against Shaw House, one from the north-east and one from the south-east though Shaw village. The first column made it into the gardens of Shaw House, where they found the troops of Lieutenant-Colonel Richard Page. With both sides screaming their battle cries at each other, Manchester's men poured in their fire and beat the King's forces out of their works. After Page ordered his men to respond, a hail of bullets and stabbing pikes forced the Parliamentarian infantry back in confusion. Sir Thomas Hooper and his dragoons and Royalist foot were located in the hedges and lanes, while Colonel Thelwall's regiment and the Reading brigade were the reserve, and they soon joined in the mêlée. The other Parliamentary column, loudly singing psalms, was equally roughly treated. It forced out a body of Royalist musketeers from a hedge in front of them, but Sir John Brown and Prince Charles's horse gallantly charged them and they fell back in confusion, having suffered the loss of a number of men. The shot now flew thickly on both sides, tearing at the bodies of men and horses. An attempt by the Parliamentarian horse to fetch away their abandoned cannon was also repulsed. These attacks were undertaken in the dusk, with drifting smoke and little co-ordination, and the desperate fight that ensued was far too late to be of any real use. The Parliamentarian troops eventually fell back and withdrew to lick their wounds.

Darkness now lay over both fields. In it the King eschewed renewing the battle the next day, and instead took the opportunity to withdraw to the north and began to move his forces towards Oxford. He abandoned both his guns and carts at the strengthened Donnington Castle and sent his army north, whilst he and his escort rode west towards Bath. They eventually reached Oxford once more on 29–30 October. The Parliamentarians only discovered the King's withdrawal the next day – another hint that all was not right with the cavalry. Waller and Cromwell were soon sent off after the King's forces, but around Blewbury they were recalled on a somewhat flimsy pretext by Manchester. Further quarrels followed in the council of war. Cromwell (who seems to have recovered some of his energy) and Waller argued for a pursuit of the King, or at least the prevention of the junction of Rupert and the King from occurring. Desertions, a lack of supplies and Manchester's reluctance all prevented this. Instead,

Donnington Castle was summoned. The governor, Sir John Boys, easily snubbed this, and, although the place was attacked, the Parliamentarian troops were soon driven off. Only then did Manchester finally allow his forces to move off sluggishly towards Oxford, but after another council of war the troops retired once again towards Newbury.

By now Charles had made Prince Rupert his commander-in-chief, and the Royal army soon set off back down the road to relieve Donnington. When Cromwell was ordered to attack this force, he claimed that his cavalry were now much too exhausted to act, and nothing much was done. By 9 November Charles had arrived at Donnington and once more drawn up his army in a strong position. In a very fractious council of war on 10 November, the Parliamentarian commanders again demurred from attacking. There Cromwell argued that 'if we should beat the King's army it would hinder his affairs in France, and might prevent the coming of French forces into this kingdom.' Manchester scoffed at this idea, and, alarmingly for Cromwell, Waller and the others, he was apparently not for fighting at all, instead claiming that 'if we should beat the King never so often yet he would be King still and his posterity, but if he should beat us but once we must be hanged and our posterity undone.' At this point Cromwell responded angrily, saying, according to Haselrige, 'My Lord, if this be so, why did we take up arms at first?'[43] Cromwell himself later claimed to have gone on to say that 'if this principle was true it condemned all our former fighting as foolish, and was an argument against fighting for the future, and as a ground for making a peace how dishonourable soever.'[44]

The Royal army finally withdrew on the following day. The Parliamentarians, disheartened, low in morale and subject to increasing desertions, now swung out with the intention of making towards Basing House, but they were unable to get there. The siege was called off, and Basing House was relieved while the exhausted Parliamentary army stood by and watched. Despite the efforts of the troops, the campaign, and the year, had ended in failure, Moreover, the war between the Parliamentary generals now infested the House of Commons.

CHAPTER 6

NEW MODELLING, 1645–1646

'The Lord is a man of war, the Lord is his name.' – *Exodus* 15:3

WINTER 1644–45: THE WAR REDEFINED

The political outcome of the failed Newbury campaign proved to be the most significant of the war. The backbiting of the commanders on the field of battle moved swiftly on to the floors of the Houses of Lords and Commons. It was clear that the war-weary majority in Parliament wanted an end to the conflict, but were split between going for outright military victory in the field and seeking a compromise peace. The English and the Scots were already divided, and further divisions had appeared over the religious question. Toleration and free religious association, or uniformity under a Presbyterian Church, appeared to be the choices on offer. The Scots and their Presbyterian allies in Parliament now also greatly feared the rise of the Independent religious sects and their more radical ideas. In particular, this fear was given a face, as the sects now had a military hero to sustain them – Oliver Cromwell.

Intensely frustrated at the way in which the war was going and how the fruits of victory in the north had apparently been thrown away, Cromwell, on his return from the campaign, consulted his allies in the Commons. Then he hurried to lead the attack on his old commander. On 25 November 1644 he stood in the Commons to list the apparent failings of Manchester since Marston Moor, and particularly those around Newbury. He was to do so again in the inquiry that followed. In the Lords, both Essex and Manchester retaliated by attacking Cromwell. Manchester accused Cromwell of continual disobedience and failure of duty, claiming that he, as a commander, had only ever acted with the advice of others. He also accused Cromwell of more sinister aims, such as social levelling, and other fanatical ideas. The idea of Cromwell being cited as an 'incendiary' was mooted in a number of secret meetings between Essex and Cromwell's other enemies, but the argument had passed beyond individuals and on to the general conduct of the war and the need to reform the Parliamentary armies. It was obvious to all that a real crisis now lay at the heart of Parliament's military arm. Victories there had been, but these had been apparently squandered, and God had withheld the final triumph. There was now a vital need for reform, and the subsequent arguments would dictate what sort of army Parliament could put into the field in the new campaigning season. Politically, the old middle group was breaking up, and peace groups were emerging with the labels of 'Independent' and 'Presbyterian'. The Scots had also switched sides, now offering their support to their Presbyterian allies and angry at the way that the Independent faction in the Parliament was moving.[1]

Meanwhile, the politically astute inheritors of John Pym's legacy, Sir Henry Vane and Oliver St John, gave the peace group a further chance of negotiations with the King at Uxbridge while at the same time continuing to forward plans for a 'New Model' army. The Uxbridge negotiations of January–February 1645 were flawed from the beginning, in that Parliament made offers that were bound to be unacceptable to the King, for example the abolition of bishops, a Presbyterian Church, the punishment of many of the King's followers and a loss of control of the military. Nonetheless, Charles I kept these negotiations going. He was well aware of the splits in the Parliamentarian and Scots ranks, and his action was 'at most a ceremonial' to win over public opinion.[2]

On the other hand, Parliament desperately needed a new army, new commanders and a new logistical base to sustain its war effort. The plan that finally emerged was to create one professional force made up partly of an amalgamation of the current field armies of Waller, Essex and Manchester. It would be made up of 22,000 men, some twelve infantry regiments, eleven cavalry regiments and a regiment of dragoons.[3] While many in the new army were impressed men, and not all the regiments were up to strength, the cavalry, having recruits usually of a higher status, and greater conviction, was better off. The real struggle was over who was to command such a force. The events of Newbury had highlighted the discord amongst the current senior commanders of the Parliamentary forces. In the Houses, one side now feared the possibility of the new army becoming an Independent force, while the other did not wish to let the new army fall into the hands of uninspired men such as Essex and Manchester.

It fell to Cromwell to break the political deadlock in a daring speech in the Commons on 9 December 1644. On the day when the inquiry chaired by Zouch Tate into the causes of the problems in the army and the accusations and counteraccusations that had ensued was due to deliver its verdict, Cromwell made his move. While admitting that he had also made mistakes in the field, he now linked the burdens of the people at war with the notion that 'Members of both Houses have got great places and commands ... and ... will perpetually continue themselves in grandeur, and not permit the War speedily to end, lest their own power should determine with it.'[4] Worldly pride and private interests, he said, must be put aside for the public good, and the most important idea now was to support self-denial, a good Calvinist doctrine. Political soldiers must be forced out and professional men, untrammelled by political constraint or the desire of office, must be given command. This speech and the subsequent debate were to lead to the idea of the Self-Denying Ordinance – 'That during the time of the war, no member of either House shall have or execute any office or command, military or civil, granted or conferred by both or either of the Houses of Parliament.'[5]

In effect, Cromwell had offered to give up his military career if others did likewise. In this he was undoubtedly making a genuine offer. He even noted that the soldiers 'look not upon me, but upon you; and for you they will fight and live and die in your cause; and if others be of that mind that they are of, you need not fear them. They do not idolize me, but look upon the cause they fight for.'[6] However, this action would also result in the exclusion of his enemies, Essex and Manchester, and other political generals whom Cromwell accused of continuing the war for their own pride and profit. The Commons swiftly approved the idea, much to the surprise of Cromwell and his allies. While the struggle continued throughout the winter, once the ordinance had passed the Commons it 'has ended all the quarrels which was betwixt Manchester and Cromwell ... as a most wise, necessary and heroic action', as Baillie noted.[7] Despite this, since the ordinance impinged on their honour, the Lords worked hard to delay and confuse it. As a result, the Commons decided to go ahead with their plans to create the New Model Army.

The question of who was to command the new force was determined by choosing the non-political Sir Thomas Fairfax as the new general. The warlike veteran Philip Skippon became his major-general, but the post of lieutenant-general of horse was conspicuously left vacant. Finance for the army was to come through the monthly assessment of £45,000 on the areas controlled by Parliament. After a great political effort, Fairfax also gained control of his choice of officers, and he was finally made commander-in-chief on 1 April 1645. While Parliament still retained other forces, such as those in the north now under the command of the former mercenary Sydenham Poyntz, and the forces in the west under Edward Massey, as well as garrisons that were equal to the forces in the field, the new army would be the main striking force in the spring.

What was going to happen to Oliver Cromwell in this reform? Ironically, Cromwell had already returned to active service. In February 1645 Parliament had ordered out Sir William Waller to assist in the relief of Taunton, but Waller's forces had refused to move until paid, and then the cavalry in particular resisted any movement until they had the familiar figure of Cromwell to command them. As a result, Cromwell was given a limited commission, and, with Waller as his general, he marched off to try to relieve the town of Taunton. The period of grace before the ordinance came into effect was extended for him as he was on active service. Various other extensions followed, as by now Fairfax had tasks enough for him. What is clear is that at some point in the period after February Cromwell had once more acquired the taste for the military life. He was to prove ever more reluctant to give up his role as a cavalry commander. He stayed on even after Waller had left the forces, organising and recruiting, and his actions as well as the activities of the Royalists were to work in his favour. It was obvious to all that he was the best man for the job of leading the New Model Army's cavalry, although there was continued resistance from his old enemies in Parliament to contend with.

Charles I was also busy modifying his forces over this winter, and was becoming well aware that he would need to strike before the New Model came into the field.[8] With the loss of the north, and many of the Royal regiments now frequently having less than 100 men in their ranks, the King needed a new strategy to sustain the war. The major undertaking was to reorganise the command in the west. This was achieved by placing his eldest son in nominal command there. He also gave Prince Charles a council of advisors, an army of Goring's cavalry and the remains of Hopton's infantry. Otherwise the King fastened most of his hopes on the activities of Montrose in Scotland and those of Ormonde in Ireland. The latter was ordered to create a peace in Ireland that would allow Irish troops to join the King at Oxford. Only by obtaining fresh troops could the King now win the English Civil War. Ormonde struggled to create an Irish agreement, so Charles I sent Prince Maurice to recruit in Wales prior to going to the relief of Chester. Rupert soon joined his brother, and together they relieved the city. While risings of Clubmen in the Midlands briefly distracted Rupert, by 7 May the King was able to lead some 11,000 men from Oxford to begin a new campaign.

PRELIMINARIES TO THE NASEBY CAMPAIGN

Instead of retirement and loss of his commission, it was his old colleague
Fairfax, on the authority of the Committee of Both Kingdoms, who gave
Cromwell new instructions in April 1645. Cromwell found himself in
command of a brigade of cavalry under orders to disrupt Royalist preparations for the summer campaign. This run would take him on a circuit of the
Oxford defences, in an attempt to capture or dissolve some 2,000 Royalist
horse on their way from Worcester to Oxford and the King. By 23 April he
had advanced to Watlington with a force of some 1,500 men. Cromwell, who
had sent Major-General Browne forward to gather intelligence, found the
road at Islip Bridge controlled by a brigade of Royalist horse (the regiments
of Northampton, the Queen, Wilmot and Palmer) under the command of
the Earl of Northampton. He moved forward in the evening in an attempt
to take them by surprise, but his forlorn hope only succeeded in raising the
alarm. Having watched all night, the next day they attacked. Fairfax's regiment (Cromwell's old regiment) were first into action, and

> '... the General's troops charged a whole squadron of the enemy,
> and presently broke it. Our other troops coming seasonably on, the
> rest of the enemy were presently put into confusion; so that we had
> the chase of them three or four miles; wherein we killed many, and
> took near two-hundred prisoners, and about four-hundred horse.'[9]

The troop seems to have advanced, fired their pistols and then 'entered into
the whole squadron and put them to confusion.'[10] Weight and mass, as well
as having the cavalry under tight control, did the rest of the work, and the
broken Royalist horse fell back in disarray. Many escaped to Oxford, some
were drowned, and the Queen's standard (a gorgeous affair of gold fleurs-
de-lis on a white background) fell into Cromwell's hands. The result of the
skirmish was a further advance towards Bletchingdon House.

Here Colonel Francis Windebank commanded the Royalist garrison. It
was a strongly fortified place, but a confident Cromwell, riding his luck
and trusting to God, now summoned it, threatening great severity if no
surrender were forthcoming. These were soon to be familiar tactics. The
cavalry were ordered up, to pretend that they were calling up bodies of
infantry to assist them. Whether it was this ruse, or the fact that Windebank's wife and some other gentlemen who had been visiting at the time
are said to have urged his surrender, or just that Windebank had no news
of any relief coming to his aid soon, he capitulated – too soon, according

to his superiors in Oxford, as on his return there he was subjected to court martial and subsequently shot. Cromwell in the meanwhile drew his own conclusions on the action, admitting that taking this garrison was not really 'my business and yet we got it'.[11] Naturally, he claimed God as his guide and took yet another chance to note in his despatch that, 'I hope you will pardon me if I say, God is not enough owned. We look too much to men and visible helps; this hath hindered our success.'[12]

Fortified by his successes, subtly guided by the Lord and keen to see further action, Cromwell now moved on to Middleton Stony and then towards Witney, hoping by this action to place himself amongst any of Goring's horse returning from the West to succour the King's army. In the process he received news of a party of infantry under Colonel Richard Vaughan slowly moving towards Faringdon – they had previously been placed at Woodstock for fear that Cromwell would attack there – and, as they were only three hours away, Cromwell instantly moved off to intercept them. His forlorn caught up with them in the enclosure around Bampton Bush and entered into a bloody skirmish, before the infantry scrambled into the town and barricaded themselves in a strong house. Cromwell and his main body came up at eleven o'clock that night and immediately demanded their surrender. This summons was rejected outright, and so Cromwell, after ensuring that they could not escape, waited until the morning. Various attacks were launched overnight on the barricades, but they were beaten back with the loss of some horses. In the morning Cromwell once again sent in for the garrison's surrender and again his terms were angrily dismissed. He offered to have them send out the civilian occupants, or else 'they must expect extremity', and after some more negotiations the garrison finally surrendered. Cromwell then took 200 prisoners, together with powder and muskets. The march then proceeded on its way towards Faringdon. On the way, Cromwell received further news of some Royalist cavalry crossing his front toward Evesham, so he ordered Colonel Fiennes after them. Fiennes soon caught up with this body of horse and broke up the party, taking about 30 prisoners and many horses in the process. Intelligence concerning the Royal army and its movements was gathered, as well as information about Goring's men in the west, including news of dissensions in the Royalist high command between Goring and Rupert.

Arriving at Faringdon, the prisoners were sent off under escort while Cromwell viewed the town. This was a much tougher nut to crack. By now he had with him the Ironsides, as well as five troops of Sydney's horse, part of Vermuyden's horse and two troops of Fiennes'. The rest were on escort duties. Lacking dragoons, however, Faringdon would be a difficult place to assault. Indeed, despite his belief that 'God does terrify them', Cromwell's summons to the garrison was immediately rejected. An initial assault was then repelled by heavy fire, with some loss in both wounded and prisoners. With Cromwell thwarted around Faringdon, Browne was sent up to him with some infantry, and Cromwell took time on 2 May to visit Fairfax to confer. As a result, he was given yet another 4,000 men in order to blockade Oxford. Meanwhile Fairfax and the rest of the army were off to the west to relieve the hard-pressed Taunton, then under the command of Robert Blake. While Cromwell was conferring with Fairfax, Goring took the chance to launch an attack on the quarters around Faringdon, and met with some success. He soon retired, however, and Cromwell continued to blockade Oxford and wait for the opportunity to shadow the King's army. When the Royal army finally left the city for its campaign on 7 May 1645, Browne and Cromwell moved off in pursuit, following it closely and suffering the occasional sharp bite to ensure that they kept at a respectable distance.

What were the intentions of Charles and his army that summer? At the rendezvous of Royal forces at Stow-on-the-Wold on 8 May, Royalist councils were divided. Various ideas and strategies were sounded out at the Council of War. While some wished to move into the south-west to strike at Fairfax, Rupert was against this, favouring instead the idea, held since the winter, of marching north to relieve Chester in order to keep open the sea route to Ireland. He also wished to skirt the unpaid and discontented Scots army – although he had them marked down for revenge for Marston Moor. Instead, he would move into Yorkshire, raising more troops on the way and subsequently clearing the north of opposition. Only after this did he wish to march south and take on Fairfax.

News of Montrose's success at Auldearn against the Covenanters also raised Royal hopes. Perhaps, it was thought, they really should move north and lend assistance. Defeat for the Covenanters in both Scotland and England (once the north was clear and Pontefract relieved) would radically change the situation, and leave the Royal army free to face Fairfax on his own. In addition, there was a desperate need to recruit further troops and supplies from the various garrisons on the way. Rupert shied away from south-western entanglements, where open dissension amongst Royal commanders was all too common, and he readily allowed Goring and his men to go there. Indeed, one commentator noted that 'he was jealous of having a Rival in Command', and the removal of Goring from the King's presence would not have been unwelcome to him.[13] The two had grown to dislike each other intensely. Unfortunately Charles, as the supreme commander of his armies, vacillated. While he was buoyed up by news of Montrose's victories in Scotland, and also had good hopes of Irish troops shortly arriving to succour him, his civilian courtiers, particularly Lord Digby, were pushing him to take on the New Model – or the 'New Noddle', as they contemptuously called it. This, they claimed, would give the King a triumphant blow that could settle the war for good.

In the greater strategic position, it was soon clear that, for the present, the Scots army in the north was a paper tiger. It became a useful counter in the strategic game, but there was to be very little evidence of co-operation over the next few months. Even so, Cromwell was ordered to detach Colonel Vermuyden with 2,500 men to join the Scots army in case the Royal army went north. Unfortunately, fearful of Montrose's activities, the Scots were soon to withdraw still further north into Westmorland. Meanwhile Fairfax, with the main army, continued his march into the west. He was now under the direct orders of the Committee of Both Kingdoms, and while he only reluctantly accepted this strategy, he did obey orders. The 'armchair generals' of the Committee insisted that the relief of Taunton be given priority. By 7 May, having made some ten miles a day, Fairfax had reached Blandford in Dorset, but news of the departure of the King's army from Oxford now led the Committee to call him back. Fairfax began to reverse course, but first he detached some 6,000 men to move on towards Taunton, only then swinging back towards Oxford, cautiously avoiding the open plains of Salisbury in case Goring's cavalry were out and about. The siege around Taunton now broke up. Fearful that the approaching troops detached by Fairfax were in fact his entire army, the Royalists swiftly retired and Taunton was briefly relieved.

Now the King made the worst of all his possible strategic decisions. Having first split his army by sending Goring into the south-west with much of his cavalry, he ordered the rest of the army north. News that Fairfax was back near Oxford, however, 'staggered our design, yet not so as instantly to return thither [to Oxford], or solely to abandon it; but only so retarded it, as to put the Army in a capacity to come to the timely Relief of that place if there should be occasion.'[14] On 14 May the New Model had reached Newbury, where Fairfax and his men rested for the next couple of days. They reached the lines at Oxford on 19 May. Cromwell and Browne had been shadowing the Royal army and trying to protect the Eastern Association from incursions, but they soon joined Fairfax before Oxford.

Rupert now advised the sensible strategy that, instead of returning to Oxford as the courtiers desired, the Royal army should move into the East Midlands, threatening the territory of the Eastern Association, as well as taking the town of Leicester and thereby drawing off the New Model from Oxford to counter this move. Goring was ordered back to rendezvous at Market Harborough, while Langdale and his northern troops joined the army at Ashby de la Zouch. Goring proved reluctant to move wholly under Rupert's orders, but Rupert's new scheme did begin to cause ripples in the Parliamentarians' ranks.

Fairfax, once more under direct orders from the Committee in London, had begun fifteen days of largely ineffectual siege of the Royal capital. Now, with news of the Royal army on the move once more, changes occurred. News soon came in of the Royal army's bloody siege and capture of Leicester on 31 May. This had been a Parliamentary stronghold, and its capture caused great panic in London counsels, where it was feared that the King might use this victory as a jumping-off point to break into the heart of the Eastern Association. In fact, Charles, now posted around Daventry, began to hesitate: he was too fearful for Oxford's safety to embark upon truly daring actions. Rupert, who was in close touch with the Governor of Oxford, had no such fears of the city's fall. Instead, he advocated that a military progress northwards through the Midlands would draw off Fairfax and his army, for Cromwell had already been ordered to Ely with four troops of horse to ready the Eastern Association forces. By 1 June Cromwell was in Cambridge, and three days later he was in Huntingdon, marshalling the defences of the Eastern Association, although not without some difficulty.

An alternative strategy now began to emerge. This was to move the Royal army towards Worcester and there to contact Charles Gerrard, who had been raising horse and foot in Wales that would prove a useful addition to the Royal army and assist in its holding on to its new conquests. Unfortunately, the mood of the King and his immediate counsellors went against these sensible military strategies, and it was decided once more to turn the army towards Oxford. Yet in doing this Rupert faced troubles of his own, especially amongst the northern Royalist troops, who now wished to go home and defend their home territories. There was something of a mutiny amongst them, and they needed a great deal of persuasion to make them stay. In the meantime, movements were also occurring in the New Model around Oxford.

The New Model Army was finally released from siege duties following the destruction of Leicester. A worried Committee now gave Fairfax full authority to pursue whatever course he thought fit, and Fairfax lost no time in moving on 5 June to seek out the Royal army and try them in battle. At the same time, he made it clear that he still lacked a lieutenant-general of cavalry, and formally requested that Oliver Cromwell be appointed to the position. This was finally agreed on 10 June, when Cromwell was ordered to join the army with all the troops he could muster, saving those to protect the eastern counties. Colonel Bartholomew Vermuyden's brigade was also recalled, especially as the Scots were proving reluctant allies, although Vermuyden himself laid down his command on his return to the army, claiming urgent business abroad. The loss of such an experienced officer at such a time must have frustrated Fairfax, but it did make it possible for him to continue to argue that the veteran Cromwell should be finally given the position of lieutenant-general of horse.

By 12 June, with the Royal army still located around Daventry and still divided over whether to seek battle, King Charles I sought pleasure in hunting. His amusement was soon disrupted by the unpleasant discovery that Fairfax's army had appeared, and was only five miles away. The King's army hastily withdrew to Market Harborough, and the senior officers scurried into a council of war. Prince Rupert now maintained that a march north to pick up troops and supplies from Newark would enable them to avoid battle for the present; Goring and his cavalry had not yet arrived, nor had Gerrard and the Welsh infantry. It must have been obvious to him that Fairfax was now seeking battle, and he believed that the Royal army needed more troops to give it any advantage. Unfortunately, the civilians, Lord Digby and Sir John Ashburnham, persuaded the King to seek battle immediately. They outweighed Rupert in the King's counsels, arguing that the safety of Oxford should be the King's main priority, and they dismissed the New Model Army as weak in both its officers and men. In the end, it was decided to swing south and bring some relief to Oxford, prior to moving north again, thus trying to satisfy all opinions.

PREPARATION FOR BATTLE

While Fairfax gathered intelligence of the Royal army's movements, orders were also sent off urging Cromwell to speedily join the New Model. In fact, he was already on his way. Cromwell first reached Bedford, and then, on 12 June 1645, he crossed the Ouse at Olney and continued his march to Northampton, where he arrived that evening. He finally reached camp, to great cheers from the soldiers, on 13 June 1645. At the subsequent council of war, it was obvious to all that Fairfax had decided to engage the enemy.

In the meantime, the Royal army had moved from Daventry towards Market Harborough for a rendezvous on Borough Hill by 13 June. They were hampered by poor intelligence, and news of Fairfax's presence, when it came, still caused some alarm. Clearly, a choice would have to be made as to whether to engage the New Model Army or definitely retire north. The latter option would have certainly exposed the rearguard of the Royal army to attack by the Parliamentary cavalry, and so after some discussion Charles decided on battle and Rupert was forced to put the troops in 'battalia' in preparation for the combat. There was still some doubt about the actual location of the New Model, so Rupert sent out Francis Ruce, the scoutmaster, to reconnoitre. He soon returned, falsely claiming to have gone two or three miles and found nothing untoward. A somewhat dissatisfied Prince now decided to explore for himself, and promptly found the New Model barely a mile from his position. As he drew up his horse at Clipston, he sent back for the main body of the army, unable to decide whether the New Model's movements before him signified a retreat or not but more than willing to exploit the situation if he could. He was to find a waiting Fairfax on the high ground above Naseby.

King Charles, dressed in complete armour of back, breast and helmet, with a drawn sword, now toured his lines as the troops marched up into their formations, and was given rousing cheers. Under Rupert's orders, a line of battle was formed up with four main bodies in the army: the experienced Lord Astley had control of the some 3,500 foot in the centre, with the infantry in tertia under Sir Bernard Astley, Sir Henry Bard, Sir George Lisle and Colonel Smith's Shrewsbury foot. They were placed with Colonel Thomas Howard's cavalry divisions (some 880 men in three divisions, with a reserve) as a second line. Rupert decided to take control of the right wing of cavalry himself (1,610–1,710 horse, plus 200 musketeers: Northampton's brigade and three other units). In the front line were Princes Rupert's and Maurice's lifeguard regiments, as well as Rupert's and Maurice's infantry regiments and the Queen's regiment. In the second line were placed the regiments of Northampton, Vaughan and Boncle. Sir Marmaduke Langdale, who also commanded one of the brigades, took control of the left wing of cavalry (the Northern Horse, Newark Horse and musketeers: 1,700 horse and 200 musketeers). The reserve, ostensibly under the King, comprised some 800 cavalry and 700 foot (the King's Lifeguard, commanded by the Earl of Lindsey, and Prince Rupert's regiment of foot, with the King's horse guards commanded by the Earl of Lichfield). This was, perhaps, not the best use of either commanders or troops available, and Rupert's usual aggressive

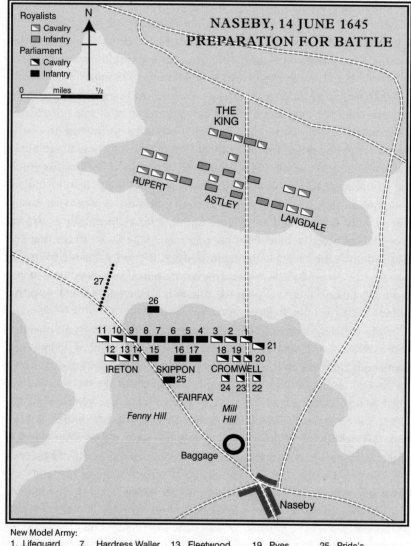

NASEBY, 14 JUNE 1645
PREPARATION FOR BATTLE

New Model Army:

1. Lifeguard	7. Hardress Waller	13. Fleetwood	19. Pyes	25. Pride's
2. Pyes	8. Skippon	14. Association	20. Fines	26. Forlorn Hope
3. Whalley	9. Ireton	15. Pride's	21. Rossiter	27. Okey's Dragoons
4. Fairfax	10. Vermuyden's	16. Hammond's	22. Rossiter	
5. Mountague	11. Butler's	17. Rainsborough	23. Fines	
6. Pickering	12. Riches	18. Sheffield	24. Association Horse	

stance would happily play into Fairfax's hands as he had virtually abdicated
responsibility for the strategic control of the battle by placing himself on the
army's right wing rather than in the reserve, where he would have been
better positioned to feed troops into the front line as he saw fit.

Fairfax was touring his lines throughout the rainy night of 12/13 June around Kislingbury, eight miles from Daventry, until about four in the morning. He had been halted for a time in the rain by an officious sentry, having forgotten the password, and had to wait until the soldier's officer came up to let him pass. Scoutmaster-General Watson, who had been working hard all night bringing in intelligence, awaited his return. Various spies, who came in to give their information in person, had reported the motions of the enemy westwards towards Warwick. Fairfax and his council of war now met at around six o'clock. As they sat down and began their debate, shouts were heard: 'A Cromwell! A Cromwell!' News came in of the arrival of General Cromwell with some of his troops, ready to take his command of the cavalry. Soon the man himself was at the council. A party under Thomas Harrison was immediately sent out to scout out Royalist positions at Daventry. By the evening of 13 June, Fairfax was at Guisborough, and Ireton was now ordered out with a party of horse to shadow the King's army as it moved and to harass them if there were an opportunity.

Intelligence regarding the enemy came in, and it seemed that they intended to do battle. With bodies of horse entering on to the ridge on the Naseby side of Harborough, Fairfax and his officers now went out to observe the field and place his men in 'battalia'. The field of battle was to be a large area two miles north-west of Naseby village. Fairfax drew up his army on a low ridge facing north and running west to east in the usual manner, with infantry in the centre and cavalry on the wings. Fairfax ordered his battle behind the ridge, and the Royalists, thinking this a retreat, moved forward, locating around Dust Hill. The New Model moved parallel with this. Skippon and Fairfax now ordered the foot, while Cromwell and Henry Ireton, the Commissary General, took the horse. In the traditional formation, the novel aspect would be Okey's dragoons, thrown forward into the hedges on the left of the army. Cromwell was to be on the right wing with some 3,900 men. Judging that there were far too many cavalry for one man to control, he had asked Fairfax to assign the left wing of some 3,300 horse to Ireton. Skippon meanwhile took the five infantry regiments in the centre, some 6,400 foot and eleven artillery pieces. Behind him there were three regiments of foot as a reserve.

The terrain constricted Cromwell's men, who had some five squadrons in the front line led by Colonel Edward Whalley. These men were mostly drawn from Cromwell's original regiment. Moreover, the late arrival of Colonel Rossiter's Lincolnshire regiment meant that at least half of those men were crowded into the right-hand side of the rear squadron of

Whalley's front line. The second line consisted of four squadrons of Fiennes', Pye's and Colonel Thomas Sheffield's regiments. For the first time, evidently learning from his experience of Marston Moor and Newbury, Cromwell decided to station himself with these men and also placed a reserve of three squadrons from Rossiter's, Fiennes' and the Associated horse. The wing was somewhat crowded and hemmed in by hedges and rabbit warrens, but it was made up of sufficiently self-assured troops with a commander who was now confidently reaching the summit of his tactical skills. He was seen spending time restlessly riding up and down 'about my business', giving out orders and greeting officers (and, no doubt, some of his veterans by name), all the while unable to stop smiling and grinning to himself and speaking to God 'in my praises, in assurance of victory, because God would, by things that are not, bring to naught things that are. Of which I had great assurance.' As he later said, 'God did it.'[15] His oddities, rather than worrying his troops, are likely to have cheered those he rode past.

In the centre, the stout Philip Skippon was busy placing his five regiments of foot – Fairfax's, Montagu's, Pickering's, Waller's (under Coatsworth) and his own – in the front line. Eight artillery pieces were also placed at intervals between the regiments, and a forlorn of some 300 musketeers was flung out before the army on the left of the front line. In his second line he had two and one-half regiments – Rainsborough's men, Hammond's and Edward Harley's (without their colonel) – with some of these troops acting as rearguard. All of them were in the traditional stance for infantry, with pikes in the centre and musketeers on either flank. Henry Ireton's left wing of cavalry was much weaker than the right wing under Cromwell, and this was his first real command, so Ireton placed six squadrons in his front line and decided to take command of them himself. He talked rapidly to the efficient and godly soldier Charles Fleetwood, and the latter took command of the second line of five squadrons.

Saturday 14 June 1645 promised to be a fine day, with a fresh north-westerly wind that died away as the morning advanced. For the troops of the New Model, many of whom were tired, cold and hungry (a number of them had not eaten for some time), this promised to be a great test. They would have been able to see the enemy within cannon shot. While some were no doubt moved by baser feelings of seeking out the rich plunder said to be in the Royalist baggage train, others, including the newly arrived Lieutenant-General Cromwell, had more godly thoughts about the preservation of religion and liberty. All would have been nervous, and most, lacking sleep, were doubtless very tired. The veterans amongst them would have been well aware of what was to come. The blustering chaplain, Hugh Peters, rode through their ranks, carrying his Bible in one hand and his pistol in the other, attempting to raise the spirits of the men by calling on them to remember that they were about the Lord's work on this day of battle.[16] The men busily prepared their weapons for combat, some quietly praying, others nervously chatting to each other in their ranks, and all grumbling about the lack of food in their bellies. The older men and non-commissioned officers were giving out advice and checking equipment, tightening girths, belts and straps, as their officers walked or rode about inspecting their ranks. In the cavalry on the wings, men were trying to quieten their restless horses. A similar scene was occurring on the other side of no man's land. Above all would have been a ceaseless murmur, the noise of trumpets and drums, the neighing of horses, the jingling of equipment and the hum of over 24,000 men gathered in an English field for battle. Some amongst the New Model troops had placed white paper or linen in their hats as tokens of recognition, and the comforting word for the day began to pass through the ranks: 'God is our strength.' The colourful standards of both sides had also been unfurled and were flapping and snapping in the mild breeze. The Royalist troops, having advanced through some bean fields, had cheerfully placed the stalks of the plant in their hats as their token for the day. Gradually the men settled down, and a bright combination of uniformed men now stood, or sat mounted, waiting for the business to begin.

BATTLE: SATURDAY 14 JUNE 1645

Around ten o'clock, on Cromwell's advice, the New Model's line shifted westward to gain the wind. This led Rupert to imagine that they were retreating, and orders now went out to attack. Fairfax appears to have decided to fight a defensive battle; at least, his position was such that he could sit and await the Royalist attack. He himself was described as pale and drawn before the battle: 'his lookes were like to a dead man.'[17] Always a nervous man, the burden of command only lifted in the heat of combat and in the midst of its dangers, Fairfax sprang into life. He was to spend much of the day animatedly riding over the field, moving hither and thither, encouraging his men, giving orders and leading attacks in the bravest of manners. At one point he even lost his helmet, and despite the dangers he fearlessly refused to take another.

Cromwell proved to be equally aggressive. It was he, it seems, who had found Colonel John Okey and his dragoons half a mile behind the field of battle ordering their ammunition. Cromwell now ordered Okey and his men forward into Sulby hedges. They rode off, then dismounted and quickly left men to hold the horses. The rest hurriedly rushed forward to seek the protection of the hedges of the left side of the field. This was a bold move by Cromwell, who hoped perhaps to outflank Rupert, or at least cut up Rupert's cavalry with gunfire as they moved past the hedges. As Burt noted, dragoons 'may give the enemy an unexpected volley of shot from some secret and unexpected place ... which having performed, to mount suddenly again, for better and sooner expedition.'[18] It may also have been an attempt to support Ireton's rather weaker left wing.

On the other hand, the artillery action in this battle was to have limited value. Rushworth tells us that neither side had the 'patience to shoot one peece of Ordnance',[19] while another commentator noted that experience of 'Marston Moor and other places' had proved artillery 'but a loss of time'.[20] The author of *Brief Memorials* noted that five pieces were discharged at the Royalist infantry as they advanced, but the gunners over-shot, and, as the smoke began to drift across the field, the guns were abandoned as the artillerymen fled to safety with the infantry.

It was on this left wing – the Royalist right – that the combat opened. Once more, Rupert abandoned his role as general-in-command and joined the majority of his horse to launch an attack here. Some damage was done by John Okey's dragoons, now firmly embedded in the hedges for protection, and they, as he noted, 'shooting and rejoicing received them', but it did not halt the movement completely.[21] They beat off any attempts to get them out of the close position they were in and took pot shots at the cavalry as they rode past. Slingsby, on the receiving end of this heavy fire, noted that the 'Musqueteers ... [did] Gall our horse ... many of ye Regiment [were] wound'd by shot from ye hedge before we could joyne with theirs on [that] wing.'[22] Some of the cavalrymen fell and did not get up.

Rupert's cavalry now halted for a time to allow his own musketeers to come up. Once these men had arrived, they poured in their fire, then the cavalry were launched at Ireton's troops. Ireton did not stand and wait to receive them, but launched his own men down the slope. Butler's men were now caught up in this brutal assault, and, even with Okey's support from the hedges, they began to crumble, the majority soon breaking and fleeing the field. Ireton fared rather better as his men battered the regiment of Prince Maurice. Ireton himself was in the front rank and, seeing

Skippon's infantry hard pressed, led a charge that unhorsed him and left him wounded in both face and thigh. A sergeant of the Duke of York's regiment then captured him. Colonel Butler was also wounded, while many of the Parliamentary cavalry simply fled. Unfortunately, Rupert's men did not halt at this point, but set off on the inevitable pursuit towards the Parliamentary baggage train. Some of Ireton's men, however, did stand, and were left milling about on the field.

Meanwhile the infantry struggle in the centre had begun. The Royalist infantry under old Sir Jacob Astley marched forward, drums tapping and officers taking care to dress their ranks as they did so. Both sides hardly saw each other until the last minute. Some of the New Model's musketeers in the forlorn fired, but overshot and then fell back. Each side then came up to the other, made one volley and then, in the enveloping smoke from the musketry, fell on 'with Sword and butt end of Musquet ... [making] notable Execution'.[23] Yet another observer noted that the sides did not charge each other until 'twelve paces one of another, and could not charge above twice, but were at push of Pike'.[24] After the Parliamentarians had made a little ground, Astley's men drove back those of Skippon; Bard and Lisle's men did not fare so well. The Lord General's own regiment successfully outwinged Lisle's men and the infantry began to fall back, leaving the bodies of their comrades strewn on the ground. They did not break, however, and Skippon now regrouped his men and followed in with the reserves, forcing them back. At this point, a musket ball pierced his armour. He fell, but rose and refused to leave the field of battle, continuing to order men forward.

On the Parliamentary right wing, the combat was a little less in doubt. Cromwell had some initial difficulties with marshalling his regiments as the terrain (rabbit warrens and furze bushes) caused some problems, but Whalley's men struck heavily at Langdale's men as they came up. They were 'out front'd & overpour'd by their assailants'.[25] Fairfax, who had positioned himself on the left wing, now ordered Cromwell's troops into combat in successive waves of Parliamentary cavalry, in an 'orderly and timely coming on, not one failing to come on in time', to rout them.[26] In his excitement, Fairfax also seems to have led one of the charges himself at this point, losing his helmet in the process. Some of the Royalist cavalry now took shelter with Prince Rupert's regiment of infantry, but the King's lifeguard, with Charles at their head, were caught up in the confusion and retired.

At this crucial stage of the battle, Fairfax and Cromwell 'faced about to that Wing, with some divisions of Horse, charged bareheaded within push of Pike, [and] routed the enemy.'[27] Whitelocke noted that Fairfax led the charge into the flank of Lisle's regiment (Cromwell had moved to the left wing to try to re-group its remnants) while his own lifeguard took them from the front. In the course of this struggle, Fairfax killed their standard bearer, but one of his men, coming up, took the standard, as well as the credit. The Royalist reserve now rallied slightly, and 'both parties ... stood very neere each other, having silence for a short space, but ours advancing to charge, the Enemy fled.'[28] It seems to have been at this point that Fairfax rallied his men for 'second good Batalia', if it were needed, and they now forced the Royalists into retreat with great loss.[29] Slingsby noted that the Royalists could not take a second charge, and were 'mightily discouraged'.[30] One of the Royalist colours taken showed a pair of horns with the motto 'Come Cuckolds'; this was subsequently captured and turned round on the enemy. The quick-witted John Okey, still in the hedges on the left, had noted the right wing's success and, ordering his horses forward, mounted his men. He then attacked. Cromwell also arrived at this point and immediately took command. He and Okey's men now charged a foot regiment and broke them, picking up their colours and 500 prisoners in the process. The dragoons then rallied and charged the King's Regiment of Horse, who 'faced about and run away and never made any stay till they came to Leicester.'[31] While unusual, Okey's actions showed what dragoons, the most flexible of all the units in the army, could do if well led. Nathaniel Burt, in his contemporary piece on dragoons, notes that their officers should 'make use of, and store up experimentall knowledge; for as this war differeth much from other warres, so doth the severall skirmishings, and occasions (therein:) and resolution goeth very farre in it, so it be grounded upon judgment, and produceth many faire effects, through God's blessing.'[32]

At the same time as Fairfax's attacks had gone in and the Royalists had begun to take flight, some of Cromwell's cavalry began to pursue them; the Royalist infantry now fled past the Royalist baggage train, soon to be ferociously plundered by the New Model infantry. Most of the Royal infantry ended their lives on Wadborough Hill, some two miles north of the battlefield. They were harassed all the way by Cromwell and his cavalry. Once again, Rupert had returned too late to the battle, and his troops were now so disordered that they could not be 'brought to charge again, not to rally any of the broken troops; and so after all the endeavours of the King and Prince Rupert, to the hazard of their Persons, they were fain to quit the Field.'[33] By then it seems it was too late, and, as the Parliamentary infantry came up, many surrendered. It had taken some three to four hours to put the whole Royalist cause in mortal danger.

What was Cromwell's role in the battle? One witness noted that he 'behaved himself to the utmost, routed the Adversary as on Marston Moore and then relieved our Army on the other Party which was like to been undone; whom God mightily honoured. And now hath given Prince Rupert his other Iron-side,'[34] but this tells us little of his activities on the day. However, the orders to Okey to move forward seem to have been given on his own initiative; Fairfax had consulted him on some of the pre-battle manoeuvres and on the question of gaining the wind, and told him to order the cavalry. This left him in charge of the tactical battle on the right wing. The rest is rather obscure. He himself noted that the result was 'the hand of God; and to Him alone belongs the glory, wherein noe are to share with Him'.[35] He did, however, give some of the palm of victory – and rightly so – to Fairfax and to the troops. About his own immediate actions, both he and Fairfax are silent. In the tactical battle, what did he do?

Cromwell was certainly in command of the right wing. He took action to marshal the regiments of the right wing as best he could, given the terrain. In combat, he seems to have learnt from his earlier battles, and now he chose to lead the second line, enabling him to observe the first clash of horse. However, during the course of marshalling his troops, which proved difficult owing to the constriction of the ground and numbers of horse, the Royalists came on suddenly. He was unfazed by this, trusting to God, and, not wishing to stand to receive them, he ordered in Whalley's regiment, on the left hand of the right wing, against two divisions of the northern horse. He seems then to have returned almost immediately to manoeuvring the reserve cavalry in order to support this combat. Whalley swiftly drove the divisions back by sword, and, when they rallied under the shelter of Rupert's foot regiment, Cromwell sent in his reserves. The Newark horse attempted to succour their colleagues, but, outflanked and worried by this bold thrust, they broke and fled up to a quarter of a mile. The tactics of Marston Moor had worked again. 'O that men would therefore praise the Lord, and declare the wonders that He doth for the children of men!' as Cromwell put it.[36]

This action now left Cromwell facing the two right-hand divisions of Langdale's horse, and four of the squadrons were detached in pursuit of the fleeing Royalists. Doubtless alongside Fairfax, Cromwell was now responsible for sending in the reserves, and was also to rally them after the charges, and there seems little doubt that he will have sometimes fought hand-to-hand himself. Now, however, his style of leadership was even more related to the moral than the physical. The substantial strategic control of the battle he left to Fairfax, while he managed his cavalrymen on both wings tactically, and 'did admirable well', in leading them into combat.[37]

WAR IN THE WEST

Naseby was a crushing defeat for the King: he had lost not only substantial numbers of men, artillery and baggage but also his secret correspondence relating to his deals at home and abroad with the Catholic powers, which was subsequently published and did great damage to the King's cause. Although strenuous fighting still awaited the New Model, one could say that these were largely mopping-up operations through the next eighteen months. The Royal forces left after Naseby may well have been less significant than they had been, and were held transfixed by their enemies or left in garrisons and fortresses. Despite this, there was to be some further hard and bloody fighting. The King himself had around 4,000 cavalry after the battle and managed to pull together some 3,000 or so infantry. While Gerrard was still located in South Wales with some 3,000 Welsh infantry, Bryon was located at Chester but blockaded by Sir Thomas Middleton and Sir William Brereton. As for the King, after Naseby his primary aims were to revolve around renewed attempts to raise further troops and hold on to territory. Charles himself seems to have been unable to concentrate the forces of his mind sufficiently to see where and how to achieve victory, although he never lost hope that he would ultimately prevail. For Rupert and some of his generals, however, the reality soon dawned that a solution had to be found to end the war on the best possible terms.

Rupert had retired to find himself in control of Bristol, the second city of the land and an obvious target for Fairfax and the New Model Army. Also located in the West Country were the forces of George Goring, besieging Taunton. Moreover, the west had other, unofficial, forces in it – the phenomenon of the Clubmen. These were groups of men who were weary of the war and of both sides in the conflict tramping over their territory. Charles's best hope would have been to concentrate his forces; instead, Goring was left to fend for himself while the King dallied in the pleasant surroundings of Raglan Castle.

LANGPORT

Fairfax was of course keen to exploit his victory and move into the west to complete the destruction of the Royalist army, as noisy advice from London was now suggesting that Taunton be relieved as soon as possible. First, however, he swiftly moved to recapture Leicester on 18 June, and

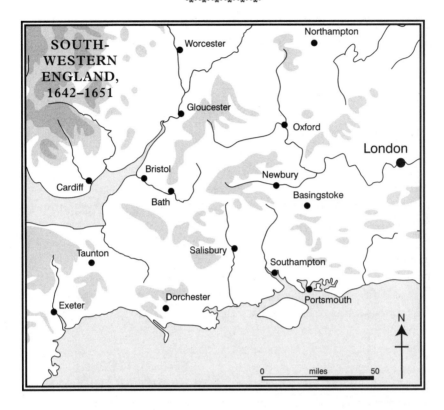

one by one the Royalist garrisons still remaining in the north began to collapse – Carlisle on 2 July, Pontefract on 21 July and Scarborough on 25 July. After a council of war, it was agreed to move the army south to relieve Taunton and, if possible, eliminate Goring's forces. The New Model took a long swing into the West Country via Gloucestershire, where Massey's troops joined them and avoided the Royalist garrisons at Bristol, Bath and Bridgwater, and arrived at Marlborough on 29 June. Fairfax, keeping London behind him and reorganising his base of supplies to Lyme and Weymouth, chose to approach the problem of Taunton by the south via Wiltshire. In Wiltshire he also had preliminary dealings with the Clubmen, but his main aim was to try to outmanoeuvre Goring. Dorchester was reached by 3 July.

Fairfax now aimed to strike swiftly and relieve Taunton, and, despite the hot weather, he moved his forces rapidly enough. News soon came in that Goring had withdrawn from Taunton but seemed reluctant to come to blows. He eventually stationed himself and his men along the Rivers Parret and Yeo, protecting his lines of communication with Bristol but

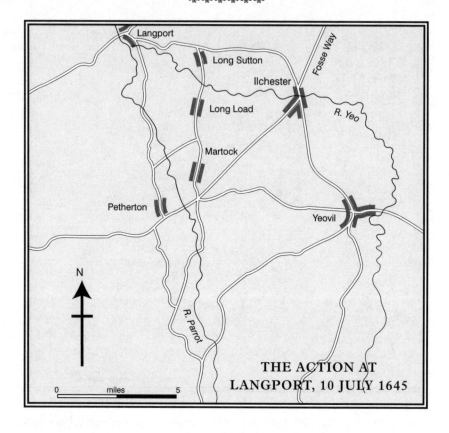

THE ACTION AT
LANGPORT, 10 JULY 1645

leaving the Royalist garrison at Bridgwater slightly exposed. Fairfax moved his forces up to Crewkerne and sent out the reliable Charles Fleetwood with some cavalry to observe the movement of the Royalist forces. They retired to an awkward position behind the Yeo between Langport and Yeovil, some twelve miles away. The Yeo had three bridges, Load Bridge (between Long Load and Long Sutton), Ilchester and Yeovil. Goring located himself at Long Sutton and sent troops to protect the crossings at Load and Ilchester. Fairfax subsequently reconnoitred the position very carefully, and on Monday 7 July he called a council of war. This agreed that cavalry forces should now try to pin Goring by threatening the Load Bridge and Ilchester while the infantry turned Goring's left at Yeovil. In fact, the weak Royalist force at Yeovil soon fell back and Ilchester was also abandoned. The Royalists then retired on Langport, but Goring did detach some of his forces under his brother-in-law, Lieutenant-General Porter, towards Taunton in a feinting manoeuvre. The reasons behind this move remain obscure, but it may well have been an attempt to divide Fairfax's forces and thus denude him of some of his troops. If so, the plan only partially succeeded. Fairfax, soon over the river and in occupation of Ilchester, endeavoured to counter the move by sending General Massey with 3,600–4,000 men to check the threat to Taunton. He then waited, concentrating the rest of his forces at Long Sutton. Hearing distant sounds of fire during the afternoon of 9 July, he sent off further force to assist Massey.

In fact, the men detached by Goring had got themselves into great difficulties. Halted seven miles from Langport, they were surprised by Massey and routed at Ilchester mainly because of Porter's negligent security. Many fled back towards Langport, and Goring was furious at Porter's errors. However, with numbers now about even, Goring was still reluctant to come to blows, and he therefore sought to withdraw to the powerful fortress of Bridgwater. He sent off his baggage and most of his artillery in the morning of 10 July, and sat covering the withdrawal on a strong position outside Langport. As Cromwell noted, Goring was rightly trusting to his ground, 'thinking he could march away at pleasure'.[38] It seemed a strong position to hold, on top of a steep hill leading into Langport, and it was also at the junction of the Parret and Yeo. Goring placed his two cannon to cover the ford and also placed musketeers in the hedges on the near side of a little brook called the Wagg Rhyne.

Viewing the ground from the other side of the valley, Fairfax and Cromwell quickly placed their troops in 'battalia'. Messages were sent to call back most of the infantry and cavalry that had been sent to assist Massey, but it seems that the commander decided not to wait for their arrival. The assault began with a strong artillery barrage, which soon wrecked Goring's cannon and began to cut up his infantry and cavalry. The New Model infantry then moved forward to chase off the Royalist musketeers placed in the hedges, and their cavalry moved to cover them. Seeing this, the forlorn hope of Major Christopher Bethel was ordered down to the ford and rapidly crossed over, four abreast. Bethel, with two troops of around 120 men and seconded by Major John Desborough, crossed over the ford and, not waiting to dress his lines, charged straight into the waiting Royalist horse and 'brake them at sword-point'. They hit the front line at pace and broke into the reserve. The Royalists soon returned the compliment with 400 fresh horse, but Bethel's men charged them also, pressing into the centre of their lines. He then turned his men about and, with Desborough's assistance, again broke the Royalist horse, which finally fled in terror. In the meantime, the infantry had followed up and moved against the Royalists. Cromwell's influence at Langport was seen in the way his men had fought. He had gazed in wonder at the strength of his cavalry: 'To see this is it not to see the face of God?' he asked. Major Thomas Harrison, another whose religious views were now in full flight, began to speak in tongues at the sight of the cavalry action and could hardly restrain himself.

Fortunately at this point Cromwell's common sense intervened and he moved up to hold both Bethel and Desborough's men back, 'that the pursuit might be orderly', only then following the retiring Royalists towards the town. There was a further action another two miles on, but the Royalists again retired, after another partial charge, losing a number of men and many horses in the ditches in the surrounding countryside. Others, who retired into Langport itself, set the town alight. Cromwell pursued them through the town, and then, some eight miles towards Bridgwater, caught many fugitives on the bridge, as well as killing and capturing large numbers of men and horses. Although Goring had made a withdrawal into Bridgwater, this was a moral as much as physical defeat for him. The campaign in the west then moved on to sieges of the various Royalist garrisons.

BRIDGWATER

During the latter part of his campaign, Fairfax had already begun to meet parties of so-called Clubmen. These locals, led by members of the gentry (as has been noted above), were a product of the country's war-weariness. At first the General handled them with his usual tact and, thanks to his excellent logistics, was able to reassure them that his army's needs would be minimal and that any supplies would be paid for. Otherwise he dispersed those who refused to give him passage. His lieutenant-general was less sure, calling them 'malignant Club-men ... who are ready to take all advantage against our parties, and would undoubtedly take them against our Army, if they had opportunity'.[39]

The army now reached Chedsay, two miles from the town of Bridgwater, which was very strongly fortified and presented a considerable obstacle. Standing in a valley with good fortifications and a broad ditch around it, which with every tide filled up, it also had a castle of indifferent strength. The place was well defended by some 1,800–2,000 men, with good stores of food and ammunition. On 11 July Colonel Welden's brigade arrived on the north side of the town while the rest of the army placed itself on the south. On Monday 14 July a council of war was called to decide whether to storm. Fairfax seems to have decided to risk an all-out assault, and preparations were made. On viewing the place, wooden bridges were ordered to be made available for the storming. A delay of some days followed, but it was clear that the town had to be taken before the army could proceed; yet a full-scale siege would be far too time-consuming, and the area was subject to hazards such as boggy ground and dangerous floods. By Friday 19 July it was Massey who took command of the brigade on the north side of the town, while Fairfax himself would command the southern side. On the morning of 20 July Hugh Peters preached a rousing sermon of encouragement to the army, and in the afternoon Mr Bowles did the same, after which the drums beat and the attack moved forward. Peters also went forward with the forlorn hope, in order to agitate them to do their duty. The storming of Bridgwater was to take place after dark, and the sign was to be the shooting of three pieces of ordnance so as to co-ordinate the attack from both sides.

At two o'clock in the morning the attack began. On the north, the attack proved to be a somewhat involuntary feint, for Massey did not strike home, much to Fairfax's annoyance, but his action did draw the defenders off. The southern part of the army went about its business more seriously. Lieutenant-Colonel John Hewson led the forlorn hope, and the bridges, prepared earlier, were quickly thrown across the moat. The soldiers then moved across, encountering a hail of shot, but, despite serious losses, they managed to reach the outer works and then to let down the drawbridge, making the defenders cry for quarter. Captain Reynolds now led in a forlorn of horse across the drawbridge, and they scoured the streets up to the second drawbridge leading into the inner town. Many defenders threw down their arms and surrendered, but others began to make barricades and drew up the second bridge. Two hours had now passed, and cannon fire of hot shot, or deliberate maliciousness, had by this time set light to the newly occupied areas. The surrounding buildings began to burn fiercely.

Fairfax, now facing the inner defences, summoned them, but was rejected. A second assault was obviously going to be needed. However, early the next morning the army made demonstrations on both sides of the town and once again Fairfax summoned the Governor. He agreed that the women and children could leave by four o'clock. After this, cannon were brought up, heavy fire was once more opened up on the garrison and the inner town caught fire. As the townspeople scurried to rescue what they could, the Governor, Sir Hugh Wyndham, finally decided to ask for terms, but Fairfax set such strong conditions that they were again rejected. With fighting about to resume, however, the Governor at last capitulated and hostages were exchanged, while many rushed to put out the extensive fires in the town. Bridgwater finally surrendered on Wednesday 23 July, and the next day was spent settling the place and ordering the prisoners.

A council of war was called on Friday 25 July to decide the army's next move. To follow Goring further into the west would be difficult, as the army now lacked ammunition and there were still several garrisons north of Bridgwater to deal with. Moreover, the Clubmen were still bold enough to cause problems. In the end, it was decided to reduce some of these Royalist garrisons first. Bath and Sherborne were chosen as the next targets. Bath quickly capitulated. Okey's dragoons were sent in to seize the gates on the bridge, and the city surrendered itself before Rupert, with some 1,500 horse, could come up from Bristol to its relief. Sherborne was bombarded and then assaulted successfully on 15 August. Tact and discretion were first used on the Clubmen to disperse them, but eventually Cromwell came across a large group of them on Hambleton Hill. He sent in a forlorn of fifty cavalry that was fired on, so, trying a more subtle approach, he then ordered in Mr Lee, formerly of their number, to reason with them. Lee was also fired on, and, even though he retreated, Cromwell ordered him in again, but to no avail. Having tried and failed to disperse them with kind words, on 5 August Cromwell sent in his cavalry with their swords. They were shot at and lost two men and a few horses, but Desborough's men caught the Clubmen in the rear and then killed twelve and dispersed the rest. Three hundred were taken prisoners – 'poor silly creatures', as Cromwell noted.[40]

A few days later Cromwell's commission was extended for another four months, for, this police action over, the port and city of Bristol was the next target for the army. Two thousand men under Prince Rupert now held Bristol, but the plague was in the city and Rupert still had insufficient men to hold the place. Nevertheless, when the army arrived on 23 August, a more formal siege than usual was begun. Fairfax deployed his guns and commenced a bombardment, having first summoned Rupert to surrender. A defiant Rupert declined this. Cromwell's cavalry also joined in the siege, 'to stand by the foot, [which] being so weak in all their posts, might receive an affront'.[41] Rupert remained aggressive despite his difficulties, and from time to time made sallies out from the walls to disrupt the army's lines. During the course of one of these, Colonel Okey was captured: in the smoke and confusion, he had made the mistake of going towards the enemy thinking they were friendly.

On 10 September the city's eastern defences were finally breached. The army went into the breach early, hoping thereby to take the forts first, then halt by daylight and assess the situation. However, once the infantry had taken the line, the horse went in. Buildings around also began to catch fire. Rupert's position was militarily untenable, and he now sought terms. These enabled him to march his men out the next day. To the King, this surrender was a cruel blow, and he felt betrayed by his nephew. On Rupert's return to Oxford, he angrily dismissed a visibly shaken Prince from all of his commands, moving north with what was left of his small army. To Cromwell, on the other hand, the capture of Bristol was 'none other than the work of God. He must be a very Atheist that doth not acknowledge it.'[42] He also took the opportunity to note that 'Presbyterians, Independents, all had here the same spirit of faith and prayer; the same pretence and answer; they agree here, know no names of difference; pity it should be otherwise anywhere.'[43] In war the soldiers had unity, and why should the coming peace be any different? Already the problem of the post-war religious settlement was beginning to exercise his mind. In the meantime, he had been detached by Fairfax to resolve the problems of Winchester and Basing House.

BASING HOUSE

After the fall of Bristol, Fairfax ordered Cromwell east with three infantry and three cavalry regiments, and he reached Winchester on 28 September. There he summoned the castle, and he took the place after a week's bombardment. Then Cromwell moved on towards Basing House. Home of the Roman Catholic John Paulet, Fifth Marquis of Winchester, who had been loyal to the King throughout the war, this formidable strongpoint blocked the strategic road to the west from London. Having withstood various sieges over the past two years, the place remained a daunting position, combining the old and new houses with modern earthworks and walls. The garrison was now mostly Catholic, with soldiers, civilians, priests, women and children all mixed in. At this time, Basing House was besieged by Colonel John Dalbier, a Dutch mercenary who had formerly served in Essex's army and whom Cromwell knew well; indeed, Dalbier had helped to train Cromwell's troops in the early days of the war.

After Dalbier's arrival in mid-August 1645, the siege had taken on a more serious outlook. The use of cannon to breach the walls and more trenches soon brought the Parliamentarian forces ever closer to taking the place, but Dalbier was short of men. Having fewer than 1,000 troops available, he was unable to encompass it. Nevertheless, his artillery continued to pound away at the New House in particular. Rumours of the riches within were rife amongst the Parliamentarian troops in the trenches, and these rumours soon spread to Cromwell's forces, so they were eager to join the siege on 8 October.

New batteries of artillery were now placed. There was something of an inauspicious beginning to Cromwell's siege, for Colonel Robert Hammond and Major King, who strayed too close to the works in the fog, were unfortunately taken prisoner. Cromwell sent in a note threatening retribution should either of the men be harmed, for he had decided on storming the position on two sides. He was not a man content to wait the siege out, and this storming would presage some of the tactics he would use in Ireland in 1649; he had already seen Fairfax use them at Bridgwater. Dalbier was ordered to take the northern side of the House; Colonel Pickering was on his left. Sir Hardress Waller and Colonel Montague's men (the Colonel himself was not there) were placed to strike the southern side.

As Monday night drew on, orders were given for the storming to take place the next day. Cromwell had decided on an early start, and the men carrying scaling ladders were to move forward at around six o'clock. The signal was to be the simultaneous firing of four large cannon. Their commander spent the night in prayer and Bible reading, seeking the righteousness of his cause, while his men bedded down where they could. They will have known that the assault would be hard, but may have already been promised free rein to plunder this 'nest of idolatrous Papists'. Those inside also knew that the assault was imminent, having seen the preparations that day.

Pickering's men were the first to begin to storm the New House area, with 'great resolution and cheerfulness'. They soon scrambled over the works and into the building itself; an attempt to blow up some of the works by the defenders misfired, and the assault pressed on. A parley was briefly offered, but the men surged forward. On the south-eastern corner of the garrison, Montague's and Waller's regiments ran for the strongest part of the works, the court of guard. Here the enemy was brutally beaten out of his position and then the soldiers dragged their scaling ladders after them, placing them on the next work. Once over these immediate works, they found both the house wall and a hail of grenades and musket balls from the desperate defenders. Waller fell, shot in the arm. At the New House, the men managed to get in through the windows. Soon all was chaos inside as they broke in. The frenzied Major Thomas Harrison, shouting out Biblical verses as he attacked, shot dead Major Cuffle, a 'notorious papist', and yelled, 'Cursed is he that doeth the work of the Lord negligently.'[44] In the bedlam that ensued, there were cries for quarter, but in the heat of the action many died before it could be given. Hammond and King were preserved from harm and liberated. The Marquis of Winchester was also captured, and his person and clothes were rifled for loot. Hugh Peters then appeared and lambasted him both for the Marquis's popery and his loyalty to the King. The plundering of Basing House was allowed to continue until late on Tuesday night, during which time the building caught fire, burning throughout the night. The flames were seen for a great distance around.

THE END OF THE FIRST CIVIL WAR

By 24 October the successful Cromwell had returned to his duties in the west. Once more Fairfax and the army council debated their route. Exeter was chosen as the next target, preparatory to entering the Royal stronghold of Cornwall. While winter began to close in, sickness also began to appear in the ranks, and it spread rapidly. Further supplies were forwarded to the troops in January 1646, and in the meantime Cromwell led a raid into Bovey Tracey. In the cold and snow, he surprised the Royalist camp there and captured Wentworth's headquarters, as well as 400 horses and 50 men. The war was now beginning to reach its final stages. Hopton had already gathered some 5,000 Royalists at Torrington, with whom he had hoped to relieve Exeter, but Fairfax came to Torrington on 16 February 1646, and after a brief skirmish his infantry smashed their way into the town, with the cavalry following up behind. Hopton was injured, but escaped. Torrington fell, although the local church, stored with gunpowder, blew up in the action, killing hundreds of prisoners and nearly taking Cromwell and Fairfax, who were nearby, with it. Meeting minimal resistance, the army crossed into Cornwall on 21 February, and the Royalists finally surrendered later that month. On 21 March 1646, Parliamentarian forces under Sir William Brereton at long last crushed the remaining Royalist forces at Stow-on-the-Wold, and on 9 April 1646 Exeter fell. The war was now effectively over, and the returning Cromwell, his reputation made by his successive military actions, was now faced with the difficult question of how to solve the problems of peace.

CHAPTER 7

THE ROAD TO PRESTON, 1646–1648

'Behold a present for you of the spoil of the enemies of the Lord.'
– *I Samuel* 30:26

POLITICS

The period following the end of the First Civil War – at least, until the outbreak of the Second Civil War in the spring of 1648 – is characterised by tortuous politics. The ending of the war in 1646 had placed Oliver Cromwell firmly at the centre of the political stage, and his hand can be detected in the events that were eventually to lead to the execution of the King and the establishment of the English republic in 1649. Here, however, our main concern is with the campaign that culminated in the Battle of Preston in August 1648, for this, Cromwell's first solo effort since he reached high command, relieved him from the military tuition of others and he was now a general in his own right. Of his later wars, Ireland was to bring him notoriety, Dunbar victory against all the odds, and Worcester a 'crowning mercy', but the generally neglected campaign of Preston in 1648 showed Oliver Cromwell's genuine abilities as an astute and aggressive soldier. A poorly led enemy assisted him, but this does not make his victory against superior numbers any less impressive.

PEACE PLANS

By June 1646, Oxford, the Royalist headquarters throughout the First Civil War, finally fell to the forces of Parliament. Civil wars invariably have ragged endings, and this one was no different. Military victory in England had come to Parliament and its Scots allies, and the victors were now eager for a swift and satisfactory political settlement so that the country could once more return to a much-needed peace. They were soon to be disillusioned.

While it was clear to many a Puritan that the God of battles had spoken against the King and he should, or so it was reasoned, now yield to terms, the King was not at Oxford when it surrendered. Instead, he had slipped out of the city a month earlier, and on 5 May 1646 Charles, already showing the ambiguity that would characterize his post-war dealings, had decided to surrender to the Scots forces still encamped around Newark.

Parliament might have indeed won the war, but the King still wished to be master of his own destiny. Furthermore, civil wars, as the victors soon discovered, produce not merely military victories but also political predicaments, and the major questions of the state still needed to be answered. How could any settlement be achieved without the King? More importantly, would the King actually allow Parliament to win the peace?

Consequently, the three years that followed were years of great political fluidity. They eventually resulted in yet another civil war that would so embitter the generals and men of New Model Army as to lead it to an act of regicide in 1649. Few men, however, were seeking this result in 1646, least of all Oliver Cromwell, whose distinguished reputation after the victories of the previous year was considerable but whose military commission as lieutenant-general of horse unfortunately ran out in July 1646. With it would go his military career, and, for Cromwell, a return to civilian life in London and the apparently endless debates of Parliament which now seemed to beckon. From what we know of his views, he seems to have accepted this idea with reluctance. The war to Cromwell had bought clarity of thought and certainty of action. The mire of politics was to bring with it a crisis of conscience and the many frustrations of politics. It was doubly unfortunate that these political squabbles were not confined to the normal channels of Parliament, where in any case the Parliamentarians needed little help to fall out amongst themselves over the way to peace: disagreements previously obscured by the needs of war also threatened the unity of the army. As a result, this latter body began to develop its own political ideology, and with Oliver Cromwell at its head it was eventually to emerge as the political arbiter of the nation.

The position of Charles I in this post-war political struggle was to be equally crucial. There is little doubt that the King sincerely believed that no real political or religious settlement could ever be achieved in the country without his agreement, and he still possessed his own particular agenda. Charles was soon craving a way back into power, with minimum obligations on his side, hoping that the eventual winner of any contest between the various factions that now emerged would, sooner or later, be forced to deal with him to resolve the country's ills. Hence the King's policy was to play for time, rejecting the many proposals put to him, good, bad, or indifferent, which would have established him on the throne with limited powers. Instead, he consistently sought to safeguard the Crown's powers over Church and State and, where he could, spread discord abroad in a series of secretive dealings. His last gamble was to bring a Scots army into England in 1648 to support his plans. This was to cost him his life.

Yet, although the King might not have seen it, a speedy settlement of the State in the autumn of 1646 was vital; it was needed because, in the friction of war, the societies of the British Isles had been slowly but surely deteriorating. Economically the state was wasted by four years of cruel conflict. A series of poor harvests, caused by increasingly bad weather (some of the worst ever seen in the country), had led to dearth and rising food prices. There were already high taxes on the basic commodities of life, and the poor were suffering great hardship. Communications and trade had to a large extent broken down, and there were outbreaks of plague abroad in the land. High taxation was, in some areas, leading to tax-strikes. This was doubly significant, for the taxes being gathered were necessary to pay the army's wages, and these were now dangerously in arrears. Even more importantly, perhaps, growing social chaos in the country needed resolution. The return of the King – and all politicians saw that some settlement with the monarchy at its head was the ideal solution – would help, but there would emerge new ideas that might seek liberation from the old ways. In these ideas, Oliver Cromwell was to play a central part. The political wars were to test him severely – possibly even more than his campaigns in the field.

'ENGLAND'S FREEDOM, SOLDIERS' RIGHTS'

'England's Freedom, Soldiers' Rights' was to be the cry in the army as it developed into a political force and debated its options in Putney Church in October 1647, but any number of political groups believed that they had solutions to the country's ills in 1646–47. First there were the Scots, to whom the King had surrendered at Newark in 1646. For their own part, they wanted no meddling in Scottish affairs, and they also called for some form of remuneration for their services in the English Civil War. Nevertheless, they were also keenly interested in the fate of England, and were anxious for a religious settlement that would result in the establishment of a Presbyterian Church. On the other hand, while generally subdued and with many of their leaders in exile, or suffering under the hand of Parliament for their actions, the beaten Royalist party were still dangerous. Resentful at their defeat and wishing for a return to the old regime, the King would not abandon them if he could help it. However, it was in the ranks of the English Parliament itself that the real problems of these years became apparent, as the development of two factions (Independent and

Presbyterian) had cracked open still further the already present wartime divisions in the two Houses.

Historians endlessly debate the difficulties of using such labels as 'party' or 'faction' in this period. This is especially true of the ideas of Independents and Presbyterians, not the least because these labels developed from religious tags, whose relevance is still dubious, and because the smooth delights of 'party' often masked the reality of the confused factionalism of the day. In other words, the use of the word 'party', of whatever label, as David Underdown has shown, often disguises more than it reveals.[1] Nonetheless, as we have seen, divisions in Parliament during the war had been (largely) between the peace faction, who wanted to negotiate at all costs, and the war faction, who wished to defeat the King first and then negotiate, with a rather larger middle group swaying whichever way they thought appropriate. While John Pym had led many of the 'centrists' through the hazards of war until 1643, when Pym had died in that year his successors were for the most part less politically astute, and while the alliance of middle group and war party had eventually brought success, any alliance was already crumbling as the war ended. After 1646, the search for a peace brought with it still more shifts, turns and new alliances.

The original Scots alliance with the Parliament in 1643 had, of course, been a crucial part of the war strategy. But those who had fought the war on the grounds of religious toleration wanted victory for themselves, not a Scots insistence on helping to establish a Presbyterian Church order in England. Prominent members of the old peace party, on the other hand, saw a way forward for their views by working with the Scots. This action brought with it the establishment of loose associations of politicians in Parliament labelled 'Presbyterian' and 'Independent'. The Presbyterians were partly the old peace party in the Parliament of the Civil War, and were led by men like Denzil Holles and some of the old middle group, with a few 'crypto-royalists' in their ranks. They were amorphous enough in their ideas, but were in the majority.[2] They wished to curb some of the unforeseen consequences of the war, especially the growing religious radicalism now beginning to be seen in the army and elsewhere. They also rejected ideas of liberty of conscience, and wanted to dismantle the victorious New Model Army as quickly as possible so as to end the financial crisis the country faced. In addition, they hoped to ship most of the troops off to Ireland (under their own suitable generals) in order to resolve the continuing crisis there. Perhaps most crucially of all, the removal of the army, it was argued, would allow them to make right and proper terms with the King, restoring him to the throne and re-establishing a form of Royal government. Ultimately, all these fundamentals were linked, as they thought, by the position of the New Model Army at the end of the war; for, as they argued, if there were no war, and the Scots army were to be sent on their way with suitable financial reward early in 1647, why was there a need for an army in England at all?

Facing them, and in a minority in Parliament, were those men who have come to be labelled 'Independents'. Of course, they also covered an equally wide spectrum of ideas, from old war party warriors and middle group moderates to now barely concealed republicans such as Henry Marten. A core Independent belief, however, was in the idea of religious toleration. They were equally keen to keep the New Model Army in being, at least until the King had been brought to terms, although the maintenance of the army was (unsurprisingly) very unpopular, principally because of the economic cost of the force and high taxes needed to pay for it. This was the cause of much resentment and misery at the local level. Besides, it was beginning to be thought by some that the Independents' real reason for wishing to keep the army in being was less to do with the nation's security, as they claimed, and more to do with their own: the army gave them a potential ally against their political opponents and the Scots.

Meanwhile the member for Huntingdon, Oliver Cromwell, now in the full flow of a Westminster MP's existence and evidently missing the simplicity of his military life, noted plaintively in a letter to his former commander Fairfax, 'We are full of faction and worse.'[3] Unfortunately for Cromwell, yet another factor began to enter the political scene in the wake of the war – the New Model Army itself. This, too, was slowly beginning to find its own voice, and, critically, it was developing into a political entity. It was this fact that was to have lasting consequences for all concerned, not the least the Independents, whose ties with it were through men such as Oliver Cromwell.

DEBATES

After a prolonged debate in Parliament, proposals to settle the State were sent from Westminster to the King, who was now safely lodged at Newcastle under the watchful eye of the Scots. These propositions were to ensure indemnity for past offences, abolish Episcopal government, reform religion in a Presbyterian manner, and ensure that the militia was handed over to Parliamentary control for at least twenty years. With other elements designed to safeguard the liberties of Parliament and of the Scots, and to punish some of the King's followers (already under way in some cases), the King resolutely rejected the so-called Newcastle Propositions. As yet, Charles was not about to agree that, having been defeated in the field, he was obliged to come to terms with his conquerors. Instead he stood his ground, especially regarding the powers of the monarchy, and made an offer to come to London for negotiations with counter-proposals of his own. Argyle and his faction, in command of Scottish affairs in Edinburgh, were unwilling to see Charles in Edinburgh for fear of the discords he might cause there. They had their own problems in Scotland, and in their impatience the Scots government now offered to depart from England, after a suitable payment, and to leave the King behind them. This was seized upon as resolving at least one immediate problem, and the next difficulty was to decide when the King would be handed over, and for how much. On 30 January 1647 the first payment of £100,000 was handed over; the next £100,000 was made available on 3 February, and with that reward the Scots army left the north and marched back over the border. Charles, in the meantime, was moved south, acclaimed by his people on the way, to whom he was now unable to do any harm. They enthusiastically looked forward to a settlement. Eventually Charles reached Holmby House in Northamptonshire on 16 February. He was effectively a prisoner, although it was now hoped that both sides could make a start on serious negotiations to resolve the outstanding issues of the day.

One of these was the problem of Ireland, where the Earl of Ormonde, the King's lieutenant in Ireland, was now unable to sustain his position and was finally forced to surrender his office in Dublin to the Parliament rather than let it fall into the hands of the Confederate Catholics. With Parliament left in sole control of the Irish problem, and with a surfeit of troops in England, which was now enjoying an uneasy peace, clearly there was an obvious solution: send some of the soldiers to Ireland to suppress the factions there and disband the rest. However, the question of who was to be sent, as much who was to go as the commander of such a force, was yet another puzzle.

In a letter of that period to his daughter, Cromwell noted that 'to be a seeker is to be of the best sect next to a finder; and such an one shall every faithful humble seeker be at the end.'[4] Seeking solutions to the country's ills was, however, proving more difficult than any one thought, as tolerance in both camps was limited. In these days, Cromwell had more than enough troubles with Parliamentary business, his own family affairs and, it seems, illness. He was a poor patient at the best of times, and the state of his health revived his religious fervour, never very far from the surface, for a time.

Meanwhile the army's development as a force to be reckoned with in politics was growing apace. The unsettling nature of the military presence at the local level led to many mutinies amongst the various troops of the north and in the southern garrisons. Short of money, they took to plunder and kidnapping local officials to protest against their neglect. Many were forced to live at 'free quarter' to survive, and, lacking their pay, they were also subject to the continued spread of sectarianism and radical thought within the ranks.

Another important consequence of the war was the spread of radical ideas through the lower ranks of society. Groups such as the Levellers began to come forward. With their ideas of liberty of conscience and political freedom, they began to challenge the established conservative political authority. While the civilian Levellers were made up largely of *petit bourgeois* – shopkeepers, artisans, apprentices, and the like – they were representative of those whom both sides in the political debate now seemed to be ignoring in their haste to reach a settlement. Their leaders included men like the tempestuous John Lilburne (the bane of any government's life), William Walwyn, Richard Overton and the crafty John Wildman.[5] These men's published ideas also began to influence the more politically committed rank-and-file of the New Model Army, for the view amongst these knowledgeable soldiers was that an army that had fought for that very liberty all now enjoyed should be given something out of the victory.

In the beginning, it is clear that many in the army were as concerned about their own material grievances as about politics, but these grievances soon began to be fused with the soldiers' own particular notions of military honour. Indeed, the army's honour was to become a key motivating factor for the events that followed. For the articulate members of the army, like those of most armies, saw the concept of military honour as vital to its existence. This honour not only revolved around the notable victories that the soldiers had won during the war, but it also lay in the many material and physical sufferings that had bonded it together with such a distinctive *esprit de corps*. Civilian politicians naturally failed to understand this, and their apparently harsh treatment and further incivility to those they saw as their servants was beginning to be seriously resented. Military honour was being slighted, and it needed vindication.

Questions were soon asked in the ranks as to how the army, without whom there would have been no peace in the first place, were now being thought of as the men who could be so easily disposed of and without appropriate reward. Moreover 'such as have [been] and are now the enemies of the parliament and kingdom are countenanced and honoured to be in places of general trust, and made judges of ... us for our lives and estates.'[6] This nexus of ideas was soon to appear as an ideological basis for military action in the political world. It eventually revolved around feelings that all Englishmen, even if they were soldiers in the army, had natural birthrights in freedom and liberty. Consequently, they should contribute in discussions as to how the country should be governed. Most in the army were agreed that, in the political system of England, the final authority of the civil government must rest in Parliament, but even here bad men, backsliders and malignants could all too easily corrupt that noble institution with their schemes and political intrigues. If politicians tended to think that politics was the art of the possible, and success usually the outcome of devious subterfuge, then the military mind dealt in certainty, in hierarchies of order and in honourable undertakings. The two did not see eye to eye. Accordingly, while many in the army had a view of Parliament as an organisation where the chief principle of social relations should be the advancement of public good rather than of any member's private interests, the politicians seemed to behave just as they always had. The army slowly but surely began to identify itself with the people. It began to see itself as not a 'mere mercenary army hired to serve any arbitrary power of state, but called forth and conjured by the several declarations of Parliament to the defence of our own and the people's just rights and liberties. And so we took up arms in judgement and conscience to those ends.'[7]

Besides, not only was the army drawn from the people and pledged to protect them and their liberties, it was also pledged to protect its own rights. An Englishman in arms was still an Englishman with all of his rights – perhaps even more so as he had shed his blood for them. Such agenda were radical enough, using as they did arguments drawn from rights theory, but when added to discussions on ideas of a new franchise for Parliament and toleration for the sects they became very radical indeed. The military began angrily to resent the Presbyterian majority in Parliament, who now seemed to be determined on slighting their previous services. Such thoughts also threatened the position of the generals – the 'grandees', as they came to be called – and led to petitioning and the election of agitators from the individual regiments of men who would best speak for the rank-and-file's interests.

THE BREAKDOWN

With the King under their control, the Presbyterian majority in Parliament could now – or so it was thought – safely turn to resolving the problem of the army; and the financial need for the Presbyterians in Parliament to rid themselves of the army was rapidly becoming paramount. The New Model was in arrears of £2.8 million in pay. A reduction of the cavalry to 6,600 horse and dragoons was already in motion, and it was now suggested that the infantry be disbanded where it was not located in garrison. In reality, a choice was to be offered to the rank-and-file, as well as the junior officers, to disband and be paid off or to enlist in an army forming for Irish service. This would have 4,220 horse and dragoons, with 8,400 infantry. The rest of the men were to be disbanded, while the officer corps was also to be deliberately selected: no officer above the rank of colonel was to be allowed, save for Fairfax, and all the officers had to take the Covenant.

The soldiers began to protest at what they saw as dishonourable treatment, especially when they were to be paid off with the minimal arrears. When they complained that they wanted their money, indemnity for their previous actions and liberty of conscience, they were roughly cited as disturbers of the peace. In addition, the remodelling of London militia and other forces in the country appeared to be constructing an alternative power base to act as a counterweight to the New Model. Such organisations began to use 'reformado' officers and discontented ex-soldiers to fill their ranks, engendering a fear in the army that they were thought untrustworthy by the politicians. To some, indeed, there was the hope that the army would divide, if it were offered some wages and the choice of service in Ireland. In fact, the calumnies being thrown in its direction merely caused it to begin to close its ranks. A new agenda was starting to emerge.

Despite these developments, Cromwell, for one, still believed that the army would disband at Parliament's command, and his words seem to have reassured those engaged in the matter. There is some question as to whether he was being insincere in this view and whether in private he was secretly encouraging the soldiers, but it is more than likely that he himself was divided between his own innate regard for Parliamentary authority and his natural sympathies with the justice of the case of the men he had once led into battle. The choices of Sir William Waller as general and Sir Edward Massey as lieutenant-general for the new force to be sent to Ireland caused even more disturbances in the ranks. Waller sensibly declined the command, and so the choice fell on Philip Skippon. This was not so bad, as at least the men knew Skippon, but he was still an imposed solution. Meetings of soldiers and politicians now took place at Saffron Walden, and at one of these, on 21 March, it was clear that a majority of the officers would not volunteer for Irish service; at another meeting, they responded to the offer by drawing up a petition stating their case. The men soon followed their example.

In this document, the soldiers' grievances over pay and treatment were matched by demands that they be allowed to petition freely (another natural right of an Englishman) and to vindicate themselves and their cause. On his return as one of the commissioners, Cromwell, setting his hand to the report they wrote, noted that 'we found the army under a deep sense of some sufferings, and the common soldiers much unsettled.'[8] The problem for the grandees in the army was that both the men and junior officers were beginning to push hard for some form of action to resolve the issues that concerned them, and, if they were not careful, the grandees might well be trampled in the rush. Pamphlets began to be seen in the streets in force, and in this noisy literature settlement seemed ever more distant. Despite attempts to quieten them, the soldiers increasingly seemed to distrust their political masters. In their opinion, for them to comply in their own disbandment at this point would be sheer folly, and consequently a general rendezvous at Newmarket was called for.

Cromwell's part in all of this was indistinct, and was particularly vague in the next move made by the army – the seizure of the King by Cornet George Joyce. There seems little doubt that both he and Henry Ireton were aware of this *coup*, for Cromwell's London residence was noted at this time for the comings and goings of officers and sectaries alike. It was also soon clear that self-preservation and the pace of events and occasion, as well as much communing with the Lord, had caused him to begin to choose his side – the army – although many thought he was actually behind Joyce's action. He was already a prominent leader of the Independents in Westminster in any case, and a mediator between the army and Parliament, but he doubtless felt deeply the wrongs being done to his soldiers. He shared many of their ideas on honour and on toleration, he had fought alongside them and seen them die, and he could not just abandon them. If such a belief system gave him a fixed point in the turbulent political world, in the end the pull of the army, mixed with Providence, was to prove to be much stronger than even his regard for Parliament.

Consequently, on 4 June 1647 Cromwell left London for the army headquarters at Newmarket, as much as to bolster General Fairfax as to forestall his own arrest by his Presbyterian political enemies. A new and more dangerous stage in the game had now begun. With the King in their hands, the army had for the first time become a real player in politics. As the regiments had already elected their own representatives or agitators (the idea emerging from the more radical cavalry), it was decided to let them sit upon the newly created army council, on which Cromwell was also given a seat. While dominated by officers, the men also found a place in this democratic melting pot.

'CIRCUMSTANCE AND OPPORTUNITY'

Fearful of the soldiers, Parliament now tried to placate them by promising arrears and indemnity, although it also moved for its own defence. The army rapidly responded with a declaration calling for a limited purge of the eleven members of the Commons it thought most hostile to its interests. As concessions followed, in early July 1647 the army grandees even began their own negotiations with the King. Their position was eventually to be set out in a document called the 'Heads of the Proposals'. This moderate solution to the State's ills offered an end to the current Parliamentary session within the year; subsequent Parliaments were to have a life not exceeding 120 days, and could be dissolved or adjourned by their own consent. Some redistribution of seats as well as a Council of State, with members appointed for seven years, were other prominent features. The Parliament would, moreover, control the militia and great offices of state for ten years. Toleration of religion, however, was at the heart of the Heads of the Proposals, and clemency was also to be shown to the majority of the King's followers. The Irish problem was to be left to the Parliament to resolve.

Most historians are agreed that the Heads of the Proposals were the best deal offered to the King in these years, but Charles, profoundly misunderstanding the nature of the men with whom he was dealing, and equally unable to understand why they were not seeking his favour or titles for themselves, preferred to delay. He also saw yet more possibilities in a counter-revolution in London. The eleven excluded members saw their hopes in another agreement with the Scots to resolve the State, and the mob of the City of London now forced the Commons to vote to invite the King to London for negotiations. Many fearful Independent MPs rushed to join the army, and the army responded by starting its march to London. The Presbyterian counter-revolution crumbled. With the army's presence in London, the situation could now be made favourable both to the Independents and to itself. The eleven members were expelled and the government of the City was purged. Eventually Charles was brought to Hampton Court and Fairfax made Putney his headquarters. The King continued to quibble over the Heads of the Proposals; he was now keen to enter into secret negotiations with the Scots, the latter increasingly concerned at events in England. While the King negotiated, Cromwell was working ever harder to settle with his untrustworthy monarch, all the while finding his own political position weakened amongst the army rank-and-file and the more radical element as he did so. They feared that they were being sold out. Indeed, the Levellers had now produced their own document, 'The Agreement of the People', and it was this, and its political consequences, that were disputed by Cromwell and Ireton and the more radical element in the army at Putney Church in October 1647.[9]

The debates held at Putney took 'The Agreement of the People' for their point of discussion. Important and complex political arguments followed on the nature of rights and the franchise. Tempers became frayed, and eventually Cromwell and Ireton outmanoeuvred the radicals. The worried grandees cut short the debates, and while Cromwell struggled to restrain the militant element in the army, Charles was already beginning his secret dealings with the Scots. In return for his satisfaction in religion, the negotiations promised a Scottish army to fight for his cause. The Scots commissioners also advised that the King should escape his captors.

On 11 November 1647, fearful of emergent radical voices and anxious to gain some room to manoeuvre, the King broke out. He eventually arrived in the Isle of Wight, having intended to flee to the Continent. However, he was now to all intents and purposes a prisoner once more. If the King's flight caused great difficulties for the army, already resentful at what it saw as arrangements being made with the King by the grandee generals like Cromwell, it made even more trouble for the generals. Several regiments now mutinied at Corkbush Fields near Ware, and Fairfax and Cromwell were forced into robust action to bring the army back into order. Meanwhile the King continued to mislead the grandees. In Parliament it was decided to provide 'Four Bills' as the preconditions for settlement. These would allow Parliament to have control of the militia for twenty years and determine the condition on which it could be handed back to the King; all declarations by the King against Parliament were to be rescinded and any honours given by the King since the outbreak of the war were to be null and void; and Parliament was to have the power to adjourn to wherever it wished.

Charles's approach to the army officers found them now unwilling to help him. Inevitably, while such demands were sent back and forth, the King and the Scottish commissioners had already concluded their negotiations in secret. On 26 December Charles finally signed an 'engagement' with the

Scots to confirm the Covenant by statute and protect those who had taken it. He also allowed a three-year Presbyterian establishment, with the provision that he control the Church. On the other hand, heresy, especially in an Independent form, was to be suppressed. In return, the Scots were to support the King's demands for a personal treaty with Parliament and the disbandment of all forces. If this were refused, a Scots army would be sent to invade England and enforce the King's will. An indemnity and form of economic union was to follow a subsequent peace. Charles, with this agreement in his hands, then rejected the Four Bills outright.

Parliament responded angrily with a vote of no addresses on 3 January 1648; no further approaches would be made to the King without their permission. An impasse now seemed to have been reached. Yet there was still a need for settlement. In the army, the rank-and-file rumblings continued, and now there were calls for justice on the 'man of blood'. The levels of discontent seemed to be spreading throughout the country. In addition, the bad weather brought food shortages, and, to make matters even worse, on 25 April 1648 news reached London from Scotland that the Scots were raising an army for war.

CROMWELL IN WALES

The Second Civil War now began, with a series of disorders in different parts of the country. Insurrections and mutiny broke out in South Wales in April, in Kent in May, and in Essex in June 1648. Part of the Fleet mutinied and went over to Prince Charles, blockading the Cinque Ports and the mouth of the River Thames, the gateway of London's trade. The State lurched once again into crisis. In Wales, the local governor of Pembroke Castle, the none-too-sober Colonel John Poyer, joined in a revolt that began as mutiny amongst the soldiery there, which was due to be disbanded. He eventually declared for the King; others quickly followed suit, including the local Parliamentary commander, Major-General Laugharne. In response, Fairfax sent an infantry regiment and two of cavalry, with Colonel John Okey's dragoons, under the command of Colonel Horton into South Wales to suppress the revolt. Laugharne tried to entrap Horton and his 3,000 men at St Fagan's, but he was defeated and then fell back to join Poyer at Pembroke Castle. Horton marched off to besiege Tenby, which was by now also in insurrection. By this time Fairfax had also detached Cromwell to suppress the Welsh uprising

Cromwell reached Gloucester by 8 May 1648. There he held a review and made a rousing speech to his troops, wherein he declared that he had

'... often times ventured his life with them, and they with him, against the common enemy of this kingdom, and a far more potent power and strength than they are now to engage withal; and therefore desired them to arm them selves with the same resolution as formerly and to go on with the same courage, faithfulness and fidelity, as sundry times they had done, and upon several desperate attempts and engagements and that for his part, he protested to live and die with them: the Lieut. Gen. had no sooner declared himself but they threw up their caps giving a great shout and hallow, crying out with one unanimous consent that they would venture their lives and fortunes under his conduct and command against any enemy either domestic or foreign.'[10]

Even though we have this extract second-hand as an example of Cromwellian military rhetoric, it remains one of the best. This speech was typical of his style to his soldiers, being short, simple, and in plain language, given to men whose merits he knew very well and was about to lead into battle. It made an appeal to the past and to their courage and honour, and to their soldierly values. He also took care to unite his own fortunes with those of his men. Once both parties were equally satisfied with their pledges of loyalty, Cromwell moved his small army into Wales.

By now the rebels held not only Pembroke and Tenby, but also Chepstow. As usual, Cromwell thought that there was a need for more logistical support, artillery and ammunition; nevertheless, Tenby and Chepstow were chosen as his first targets. He took the latter town on 11 May, but for the next three days he sought in vain to enter the castle. Unwilling to delay any longer, Cromwell finally detached troops to attack the place while he went on to Pembroke. Chepstow Castle eventually fell on 25 May, while Tenby surrendered to Colonel Horton at long last on 31 May, most of the prisoners being shipped off to the West Indies.

Conversely, the great medieval fortress of Pembroke Castle proved to be a tougher nut to crack. It was held by the hard-drinking Colonel Poyer and his 2,000 men, and surrounded on three sides by the sea and twenty-foot-thick walls. Cromwell had some 3,000 men at his disposal, but he was already short of equipment and stores. He rushed forward in his usual style, but his first attack on 4 June failed: not only were the defences too strong, the siege ladders had been made far too short for the assault. Now he waited impatiently for artillery in order to conduct a proper siege. Various misfortunes then struck the artillery transports, causing still more delay, and even when the artillery finally arrived the siege made slow progress. Cromwell and his troops were going hungry – the infantry, he noted, were subsisting largely on 'bread and water' – and various police actions in the surrounding countryside to subdue the local population did not help matters. The war was now turning into a very dirty conflict indeed, and the soldiers, angered at having to fight the war all over again, were acting with ever more ruthlessness. In addition, Poyer's sorties into the siege lines also kept them busy. News of the affairs of the nation was also reaching Cromwell. While he was delayed at Pembroke, the Earl of Norwich with 500 men had tried to enter and win over London, but had been pushed back into Essex, where others soon joined him. He took refuge in Colchester. Fairfax now had a serious campaign of his own on his hands. Eventually he began a blockade of the town that was both laborious and as cruel to his own men as to those besieged inside.

This only left John Lambert and his limited forces in the north to deal with any potential Scottish invasion. Most of the northern forces had already been disbanded, and Lambert's position was still more serious because the Royalist soldier Sir Marmaduke Langdale had seized Berwick and another group of Royalists under Sir Philip Musgrave had taken control of Carlisle. Neither place had been garrisoned, as earlier agreements with the Scots had denuded them of troops, and some of the walls had been slighted. A frustrated Langdale had already agreed to hold off from engaging any enemy until the Scots army arrived; as a result, it restricted his actions. Moreover, his choice of troops was soon being criticised by his tardy allies as his men apparently included many Catholics and some who had not taken the Covenant. As a preliminary exercise in Allied relations, this was not very successful, but the border with Scotland still remained open to a Scots army.

At Pembroke, the heavy siege weapons had finally arrived and begun to be placed. This at least allowed Cromwell to make serious threats to the garrison. When, at long last, the artillery opened up, Poyer (Laugharne was ill) surrendered on 11 July. The rebels were eventually given relatively generous terms (although their leaders were severely treated), mainly because on 8 July 1648 news came to the camp that, after many long delays, a Scots army had invaded England.

THE SCOTS ARMY

Internal Scottish politics had ensured that the invading forces were not made of the same stern materials as their predecessors.[11] The Scots themselves were sharply divided between those who favoured the treaty of Engagement with the King and those who rejected it. Although still keen Covenanters, Argyll and the Kirk were strongly against this particular war. Indeed, the Kirk saw it as sinful, for the King had refused to take the Covenant, and it also viewed Royalist allies as simply malignant or, worse still, Roman Catholic. The surrender of the King to the English in 1647, as well as a general war-weariness, were also factors in Scottish opinion, and few were willing to pay out further taxes for yet another conflict, whatever the cause.

It now fell to the forty-two-year-old James, 1st Duke of Hamilton to take action. Although he had not taken the Covenant, Hamilton had gained temporary control of the Scottish Parliament, but to raise an army to invade England proved rather more difficult. Politically, he still had to face the powerful Archibald Campbell, Marquis of Argyll. Argyll was the Highland clan chief of the Campbells, and a covenanting survivor of note. He was resistant to these ideas, and in any case he had his own plans. The Kirk, on the other hand, denounced everyone who was in any way involved, and guaranteed God's curse on his or her head. In its view, the English Independents and their army were dammed in any case, and God would deal with them in His own way; no agreement with the King could take priority over this. In military terms, Hamilton also had difficulties. There was to be no Leven, who was too old, and disinclined to serve no matter what, and no David Leslie, whom the Kirk had made withdraw alongside other experienced officers. Montrose, the most able Scottish soldier of his day, was still in exile in France. Montrose pitting his military skills against Cromwell would at least have been an intriguing confrontation, but it was not to be. Instead, Hamilton himself became the general in command, but, while brave, he lacked any real talent for war, being weak of will, militarily indecisive and far too conciliatory. Nor were some of his senior officers much better. The high-handed James Livingstone, Earl of Callander, was experienced, but Dutch-trained to the point of pedantry. While he was made lieutenant-general of the army, he was no friend of Hamilton. Throughout he remained reluctant to take orders, considering himself a far better general than his commander. Hamilton seems, on the surface at least, to have agreed, for he tended to be intimidated in Callander's presence. John, Earl of Middleton, was given command of the horse, and he had seen action in the Covenanting and the Parliamentary armies until 1645. The infantry command went to William Baillie, who had seen service in the Bishops' Wars and had fought well at Marston Moor. In 1645, however, he had taken on Montrose and performed badly. The often drunk but intensely fierce Sir James Turner found himself as adjutant-general, although, as he said, also 'doeing the dutie of Major Generall of the infantrie, since there was none named for it.'[12]

Unhappily, the Kirk again resisted the levy of troops at the ground level, and delay followed delay, only two-thirds of the men Hamilton had hoped to raise finally coming in to the colours – and most of them were raw troops. Ammunition and food were in short supply, and one internal rebellion had already been put down in south-west Scotland before the Scots army finally stumbled across the border on 8 July 1648 in the worst summer weather in living memory. Rain, storm and flood were now to hamper military operations throughout the campaign. Captain John Birch, who had raised a company of Lancashire men to oppose the Scots' invasion, noted the 'exteamity of wet and foul wether [and a more] miserable time for souldiers as I have seene at any time'.[13] Indeed, it rained unceasingly; Sir James Turner noted that 'it was not possible for us to keepe one musket often fixed, all the time wee were in a bodie in England.'[14]

Extra men were now sought by Hamilton from the Scots army in Ulster to bolster the ranks of his force, and although this proved difficult to achieve, eventually a body of 3,000 under George Munro was sent over to England. In spite of this, the Scots army lacked a reliable logistical base, and Hamilton's soldiers were to spend most of their time plundering the land and people around them as they marched forward. Understrength and comprising raw troops, with cruel weather, heavy ground, few cannon and little ammunition, it seemed a doomed escapade from the beginning. Nonetheless, the 9,000 blue-bonneted troops, many with their women and families in tow ('sutty vacabound women that followed the Duke's camp ... [and] vexed the pore country sore'), crossed near Carlisle under the white banner of Hamilton and proceeded slowly down the west coast, expecting reinforcements from both the Ulster Scots and Langdale's Royalists.[15] Langdale joined Hamilton's army at Carlisle with 3,000 infantry and 1,200 horse of mixed quality, but few other Royalists joined up. Expecting supplies from France and Scotland, the advance soon ground to a temporary halt between Penrith and Appleby. As soon as Munro with his well-trained and 'resolute' 2,100 infantry and 1,200 cavalry joined the army at Kendal, arguments began over precedent.

Munro had already been nettled by the difficulties in getting his men over from Ulster (they were pursued by English ships). The local population and the Kirkmen then abused them as they passed through

Dumfriesshire. Once Munro (who was reluctant to take orders) and Callander (a difficult man at the best of times) came face to face, they did not like the look of one another: Munro wanted an independent command and Callander wanted to give him orders. Hamilton was loath to resolve the problem between the two, but eventually he let Munro and his men, with two English regiments, depart to guard the artillery train supposedly following the army out of Scotland. Hamilton's weakness as a commander also began to cause friction between the English and Scots in the army. Duels kept breaking out. By now the Scots army had some 10,000 infantry and 4,000 horse alongside Langdale's 3,300 men, but the Scots soldiers were so undisciplined that they terrorised much of the local population and stole their property; this as good as ruined their cause before it had begun. Hamilton had little control, one sour English commentator reporting these words: 'Let the Lads get once into England, and then shift for themselves, and behold their shifts, they shift into Scotland all the Cowes, oxen, and Sheepe they meet with, and leave not any moveables un-shifted.'[16] Another observer noted the devastation of the area the Scots army passed through: 'Westmoreland and Cumberland are so harrowed, that the Scots and Langdale … [cannot] subsist, but will be forced to seek other Quarters in Lancashire and elsewhere.'[17] If Hamilton could not, or would not, control his men, this treatment of the local population – who were supposedly sympathetic to the Royal cause – also damaged the gathering of intelligence as to the operations of their enemy.

Meanwhile twenty-eight-year-old Major-General John Lambert was skilfully shadowing the Scots army with his own smaller force of 3,500 men and some 1,000 foot and 300 horse of Lancashire. Lambert thought that Hamilton would eventually try to move into Yorkshire, and there was indeed a continued debate in the senior ranks of the Scots army about just such a move. Despite being in 'great want of victualls, noe drink at all but water, either for officer nor souldier', and notwithstanding some clashes with the Scots, Lambert managed to pull back to await the coming of Cromwell. Nor was Hamilton enterprising enough to attempt to bring him to battle before Cromwell arrived.[18] A victory might also have rallied others to his cause, but inertia seemed to have rooted the invasion to the spot.

By this stage, 15 July, Cromwell had begun his march from South Wales. He sent the cavalry ahead and came up behind with the infantry as fast as the men could march. The little army had poor supplies, ragged clothes, few stockings and worn-out shoes, and were growing very weary with hard marching. Wrote one soldier:

'... our marches long, and want of shoes, and stockings gave discouragement to our souldiers, having received no pay these many months to buy them ... unlesse we plunder; which was never heard off by any under the Lieut. Generalls Conduct, nor will he; though they march barefoot, which many have done since our advance from Wales.'[19]

Despite all the difficulties, Cromwell drove them on, eager to come into the north. By 24 July he and his weary men had reached Gloucester. Desperate for supplies for his redcoats, Cromwell wrote to the Committee at Derby House to send such on ahead of him. He waited some days at Warwick Castle, but then pressed on to Leicester, which he reached on 1 August. There the first supplies were found, and a commission for his command of the northern troops. Unlike the Scots, even with the able Lambert already in post, there was to be no question of a divided

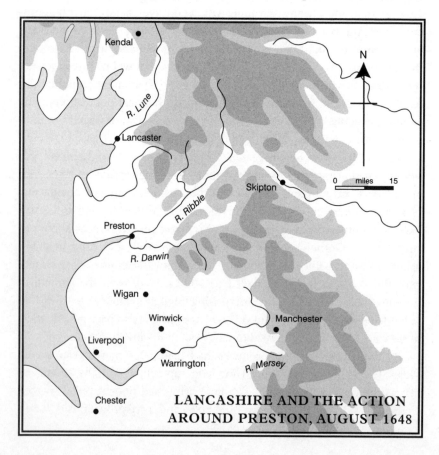

LANCASHIRE AND THE ACTION AROUND PRESTON, AUGUST 1648

command in the Parliamentary ranks. Cromwell at once wrote to Lambert that, if Hamilton renewed his advance, Lambert should shadow him, shunning any action as far as possible until his new general's arrival. As Cromwell advanced, he also gathered trained bands of about 5,000 men to add to Lambert's force. In all, he now had about 8,600 men to face Hamilton's 20,000 or so.

There was still much discord in the Scots army. The council of war at Hornby on 13 August was fractious, and undecided as to how to proceed. Strategically, the Scots should be heading south, yet Middleton and Turner wanted to go via Yorkshire first, for, as Turner noted, 'I understood Lancashire was a close country, full of ditches and hedges, which was a great advantage the English would have over our raw and undisciplined musketeers.'[20] Hamilton and Baillie wanted to continue through Lancashire, take Manchester and link up with the Welsh Royalists under Lord Byron. The commander-in-chief, said Turner, was 'never ... [so] tenacious in anything during the time of his command but in that.'[21] The surly Callander was ambivalent and kept his own council. A march through Lancashire was the eventual choice. As it was, the army soon became stretched out between Lancaster and Wigan, with Preston as the centre. Logistics dictated some of this, Middleton and Callander arguing that the army needed more fodder, and so the cavalry were sent off as a vanguard, but poor generalship and 'want of intelligence helped to ruine us.'[22]

By 12 August Cromwell had reached Leeds. There he called his own council of war to plan a strategy. He was joined by artillery sent from Hull, and this he almost immediately cast off to Knaresborough in order to save time in any advance, for he soon decided to launch a rapid offensive despite the apparent disparity in numbers. Lambert and Cromwell moved on towards Preston through Otley and Skipton in order to probe the Scots army's flank. They had reached Skipton by 13 August, and by the roadside at Hodder Bridge on 16 August they held another council of war. So far, the rapid marches had been swift and secure. Cromwell had apparently outflanked Hamilton's lumbering army and was now poised to strike. Whether this was deliberate strategy or not is debatable: as we have seen, Cromwell's tactical imperative, held at least since Grantham, was to attack the enemy wherever he was and seek a decisive victory when he found him. It was all to the good that Hamilton was lumbering forward to give him just such an occasion.

The suggestion that the army should instead remain south of the Ribble and move to block Hamilton's slow progress through Lancashire and towards London at Whalley was easily dismissed. At best this might have only have given Cromwell a partial victory; it was far better that the army strike hard at the enemy at Preston, thereby cutting off Hamilton from his base in Scotland. Cromwell had from the beginning decided that to 'engage the enemy to fight was our business', and was now about to seek out a decisive battle. Moreover, it may be that this was less bold a move than many have thought. Captain John Hodgson had earlier noted that 'we had spies amongst their army daily, that brought us true intelligence of their numbers, as near as could be computed, and their posture and demeanours.'[23] Even so, it seems that Cromwell was also being pushed into action by, as it turned out, the erroneous belief that Munro's men would advance to join the main Scots army. In fact, Munro was well to the north with 4,500 Ulster Scots and Royalists, but, given the intelligence available, Cromwell's strategy was now clear: advance along the north bank of the Ribble and attack the enemy directly with as much force as he could muster at Preston. After a further advance, the small army halted nine miles from Preston and bedded down for the night.

Meanwhile Langdale, with 3,600 Royalist troops, was six miles east of Preston, guarding the left flank of the Scots army. That evening Langdale finally learnt of Cromwell's advance, although the details were still vague, and, as Hamilton's army was far too widely dispersed along the line towards Wigan – indeed, most of the Scots forces were approaching that town – he hastened with his news to Hamilton, who was with Callander and the infantry on Preston Moor outside the town. Langdale informed Hamilton of the danger, but Callander, supervising the Scottish infantry's march south, ridiculed the report, instead claiming that the opposition was merely a light force sent to test the flank. The Scots believed that the enemy had divided, sending a force to protect the town of Manchester, the invaders' ostensible target. Hamilton failed to go to see for himself, and Langdale returned to his men. The moment to strike was therefore auspicious, and, if prompt, Cromwell could use his local superiority in numbers to seize the initiative and force the enemy to fight on his terms; he could then crush Langdale and afterwards defeat the scattered Scots army in detail.

17–19 AUGUST

Early on 17 August, Cromwell began a fierce assault on Langdale's troops. Langdale's men had already begun to retire in the early hours when they observed a small body of horse coming upon them. They soon found themselves subject to sharp attacks by Cromwell's forlorn – 400 infantry commanded by Major Pownal, and including the Yorkshireman Captain John Hodgson. Two hundred cavalry commanded by Major Smithson were also sent forward. Pownal and Hodgson were waiting for their men to arrive when Cromwell himself rode up and ordered them to engage in skirmishes to pin down Langdale's troops as he brought up the rest of the army. Both officers began to protest that only half of their men were in place and 'desired a little patience; he gives out the word March!'[24] Chastened, they moved off briskly. A group of Langdale's troops shot at them, but aimed too high; encouraged, the Cromwellian infantry moved forward. Hodgson ran to the next hedge with some of his men, and there found some of the enemy, who promptly threw down their arms and fled. The next formed body was a stand of pikes, so they approached them more cautiously. Hodgson found an 'ambuscado' waiting for Smithson's cavalry, but the enemy then drew off, and, as they did so, he leapt over a ditch and chased after their officer, but he escaped. Smithson's men now came up, and together they engaged the enemy. Smithson and some of his men were caught in a mêlée with some Scots lancers and retired, but during this mêlée Hodgson was pleased to dismount an enemy officer and seize his horse.

After a while, Langdale called a halt some two miles from Preston and sent his men into the enclosed fields and hedges. The ground was now very waterlogged, and the position also crossed a deep lane that led on to the town. Once more Langdale sent back to his commander. Hamilton was busily supervising Baillie and the infantry across the River Ribble at Walton Bridge; Middleton was already at Wigan with the cavalry. If he immediately began to close up his troops, Hamilton would have an advantage in

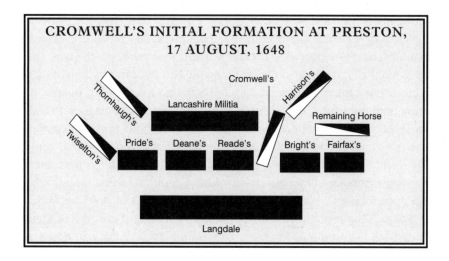

CROMWELL'S INITIAL FORMATION AT PRESTON, 17 AUGUST, 1648

numbers. He went once more to view Preston Moor to see if it were suitable for battle. In the meantime, Callander ordered Baillie to continue to move his men south over the bridge, and he then rode to the moor to berate Hamilton. In the discussion that followed, Callander overbore the Duke, arguing that they had insufficient cavalry and must move south to join up with Middleton, before giving battle on a ground of their own choosing. Hamilton finally gave way and the infantry continued south, but, rather than totally abandon Langdale's Englishmen, he felt responsible enough for them to remain on the moor with his horse guard, and some infantry were left to cover the bridge. Langdale later stated that the Duke was initially 'incredulous' that he now faced the whole of Cromwell's army, and sent Sir Lewis Dyve forward to confirm this. Langdale told him in no uncertain terms that his forces really were facing the whole of the Cromwellian army, and that he desperately needed reinforcements, as well as powder and ammunition. Others later said that the Duke, or Callander, had been all for abandoning their Royalist allies, saying contemptuously 'Let them alone – the English dogs are but killing one another.'[25]

Cromwell had chosen a tactical formation previously seen at Langport, mainly because he realised that the ground was far too heavy and wet for the cavalry and that, in the end, this battle would be a 'hedge dispute' for his infantry. He placed Harrison's and his own cavalry regiments to charge down the lane in his centre, with his infantry on the flanks. On the right were Reade's, Deane's and Pride's infantry. and on the left were Bright's and Fairfax's foot regiments. Ashton and the Lancashire foot (with Captain Hodgson and his newly acquired horse) were in reserve on the left, and in support on the far right were Thornhaugh's and Twistleton's regiments of horse. The remaining horse was to the left. Much of this deployment took time owing to the weather and muddy ground, and it was around four o'clock before the cavalry began to drive down the lane and throw the Royalists back – and even then the Royalist infantry fought with grim determination as a tough infantry battle now developed. In spite of being outnumbered, Langdale's men put up a desperate resistance. Pride's and Deane's regiments had outwinged the enemy and saw little enough action. Cromwell had placed them there, fearing that Munro would come down and outflank him. In reality, the latter was far from the action, but it shows the gambler in the aggressive soldier Cromwell had become that he was even willing to risk being outflanked in order to come to the enemy.

Instead, the centre of the action lay on the lane and on the left. Here Langdale's men continued to put up a stout resistance. After four hours of hard fighting, with push of pike and close musketry, and 'incredible Valour and Resolution', Lambert finally ordered Hodgson to bring up the Lancashire regiment. Hodgson had been blundering around in the fire and smoke, and, when he arrived and gave his out his orders, he seems to have confused them, for Major Jackson began to dither. One of his sergeants then grew impatient at the talk and broke in on the conversation to ask Captain Hodgson 'where they should march? I showed him the party he was to fight, and he, like a true Englishman marched, and I caused the soldiers to follow him.'[26]

Lambert eventually broke the enemy with the Lancashire trained bands, and Langdale's men now began to fall back rapidly towards Preston and the Ribble Bridge, Cromwell hastened his men after them into the town. Many of the Royalists were now 'killed, some being trodden into the dirt in the Lanes with the horses feet, the wayes being soe deep.'[27] Many were also killed in the fields on the east side of Preston and driven down to the Ribble Bridge. Harrison's men charged into Preston. Langdale fell back, cursing his luck and noisily blaming the Scots for their lack of support. He later claimed that, with a thousand more men, he might have outflanked the enemy and won a victory. Hamilton was also caught up in the rout. He ordered whatever cavalry he had north towards Munro, while he tried to cross the river to re-join his command on the south bank. The ford he had chosen was so swollen with the heavy rain that he was caught and soon came under heavy fire. Bravely, he led three fearless charges to give his troops some breathing space, before plunging into the water and crossing to safety.

Baillie's infantry, meanwhile, was still moving south over the Ribble Bridge. As Langdale's Royalists broke and fled into Preston, Cromwell's army continued the pursuit into the town. The Lancashire foot regiment now cautiously made its way down a small watery lane on the right rear of the Royalist position towards the Ribble, to take the opposition in the flank. The Scots had neglected to protect this, even though Langdale had pointed it out to them. Cromwell now ordered an attack on the Scots at Walton Bridge with Fairfax's and Ashton's regiments. Fierce fighting again took place with pike and butt-end of musket as the Cromwellians smashed into the Scots around the bridge. Captain John Birch, in command of the Lancashire Brigade's forlorn, had a tough fight: 'almost all my officers markt, none killed, divers souldiers shott and hurt, some very dangerously, most performed very well.'[28] Eventually the stubborn Scots gave way and were chased off in a disorderly fashion towards Walton, some of them taking time to make off and plunder the nearby houses while their comrades were being slaughtered. It was later rumoured that they had buried their stolen goods in the fields close by, hoping to return to them, and after the battle the good folk of Preston spent many a long day searching in the mud for their belongings. Hamilton had by now fallen back towards his men, and Langdale, with some horse, was forced away from the field towards Chorley, where he eventually found Middleton preparing to advance.

As night fell, Cromwell and his exhausted troops secured the bridge. His bold actions had now split the enemy in two. Hamilton and his army were cut off from Munro and Scotland, and from any retreat that way. Cromwell aimed to renew the struggle next day. In the pouring rain, his men immediately slumped down where they could, grateful for the lull in the action. Cromwell posted Ashton with all the men he could spare to guard Preston with the 4,000 prisoners he had taken that day, bluntly ordering him to put them to the sword if Munro should come up. Meanwhile, on the other side, a fractious late-night council of war was convened. Sitting on their horses, Baillie and Turner argued that they should continue the fight, but the surly Callander interrupted and said he wanted to retreat in the dark to meet Middleton coming up from Wigan. He overruled the others, and the dishevelled Hamilton now ordered his 11,000 'wet, wearie, and hungrie' men on a retreat south in a drumless march, hoping to break contact with the enemy.

Cromwell's men, still weary after their hard fight and waiting for the cold dawn, 'did not so well attend the enemies going off as might have been.'[29] The Scots abandoned their carts of ammunition (the pressed local wagon men had fled precipitately with the horses at the first opportunity), only stopping to set them with a fuse that failed to go off, so they too, alongside numerous traumatised and exhausted Scottish soldiers, fell into Cromwell's hands. One of the wagons, with Hamilton's own plate on board, overturned and spilled its contents in the mud and was eagerly seized by the Cromwellian troops. As the main bulk of the Scots army moved south via Standish, scores of men fell by the wayside or fled into the night.

Unfortunately, Middleton had meanwhile come up by Chorley, only to find Hamilton's main army gone and Cromwell's forces now in possession of the bridge over the Darwen. He promptly fled after the main army. Cromwell sent off some cavalry in pursuit, and bitter skirmishing took place all the way towards Wigan Moor. In this running battle, Scots lancers killed the promising Colonel Francis Thornhaugh, who pressed too close at Chorley and was run through the body, thigh and head. At Wigan Moor, in the drenching rain, Cromwell, with 3,000 infantry and 2,500 cavalry, caught up with his opponents. Hamilton promptly ordered a further withdrawal that evening towards Warrington, leaving Middleton behind as a rearguard. In the dark of a chaotic retreat, some of Turner's men became so alarmed by the approach of Middleton's men scurrying back to their lines that they thought they were Cromwell's troops. Turner managed to halt the cavalry, but the panic-stricken infantry refused open their lines for them, and two of them attacked Turner with their pikes, wounding him in the thigh. A furious Turner then ordered the cavalry to charge the Scots pikemen, some of whom broke and fled into nearby houses while others were merely knocked down by the horsemen. Turner, wounded and exhausted, refused to stop for rest, but pressed on to Warrington. Wigan, in the meantime, had suffered the ignominy of being thoroughly ransacked by the withdrawing Scots troops.

As these scuffles sputtered away all through the grimy wet night, Cromwell's worn-out troops were lying in sodden fields close to the enemy. While some rested where they could, Cromwell ordered constant probing against the enemy along the waterlogged and muddy roads. As dawn came they moved off again, and, in a narrow lane outside Winwick, Cromwell caught the Scots once more. This time the mud-spattered and half-starved Scots infantry marshalled their pikes and fought back for many hours, until finally they were pushed back with the help of some locals, who showed Cromwell's men a route around the position. Some of the Scots then retired into Winwick Church, but they soon surrendered.

Three thousand Scots had now fallen. Many had been wounded, or captured, and the remnants of the army retreated once more, this time into Warrington. Cromwell ordered a further advance to that place, and again caught up with them. Hamilton and his remaining cavalry now abandoned the fight and fled towards Chester. The commander-in-chief left behind Baillie, who was at first unaware of their flight. When he finally learnt the news, he was furious at the desertion and loudly 'beseechd any that would to shoot him thorough the head'.[30] Nobody obliged, and eventually he calmed down sufficiently to try to seek terms for his abandoned infantry. Sir James Turner, reluctant to become a prisoner, had his wounds dressed, and then mounted his horse and rode off after Hamilton.

Sensibly, given the state of his shattered troops, Cromwell now gave the Scots terms and sought to take them as prisoners of war. The local people were not so generous, and took their own revenge on the invaders for their plundering and looting on their march. Many Scottish soldiers were now silently murdered in the chaotic scenes that followed. In fact, so bad did this civilian settling of scores become that Cromwell was forced to issue passes for his own men for fear of their ending up the same way. Although Cromwell and his men were so 'harassed and haggled out of this business, that we are not able to doe more than walke an easy pace after them', he now sent Lambert off in pursuit of Callander and Hamilton.[31] The latter overtook them at Uttoxeter, where they were finally caught; many more surrendered, including Hamilton himself, who was now sick and unable to move. Callander and Langdale broke off and managed to escape with some of the force, but at Ashbourne, in Derbyshire, Callander was faced with a mutiny of his remaining troops. Eventually they were all taken prisoner and lodged in Nottingham Castle. So, noted one sour English commentator, the army that 'was expected to fill whole volumes with its exploits ... scarce affords matter enough for one single sheet of paper, except their outrageous villainies be inserted.'[32] Cromwell meanwhile had turned north once more to begin his pursuit of Munro's command, and his march soon brought him north of Berwick and into Scotland.

The three days of Preston were unquestionably Cromwell's greatest victory. We can now begin to measure his generalship for the first time against the customary principles of war. For example, in the principle of the 'selection and maintenance of the aim', Cromwell's unmistakable intention, once he had rapidly marched north to join with Lambert, was clear and simple: seize the initiative and engage in battle. That he was able to do so and, with inferior numbers, gain a local advantage eventually to destroy a numerically superior force in dreadful weather was due at least in part to his ability to maintain the morale and discipline of his army. His faith in himself and their faith in him, and in the cause, meant that he was able to meld this rather small disparate force into what Captain Hodgson called 'a fine smart army, and fit for action'.[33] Cromwell was greatly assisted in his work by the treatment meted out by the Scots to the land through which they were marching, creating conditions of hostility to the invasion by their attitude to the local population. The so-called liberation turned into a conquest. Their intelligence-gathering more or less collapsed as a result, the invaders having alienated so many of the local population by their constant looting and other crimes that neither help nor assistance seems to have been offered. The Scots forces were blind at times, being unaware, for example, of Cromwell's actual position until the eve of battle. His rapid march also meant that Cromwell was able to act positively throughout this campaign, and the war, as most wars are, was really won through continued offensive action.

Cromwell was able to destroy a much larger army by his belligerence and moral superiority. In this instance, the aggressive tactics of the cavalry officer had paid off, although this was not always to be the case. His positioning of the army on the flank of the enemy so as to cut the Scots force in two was also redolent of a general who had now sufficiently matured to be able to think in greater strategic terms. The surprise was his able use of the idea of the strategic concentration of force and good intelligence, at the critical points. This was a result of a transference of battlefield tactics to the wider strategic sphere. As ever, we may also see the usual instinctive eagerness to come to action as quickly as possible. His march north was rapid, it outflanked his lumbering opponents, and he was able to make the critical effort at the right time. Any pre-planning – and this may have been still limited – was adjusted to the circumstances in which he found himself in Lancashire: opportunity, or God's Providence, had delivered the Scots into his hands. Above all, there was good co-operation at all levels in the army. Lambert and his junior officers, as well as the redcoats in the army regiments and the local Lancashire militia, ably supported Cromwell. The Lancashire militia performed with great daring throughout the battle. Hodgson in particular praised them, noting that 'the Lancashire foot were as stout men as were in the world, and as brave firemen. I have often told them, they were as good fighters, and as great plunderers, as ever went to a field.'[34] Discipline and organisation had served the army well. Tactically, the formation that eventually faced Langdale was a result of expediency, but was also reminiscent of Langport. This time it was the infantry that took the brunt of the fighting – which was natural, given the circumstances, and the character of the terrain.

It must be said that, in Hamilton, Cromwell had also found a much inferior opponent who had squandered any real numerical or strategic advantages he may have had early in the campaign. Hamilton was eventually to pay for his failures on the scaffold in 1649. Any advantage or superiority was wasted by poor dispositions, and in the end the Scots were far too widely dispersed to come to each other's aid, even if, as in the case of Langdale's men, they had wished to do so. As we have noted, intelligence-gathering was a total failure. Political problems at home and friction amongst the senior officers meant that the army crumbled alarmingly when faced with Cromwell's aggressive strategy, and its lack of unity caused the expedition's failure. Callander was a disruptive influence, and utterly contemptuous of his commander. Langdale, bitter at the lukewarm support he had received, lived to regret his alliance with the Scots, loudly claiming that he had been abandoned in the face of Cromwell's attack. Hamilton, although he was personally brave, proved to have neither the skill nor the ability to control his generals or his troops. The last word should naturally be left to the victorious Oliver Cromwell, content as usual to give the victory to God: 'Surely Sir, this is nothing but the hand of God, and wherever anything in this world is exalted, or exalts itself, God will pull it down, for this is the day wherein He alone will be exalted.'[35]

Politics in Scotland now became the key to ending this war. Hamilton's catastrophic defeat brought Argyll once more in power. On 22 August 1648 Cromwell and Argyll met at Mordington, where it was agreed that Carlisle and Berwick would remain in English hands and the Engagement would be repudiated. Cromwell then sent some of his troops under Lambert into Edinburgh to support Argyll's party, after which he set off south to resolve the problem of Pontefract (still holding out for the King) and the still more knotty problem of what to do about the real cause of this unnecessary war – Charles Stuart.

THE REVOLUTION: 1648–49

Long before the results of this conflict were known, Parliament had once more decided to treat with the King. The Vote of No Addresses was repealed, and negotiations began again with the King in the Isle of Wight. For their part, many of the Parliamentarians were now seeking some form of settlement before the army came home. Negotiations were opened at Newport, and, as usual, Charles, without much sincerity, strung out his demands for as long as possible. However, the army was tiring of these endless political manoeuvres, and was bitter at the unnecessary bloodshed caused by the war. Fairfax, potentially the most powerful man in the country at this time, was no politician, and indeed was to prove hesitant throughout what followed. Others were not so cautious. The politically conscious rank-and-file were now bubbling over with anger and enthusiasm.

Cromwell, conversely, was suffering one of his periodic fits of irresolution. He took to leisurely campaigning in the north around Pontefract, and he chose to remain there as the political crisis built up; he was in two minds about the King – fired by religious zeal after his victories, but held back by his conservative attitude. It was now left to his son-in-law, the more radical Henry Ireton, to act to resolve the conundrum of politics. Ireton was a motivated, intellectual man, fired by Puritan zeal, but enough of a Machiavellian politician to encourage, wheedle and push the Council of Officers and Fairfax into thoughts of a final military intervention. He got the army to agree to purge the body politic of its corrupt members. First, Parliament, essentially a good institution (thought the military), had to be purged of those malignant elements that were determined to come to terms with the King in spite of the army, its victories and the King's defeat. Then the King – that 'man of blood' – had to be dealt with, this time being punished for his crimes. However, once the military had finally entered civil life, it would prove difficult to remove them, so Ireton was playing a most dangerous game. Ireton's 'Remonstrance of the Army' was now the opening salvo in a political war with the Parliament; it appealed to the sovereignty of the people and also called for the trial of the King, and was influenced by Leveller thought. The next act was to take the King into custody once again and move the troops into London in order to dissolve Parliament itself. The latter was eventually reduced to a purge of the malignant members of that body by the army.

Wednesday 6 December 1648 was the day of the *coup*. Colonel Pride stood at the door of the Commons and arrested those members of Parliament considered dangerous. During the course of the evening, Cromwell finally arrived in London. He had chosen to remain at Pontefract until 28 November, although in touch with Ireton. On his arrival, he commented that 'he had not been acquainted with this design; yet since it was done, he was glad of it, and would endeavour to maintain it.' He had feared using military force to impose a solution, but now Providence had shown the way he was as committed to the act as everyone else. With Parliament and the City under control, the next move was to bring the King to trial, but, once again, Cromwell was hesitant and unadventurous in his views. If there could still be a settlement and compromise with the King, he would have seized it, but this was again undermined by the attitude of the King, as well as that of his more militant soldiers. In the end, Providence, that most important element in his generalship (and indeed in his whole life), carried him forward towards regicide.

Thus it was that on 1 January 1649 an ordinance for setting up a High Court of Justice to try the King was passed by the purged Parliament. On 21 January the King's trial began. Charles made a vigorous defence of his position and the illegality of the act, but an equally vigorous response came from the court. The result was already ordained; Charles Stuart was sentenced to death on 27 January as a 'tyrant, traitor and murderer'. His execution swiftly followed, on 30 January. After this, and in the face of a horrified nation, the process of dismantling the Royal regime continued. The House of Lords was abolished on 6 February, and the monarchy itself went the next day. The journals of the Commons tell the tale:

> 'Resolved, that it hath been found by experience, and this House doth declare, that the office of a King in this nation, and to have the power thereof in any single person, is unnecessary, burdensome and dangerous to the liberty, safety and public interest of the people of this nation, and therefore ought to be abolished.'[36]

A republic had been fashioned, but who was now to defend it against its many enemies?

CHAPTER 8

IRELAND, 1649–1650

'And ye shall compass the city, all ye men of war ...' – *Joshua* 6:3

CONTROVERSY

The Irish war of 1649–50 involves the most contentious campaign in Oliver Cromwell's military career. The controversy revolves as much around the moral dimensions and values imparted into the events themselves, by commentators on both sides of the argument, as around the reality of a very brutal war. Various historians have, on either hand, attempted to excuse, excoriate or otherwise deal with Cromwell's own actions in this campaign; and it must be said that they have seen the affair as a blemish on an otherwise remarkable political and military career. In fact, to some extent at least, what occurred in Ireland in places such as Drogheda and Wexford is as ascribable as much to faulty generalship as to deliberate policy. For the Cromwell of the English Civil wars now brought his soldiering to Ireland, where we find familiar elements of aggressive warfare. Although on this occasion he was the commander-in-chief, he was also subject to influences often out of his control – time, weather, disease, expense and supply. These frictions certainly created intense fears in him of a severe attrition of his forces in a country notorious for the dissolution of armies at the best of times, and a keenness to end this particular conflict as swiftly as possible.

If swift victory at minimal cost were his aim, then the methods used would reflect this. Through no fault of his own, the campaign would bring none of the large-scale battles found in England, but instead Cromwell was caught in a grind of minor skirmishes and sieges, the latter being a form of warfare in which he was undistinguished – and, it might be said, a form of warfare of which he had little real appreciation. More than once, therefore, he overplayed his hand, choosing brutish tactics to resolve immediate problems, whatever the cost in men and civilian casualties. To be fair, in most cases he did attempt to get the garrisons to surrender first.

Controversially, however, Cromwell in Ireland seems to have been engaged by a sense of divine mission. He came over to the country with

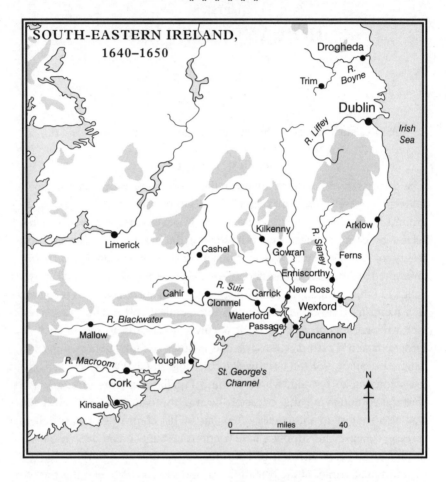

SOUTH-EASTERN IRELAND,
1640–1650

fixed attitudes towards to the situation he would find there. Many of these attitudes, of course, he held in common with other Englishmen and women of his day – an intense hatred of Roman Catholicism as a creed, and of Irish Roman Catholics in particular, as well as a burning desire to avenge the massacres of 1641, events which he, along with countless others, believed had seen many thousands of Protestants cruelly put to death. Ireland, to Cromwell, was also a land brimming with thwarted potential. The farmer's eye saw a fruitful land populated by a strange people, who in his eyes did not deserve to be treated well because of their wasteful lives. Finally his response to the Catholic clergy, who had dared to try to speak for the Irish people in December 1649, provides, in many ways, a summation of his attitude to the 'Irish problem' of his day. It was not pleasant reading, being self-righteous, overbearing and imperialistic in its posture. Why had he come with an army to Irish shores, they asked? The answer was plain:

> 'England hath had experience of the blessing of God in prosecuting just and righteous causes, what ever the cost and hazard be. And if ever men were engaged in a righteous cause in the world, this will be scarce a second to it. We are come to ask an account of the inno-cent blood that hath been shed; and to endeavour to bring them to an account (by the blessing and presence of the Almighty, in whom alone is our hope and strength), which, by appearing in arms, seek to justify the same. We come to break the power of a company of lawless rebels, who having cast off the authority of England, live as enemies to human society; whose principles (the world hath expe-rience of) are, to destroy and subjugate all men not complying with them. We come (by the assistance of God) to hold forth and main-tain the lustre and glory of English liberty in a nation where we have an undoubted right to do it; – where in the people of Ireland (if they listen not to such seducers as you are) may equally participate in all benefits, to use liberty and fortune equally with Englishmen, if they keep out of arms.'[1]

Given such motives, the campaign was bound to be a bloody affair. The Irish war was, perhaps more than most, a cruel one. It was cruel because to some extent it was an ethnic conflict. It had a long history that was already a somewhat bloody exercise in death and destruction. So, in order to understand it, we must briefly give our attention to its historical context.

1641 AND THE WARS BEFORE CROMWELL

From 1603 to 1641, the English Government's attitude to one of its more troubled partners on these islands had been mainly exploitative. In this period, the majority of the population in Ireland was described as Irish or 'mere Irish' and was essentially of Gaelic stock, keen on retaining its remaining tribal bloodlines, language and traditions. The people were also Catholic. From the twelfth century onwards, however, there had been an additional influx of new Anglo-Norman settlers, and by the seventeenth century these families had come to dominate the country's institutions, land and political life. They were the 'Old English'. They, too, were largely Catholic in their religion. For both groups in an era of religious reforma-tion, this was to prove difficult and lead to persecution, rebellion and revolt. Revolt, religious or otherwise, had been commonplace throughout Irish history, but few were very successful for long, and by the seventeenth century the English Government was adopting ever more centralising measures to ensure their control of the country.

One means of doing this was through a 'Plantation' policy, largely, but not exclusively, initiated in the early seventeenth century. In one way this could be seen as a reforming policy, although it was all too obviously governed by the intention of making Ireland, and thus the Irish, into England as far as possible. The tenor of this attitude was to make it clear that English institutions were far superior to anything the native Irish could ever devise, whether in terms of land, society or government. Plantation was one of the main methods by which the Stuart government hoped to resolve the longstanding issue of Ireland. Following the defeat and flight of the Catholic leaders over the period 1607–08, land also became available in Ulster. Most of it could now be given to good solid Protestant stock, whether Scots or English. Settlers could buy the land, colonise it, 'civilise' the natives (or expel them), strengthen Protestant control, and thus make Ireland secure. Moreover – and not incidentally – the country would make a profit for an ever-impecunious Crown. One historian has rightly called this scheme a 'massive exercise in social engineering', and so it was.[2] Yet, like most social engineering ultimately it failed. Certainly social dislocation followed the Plantation, particularly in Ulster, and 'British' tenants came in to replace the native Irish population, but the latter did not just go away, and because of their suffering they naturally grew ever more resentful. Impoverishment, debt and harvest failures added to the problems. Moreover, the next thirty years or so saw a mixed reception for the Government's ever-shifting polices and the King's ministers who carried it out. In particular, the rule of Wentworth, with increased taxation and a policy of 'through', raised much resentment amongst the Old English, new Protestant settlers, as well as the native Irish. This rose to a crescendo in 1641, a crucial date in Irish, in English and in Oliver Cromwell's history.

The plan to seize Dublin Castle, the seat of Royal authority in Ireland, with a rising in Ulster to follow this, was unsuccessful in 1641. If the conspirators were foiled, the serious rising that began in Ulster at the same time spread quickly throughout Ireland, taking with it many of the Plantation strongholds in the north-eastern part of the country. Slaughter on both sides became commonplace. While the savagery was sometimes exaggerated, these acts were bad enough, the stories of atrocity making a 'wonderful impression upon the minds of men' in England.[3] Deep-seated fears of an Irish invasion also emerged, and the rising of 1641 engendered a miserable series of wars in that country in which little quarter was either given or received.

As we have seen, the government of Charles I proved to be powerless to intervene once the Irish situation had entangled England into a further crisis between King and Parliament. This allowed the Catholic insurgents eventually to create a government of their own – a formal confederation, 'an alliance of individuals, bound together in pursuit of common purpose' – located at Kilkenny. Both native Irish and Old English settled some of their differences and lived in an uneasy alliance.[4] They created armies, engaged in European diplomacy, attempted to retain power, fought amongst themselves, and generally tried to influence the outcome of the Civil War both at home and in England, as well occasionally combining to resist outside intervention. The Protestant Plantation settlers struggled to survive in this new world, fighting Catholics, holding on to as many garrisons as possible and seeking help, supplies and men from the King, Parliament or the Scots, as need drove them.

As a result, four armies trudged the land. There was a Scots army under Sir Robert Munro. This force had intervened in Ulster in April 1642. There were also 'British' forces left in Ulster and Munster, loyal, for the most part, to the Parliament. Thirdly, there were the Royalists, who were loyal to the King and looked to James Butler, Marquis of Ormonde as their leader. Ormonde was a Protestant and a leading magnate in Ireland. Following Stafford's departure in 1640, he became the mainstay of royal authority there. While he was deeply loyal to the Stuarts, his honourable attitude all too easily got lost in the mazes of Irish politics. As a military man he proved rather ineffective. Indeed, Cromwell, on seeing his portrait, thought him more 'like a huntsman than anyway a souldier'.[5] Lastly, there were the Confederate armies of Ulster, Leinster and Munster. The Confederate forces certainly possessed enough men and munitions to overcome the other forces, but their almost constant internal squabbling meant that a co-ordinated strategy was difficult to find.

After 1641, following the shock of the rising, the arrival of English and Scots military manpower enabled the British (of whatever political complexion) to make some gains against their Catholic opponents. Led in part by Ormonde, they tried to deal with the wave of the Catholic forces; but the outbreak of war in England soon left the British and Royalists alike cut off from supplies and reinforcements. The English in the south soon moved into garrison warfare, wherever possible holding on to what they had. The Scots army sent into Ulster tried to bring the Confederates to battle, while the latter tried to avoid it where possible. The Catholic cause was fortunately cheered by the return from the continent of Irish veteran soldiers, two of the most prominent generals being Owen Roe O'Neill and Thomas Preston. Preston and O'Neill had both seen service in the Spanish forces and were able enough soldiers, but unfortunately neither man was content to serve under the other, nor, it often seemed, do much to help one another in the wars. However, the creation of the Confederation of Kilkenny in late 1642 finally brought some co-ordination to the Catholic effort. Although the Confederate politicians were soon to break out into factional infighting, the creation of O'Neill's army of Ulster and Preston's army of Leinster at least allowed for some organisation of the troops. Other elements of strategy in the Irish wars were to deny the opponent supply: territory was seized, crops destroyed and towns besieged. Grand strategy was, if not entirely neglected (Dublin always remained a key strategic target), not obviously at the forefront of their minds. By the spring of 1643 Preston had been able to push back Ormonde's garrisons and begin a march on Dublin. Meanwhile O'Neill had also gone on the offensive in Ulster.

In the summer of 1643, with the Confederates beginning to control most of Ireland, Charles I intervened, seeking troops for his stalled campaigns in England. He ordered Ormonde to send as many Irish troops to him as possible, and to engineer a ceasefire with the Catholic confederation. The subsequent negotiations were weighed down mainly by questions over religion. Would the King offer liberty of worship and an officially recognised Catholic church in Ireland to save his crown in England? Ormonde was reluctantly placed in the midst of these negotiations, and the eventual result, in September 1643, was a year's cessation of arms. No real concessions had occurred, but a *de facto* recognition of the Confederates had taken place. The Scots, of course, now allied with the English Parliament through the Solemn League and Covenant at home, were no party to this deal, and they found they had a new opponent in Ormonde.

This truce naturally appalled many Irish Protestants, but it also divided them. It led Lord Inchiquin, for example, who was based in Munster, to declare for Parliament in July 1644. This was as much for his personal feelings of being slighted in his honour as his view of the wider political problems of the country. The Confederates in any case planned to attack the Scots in Ulster, but rivalry between O'Neill and Preston eventually led to the appointment of the Earl of Castlehaven as commander. Still more division followed, and little was really achieved. All sides eventually sent delegates to the King at Oxford in the spring of 1644, hoping for some political determination as to Ireland's fate; Charles, as usual, prevaricated. Troops had already been shifted out of Ireland into Wales, and some left to join Montrose in Scotland. Otherwise, the negotiations dragged on, to varying degrees of optimism, until the King's death in 1649. Charles, in the main, wanted still more Irish troops, especially after the defeat at Marston Moor, but was nervous of paying the religious collateral demanded. The Confederates wanted deeds rather than words.

Meanwhile, the Catholic Confederates were seeking help from abroad. They turned, naturally enough, to the great Catholic powers of the day. Neither France nor Spain could agree to help them; both were too locked into their own rivalries to care. Pope Innocent X in Rome, on the other hand, did intervene. His response was to send a Papal Nuncio to Ireland, and, as a consequence, the Confederates were soon to be caught up over questions of their loyalty to their Church and the apparent need to stay equally loyal to the monarchy. Charles, however, ordered Ormonde to conclude a peace with the Irish.[6] Ormonde, a loyal Royalist and a Protestant, remained ambiguous about the whole idea of making peace, and in 1645 the King's defeat at Naseby intervened. Charles, now even more desperate for men, decided to send a personal envoy (the Welsh Catholic Earl of Glamorgan) to Ireland over Ormonde's head, to get Irish troops by any means he could. In return for toleration, Glamorgan wanted 10,000 men. In spite of this opportunity, the arrival of the Papal Nuncio, Giovanni Batista Rinuccini, in December 1645 was to split the Confederates.

Rinuccini's primary role was to ensure the re-establishment of Ireland as a Catholic country. Glamorgan appeared to offer this very thing, but the agreement soon leaked out. Not only was the London Press outraged: Ormonde had Glamorgan arrested on his return to Dublin on 26 December 1645. Although he was soon released, a second attempt to come to an arrangement also fell through when the ever-distrustful Rinuccini acted to block it. He saw the arrangement for the Catholic Confederation as neither reliable nor suitable. The confused politics in the Confederate capital were not even assisted by O'Neill's victory over the Scots at Benburb on 5 June 1646. While Munro was subdued, the rumblings of war continued. Now, when the Confederate peace faction took up direct negotiations with Ormonde and the Irish Royalists signed a peace agreement, Rinuccini blocked that too, even moving to excommunicate those who joined the 'First Ormonde Peace', as it became known. A *coup* in Kilkenny established a new council, which ordered O'Neill and Preston to advance on Dublin, but the generals' infighting lost them this chance, and, seeing his position as untenable, Ormonde then opened negotiations with the Parliament in London to withdraw from Dublin. The talks were eventually successful in June 1647 (although the New Model army's interventions in London did not make it very clear to whom Ormonde would actually surrender Dublin). In any event, on 7 June 1647 Dublin saw the arrival of Colonel Michael Jones and some 2,000 men, and Ormonde, for the time being, left the scene.

Michael Jones was not new to Ireland: he was Anglo-Irish, the son of the Bishop of Killaloe. He had left Ireland to learn the law at Lincoln's Inn in the late 1630s, but had apparently spent most of his time gambling, 'being rooked by gamesters, and ... acquainted with [an] ... unsanctified crew to his ruine'.[7] Despite this, with news of the Irish rebellion Jones had turned his thoughts to his homeland, returning there and joining the cavalry. He served in the Irish Royalist forces in the early years of the Irish rebellion, and established himself as a man of bravery and a reasonable tactician, although rather too prone to engage in chivalric single combat when given the chance. With the cessation, Jones was one of those sent to speak for the Protestants in Oxford, but by 1643 he had switched sides and then saw distinguished service in the cavalry in the north-west of England and Wales, most notably at the storming of Chester in September 1645 and at Rowton Heath on the 24th of that month. By February 1646 he had become Governor of Chester, before once more being sent to Ireland.

Jones's first test was not long in arriving. Preston moved forward with 6,000 men to attack him in August 1647, but was badly beaten by the agile Parliamentarian at Dungan's Hill (8 August 1647). Jones now proved himself a skilful and aggressive commander, despite his limited resources. He naturally attributed his victory to God, for deep down he was a religious man, but Preston's heavy defeat was one of the two that he would suffer that same year, and it was more likely due to his own incompetence than any divine interest. Only a lack of funds and supplies prevented Jones from really exploiting this victory.

That same summer, Inchiquin had spent his time wrecking the area around Tipperary. On 13 November 1647 he defeated the army of Munster at Knocknanuss, but in the spring of 1648 he once again changed sides and declared for the King, a move much influenced by events in England. Now Inchiquin sought an alliance with the moderate Old English

Confederates. As a result, Rinuccini excommunicated them, convinced it was a plan to bring in Ormonde once more, and both sides took their case to the Pope. However, Owen Roe O'Neill, the military commander in the army of Ulster, threw his hand in with the nuncio. As 1648 ground on, Ormonde returned and made yet another offer of peace, greatly assisted by the news that the King was to be placed on trial for his life. The agreement, or Second Ormonde Peace, finally left the Catholics with a promise of legal recognition for their place in society and their church, but the execution of Charles flung everything into disorder. The Confederate government was dissolved, and twelve 'commissioners of trust' were now established under Ormonde as lord lieutenant. The angry nuncio, foiled in his plans, withdrew from Ireland. Nevertheless, by 1649 many in the new English republican government were looking for a different solution to the Irish problem. Ormonde, in the meantime, began to concentrate his forces and move towards Dublin with the armies of Inchiquin, Preston and Castlehaven. By July 1649, Drogheda, Dundalk, Newry, and Trim had been taken, and plans were being made for the siege of Dublin, where Michael Jones's small garrison awaited them.

RATHMINES: 2 AUGUST 1649

Ormonde's forces were now some 11,000 strong, and by 19 June 1649 he had reached Finglas, north of the present site of Phoenix Park. His main aim was to invest Dublin. In July, Inchiquin joined him. Leaving 2,500 men on the north side of the River Liffey, Ormonde moved the rest of his forces south towards a new camp at Rathmines. On 26 July Jones received new reinforcements. These were the first elements (some 2,000 foot and 600 horse under Colonels Venables and Reynolds) of the army of Oliver Cromwell, waiting on the other side of the Irish Sea. Rumours – apparently deliberately spread – also reached Ormonde that Cromwell's forces were to be sent into Munster, and so he detached Inchiquin and nearly three regiments of horse there to foil any invasion.

Ormonde's remaining troops were a somewhat miscellaneous gathering, and even he had misgivings about some of them. Sir Lewis Dyve later believed that there were 'lurking seeds of discord between the King's and the Nuncio's parties' in the army, and even plans for Owen Roe O'Neill's forces to start a new war if Dublin fell.[8] A council of war also left Ormonde and his officers still uncertain as to what to do next; some were for retiring towards Drogheda and playing a waiting game, but most were for moving from Rathmines altogether. In the event, the decision was to try to seize nearby Rathfarmham Castle, which fell on 28 July. Following this heartening victory, a new plan was now devised to cut off Jones's cavalry and store of cattle from their grazing grounds near the Donnybrook road and work down towards Ringsend, thus also preventing Cromwell from making a landing there if he should come to Dublin. A vital position in this scheme was the partly slighted Baggorath Castle. It was decided to seize and fortify this point and then link it with a new fort to be situated on the edge of the Liffey. The guns would then also cover Dublin Bay.

On 1 August, Major-General Patrick Purcell was sent with an engineer, Mr Welsh, 1,500 foot and 800 pioneers to take and recover Baggorath. He proved remarkably dilatory in his manoeuvres, considering it was only half a mile from the camp, and he spent most of the hours of darkness amongst the damp fields and lanes struggling to reach his target. In the event, Purcell only arrived there in the early hours of the morning, and then, according to some, kept 'such negligent guards, that many judged it was done on purpose.'[9] In the meantime, Castlehaven and Lord Taafe followed up with 2,000 horse and some fusiliers. Ormonde himself rode up to the post at daybreak, having spent the night writing despatches, only to find Purcell's forces just arrived and Jones's forces disposing themselves outside Dublin in the distance. Jones placed his men behind some houses on Lowsy Hill and in the shallow ground between the Royalists and the strand. It seemed necessary to Ormonde to continue the fortification; accordingly, he gave orders to Sir William Vaughan, who had joined Purcell on his rambling march with his horse, and Purcell himself, to place their men to protect the works. Ormonde appeared confident that Jones would soon be forced to attack the works, at which point he showed his almost criminal incompetence as a commander when he not only neglected to place the men himself, but, shortly after giving his orders to Vaughan and Purcell, pleaded lack of sleep and exhaustion and decided that he should take some rest. As he rode back to his tent, he ordered his regiments to stand to arms, but, on reaching his tent at nine o'clock, he promptly went to sleep. Unknown to him, and evidently taking their general at his word that Jones would not attack that day, some of the officers also quitted their posts as soon as he had retired.[10]

In fact the aggressive Jones, a far more able general, almost immediately seized his chance. Initially he had only intended a 'beating up of the enemy's quarters';[11] a general engagement came about mainly on account of his 'extraordinary expedition', and Jones now struck at Ormonde's troops with 4,000 foot and 1,200 horse.[12] The works at the castle were entered, and resistance there soon crumbled. The guards of the camp also fled. Almost simultaneously, the right wing of Vaughan's, Castlehaven's and Taafe's horse was routed, Vaughan's death at the head of his men in the first charge causing the Irish horse to fly leaderless to the rear. Purcell's foot and Gerard's fusiliers were also overrun after a stiff fight. It was now ten o'clock in the morning, and the initiative had completely swung into Jones's favour. Seeking to retain this, he began to move his re-grouped troops towards the centre right, while his reserve was placed holding the Royalist left wing. He also sent some of his forces on towards the Donny-brook, to sweep in to the rear of Ormonde's centre, made up of some of Inchiquin's foot and commanded by Colonel Giffard.

Ormonde had been rudely awakened from his slumbers by gunfire, and he rushed out, half-dressed, to join the centre of his rapidly crumbling line. Attempting to place the men in some sort of order, he soon found that Jones had not only broken the right wing, but sent cavalry in his rear and that two of his regiments had begun to succumb to panic. Gifford's regiment put up a stout fight against Jones's cavalry and even disordered the attackers, but the retreat of the other two regiments meant that they began to slip away or accept quarter. Ormonde, gallantly leaping ditches in his haste to rescue the battle, tried to get to his left wing, but they had also begun to disintegrate. Ormonde, with a number of spent musket balls bouncing off his armour, attempted to rally them by valiantly advancing alone towards the enemy. As he moved forward, the men behind him, seeing their other comrades running, took flight. Ormonde tried once more to rally his men, but it was hopeless and eventually he was forced back. Abandoning the struggle, Ormonde and some of the horse now dashed off towards the fort at Ballysonan, some twelve miles away. As luck would have it, at their approach the governor of this place was convinced that Dublin had fallen, and he quickly surrendered to Ormonde. Sending messages to Lord Dillon, still situated on the north bank of the Liffey, to inform him of the disaster, Ormonde told him to fall back. He then retired to Kilkenny. A week later he was once more at Trim, attempting to rally what was left of his demoralised forces.

In a mere two hours, Jones had changed the situation in Ireland with a notable victory. Naturally, it was 'the Lords doing, and it is marvellous in our eyes.'[13] The Royalist forces had lost about 600 men killed, as well as their guns and substantial supplies. Jones, who exaggerated his opponent's casualties somewhat, took prisoner some 300 officers and 1,500 common soldiers. His own losses, he later noted, were 'little, there being not twenty missing, but many wounded.'[14] One contemporary claimed that 'The Plunder of the Field was so rich, that the Camp was like a fair; Cloth, Silk, and all manner of Clothes to be sold, and at Dublin, the Officers did not know their own Soldiers, they were become so gallant.'[15]

Ormonde was horrified to learn that some of the prisoners were killed shortly after the action ended, and after they had been given quarter – some of them even after they had been brought as prisoners into Dublin.[16] It must be said that Jones, brought up in the hard school of Irish warfare, seems not to have been too scrupulous in this regard, but he could afford these lapses, for, as a contemporary observer pointed out, he was 'both victorious, rich and fortunate, that a man may lawfully say that fortune was his handmaide.'[17] Ormonde, on the other hand, refused to blame himself for the defeat, and instead he held responsible 'Faithlessness, Negligence, Ignorance, or Cowardice of some of the Officers and Souldiers'.[18] He was later annoyed to be thought guilty by some of his critics of making his camp more 'an Inne of Play, Drinking, and Pleasure, rather than a well-ordered Camp of Souldiers', and defended his own abstemious habits, claiming that, when in the field, 'We account recreation no fault, or unusual in well-governed camps.'[19] It must be said that others rose to his defence, and instead blamed his unreliable army. Despite this, Ormonde's tactical mistakes were obvious enough, and he had been entirely outmanoeuvred. Dublin was now cleared of any immediate threats from the enemy. What is more, on 15 August 1649 Oliver Cromwell finally set foot in Ireland.

THE IRISH CAMPAIGN

After Rathmines the door to Ireland swung open, and it now remained to be seen if Cromwell would enter to resolve the condition of the house or simply demolish it. This would be a testing campaign – the second campaign in which Cromwell would have overall control – and, rather than react to an invasion, as in the previous year, he would have to create his own strategy of re-conquest. To give him political and military authority, he was now made Irish commander-in-chief, and was also made Lord Lieutenant. His best military option ran along familiar lines – to try to finish the war as swiftly as possible, and conduct a very aggressive campaign, allowing this potentially valuable resource to fall once more into English hands. He would try to do this with the minimum of expense for the already impoverished English republic, but he also insisted on ample supplies of funds, and worked hard to squeeze as much as possible out of the new government and the City. He insisted on this, for plundering was, he thought, the quickest way for any army to disintegrate. In addition, intrigue and diplomacy were intended to pave the way amongst the various Irish factions. Cromwell was willing to buy the loyalty of many who were now deliberating whether to desert his enemies.

Who was to be his second-in-command was yet another difficulty. Instead of the more likely John Lambert, Cromwell finally recommended Henry Ireton for the post. The latter was politically astute, and able enough, but Lambert was the better soldier, and had previously been considered for command in Ireland. Ireton, however, would defer to Cromwell in military matters. He and Cromwell were also politically and religiously close, and this was partly an exercise of patronage to his son-in-law in a time of uncertainty for his career. Ireton had been regarded by many as the architect of the regicide, which indeed he was, and had suffered the consequences. He had been rejected for the new Council of State, where his previous actions, leading to Pride's Purge and the regicide, had been resented. As a soldier he was dutiful and energetic, but otherwise his military talents were limited.[20] Cromwell also recruited the Irish noble Roger Boyle, Lord Broghill, to his cause. Broghill was living in exile in Somerset at the time, but had previously served in Ireland and had much influence there. Traditionally, Cromwell is said to have recruited him by threatening him with the Tower, accusing him of secretly trying to obtain a commission from the exiled Charles II, the alternative choice being to serve under his command in Ireland. The opportunistic Irish noble either gave into these threats or, more probably, deferred to the rising Cromwell's personal charms. In any event, Broghill became a valuable ally.

Ireland, in Cromwell's opinion, now awaited God's deliverance, if He wished it to occur, and God's servant was determined that His will would be done. Cromwell's sense of divine mission was very strong prior to, and indeed throughout, the campaign. He had written on the day of his embarkation from Milford Haven to his friend Richard Mayor: 'Sir, pray for me, That I may walk worthy of the Lord in all that He hath called me unto.'[21] There would naturally be difficulties – tests laid by God for the unwary in the war. These included disease, the weather and the poor condition of the Irish roads. All of these would cause a wearing away of his forces, hence his insistence on plentiful supplies, money and reinforcements, even before he left England. The actual forces were yet another problem. Cromwell had been offered the command and the Lord Lieutenancy of Ireland on 15 March 1649, and he had pondered for some time as to whether he should take it. When he finally accepted, on 30 March, he was given a command of some 12,000 men. By the time the new force reached the West Country and its embarkation points, there had already been desertions and mutinies enough to contend with.

Recruiting a force for war in Ireland had been fraught with difficulties. The Levellers' influence in the army remained strong, and radical ideas had reached a new pitch following the execution of the King. The troops, still short of pay, were also much disturbed by the prospect of Irish service. Pamphlets sympathetic to the Levellers' views indeed wanted Ireland to be free to find her own way forward: 'What have we to do in Ireland, to fight and murder a people and nation (for indeed they [the grandees] are set upon cruelty and murdering poor people, which is all they glory in) which have done us no harm ... We have waded too far in that crimson stream already of innocent and Christian blood.'[22] Campaigning for the revival of the Council of the Army and petitioning, with new representatives for the men, also seem to have been stirred up by Leveller agitation. The Leveller leaders were subsequently arrested, and a lottery facilitated the selection of the regiments to go ahead on 20 April 1649. Four horse regiments were eventually chosen – Ireton, Scroope, Horton and Lambert – with five troops of Colonel Okey's dragoons, the latter commanded by Major Abbott. Also chosen were four foot regiments, Hewson, Ewer, Deane and Cooke.

Not all the men were happy with God's Providential judgement: they were already troubled with grievances, whether of pay or politics, and the first mutiny began amongst the soldiers of Whalley's regiment on 25 April 1649. Fifteen of the men were consequently court-martialled, but only one died – the young Robert Lockyer, their alleged ringleader. He was shot on 27 April, having first noisily attempted to persuade the firing squad of the iniquity of their action. His mass funeral took place two days later, and was turned into a Leveller political rally. Further agitation now followed, and in the ranks of Scroope's regiment some men refused to move to Bristol until the liberties of England had been secured. This view rapidly spread. In Banbury, a quick-tempered ex-corporal, William Thompson, led the disturbances in Reynolds' regiment. Colonel John Reynolds, soon to be fighting valiantly in Ireland was sent down to bring his men to heel.

Reynolds was the third son of Sir James Reynolds, and had been well educated as a lawyer. He joined the Parliamentary forces at the outbreak of war, and had proved to be a gallant officer. In the New Model, he was made a captain in first Vermuyden's and then Cromwell's regiment of horse. At Bridgwater, he had ably commanded the forlorn hope of horse. Afterwards, he had some relations with the agitators, but he was over-looked in a promotion to major in Cromwell's regiment and so he left. He then commanded a regiment of horse. On 24 October 1648 he was commissioned as a colonel in the cavalry for Irish service. On discovering that his regiment was unsettled, in May 1649 he went down to their quar-ters with three troops of loyal horse and scattered the mutineers. Thompson escaped to Salisbury, where further problems now arose.

In London, Fairfax and Cromwell had already persuaded their troops back to their duty, and were assisted by doling out some of the back pay due to the men. With their men in hand, they then set out to resolve the problems at Salisbury with a mixture of tact and brute force. Some of the mutineers moved off to Marlborough, and then north towards Oxford, hoping to link up with other mutineers. On 14 May they arrived at Burford. It was there that Fairfax and Cromwell caught them unprepared late at night. For the most part, the trapped men immediately surrendered, and courts martial now accounted for some of the rebels. Two cornets, Denne and Thompson (the latter being the brother of William), as well as two corporals, Church and Perkins, were shot outside Burford Church, Perkins shouting his defiance. Having been roughly brought back into line, the remainder of the men were forced to watch their comrades' execution and were now thought sober enough to be pardoned. William Thompson had already escaped with some of his associates, and it was left to Reynolds' men to run him down on 17 May near a wood at Wellborough. Bravely, Thompson refused any thought of quarter and charged his enemy three times, killing one officer and wounding another, before he was finally cut down by a bullet. It seemed as if the mutiny was now over.

Scroope's regiment was disbanded, while Lambert's remained in Eng-land; Reynolds' newly raised regiment and a new cavalry force raised for Cromwell replaced them. Cromwell was now to return to his old double regiment of twelve troops, and this eventually became two regiments. Another six new regiments of infantry were also raised (Venables, Tothill, Huncks, Ireton, Stubber and Phayre). These troops would join Jones's forces of around 7,821 foot and 2,168 horse, thirteen regiments of foot (seven drawn from Ormonde's old army) and two or three of the horse having been sent over in 1647–48. By the time Cromwell arrived, some of these were dispersed into garrisons, and many were at half strength because of desertions and other causes. Six of these infantry regiments were subsequently made into three, and the remainder were dispersed.

Cromwell also took over two regiments of horse, Jones's and Coote's. With the mutinies in the army over in Cromwell's favour, it was now clear that divisions in the enemy camp were still growing daily. The effect of the battle of Rathmines, 'This late great mercy of Ireland',[23] had left Ormonde's forces in real disarray, if not broken altogether. His army would prove difficult not only to reconstitute, but also, given their morale, to hold together in the field.

DUBLIN: AUGUST 1649

As the commander of the Irish expedition sailed out of the harbour, it may be that Cromwell felt that, on this occasion, the Lord was not going to be with them, for, as Hugh Peters noted, Cromwell 'was as seasick as ever I saw a man in my life'. Despite this, the fleet was soon anchored in Ringsend, and the general was greeted with salutes as he disembarked, grateful, no doubt, to be on dry land again. Cromwell evidently felt well enough to give a speech on landing, and again God was invoked for the great work ahead against the 'barbarous and bloodthirsty Irish'. He also claimed that he intended to propagate the 'Gospel of Christ', as well as restore the Irish nation to its 'former happiness and tranquillity'.[24] Sword in one hand and Bible in the other, Oliver Cromwell came not only to wreak vengeance on his enemies, but also to pray over them.

Michael Jones had done his work sufficiently well that the immediate prospects and needs of the expedition could soon be met. Cromwell had a safe haven in Dublin from which to base his activities. On 23 August, the rest of the fleet, laden with Ireton's men, joined them; it had skirted the coast of Munster, but, finding no point of entry, had turned up at Dublin. The preparation and organisation of the 'weather-beaten men and horses' was the next task: the effects of even a short voyage had left men and horses 'so sick at sea that they cannot well march any sooner.'[25] Severe discipline was now to be instilled into the new command. Cromwell was aware of the previous depredations of soldiers in Ireland, and proclaimed that his men at least should refrain from molesting the local people and should always pay for their supplies. To local surprise, they usually did. As in his command in England, plundering was not to be tolerated; indeed, it would be severely punished. Perhaps it was an attempt to win over the hearts and minds, or at least the pockets, of the local populace around Dublin. With this in mind, the constant demand for money and supplies, as well as reinforcements, continued to emanate from the new Lord Lieutenant.

What was to be the army's first target? Logic and strategy dictated that the south-eastern and southern parts of Ireland – the Confederate heartland – and the dubiously held province of Munster were to be Cromwell's real strategic goal. First, however, the northern approaches to Dublin had to be secured, in order to prevent any conjunction of Ormonde's forces with those of Owen Roe O'Neill. With this in mind, the town of Drogheda seemed the most suitable target. Not only was it strategically placed, but intelligence indicated that the enemy was building up his strength there, so a move towards it might well tempt Ormonde into the battle that Cromwell really desired. For, as usual, Cromwell wished to strike at the enemy field force as speedily as possible and crush it. Seizing Drogheda would enable him to do this, and also to control the gateway to the north.

Drogheda, however, was being strengthened day by day, so, if no battle were possible, a siege would be inevitable. The danger here was being stuck before the town walls in poor weather and with inadequate resources. Ireland had always rapidly punished dilatory commanders and subjected their armies to high wastage rates from dysentery and other diseases, and Cromwell sought to avoid this. A swift decision was the order of the day: no long-term siege was planned. Cromwell would use his artillery batteries to breach the walls and launch his men on, it was to be hoped, a not too bloody assault to take the town. The acts proper to seventeenth-century siege warfare were to be foreshortened: the reconnaissance to view the position, circumvallation, saps and parallels, and the use of experienced engineers and gunners to lay the batteries were to be discarded. He would end the affair as hastily as possible, saving his government money, men and material in the long run, by blasting his way into the town.

We may well ask why else he chose these methods, more or less throughout the campaign. On one level, it is very clear that Cromwell did not have the time or patience – nor, it seems, the personality – to engage in full-scale sieges. His old commander Fairfax had been able to temper his aggression and engage in a full-scale siege at Colchester the previous year; but then Fairfax had been brought up in the correct form of early seventeenth-century generalship, although even he was not averse to storming a place if he could. There were also precedents for this. Gustavus Adolphus, as depicted in the *Swedish Intelligencer*, was not one to 'stand entrenching and building redoubts at a mile's distance; but clap down with his army presently, about a cannon shot from it. There he would begin his approaches, get to their walls, batter and storm presently.'[26]

Furthermore – and, perhaps, more significantly – Cromwell needed to take Drogheda, as the first of the targets, in order to teach a moral lesson to the 'barbarous Irish': if he were successful, it would brutally illuminate God's plan for Ireland; and it would show His vengeance for the crimes of 1641, and provide other towns that may be thinking of resistance with much food for thought. The use of terror was a tactic in Cromwell's plan. It even had Biblical precedents, and this was, after all, in his eyes, a 'holy war'. The choice of battery and assault, however, would almost certainly mean that Cromwell, wild in his approaches sometimes, would lose control of his men – and perhaps even of himself once they went in.

We do know that a constant round of prayer was already taking place in Cromwell's mind. On 26 August, sources noted that the Lord's Day was spent in 'publick exercises', while the afternoon was spent in 'Prayer and seeking Councell from God concerning their intended march in the week following.'[27] The general trend of the campaign would soon become apparent. He would trust to God, the siege batteries and the courage of his men to resolve the problems. Of course, Drogheda could always surrender on terms.

DROGHEDA: AUGUST–SEPTEMBER 1649

Today Drogheda (*Droched Atha*, the Bridge of the Ford) is a busy town on the banks of the River Boyne, some 25 miles or so from Dublin. It still occupies a strategic crossing on the river, and acts as a gateway to the north of Ireland. It is cut in two by the Boyne, and in 1649 a wooden drawbridge connected the two halves. The northern half of the town – the English town – had its own wall, created in a rough semi-circle, with seven gates and nineteen towers. The southern half, or Irish town, was a smaller area, again in a rough semi-circle surrounded by a curtain wall some twenty feet high and six feet thick at the base, with a walkway at the top. There were five gates and eleven towers on the southern side of the wall, and to the south-east of the wall there was a deep ravine. The southern section was the strongest part of the fortifications. Located within the boundaries was a stronghold in the shape of Mill Mount, and in the southeast corner stood a large church, St Mary's. Mill Mount was described as 'a high mount, with a Fort upon it, the principal place of strength in the town'. From the top one can still get a very good view of the surrounding country, now mostly built over, and of the town itself as it dips down on both sides towards the river. A visitor in 1635 noted that 'divers fair, neat, well built houses' lay within the town. It was of medieval origin and a 'rich town [whose] … inhabitants [were] more civilised and better apparelled' than many elsewhere; it was also noted that many among the population were 'popishly affected'.[28] The fortifications were outdated by European standards, but had withstood sieges before, although they had not yet faced the artillery Cromwell would bring to them.

Ormonde's strategy was to advance on Dublin by co-ordinating his forces (Montgomery in Ulster, Clanrickard in Connaught and Inchiquin in Munster). Negotiations were also reopened with O'Neill, and these were to continue until 5 September, by which time they were to be too late for Drogheda. The Royalist garrison of the town had not been idle, and the council of war now decided to hold the place, hoping thereby to delay Cromwell sufficiently so that 'Colonel Hunger and Major Sickness' could take effect on his troops. While Cromwell besieged the place, it would also allow the garrison to sally forth on raids and Ormonde to manoeuvre his forces in conjunction with them. Ormonde had already begun to strengthen the garrison with new men and by appointing a new governor, Sir Arthur Aston.

Aston was a one-legged, Roman Catholic, English professional soldier, self-assured and an unfaltering Royalist who had seen plenty of active service in eastern Europe and had even been complimented by Gustavus Adolphus of Sweden for his soldiering. At Edgehill, Aston had been in command of the dragoons and did good service there. Afterwards, he served as Governor of Reading and Oxford and had added to his reputation. He had lost his leg in a riding accident in September 1644 while showing off before some ladies; he had fallen, and the wound had afterwards turned gangrenous. The removal of his leg did not make his testy manner any better for those around him; indeed, the good folk of Oxford had cheered loudly enough when Aston was finally removed from their presence, for he was noted for his uncompromising and forbidding manner with enemy and ally alike. By 1646 he had arrived in Ireland, and in July 1649 he was on Ormonde's council of war. Clarendon later noted his rough nature and his grasping want of money, but otherwise Aston would be stout in defence and an apt choice for the governorship of Drogheda. He was not very popular with the townsfolk, many of whom, including his own mother, were soon to be agitating for the town's surrender. However, Aston, given sufficient supplies, thought the place strong enough to hold for some time.

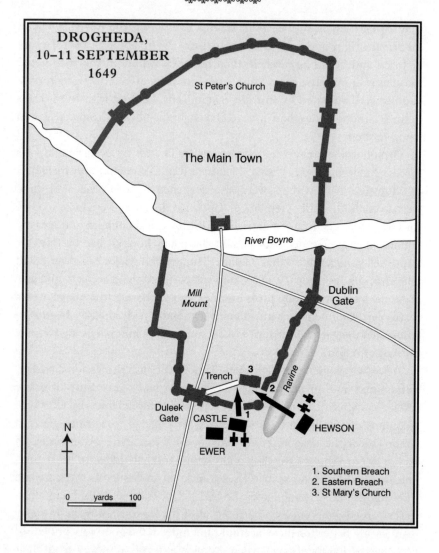

The Council of War agreed, planning to hold Drogheda to deflect Cromwell from any southern advance and to weaken his forces in lengthy siege. Aston thought he was clearly there to

'... tire out, and break the enemy ... by badness of the Weather, Watching, and Hunger; then expose them to be harassed and alarmed by the Lord Lieutenant's Horse, and the Foot that were shortly to be recruited, until the Royalists being reassured and encreased in force, might ... fight them in a pitched Battel.'[29]

Reinforcements could also be fed into the town from the north: any besieging force could ill afford to split its forces by crossing the river and trying to assault the town in two places. Aston's main problem was his lack of supplies. He sent a constant round of letters to Ormonde begging for more shot, ammunition, money and 'belly foode'.[30] Nor was he that sure of his troops, as he noted (in his somewhat idiosyncratic spelling): '... if our soildiers will but doe whot I am shure thay may doe I hope the ennmey will finde sum goode resistance. But yesterday theer ran foure away.'[31] In another letter he noted, 'I pray my horse does not jade it. Thay seemed sumthing out of counternance; it may bee within the walles thay will renue thear curradges.'[32]

The forces now placed in Drogheda were at first an attempt to substitute Protestant cavalry with Old English and Catholic troops. Numbers rose as Ormonde and Aston marshalled their men, and by 30 August some 2,552 (infantry, cavalry and artillery) were in garrison there. Others came in during the siege, finally raising the garrison to 3,000 men. The regiments included those of Wall, Ormonde, Bryne and the Westmeath regiment, Warren's regiment and Dillon's, with various sundry troops. The garrison was consequently a largely mixed force of Old English and New English, both Protestant and Catholic. Amongst the ordinary soldiers were very few native Irish, but most of the troops were loyal in some way to the exiled King and to the maintenance of English interest in the island. What is clear is that they were far from being Cromwell's 'barbarous' Irish.

THE ADVANCE TO DROGHEDA

On 31 August 1649 General Cromwell assembled his troops and marched out of Dublin, with 'trumpets sounding, Drums beating, and Colours flying'.[33] The men were then drawn up about four miles from the city, where various solemn speeches were made to them about the 'great work at hand'. A selected party of horse under Colonel Reynolds was then sent ahead to scout some three miles in front of the army's advance. Regiments were chosen for the expedition – some six of foot and eight of horse, with one of dragoons, about 10–11,000 men in all. The cavalry were well mounted, and the rest, so it was said, were eager for battle. The heavy artillery pieces were to be sent by sea with the supplies. The train of artillery consisted of two cannon of 8 inches, two cannon of 7 inches, two demi-cannon, two twenty-four pounders, three culverins, two demi-culverins and ten sakers, totalling eleven siege-guns and twelve field pieces.[34]

The advance halted that night some six miles from the city, and the next day Reynolds was sent further out towards Drogheda with 1,000 horse. That evening the Redcoats pitched camp at Ballygarth, some twenty miles from Dublin, where some deserters joined them, much to Cromwell's satisfaction. There was some scattered skirmishing on the way, but, in general, the opposition withdrew before the advance, and the march to the walls of Drogheda was an easy one. The walls of the town were finally reached on 2 September 1649. Once there, the troops set up their tents that Cromwell, with considerable foresight, had insisted they carry. Fortunately, the weather was reasonable at this stage, although it is possible that there was already sickness within the ranks. One observer noted that some of the troops were sick with 'the too much use of that, which moderately used, would make them continue much healthier' – that is, drink;[35] not even a man-manager such as Oliver Cromwell could have kept English soldiers from drinking alcohol. The lines were soon laid within a musket shot or two of the southern walls, and Cromwell and his officers then went to view the position. Most of the siege guns were still at sea, and, to make life interesting for the defenders, some small field pieces that had marched with the army now opened up, playing their shots on the walls, while, despite the distance, the defenders returned fire with their muskets.

Scouts cautiously skirted round the fortified town, and some of the horse and foot crossed over to the other bank of the Boyne at a ford further upstream. Some skirmishing took place, for Aston was quite bullish at this point, and he was certainly not content to leave his enemy to his own devices. Frequent sallies were consequently made from the walls, with the intention of disrupting the besiegers' preparations and raising the morale of the besieged. They were bloodily repulsed. One success did occur when a foraging party, after cattle and supplies, was fallen upon and some thirty to forty men were taken prisoner. Aston subsequently declared that 'The enemy receive (since our sallies) alarms very lightly, and our men are mutch incurredged by them.'[36] Round about Drogheda, Inchiquin was also beginning to skirt the countryside, burning and destroying the area so as to make it difficult to gain supply. In spite of this, Cromwell's forces had the advantage because of their access to the sea. Unfortunately, Cromwell could not besiege the whole place, so he decided to set his batteries against the southern walls in order to make a practical breach through which an assault could be launched.

By 9 September the heavy guns had arrived. They were soon placed: one battery was some four hundred yards or so to the east of St Mary's churchyard, the other was positioned to the south of the wall. Cromwell then communicated his intentions to those inside. In his summons, he made it very clear that, if surrender were refused, 'you will have no cause to blame me'. In thus plainly setting out his stall for the enemy, Cromwell had shown the first signs of the attitude that was to persist throughout the campaign and eventually was to go badly wrong. In this case, Aston immediately mocked the English commander's formal opening to the siege, claiming 'That he had received the Charge of the Town too lately into his trust to surrender it so soone upon bare summons only; And that he must give another Account of it.'[37] A sally was immediately sent forth to reenforce his words, but was severely repulsed. Aston had earlier noted the unsuitable nature of the town for sallies, but he had persevered with them, however costly in men and ammunition, in order to disrupt the Cromwellian preparations.[38] He still doubted the morale of some of his men, but noted that "'Tis only the remberance of which I saw before Dublin that make me misdoubte theer performance.'[39] Despite this, and the continuing lack of supply, he was still optimistic of holding out for a long time.

The personal white flag of Cromwell was now lowered, and a blood red flag rose in its place. With this, the bombardment commenced in earnest. By nightfall the two batteries had begun to make significant breaches in the walls. The batteries steadily fired some two to three hundred shots towards the town and also smashed the steeple of St Mary's church to prevent its being used to observe their actions and as a vantage point for enemy snipers. Otherwise the target was 'that part of the town wall next to a church called St Mary's, which was the rather chosen because we did hope that if we did enter and possess that church, we should be better able to keep it against their horse and foot until we could make way for the advance of our horse.'[40] Cromwell seems to have taken little account here of the ravine underneath the walls, over which his men would have to scramble. The south-facing wall was, in any case, positioned rather higher in the terrain and more thickly protected. The implication was that the initial assault was only meant to seize and take the church as a stronghold within the walls, prior to moving on to the next stage. In this, the plan resembles the Bridgwater assault of 1645. The action would have been debated in council of war as was the usual custom, but no account had apparently been taken that the town's defences might collapse very quickly.

The defenders had also recognised St Mary's church as a vital strongpoint and had constructed some defensive trenches between it and the walls to the west and the east. The two batteries located 'for that part of the wall against the east end of the said church, the other against the wall on the south side' enabled them to provide enfilading fire.[41] The round shot soon beat down the 'corner tower' and began to open up reasonably good breaches in the east and south walls, although these were still too high for cavalry to enter. The assault would thus be left to the infantry, and the cavalry would follow them in. This would leave infantrymen vulnerable to any cavalry inside, but it could not be helped. That day Aston wrote his last letter to Ormonde. In it he noted that his soldiers 'say well; pray God doe well. I will asshure your Exlns that there shall be no want in mee, but yor Exlns speedy help is much desred.'[42] As it turned out, Ormonde had little help to give.

In the late afternoon of 11 September, the men of the various regiments began to assemble for the assault. They would generally have been chosen by lot, and armed with faggots, scaling ladders, swords, guns and pikes. One assault would take place on the east of the position over a deep ravine and up to the walls; the other assault was on the south, opposite the corner of the southern wall. Amongst the first regiments chosen were those of Colonel John Hewson, on the eastern side. Colonels Castle and Evers, with their men, were to take the southern breach. The regiments of Venables and Phayre were placed in reserve. Once inside, the infantry regiments would head for the church of St Mary's.

Hewson's regiment seems to have been in the van of the eastern breach. It was an original New Model regiment, its former colonel being John Pickering, who had died of fever in November 1645. The tall, one-eyed John Hewson, who had succeeded him, was a tough veteran soldier of some note. According to some, he had been of lowly origins in civilian life, reputedly having been a cobbler. Nonetheless, Hewson had subsequently served bravely in the armies of Essex and Manchester. He became lieutenant-colonel to Pickering in the New Model in 1644, and had led the forlorn hope in the storming of Bridgwater in 1645. The regiment had then had its fair share of sieges, having also been at the storming of Bristol that same year and suffered considerable losses. Hewson was an independent in religion, favouring the Baptists, and he had also supervised the growing discontents in the regiment after the Civil War had ended. While most of the men neither wanted to disband nor serve in Ireland in 1647, they remained obedient enough. The regiment was involved in the Second Civil War as part of Fairfax's command, and took part in the 'desperate' storm of Maidstone on 1 June 1648. Fairfax noted their 'valour and resolution', and complimented both Hewson and the regiment. Later, Hewson became one of the King's judges in the trial of January 1649 and signed the death warrant of Charles I; indeed, the King's guard had been largely drawn from his regiment.

When fate chose the regiment to serve in Ireland on 30 April 1649, 300 of the men were dismissed, preferring not to go, but the ranks were soon filled. Hewson had his fellow regicide Daniel Axtell as his lieutenant-colonel, and Major John Carter and Captains Atkinson, Jenkins, Brayfield, Samuel Axtell, Graime (or Grimes), Smith and Gale were his officers. Two former agitators also became officers in the regiment – Lieutenant Edward Game (or Garner) and Quartermaster Daniel Hincksman (or Hinchman). A mixture of veterans, new recruits and old soldiers from other bodies now formed the regiment. Some of these men would have been experienced infantry and, for a foot regiment (notoriously less particular in their enthusiasms), they were highly motivated. They would be well aware of what was about to happen: orders would have been seen being given to their officers, who would in turn have quietly informed the men. Signs for the day had also been issued. The words given to the army that day were 'our Lord God', the enemy's word being 'Ormonde'. At Ypres in 1658, the men asked Major-General Morgan if they should 'fall on in order, or go happy-go-lucky'; he chose the latter, and the men took the place. Trust in one's troops was always necessary in such assaults, and testing their bravery could be potentially traumatic for any commander. The army had been noted for its courage in previous assaults in England, and so Cromwell also would have been confidently relying on this courage to take them into the breach. This courage was, of course, a finite capital for any general to draw upon, as we shall see, for, if things went wrong and the men were bloodily repulsed, they could refuse to go back into the breach. Later in the campaign, there was also to be evidence of growing resentment amongst the infantry that the cavalry, better equipped and armoured, as well as better paid, was not taking its fair share of these deadly assaults.

No doubt with many a dry mouth and queasy feelings in the pits of their stomachs, they now waited. Nervous tension and the sweat and stink of the men in their heavy woollen redcoats grew around them as they quietly prepared for the assault. Some men would doubtless have been praying softly to themselves; others would be listening to the very few chaplains, who had joined the expedition, exhorting them to their duty (and equally willing to rebuke them afterwards if they had not carried it out). Lucky the man who would hear Hugh Peters in full flow. More likely, they listened to their fellow soldiers, or to their junior officers, their rousing, Biblical words providing great comfort. Once they were in the breach, their orders would have been clear enough – to kill all the Irish soldiers in sight and enter the town and hold the church. Otherwise, success lay in the hand of God.

As the drums began to roll and the trumpets to bray, the signal for the advance was given. Amidst shouts, the odd psalm and the rattle and clatter of equipment, they moved off. The fighting in the breach was to be tactical work and General Cromwell himself, beyond approving of the choice of the regiments going in, would at first have had little to do but pray, trust in God and act when necessary to push forward the reserves. We know that he was not far off, near the battery watching the assault.

Between four and five in the afternoon, some 700 to 800 men rapidly approached the eastern breach, but they soon met with difficulty and all began to crowd into the small area. There would have been much pushing and shoving as the redcoats went down into the ravine under fire and then up towards the wall. Not surprisingly, they seem to have lost their cohesion, reaching their objective in a somewhat disorderly manner. The defenders, led by Colonel Wall, fired more shots at them, bringing some of the men down. Colonel Castle, on reaching the southern breach with his troops, was shot in the head and later died. Most of Evers' regimental officers also fell. Captain Brandley and his men assaulted a tenalia on the outside of the wall that flanked the breach. Following a short struggle, he got his men into this and slaughtered some forty or fifty defenders. No quarter was given, but neither could any way be found into the town by this outwork.

A hot dispute now broke out at the eastern breach, and the defenders there maintained their posts with great gallantry, even managing to push their opponents back down the slope. Indeed, as the attackers began to stagger back in some disorder, they met the troops of Colonels Venables and Farre coming forward, as well as Cromwell himself. Fired with emotion, he had now decided to join the assault personally, and moved forward on foot to rally his soldiers. He ordered them to turn about and, encouraged by the presence of their commander, they charged into the breaches, once more determined to 'exceed one another in the demonstrations of valour'.[43] In this assault, Cromwell was ablaze with God's vengeance and absolutely fearless. He had led by example in the past, and this time was no exception. The troops gradually began to push back the defenders, some commentators noting that the action took all of fifteen minutes or so. The defenders' senior commander, Colonel Garret Wall, was now killed by a shot in the chest. His men began to waver and then broke. It was said that Colonel Warren was caught up in this mêlée, only to be cut down by a shot that took both his feet off. Lying there, he continued to struggle until he was finally overwhelmed by weight of numbers and killed. Some of the defenders now fled wildly back into the town, retreating over the wooden drawbridge to seek the safety of the northern part of the town, while others retired to the Mill Mount.

In one sweep, the Cromwellian troops now took the wall, church and trenches set up on the left and right of the church. Was quarter offered at this point and then withdrawn? Some said that Jones, now Cromwell's second-in-command, told Cromwell that he now had the 'flower' of Ormonde's army in his hands and changed his commander's mind on the question of quarter. It is more likely that the assault, once successful, moved too quickly even for Cromwell, or anyone else, to hold back the men, even had he wished to do so (and there are good grounds, as we have seen, for suggesting he did not). Vengeance for the events of 1641 was still continuing to play upon his mind days later. His blood would have been up as a result of his actions in the breach. In previous actions such as that at Basing House (the sack of the house) and at Preston (the order to kill the prisoners if Munro came up), there had been hints of what was to happen in Ireland. There are also good grounds for suggesting that some of his officers offered quarter and were then overruled. Ormonde later noted that the cry of 'No quarter' was 'against even the desire of his common soldiers.'[44] Yet, as John Keegan has pointed out, 'Battle for the ordinary soldier is a very small-scale situation, which will throw up its own leaders and will be fought by its own rules – alas, often by its own ethics.'[45] What followed was a prime example of this.

The plan to halt and hold the church seems to have been abandoned as the soldiers pressed on into the town. Mill Mount, 'a place very strong and of difficult access', commanded the southern half of the town. It was a high mound of earth, a motte, with a wooden palisade around the summit on which was also a windmill. A later Martello tower now occupies the position. Aston, his officers and some of their men had taken refuge here. It appears that Daniel Axtell, who went up the mount, promptly shouted some terms of surrender, but they were either refused with 'big words', or accepted and the surrender then ignored. Some Royalist sources claimed that the officers had first been offered quarter and then retired to the top floor of the windmill when the assault began on the mound. In any event, the Redcoats smashed their way in and 200 or so defenders were disarmed, some being summarily butchered. By now Cromwell had certainly ordered 'No quarter', but the officers were not killed straight away.

While rumours that the bodies were mutilated may be so much Royalist propaganda, it does seem that Aston found himself the object of particular wrath. He was caught and, so it was said, beaten to death with his own wooden leg. The soldiers, insane with rage over the death of Colonel Castle, abused his body. Some of them thought he carried gold hidden in the leg and so looted his corpse. Sir Edmund Verney, as well as Colonels Warren, Fleming and Byre, was also killed. According to one account, Verney was captured, but, while walking with Cromwell's entourage three days after the assault, was simply taken aside and knifed. An officer named Boyle was said to have been captured, and, four days later when at dinner, he was called out and shot. Inchiquin maintained that some of the officers were still alive at least twenty-four hours after the assault and were put to death very late on – too late, indeed, for the laws of war. If this were the fate of the officers, then the men would have been treated equally badly. What is clear is that Cromwell did nothing to prevent this butchery. In fact, he later noted that, 'being in the heat of action, I forbade them to spare any that were in arms in the town.' The heads of Aston and his commanders were now cut off and placed on pikes. They were later sent to Dublin. Even Ormonde, now somewhat hardened by Irish warfare, was appalled by the action. He noted that, 'when they had once all in their power, and feared no hurt that could be done them, then the word no quarter went round, and the soldiers were many of them forced against their wills to kill the prisoners.'[46]

As the troops continued to pour in through the breaches and towards the wooden drawbridge, Venables' men, led by his captain-lieutenant, Thomas Chetam, and Ensign Done, used their pikes to prevent the bridge being raised. The redcoats then swarmed over the bridge, slaughtering all in their way. The dead began to litter the streets.[47] Cromwell and most of his officers seem to have had little control over them, and the army now ran amok. The commander's failure here is very notable: he later gave the impression that he almost relished the slaughter through his use of Biblical language, seeing the actions as committed by those of the chosen of God, His saints laying righteous judgement on the heathen. The men themselves, under strict discipline since their arrival in Ireland, were finally let off the leash, and what followed were crimes even within the contemporary laws of war as Royalist soldiers and civilians alike died.

ACTION AT THE NORTHERN END OF DROGHEDA

The action now moved into the northern end of the town. Many of the fleeing Irish soldiery took cover in houses and in some of the notable buildings on the northern side of Drogheda. At least eighty to a hundred men got into the church of St Peter's and fled to the steeple and the roofs. Some also took refuge in the West Gate and in a round tower next to St Sunday's Gate. Directed to yield the steeple, the terrified occupants naturally refused, so Cromwell angrily ordered the place burned to the ground. Hewson at first thought of trying to blow it up, but eventually settled on piling up the seats in the church and setting light to them. Many in the steeple were now burned alive in horrific scenes that Cromwell, in his guise of the flail of the Lord, seems to have relished. As the church burned, some of those who did come out were immediately slain by the enraged soldiery. Night now fell on the town of Drogheda, and under its cover we can only guess at some of the events.[48] The men in the other towers were also summoned but, not surprisingly, they also refused to come out. Guards were placed on the towers, but during the night shots were fired at them and some were killed. After this, anyone who surrendered was roughly treated. The officers were simply knocked on the head – on Cromwell's orders according to some, and in spite of being offered quarter in some cases – and every tenth man was killed. Some surviving soldiers did have their lives spared, but were fated to be shipped off as prisoners to the West Indies. It is clear that some of the officers survived the original assault, and some of these were later put to death, despite being prisoners. One who did survive was the young Cornet Richard Talbot, a man who, under James II, was to become Duke of Tyrconnel and to have his own influence on Irish affairs. He owed his life to Colonel John Reynolds.

The question of civilian casualties in the sack of Drogheda is a further point of disagreement amongst historians. In any such event, large numbers of the non-combatants would naturally suffer, and even Cromwell noted that 'many inhabitants died'.[49] Any Catholic clergy discovered in the town were simply murdered. While the stories of Thomas Wood, later told to his family, may sometimes be taken with a pinch of salt, it may be that at least 1,000 civilians perished in the action. At the least, the killing was still going on two to three days later, and little was being done to prevent it. Hewson, travelling the town in the aftermath of the assault, saw 'at least 3,000 dead bodies in the Forts and streets, whereof there could not be 150 of them of our Army'. His own regiment had lost some 60 men, while most of the officers of Ewer's regiment had fallen. Hugh Peters was even more precise in his tally, claiming that 3,552 were slain, and he noted in his own particular way that he was writing having just come from giving 'thanks in the great church'. In Dublin itself, the 'guns went off for joy' at the news. In London, the ministers were ordered to preach on the great success. *The Kingdome's Weekly Intelligencer* noted that 'the taking of Tredagh ... may be an instruction to the other Garrisons in Ireland to obey hereafter at the first summons.'[50] Thus ended, militarily speaking, the 'flower' of Ormonde's army. The moral implications of Cromwell's actions that day, however, were to rumble on for much longer.

TO WEXFORD AND THE SOUTH

The countryside around Drogheda was soon secured up to twenty miles. Trim and Dundalk fell, and Ormonde and his scattered forces retired from the area with rapidity. Two days after Drogheda fell, Venables was sent north with some of the forces to seize these areas. Cromwell retired south once more with his men, no doubt laden with booty, to Dublin in order to prepare for the next phase of the campaign. This was to bring him into the heartland of Confederate territory. With Drogheda in his hands, Cromwell now had the initiative, and he was not slow in exploiting it. His general strategy was now clear: master the coast and use the Navy for supply and transport, and then, by degrees, enter into the hinterland of the country.[51] His next target was to be the seaport of Wexford.

Meanwhile Ormonde sought to gather his forces and to seek aid from Montgomery and O'Neill. Cromwell prepared the army to march south; he left Hewson behind as Governor of Dublin and moved his army off on 23 September 1649. As his men pushed into the Wicklow Mountains, there was some skirmishing and losses in horses, but the force arrived safely outside Arcklow on 28 September. The place was promptly summoned, and it surrendered the same day. By 29 September the advanced guard had reached Ferns Castle, which rapidly surrendered. Once a garrison was in place, the army then crossed the River Slaney and followed the line of the river south to Enniscorthy. This also fell.

The weather now began to turn wet and stormy, and this added to the sickness already beginning to be seen in the ranks. Still Cromwell pushed on, moving via the right bank of the River Slaney and the villages of Muchwood and Ardeandrigh. The army outriders finally made camp at the north-western corner of the hinterland of Wexford, and the main body of the army entered the camp on 2 October 1649. Scouts were now pushed out, and the next moves were pondered. With rain, wind and dirt getting everywhere, and supplies beginning to run low, the besieging redcoats' camp rapidly became a quagmire. There is little doubt that grumbling in the ranks increased as well. Once more Cromwell had shipped most of his supplies and heavy guns by sea, much as he had done for the siege of Drogheda, but these could not be landed for a number of days, owing the stormy weather. Dysentery had also broken out, and, with his men beginning rapidly to succumb to disease, the forces available to Cromwell – now only about 6,000 men – were being considerably depleted. The enemy also contributed to the difficulties by shooting at the camp where they could and massing some forces about twelve miles away at Ross. The fear grew that the camp might be raided or 'camisadoed'. To prevent this, action was taken by Jones and his men to seize the fort of Rosslare. While the fort was a defensible position, at Jones's approach the garrison immediately withdrew and deserted both it and its guns. Clearly, the opposition was not very effective for they also abandoned a ship nearby. Deane and his ships now came in sight, and, despite stormy weather preventing the landing of stores and guns, they maintained a visible blockade. On 3 October 1649 General Cromwell decided to summon Wexford.

WEXFORD

Wexford lay on the outflow of the River Slaney on a large harbour. The town was situated at the southern end of the harbour, and was connected by ferry to the northern bank. It ran north to south, and was defended by stone walls, bolstered by earth ramparts. A contemporary noted that the 'Wall of the Town is very strong, being rampier'd with earth very thick.'[52] Outside the walls, on the south-eastern corner, lay a castle on higher ground. This, noted one observer, 'stands close by the Works, & commands a great part of the Line.'[53] It also commanded the town, and was an obvious point of decision for any besieging force. On the other hand, Wexford, properly defended at least, could have been a tough proposition for the Cromwellian troops to break into. Given the situation, Cromwell would have neither time nor again the inclination to besiege it fully for very long. His original plan seems to have been to seize it, possibly as winter quarters; certainly, it would provide a secure southerly entry port for recruits from England. Moreover, it was a port plentiful in its time in ships and seamen of a particular kind, for Wexford had a history of piracy and privateering in the Civil Wars. These privateers were of many nations – Flemish, Irish, French and even English – and some had been chased out of Dunkirk in 1646 and had successfully re-established themselves in the town. From here, they did great damage to English shipping, as well as to that of other nations. Its capture would thus remove this nest of pirates from the new Republic's trading interests.

In 1649 there were, however, many divisions in the town between the garrison and the townsfolk. Colonel David Sinnott, the new Governor, wrote to Ormonde thus: 'I find noe resolution in the Townesmen to defend the towne, but to speake truth nakedly I find ... them rather inclined to capitulate and take condicons of the Enemy.'[54] The fear was that failure to capitulate immediately would result in another Drogheda. Ormonde certainly considered burning the town and withdrawing his troops to fall back on Ross, especially as Rosslare Fort was described as 'not finished and the Towne weake'.[55] In the event, it was decided to hold Wexford. Plans to attack Cromwell's camp when he arrived were drawn up, but they had little effect. Lieutenant-General Michael Jones and fifteen troops of horse saw off Ormonde's only approach towards the camp.

In the meantime, Sinnott's chosen tactics were much as Aston's had been – an attempt at Fabian delay, whilst seeking reinforcements from Ormonde. He began negotiations with a townspeople still divided over whether or not to surrender. Outside the walls, Cromwell was now in haste to end the affair, being, it seems, willing to take the town on terms if he could. Eventually, on 9 October, his army, sick of its poor ground, decided to shift, and began to set up its batteries in the vicinity of the south-eastern corner of the town wall, opposite the apparently strong castle that stood there. During this manoeuvre, Ormonde arrived with his forces on the other side of the harbour, and he and Sinnott discussed the situation with the townspeople. Further reinforcements of some 1,500 foot, mostly Catholic, were sent into the town as a result, and Sinnott promptly broke off the negotiations.

By 10 October, Cromwell's batteries were ready, and the next day they began a steady fire, mainly on the castle. The redcoats were quietly drawn up in battle formation awaiting the result of the artillery's action. One of them noted that the 'Ordnance played their parts very handsomely.'[56] Some 100 shot were launched from eight pieces of artillery and two mortars, and by noon the castle walls had begun to crumble in two or three places. A loss of nerve, or the fears of the townsfolk, seems to have led Sinnott to reopen negotiations. Again, Cromwell was willing to listen, but the terms sent out to him were roundly rejected as impertinent. His own terms were drawn up: soldiers and NCOs were to be given quarter, and had leave to go back to their habitations; officers were to be given quarter and made prisoner;

and no violence was to be done to the townsfolk or their property. He gave them one hour to decide. In the interim, and before he had actually sent his terms in, Captain Stafford, the commander of the castle, decided to act on his own behalf and offered to give up his post to the redcoats. This collapse was quickly seized upon, and the Cromwellian troops were soon raising their own flag over the walls of the castle. Seeing guns being turned their way and also seeing the raised flag, the men on the town walls now began to panic. A number began to desert their posts, some of them jumping over the walls to get away, most – 'men, women, Officers, and souldiers' – fleeing into the town for the harbour.[57] Before the town's commissioners had time to return with Cromwell's terms, the redcoats, seeing the tide of fortune turn, did not wait for orders but moved quickly forward, armed with scaling ladders, to assault the town walls. Once they were inside, there was some stiff resistance in places, but the Cromwellians now had the town at their mercy and it took little over an hour to capture it. As they worked their way through to the market place, they met small groups of soldiers and towns-folk and gave them little quarter.

As a policy this time, 'No quarter' was not ordered, but neither was it prevented. Once more Cromwell had little control of his army. For himself, he later wrote that God had spoken through His 'unexpected providence … His righteous justice, brought a just judgment upon them, causing them to become a prey to the soldier, who in their piracies had made preys of so many families, and made with their bloods to answer the cruelties which they had exercised upon the lives of divers poor Protestants.'[58] Many in the population now fled to the boats in the harbour. The vessels were soon overloaded, and some sank in the water; the Cromwellian troops also shot at them, drowning at least 300 people, some of whom were women and children. They received little sympathy from the soldiers, and the action was seen by some of the Cromwellian troops as a suitable retribution for the drowning of Protestants in 1641. Some 1,500–2,000 soldiers, priests and civilians now died in the slaughter as the army sacked the town. These killings seem to have been random acts of violence by the soldiers rather than the execution of deliberate orders, as at Drogheda, although no doubt a prayerful Cromwell stood by while the acts occurred as he had even forgotten how logistically useful the town could have been. Rather, he seems to have given his men two hours to loot the place, and much 'spoyle and havock was made of many rich commodities' as a result.[59] At this point, rather late in the day, 'my Lord caused a proclamation to be published, "That all further violence, and plunder should cease upon perill" of their lives.'[60] Later one observer, rather piously (or hypocritically) noted, 'we would have saved it [the town] but could not; the judgment of the Lord was upon them.'[61] Hugh Peters, walking the streets of Wexford, said: 'I saw the spoyler spoyled, the Drowner drowned, they that have made naked, were themselves made naked, and which was strangest, I saw Hoggs gnaw their flesh, and suck their blood ... their ill gotten goods so scattered into strange and severall hands, that we know not who hath them.'[62] With many houses now bereft of their former residents, both he and Cromwell now thought the place eminently well suited to Plantation setters from England.

On the other side of the harbour, Ormonde and his troops – 1,800 horse and 1,500 foot – watched in horror at the rapid collapse of the town, and they made off in haste. Ormonde yet again put the failure of resistance down to 'the cowardice of the soldiery and treachery of the townsmen and inhabitants'. [63] Now Wexford had fallen as Drogheda had fallen, and Cromwell and his men swung round to march on Ross. It surrendered on terms on 19 October 1649, and, despite the growing sickness in the ranks, the general's brutal campaign of conquest was clearly beginning to take effect. For Cromwell there could be only one reason behind this: 'The Lord shows us great mercy here, indeed He, He only, gave us this strong town of Wexford into our hands.'[64] If so, Cromwell showed his own peculiar mercy by standing aside and letting it happen.

AFTER WEXFORD: THE FIRST PHASE

The campaign following the fall of Wexford became increasingly one of attrition on both sides. Ormonde's forces were now continually on the back foot, hoping, it seems, to delay Cromwell as much as they could, and desperately relying on weather and disease to affect the Cromwellian army sufficiently to allow the campaign to stagnate. In a paper of November 1649, Ormonde noted that Cromwell's 'army decays incredibly and will become very inconsiderable unless he be strongly and timely recruited out of England, and had already been wasted had not townes been poorly given him.'[65] Moreover, Cromwell's tactics were now to lead him into difficulties: the cost of the campaign was increasing, his blunders were to cost many of his men their lives, and he became ever more frustrated as the resistance of the Irish began to stiffen.

New Ross, situated on the River Barrow, would allow the army access into the Munster hinterlands. In addition, it would enable the forces to switch their supply routes into the port and second city of Waterford, if it could be taken. Waterford was a noteworthy city, heavily defended by a double wall with gates and towers. Outside the Westgate lay a citadel on Thomas's Hill with four bastions and guns and moated on three sides. The fort of Duncannon on the eastern bank, and Passage on the western, also guarded the entry into the harbour. A Roman Catholic city, Waterford needed to be taken before the troops marched into Kilkenny. Taking Waterford would also provide an additional point of entry into Munster, where, by courtesy of Lord Broghill, much diplomacy was already under way.[66]

The first move was to try to take Duncannon fort. This was under the command of Captain Roche, a Catholic officer, who bluntly told Ormonde that the fort could not be held. Colonel Edward Wogan, a Welsh soldier who had originally fought for Parliament and then changed sides, was soon sent in as his replacement. Wogan was a much more robust character, though not well liked by the garrison, and when Cromwell summoned the new commander he was brushed off. The siege of Duncannon that followed did not go well for the Cromwellian army, and there it received its first real check. Wogan and his troops made frequent sallies, and finally, on 5 November 1649, the redcoats were forced to withdraw in some disorder, leaving behind them some supplies and two brass cannon.

A bridge of boats being erected at New Ross offered new opportunities. Cromwell and the army now made to cross this in order to outflank Waterford from the north. Inside the city, while the defenders sought to strengthen the place, the citizens were beginning to prove difficult, refusing to accept any troops except those loyal to the Catholic cause. In the interim, Cromwell had fallen ill and was 'crazy in his health', alongside many of his men. Rumours of mutiny and demands from the troops to be placed in winter quarters now began to emerge. However, on 20 November, Reynolds and some of the dragoons were sent to seize Carrick, upstream from Waterford. Reynolds exercised great skill and took the place without losing a single man. This now gave Cromwell another way over the River Suir, and he sought to protect the crossing by placing a garrison there.

On 21 November Cromwell and his main force set out for Carrick to cross over and then move south towards Waterford. A trumpeter was sent out ahead to summon the city, but the ploy did not work. The Mayor, John Lyvett, instead demanded a fifteen-day cease-fire and negotiations with Cromwell, while the latter halted his forces. Lyvett also wrote to Ormonde asking for 300 Ulstermen under Richard Farrell to be sent into the city. By 24 November, when Cromwell reached the city, he found the suburbs burning. This enabled the defenders to take pot shots at the besieging forces. Cromwell based himself at Kilbarry, south of the city, and once again summoned Waterford. Yet again he was rebuffed. He then offered four or five days' cease-fire and safe conduct, so long as no troops were sent into the place during the negotiations. By this time, however, Farrell and his men had already got into the city. One move could be undertaken, and that same day horse and dragoons were sent to try to take Passage Fort in order to control the west side of the harbour. It fell with the promise of quarter, and this enabled the Cromwellians to begin their blockade. In the meantime, the enemy moved to try to cut the army's communications by an attempt on Carrick as Inchiquin and his Munster troops laid siege to the place on both sides and tried to storm it. Reynolds and his regiment beat them off with the assistance of some 200 infantry. Cromwell sent Jones and some more men to relieve them, but the enemy had already dispersed before he arrived.[67]

The weather worsened, and in the heavy rain the Irish roads began to turn to quagmires of mud. This meant that the heavy guns could be brought up to the siege of Waterford only with great difficulty. Disease continued to stalk the army. Cromwell now had some 4,000 infantry, 2,000 horse and 500 dragoons, many of whom were suffering from dysentery and other ailments. On 27 November he ordered a garrison placed between Carrick and Waterford to try to secure his communications. On 28 November another threat was made to Carrick and was seen off, and by 1 December Cromwell had at last decided that enough was enough. He would retreat. So many men had fallen ill that they were all in grave danger. The next day, in the face of rain squalls, the army abandoned its camp and managed to stagger back some fifteen miles. Wogan and Farrell took the opportunity to attack Passage Fort on 13 December, but they were thrown back. Some good news came to Cromwell of the fall of Dungarven to Broghill, but this was more than matched by the loss to the army of Michael Jones. Jones had fallen ill during the retreat, and he died on 10 December 1649. Cromwell's campaign had all too obviously stalled, and the army, with some relief, now sought its winter quarters.[68]

THE SOUTHERN CAMPAIGN RENEWED: THE SECOND PHASE

The second phase of Cromwell's southern campaign was to open early on 29 January 1650. Once more Cromwell was impatient of delay, and was now ever more fearful of his recall, about which rumours were reaching him, before he had settled Ireland. The political situation between England and Scotland was becoming dangerously tense as relations began to break down and war between those parts of the three kingdoms seemed again to be in the offing. Moreover, the Irish weather had suddenly turned favourable, and Cromwell was eager to end a campaign that had begun so well in his eyes but had been brought to a standstill in south-east Ireland. This second phase of the campaign would see the army move from its coastal operations to strike deep inland into the heart of the enemy. After their rest, Cromwell's forces were in relatively good shape, though much less fit and numerous than when he had begun in August 1649. Reinforcements had arrived, and supplies and food had worked wonders, although the troops' pay was still irregular and contributions were now being taken from the country. Together, circumstances enabled them to begin their moves.

For the moment, Ormonde was located at Kilkenny and his forces were scattered thereabouts. The old Confederate headquarters at Kilkenny was to be the main target of the second phase of Cromwell's campaign, although there were still many fortresses and garrisons to eliminate on the way. Cromwell now split his forces into two main columns. Fifteen or sixteen troops of horse and dragoons, as well as 2,000 foot, under Reynolds' command, were to enter Kilkenny county by way of Carrick, with Ireton to follow them with a reserve. The other column was Cromwell's own. He was to take his forces, some twelve troops of horse, two troops of dragoons and 200–300 infantry, to Mallow in order to cross the River Blackwater and move through Tipperary towards Kilkenny. Broghill was to be left in south Munster, while Ingoldsby was to move towards Limerick and protect Cromwell's flank. Cromwell's route was to be marked by a number of bitter and bloody little sieges, as each castle or fort was called upon to surrender and the artillery was brought up to ensure that it did so. This piecemeal siege warfare would eventually isolate Kilkenny from its hinterland garrisons.

Initially, their route took them to Conna, five miles west of Tallow, then to Casteltown Roche. The force eventually crossed the Suir at Rochetown, three miles from Cahir, and then made for Fethard in County Tipperary. Here, arriving late, they were at first ignored by the garrison, who in wild and windy weather preferred a night indoors and did not care to surrender. The next day, seeing the opposition, they changed their minds. The sick were left to be tended, and the army then moved on to Callan. This was also the rendezvous for the other column (Reynolds', Ireton's and Sankey's forces), and a siege was soon begun on the castles and their walls here. Inside were some 1,500 men. Once more the fortifications fell. By 24 February 1650 the army was before Cahir, and this, with Killeanan, six miles north of Clonmel, was next to fall by cannon shot. Other lesser forts in the area were removed piecemeal by army detachments of various sizes.

In the meantime John Hewson had begun a simultaneous advance from Dublin. He headed for a new rendezvous at Gowran with all the troops he could muster, and, having already made some sallies from Dublin, by 24 February he had made his way with some 200 foot and 100 horse, as well as three small guns, over the River Naas and then to Ballyshannon. Another strong garrison surrendered here after cannon had damaged the walls. Hewson's next act was to storm the Monastery of Timloe, adding yet another atrocity to the seemingly endless list of such events. The monks were dragged out and simply put to death, but later, at Castle Derent, Hewson's provisions ran out and he was forced to return to Dublin. Three days later Hewson was on the march again, first towards Kilkea and then to Leighlinbridge. By this stage Cromwell was at Thomas-town, but had ordered a general rendezvous at Gowran some seven miles from Kilkenny. Breaches were soon made in the walls there and the place surrendered, the defenders choosing quarter over obedience to their officers, who were subsequently taken out and shot.

Kilkenny had now become the main target.[69] Cromwell had high hopes of taking the place by *coup de main*, as one of the officers inside had secretly offered to betray the place, but unfortunately he was discovered and swiftly executed. Cromwell therefore decided to retreat to Cashel, his new headquarters, and await his heavy guns. Ormonde had been furiously attempting to strengthen Kilkenny, but the plague was raging in the city streets and daily weakening its defences. To Cromwell, of course, this was God's judgement on the Irish, and he hoped that the disease would soon undermine the garrison. When the advance was finally renewed, the army moved to Gowran and then to a mile outside the city walls. By 23 March Cromwell was before the walls, and he immediately summoned the city. His summons noted God's punishments in the form of the plague on those he saw as rebels, but how he was still willing to offer terms to the defenders. Despite the usual threat and bluster being added as to what would happen if any terms were refused, the defiant garrison turned him down and the siege commenced.

At first the redcoats tried to take Irish town, but they were bloodily driven back. St Patrick's Church was then seized, and ordnance was placed there to play upon the town, but still the inhabitants were defiant. At around 5 or 6 o'clock in the morning of 25 March, the main guns finally opened up on the walls of Kilkenny. They continued firing their shot until noon, when a break was made, but the garrison commander succeeded in erecting works inside the breach and posted his men behind these. Lieutenant-Colonel Axtell was given command of the forlorn hope, with Hewson as his reserve. Evers and 1,000 foot were also sent, to take St Cenice's Church. The assault began in the afternoon. Inside, the citizen soldiers were placed to man the Irishtown, while the more professional garrison held the city walls. Faced with charging redcoats, the townsfolk soon deserted their posts and the soldiers raced in to take possession of the Irishtown. At the breach, however, things went badly wrong. Twice the assault was driven off and numbers of men fell. Hewson was wounded, as was Axtell. The breach was frantically repaired as the anxious garrison held on. Ordered to advance once again into the breach, the now exhausted troops bluntly refused and the day ended in defeat.

Even Cromwell was aware that, this time, his somewhat brusque tactics had failed. He resorted to negotiations once more, and the grim siege continued. On 27 March, Colonel Gifford and eight companies of foot crossed the river to try to seize part of the city. While this operation was successful, a similar attempt to cross St John's Bridge and blow up the gate was badly cut up. Some 40 or 50 men were shot down as they attempted to reach their objective, and work began on setting up a new battery. At this point, both sides wearied of the siege and a parley was agreed. A cessation of hostilities soon followed. At long last, at noon on 28 March, the town and castle surrendered. Ireton had arrived that same day with another 1,500 men, but it was the citizens of Kilkenny rather than Cromwell's army that had created the end to this particular siege. Cromwell's blunt tactics on this occasion had failed – and worse was to come when his forces reached Clonmel.

CLONMEL

Cromwell and the army, still fearful of the plague raging in Kilkenny, did not linger in the vicinity for long, and the army returned to Carrick. Various strongholds were still left in the neighbourhood, and these began to be mopped up. The next significant target, however, would be Clonmel, where Cromwell's forces finally arrived on 27 April.[70] The Spanish veteran Hugh O'Neill, nephew of Owen Roe, had some 1,500 foot and 100 horse, under Major Fennell, to garrison the town. His artillery pieces were few, but most of the troops were reliable and they were well-officered. Clonmel was well protected to the south by the River Suir and a high wall else-where, lying east to west on the river. The fourteenth-century walls ranged from twenty-five to thirty feet high and were five feet thick. Four gates and numerous turrets strengthened the walls and gave access to the town. In the north-west corner lay St Mary's Church, east of which was the longest stretch of wall and the weakest point of the defence to modern artillery. A breach here would enable the attacker to pour into the main body of the town and swing round to open St Mary's Gate. Despite this, the garrison remained defiant behind the walls, although the townsfolk were less enthu-siastic, fearing another Drogheda with themselves as victims. They spent much of the time complaining to Ormonde about the soldiers quartered on them, as well as the levies made of their purses. With Cromwell's approach, however, O'Neill was given a free hand to organise his defence. Ammunition and arms were still in short supply as the Cromwellian troops marched in to camp before the walls. The town seemed to be doomed.

As was now his usual practice, Cromwell immediately summoned the place, this time offering more reasonable terms. They were treated with contempt, and so his artillerymen began to set up their batteries. Reynolds and Sir Theophilus Jones, with 2,500 horse and dragoons, were sent out as a corps of observation to prevent any relief coming into the town. O'Neill now began to show himself to be an aggressive commander, and several sallies were launched against the besiegers as they worked, causing some serious losses. Cromwell is said then to have tried a different strategy. He entered into a dubious bargain with Major Fennell for £500 to open one of the gates on the north side. However, Fennell was betrayed, and on the promise of a pardon he made known the whole plan. This enabled O'Neill to cut up the assault that went in at his leisure. With typhus now beginning to ravage those both within and without the walls, things were becoming desperate. Cromwell sent for Lord Broghill and his men as the bombard-ment of the town continued. The loss of men to the besiegers began to mount up. News came in of events in Scotland and the general's own recall. In his determination to be free of Clonmel, and perhaps be done with Ireland, Cromwell drove himself and his men into hasty decisions. Fortunately, Ormonde's attempt to send relief to the town now proved fruitless, and Lord Roche's troops in County Cork were defeated near Macroom on 10 April by Broghill. Many Irish Royalists also began to capitulate. When Broghill and his men finally turned up at Clonmel, they were roundly cheered.

When a breach was finally made in the wall, it was still obstructed by rubble. Cromwell's strategy would be to make some diversionary attack at the St Mary's end of this wall, before a force went in at the breach. Once inside, the men could swing round to open the St Mary's Gate. Unfortunately for the general, O'Neill had also secretly planned a counter-move: he was setting up an ambush behind the broken walls. The civilian population was now labouring furiously on the construction of a trench and firing positions, hidden out of sight behind the breach. O'Neill then placed some of his guns on either side so as to give enfilading fire.

On 9 May 1650, at eight o'clock in the morning, the assault column of some 3,000 Cromwellian troops began to move forward, keeping up their morale by singing hymns and psalms as they marched. When they reached the breach they began to clamber in, only to find themselves trapped by an unrelenting fire. Pike and musket shot now began to cut them down. As more and more assault troops pushed forwards, the forlorn, still under heavy fire, tried to retire, only to be pushed further inside the breach by troops trying to get into the town. They were increasingly caught by the waiting artillery and by heavy musket fire. Several of the guns used chain-shot against the attackers, and this caused still more carnage as it struck the struggling mass of men. With the dead and wounded beginning to pile up, the survivors finally stumbled back through the breach and fled.

Cromwell, standing nearby, saw his men falling back and was furious. He stormed up and ordered them forward once more. This time, however,

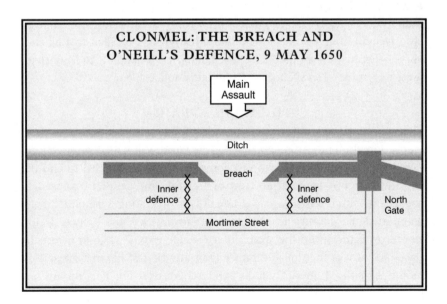

CLONMEL: THE BREACH AND O'NEILL'S DEFENCE, 9 MAY 1650

Main Assault

Ditch

Breach

Inner defence

Inner defence

North Gate

Mortimer Street

the infantry had had enough. Their morale was already low and the losses had been formidable. Neither their general's pleadings, nor his charm, nor the flats of the sergeants' sword blades, could work their effect. The men refused to move. An enraged Cromwell now hastily rode off to order forward a strong party of dismounted cavalry. The heavily armoured troops went bravely into the breach, but yet again a withering fire cut them down, Colonel Culin and many of his officers falling, and Lieutenant-Colonel Langley, trying to mount a wall, lost his hand in the mêlée. The troops continued to pour into the trap and once more were severely punished. Between 2,000 and 2,500 men had now fallen in the breach at Clonmel, and it was said that nearly all the officers in Ireton's regiment fell. Still the town resisted. By now the army was near mutiny, and despite Cromwell's urgings they refused to go forward. An uneasy Cromwell was forced back on shameless bargaining from a bad position.

Inside, however, O'Neill had already used up so much of his ammunition in the assault that his supplies were getting low. That night he decided to withdraw the garrison over the Suir and leave the townsfolk to gain the best terms they could. As negotiations began next day, the shrewd mayor omitted the fact that the garrison had actually withdrawn. A generous set of terms was soon agreed, and then Cromwell discovered that he had been outwitted and that, to his rage, the garrison had already left. While a furious Oliver damned the mayor, he did keep to the terms and contented himself with launching some of his forces after O'Neill's fleeing troops. The retiring Irish now lost some 200 men as a result, but Clonmel was undoubtedly a severe tactical defeat for Cromwell. It was time for him to leave Ireland in any event, for he had already been recalled to England, where other matters awaited. Cromwell departed Ireland on 26 May 1650, never to return.[71] His silence on Clonmel is noticeable.

THE IRISH AFFAIR

The war continued, although Ormonde's inadequacy as a general grew proportionally. The campaign that Oliver Cromwell had now effectively abandoned fell to Henry Ireton to complete. Ireton struggled to end the war as his troops entered the west of Ireland. The conflict managed to stagger on, with the Irish forces gradually disintegrating. Ormonde finally abandoned the country in December 1650 and left for France. Ireton moved on Limerick in the spring of 1651. He took a while to invest the place, and it was then plague rather than any skill of his that assisted in ending the siege. Limerick fell on 27 October 1651. The next month saw the army in Clare. Here Ireton himself fell ill, and he died on 27 November. He was succeeded by the republican Edmund Ludlow. Organised resistance soon collapsed in Ireland, and the resolution of the 'Irish problem' could now begin with a confiscation of property and a transportation of the native Irish.[72]

How, in the end, can we judge Cromwell's actions in Ireland? Militarily, he began with an attempt to establish a moral ascendancy over the mixed bag of disunited Irish armies that faced him. Michael Jones had already done his work sufficiently well at Rathmines that the divided Irish forces were to be little match for the elements of the New Model Army and its logistical system that Cromwell took to Ireland. Cromwell must at first have anticipated a swift series of victories in the field that could transform the Irish situation. There is little doubt that he also planned to use politics and violence to inflict a moral lesson where he could. Yet Drogheda was an appalling atrocity, even by seventeenth-century standards, which in the end seems to have stirred misgivings even in Cromwell himself. We can see this in the plethora of excuses doled out by him afterwards. While historians argue about the numbers killed and the rules of war, the commanding general's actions and his lack of control cannot be excused. His anger and hatred had got the better of him. Wexford was a different case. Here Cromwell controlled his temper and would have taken the town on terms, but his men pre-empted him. That said, he was dilatory in preventing the deaths that occurred, seemingly regarding them as part of God's punishment as a Providential opportunity. The later months of the campaign were to turn into a war of attrition that frustrated Cromwell and cost him numbers of troops and damaged his own health. A brutal struggle developed as he sought to take enemy garrisons one by one. Clonmel, however, was a warning that tactical bullishness – a prominent characteristic in his later warfare – was not in itself enough, as he was to discover in the Scottish war of 1650–51.

CHAPTER 9

THE WAR AGAINST
THE SCOTS, 1650–1651

'There is a noise of war in the camp.' – *Exodus* 32:17

THE CAUSES OF THE SCOTTISH WAR

The defeat of the Duke of Hamilton at Preston in 1648 had restored Argyll and his colleagues to power in Scotland. Naturally enough, they sought revenge against their erstwhile opponents, but looked on with dismay at the political events that were occurring in England. The execution of Charles I, who was, after all, the King of Scotland also, was seen by them as a most reprehensible act, and the recognition of his eldest son as their new King on 23 February 1649 was their opening response to it. Not surprisingly, in the convoluted world of Covenanting politics this recognition had numerous caveats. It was a recognition designed to operate within the idea of the new King taking the covenants and establishing Presbyterianism in England, as well as purging his advisors of malignants. Long negotiations were to result from the demands made of the young King. While Ireland remained a political possibility for Charles II, he tried to keep the Covenanters in play, but, with this route finally cut off by Cromwell's campaigns, and with little help forthcoming from his Continental cousins, he was left with Scotland as the only route by which he might immediately regain the English throne.

There was still, of course, the ever-confident James Graham, Marquis of Montrose, eager to draw his sword once more for the Royalist cause and to take revenge on his enemies in Edinburgh. Charles now encouraged Montrose to invade Scotland while he kept up the negotiations with his opponents. Montrose's defeat and capture, followed shortly afterwards by his execution, left the King with no choice at all. Even before this, Charles had agreed a treaty, and he finally landed in Scotland on 23 June 1650. In so doing, he had betrayed Montrose with that subtle political expediency that was to mark his character throughout his life, but he also became the virtual prisoner of the Covenanters. Charles II was unlike his father. He was tall, dark-featured and intelligent, and these years were to prove formative for the King. Out of them would emerge a somewhat sour and devious character, frequently disguised under the myth of the 'Merry

Monarch'. His hope in going to Scotland in 1650 was either to sway the Covenanters by his presence or to appeal to the wider Scottish nation. Failing either of these, there was still the hope that forces in England would rise and give him a more reliable power base. In fact, extensive political twists and turns, protracted sermonising (on one day he was subjected to 'six sermons preached without intermission'), denunciations of his parents, purges of his servants, hypocrisy, endless lies and humiliations (Charles was 'not allowed so much as to walk abroad on Sundays') – all were heaped on the young King's head. Furthermore, the recognition of Charles II had turned the eyes of the English republicans north, for it was virtually a declaration of war on them, and the idea of pre-emptive conflict was now prominent in their councils. For they knew, as well as Charles, that an invasion of England would at some point inevitably follow the King's appearance in Scotland.[1]

FAIRFAX AND THE WAR

The arrival of Oliver Cromwell from Ireland in May 1650 (to great acclaim: the Press seems to have stifled any qualms about the latter stages of the still unfinished campaign) was part of the next stage of his military career. His presence was soon felt at the Council of State, where he now sat by right. This group debated the Scottish situation with new urgency. It was soon clear, however, that the commander-in-chief, Sir Thomas Fairfax, was having serious doubts about any pre-emptive military strike against the Scots and their King. In order to try to retain some vestiges of unity in the Republic's counsels – and, it seems, to assuage the commander's reservations – solemn fasts and prayers were made, but on 22 June Fairfax finally made it known that he would not lead the invasion force. A delegation was sent to try to persuade the general to accept the command. This consisted of Cromwell, Lambert, Harrison, St John and Bulstrode Whitelocke. There seems little enough reason to doubt Cromwell's sincerity in what followed, even though it was soon obvious to all that Fairfax could not be persuaded and that his lieutenant-general would naturally take over the command. Fairfax's tortuous conscience had seen him through the Second Civil War, regicide and the establishment of this innovative idea of a republic, but it could not be bent to persuade him of the righteousness of an attack on Scotland, even with the possibility of a Scots invasion in the offing. The meeting of 24 June, detailed by Bulstrode Whitlocke, ended at length with Fairfax's flat refusal to lead any such force. Instead, he chose to lay down his command, and the immediate response to him was prompt enough. Oliver Cromwell was at long last given supreme command as captain-general and commander-in-chief of the Republic's forces. Preparations for the invasion of Scotland were already under way, and congratulations came in from all sides for the new Lord General.[2]

PREPARATION FOR THE CAMPAIGN

In reality, the Lord General's army had already begun to rendezvous round York, where Cromwell himself arrived on 29 June 1650. John Lambert was now made his major-general, with the familiar Edward Whalley as commissary-general and Charles Fleetwood as lieutenant-general of horse. Cromwell also took with him George Monck, the former Royalist and professional soldier. Cromwell seems to have admired Monck's expertise and took care to patronise him, whatever his antecedents. By 1650 John Lambert, on the other hand, was also an experienced soldier. As Cromwell had been lucky with his subordinates in 1649 (Jones being a prime example until his untimely death), so he was in 1650–51. Lambert was an asset to him. A far different character from the complicated Oliver, he was a daring, handsome, brave and intelligent soldier. A known quantity from his actions at Preston, in other respects he was unusual. He was a lover of fine art, literature, horticulture and good clothes. With his handsome wife and bold attitude, he was also much beloved by the soldiers. Indeed, later some were to say that Dunbar was as much Lambert's victory as Cromwell's, and it is clear that the latter relied on Lambert for his advice. George Monck was another matter. Solid and reliable, he had served on the Continent and in Ireland and had spent some time in the Tower, writing about the practical side of war and making love to his future wife. Cromwell rated the Devon man's military abilities very highly, although the attempt to give Monck the recently resigned Colonel Bright's regiment as his own backfired when the men refused to have an ex-Royalist as their colonel, instead calling for Lambert. As a result, Cromwell raised a separate regiment for Monck and still took him on the expedition.[3]

Cromwell's new command now mustered around 16,000 men – eight regiments of cavalry and eight of foot. The infantry regiments were his own (under the command of Lt-Col Goffe), Pride's, Bright's, Maulever's, Fairfax's, Coxe's, Daniel's and Monck's. The cavalry regiments were Cromwell's own regiment and those of Lambert, Fleetwood, Whalley, Hacker, Lilburne and Twistleton, and Okey's dragoons. The cavalry came to about 5,415 and the foot 10,249, with a train of around 690 men. In the course of the campaign, Cromwell was to suffer a high rate of attrition, steadily losing something in the region of 4,000–5,000 men through sickness, the wet weather, cold and hunger. Despite this, the logistical elements were well founded, and, as in Ireland, they relied on the coastal routes protected by the Navy.

On the other side of the hill, the numerous Covenanters around Charles II quickly stifled the King's natural optimism. Already the young monarch was being taught many lessons in political life. He was to be no more than a figurehead, and the Scots began to build up their forces under Leven and David Leslie. Leven was in overall command, but virtually redundant, and in reality it was the shrewd David Leslie who was to be the strategist. A soldier who had trained under Gustavus Adolphus, Leslie was to prove to be a prudent opponent – too much so, some might say. He was cautious, but not altogether unskilful in the art of war. He also knew Cromwell, having fought side by side with him at Marston Moor. Unfortunately, Leslie's strategy was eventually to be hamstrung by an interfering Kirk and politicians. This could only go so far, as even the placid Leslie rebelled when the bullish Archibald Johnston of Warriston suggested that 'a sub-committee with general officers and counsel of warre might consult how to dispose of [the] forces … He [Leslie] gave a sharp aunsuer and I as free a reply.'[4] With such dissent in the Scots camp, matters could be difficult, but Leslie was too much the professional and too wise to seek an immediate battle with Cromwell, choosing instead to engage in a skilful war of attrition and to rely on logistics to do the rest. In many senses he had little choice, for his new army was made up of an amalgamation of Kirk-backed officers and raw troops, got together for this particular war. While the base was good material, the officers were subject to frequent purging by the Kirk for their sins and some of the regiments were very raw, being newly raised. As a consequence, Leslie decided to implement a safe policy and pursue a strategy of a defensive war. He sought a strong position to entrench and fortify a line between Edinburgh and the port of Leith that would allow him to cover the capital and to train his men while waiting for the English forces to dissolve. Like his counterparts in Ireland, he hoped that grinding down the enemy would sufficiently weaken the English as to enable him then to seek a decisive blow. To facilitate this, Leslie began to strip the country south of the capital of supplies and men: sheep and cattle were rounded up and driven north, and corn was carried into Edinburgh, so as to make sure that these were inaccessible to the invaders. The propaganda of the pulpit also came into play, being used to educate the local inhabitants about the cruelties of English soldiers. Leslie would have been aware of Cromwell's strategic view – to seek out the enemy army wherever it was and destroy it in battle – and the professional in him will have hoped to use the English general's natural aggressiveness to his own advantage. If Cromwell fell upon the new lines, it would stifle the English advance and frustrate their general still more into hasty action. It also might lose him a large number of men in action, or simply hasten the natural process of attrition in any Early Modern army. Eventually Cromwell would be forced to retreat, and then he might be defeated; and defeat would bring with it the wider rising desired in England itself. Consequently, the war of manoeuvre that followed was to be shadow-boxing in the best European tradition. Leslie would use his interior lines and try to stay one jump ahead of his English counterpart's actions.

CROMWELL'S STRATEGY

Cromwell himself chose the shortest route into Scotland, via Newcastle, through Berwick and northwards along the Scottish coast into the country's heartland, where lay the capital of Edinburgh. It was familiar territory to him, as he had passed that way after Preston in 1648. There would also be a political side to this campaign, with frequent appeals to the religious leaders of the Covenanters; they were, after all, not the Irish, but in his eyes merely deluded. Even so, it is clear that Cromwell was engaging in his usual strategy of seeking an encounter battle, confident that if he could crush Leslie's army he could then win a political victory. The onus was naturally upon him to bring the Scots to battle: it was, after all, his invasion.

While the dashing Lambert had been preparing the army since May, in early July the force moved forward to Newcastle. Intelligence concerning the Scots' activities had also been coming into the scoutmaster George Downing, and it was thought that Leslie would undoubtedly defend his capital and perhaps be forced to give battle outside it. Cromwell, his usual aggressive self again following the late frustrations in Ireland, was in haste to seek him out, as Scots numbers were reputed to be growing daily and their raw recruits were training furiously. Men were eagerly sent forward to scout the border, while their general prepared at Newcastle. In deciding to use the eastern coastal route, Cromwell was also doubtless drawing upon his logistical experiences in Ireland, for once again the decision was taken to supply the army by sea. Fifteen ships had been recruited to undertake the logistical task; eventually 140 were to be used to ship food, ammunition and guns, as well as men, into the Scottish war. In part this was, as he noted to his officers, because there were many 'inconveniencies [to] … meet with in the nation as to the scarcity of provision'.[5] Thus the coastal route was apposite. It would also allow the army to use the sea port of Dunbar as a primary base and supply centre until the major port of Leith could be taken. The logistical aspects of the campaign cannot be really faulted, although they were to fail on occasion. As in the Irish campaign, Cromwell's insistence on effective supply was eventually to pay dividends with the local population, although the soldiers' remuneration was sometimes erratic and this led to frequent desertions.

WAR

By 16–17 July 1650 Cromwell had moved forward to Alnwick, and by 21 July the columns of troops were reaching their forward concentration points at Berwick. The next day (22 July), the army began to cross the border at Mordington. As the beacons flared across the border, once more announcing the arrival of an English army upon Scottish soil, the honour was given to Cromwell's own regiment and that of Pride to be first to across the Tweed. Cromwell had already made a rousing speech to his men, 'declaring the grounds of the present expedition, and something in relation to his coming over from Ireland, and the providence that had designed the command to him'.[6] The soldiers greeted this short and simple speech with 'great acclamations; and … they went on shouting as they entered Scotland.'[7] Some 16,354 confident men now moved into Scotland. July 23–24 saw them halting at Mordington, and on the 25th the army continued its move towards the confined, uneven Cocksburnpath between the Lammermuir Hills and the sea. It was thought that the Scots might try to stop the progress of the army on this narrow shelf of the coast, but, as it turned out, the army was soon quartered in an apparently unoccupied zone, with very few Scots, and even less by way of supply, to be seen.

The maintenance of discipline was now high on Cromwell's agenda, for he was intent on ensuring good relations with any locals who did eventually turn up. He ordered any stragglers from the regiments to be severely punished. In fact, the area proved barren of most of the population. Whitelocke reported that

'… in all their march they saw not one Scotsman under sixty years of age, nor any Scots youth above six years of age … They are all fled from their habitations upon the ministers telling them that the

English would cut the throats of all between sixty and sixteen years old, cut off the right hands of all the youths under sixteen and above six years old, burn the women's breasts with hot irons, and destroy all before them.'[8]

The veteran Captain John Hodgson, once more under Cromwell's command and tramping along the Scottish lanes, claimed that the ministers 'represent us to the people as if we had been monsters of the world'.[9] Leslie had ordered them out of the area, and the advancing army now met only a few women who pleaded for mercy and bemoaned the fact that their men had been ordered to the muster. A few prisoners were eventually taken, but these were soon released on parole. By 26 July the army had reached Dunbar, where they found elements of the English fleet already waiting.

The red-coated English soldiers were not generally impressed with the country they had found so far. One noted how the Scots talked 'religiously, and with a great show of piety … [but] the very next moment … lye, curse and swear'.[10] Moreover, the empty beds they occupied proved lousy (the redcoats mischievously nicknamed the lice 'Covenanters') and the food was also poor; more importantly, the drink 'hath such a filthy tange, and so laxative that it brought the flux', and the women were 'ill favoured and durty'.[11] The weather was also worrying, and, to make all the marching worse, it soon began to rain heavily, dampening the soldiers' spirits still further.

Rumours now reached Cromwell that the Scots were intent on disputing the passage of Haddington on Gladsmoor, but, on reaching it, only small scouting patrols were found. Cromwell then ordered Lambert forward with 1,400 men to press on to the port of Musselburgh, proposing to follow him with the rest of the army and heavy artillery. At Musselburgh the force rested once again and viewed the Scots' position some four miles further on. On 29 July the army advanced in line of battle, Cromwell intent on fixing the Scots forces on the old battlefield of Pinkie and resolving to fight them if he could, but, again, this proved a fruitless move. Four English ships cannonaded Leith and the army managed to seize Arthur's Seat by way of compensation, but the position before which Cromwell now found himself was too strong for a direct assault. It may be that the chaos of Kilkenny and Clonmel earlier in the year was still playing on his mind, and he refused to risk his men on a direct assault, especially as Leslie was waiting for this very thing. Instead, if he could, Cromwell would try to manoeuvre the Scots out of their lines.

Meanwhile Leslie's forces were still in need of some training, and he continued to strengthen his line of entrenchments, now stretching from Holyrood and Abbey Hill in Edinburgh towards Leith. The position was undoubtedly a strong one and could not be immediately outflanked. A frontal assault, on the other hand, would lead to massive casualties, and once more Cromwell was not tempted at this point to put his men to the test. Instead, he grumbled that the Scots 'could not haive a good cause who keeped in trenches and durst not trust God with the decision of it'.[12] In any case, Leslie had his own problems behind his lines (interference by the Kirk and by politicians was increasing daily), making him reluctant to emerge just yet. The Kirkmen were especially unsure about the many heathen bodies in the army, and wanted more godly military men put in their place, although they were overjoyed that they had tweaked the noses of Cromwell and his sectarian officers of the English army, who, they said, had bragged 'they should ... stoppe the blakmouthes (meaning God's servants, whom they call priests and carters by disgrace) from rayling ... [and they] would in their busk coats preach in the pulpits of Edinburgh.'[13]

In the end, some skirmishing between the cavalry was the only action, although the village of Lang Niddery was taken. The weather then intervened and the rains began to come down again.

That night it turned very wet – 'so sore a day and night of rain as I have seen,' noted Cromwell[14] – soaking both men and horses alike, and Cromwell finally decided to pull back to Musselburgh, where food and shelter waited. By 10 or 11 o'clock, the somewhat ragged and damp retreat had begun, with Lambert in command of the rearguard. In this retreat, gaps began to open up in the army's lines. In the confusion, the Scots cavalry saw this, and, riding out from Leith and Cannongate, they moved in to exploit the gaps by attacking the rearguard. The column on the right eventually forced Captain Evanson's troops back, until Cromwell's own regiment came up and drove off the aggressors, but the Scots moved more forces forward, and, after severe fighting, the English rapidly retired. Only when Whalley brought up four troops of his own horse and Lambert's regiment were the enemy finally driven back into their trenches. Fresh bodies of horse emerged from Leith, but they were also seen off, despite some continued disorder in the redcoated ranks. John Lambert, dashing everywhere during the day, was run through the arm by a lance and also wounded in his thigh. His horse was then shot from under him and he was even taken prisoner for a time, but he was soon rescued by Lieutenant Empson and five or six soldiers of Cromwell's regiment. Empson was an officer whom Cromwell later promoted, despite claims that he was 'a better preacher than a fighter or soldier ... Truly I think he that prays and preaches best will fight best ... he is a good man and a good officer; I would we had no worse.'[15]

Colonel Hacker's men eventually saw off the other column of Scots, and by the evening the weary and muddy English forces had reached Musselburgh once more. There they discovered that some 500 Scots had managed to get into the town and had begun to erect barricades. Charles Fleetwood's horse went in and drove them out. While an attack was expected the next day, a strong party of Scots horse (between 800 and 1,500) took advantage of the cover of darkness to assault the English lines and battered the English outposts. They were led by Major-General Montgomery and were made up of many English Cavaliers loyal to the King. Later, some said that their intention had been to capture Cromwell himself. Whatever the truth, they caused considerable damage in the English lines. Lilburne's regiment was initially deceived by their English shouts of a false alarm, and both they, and a unit of Fleetwood's men, were swiftly bowled over. Shouting 'Give no quarter, but kill all', they raced into the English lines, before English cavalry and dragoons came up and routed them, taking some 80 prisoners and killing 50–60 men in the process.[16] Cromwell was not dismayed, but, seeing them driven off, thought the thing 'a sweet beginning of your business, or rather the Lord's'.[17]

If anything, this action made Leslie more cautious than ever, especially as it also led to the further purging of his army by the Kirk. Charles II, who had been at Leith at the time, cheering his troops on, was packed off to Stirling to be out of the way, with Warriston loudly asserting that his presence only meant 'carnal confidence' amongst the troops and that 'God was jealous of His glory, and was lykly, for that night's work ... to undoe us.'[18] The English Press took great pleasure in mocking 'young Tarquin', as they labelled him, as 'wholly passive, led up and down by the nose, as they please to give Orders ... whilst Hee remains a King in Name, Themselves may indeed be the Princes.'[19] With Charles gone, some 4,000 or so 'malignant' cavaliers also were dismissed from the Scots army at a time when the latter could ill afford such actions. Naturally, a hiatus of several days followed as confusion reigned in the Scottish camp.

With bad weather continuing, and the Scots once more 'sulked in their dens', Cromwell turned to debating the issues of the war by letter with the Scots ministers.[20] His 'hearts and minds' campaign proved vain. Moreover, supplies could not be landed at Musselburgh owing to the weather, and so, during the night of 5/6 August, Cromwell decided to retreat once again towards Dunbar. In the numerous prayer meetings that now began at Dunbar, three strategies began to emerge. Dunbar itself held the promise of waiting in leaguer on events, but Cromwell was too impatient a commander to sit kicking his heels and giving over any more of the initiative to Leslie. A second strategy was to force Leslie's lines by direct assault, a course against which the sensible George Monck strongly advised his commander.[21] Thirdly – and still the key to Cromwell's strategy – there was the possibility of forcing a decisive battle. If Leslie could be partially outflanked, he just might be tempted.

Re-supplied, the army once more moved out of Dunbar towards Musselburgh, where they arrived on 12 August. The area was still desolate. A new attempt was now to be made to prod Leslie into coming out from behind his defences. On 13 August, with three days' rations in their knapsacks, Cromwell's men began their march into the Pentland Hills in a feinting manoeuvre that would see them occupy a post south of Braid House that could bring them into Queensferry and even Stirling if they chose. By 17 August all the troops were camped in the hills, and 140 foot and 40 horses put into Stony Hill. From here the army moved south-west again, and the next day Collington House, some three miles south of the city, was taken. One of the Scots forlorn even fired upon Cromwell, who was reconnoitring their position 'in the hope to draw them out'.[22] The musketeer missed, and the general, greatly cheered, hooted in derision at such bad marksmanship.

CORSTORPHINE HILL

In response, Leslie now advanced to Redhall, home of Sir James Hamilton and some three miles from Edinburgh. He then moved to protect the Stirling road at Corstorphine Hill. Eager for battle, Cromwell moved his forces up. Redhall was subjected to a six-hour bombardment on 24 August while the Scots army stood by and watched; Monck's regiment eventually broke in and, shouting 'No quarter', captured the place.[23] Cromwell then recommenced his forward movement, and Leslie slid west to prevent the enemy cutting the route to Stirling. The two vans of the armies clashed near Gogar, and then the English drew up in line of battle, 'divers of our men,' wrote one Englishman, 'having cast away their Basket[s], with their Tents out of a confidence they should fight.'[24] Another noted that 'notwithstanding all their bravadoes the day before [it appeared] they were resolved to give us a faire meeting.'[25]

Leslie's sense of positioning was very strong. He had placed his army behind boggy ground, and the location was almost impossible for cavalry. While the English troops stood in 'battalia' all day long, a cannonade began of two to three hundred shot. Men on both sides were killed or wounded for little purpose. Major Hobson's troop 'was drawne close together to prayer, and just as the Amen was said, their came in a great shot among them, and touched neither Horse nor man.'[26] This touch of the hand of God strengthened their morale, and there was some skirmishing, but, with supplies getting short once more, a frustrated Cromwell was finally forced to retire in the direction of Musselburgh. On the Wednesday morning he began to move off. Leslie, spotting this move to the east, thought it was an attempt to cut him off from Edinburgh and now moved to block Cromwell's passage. Cromwell, fearing he would be outflanked, fired off a few cannon shot and hastened his men on in the wet and windy weather. As they splashed along the muddy lanes, they grumbled that the Scots intended to interpose themselves 'between us & our bread & cheese', but otherwise declined to fight.[27] One soldier thought that 'our lying there upon these cold hills brought sickness upon the souldiers, the flux and other sickness beeing [now] much among' them.[28] Even Captain John Hodgson noted that the soldiers were by now 'a poor, shattered, hungry discouraged army' – a much more despondent company than those who had cheered themselves and their commander across the border some weeks before.[29]

By 28 August, Cromwell was at Blackford Hill, two miles south of the city, with the Scots army watching warily on Calton Hill. Cromwell posted two guns to protect his march and was going to force his way through, but the Scots demurred from the attack once more, despite the fact that the English army was marching across their front towards Musselburgh. Even so, Leslie had yet again outmanoeuvred his old comrade-in-arms, and had still avoided battle in the process: 'unworthy juggling,' one soldier thought it; good generalship, others might have said.[30] The continual grinding down of the troops by an aimless strategy and by the inclement weather was now doing some damage to Cromwell's forces, and fears of a recurrence of the attritional campaign in Ireland began to become observable in some of his officers. If Cromwell did nothing else, however, he tried to see to his men, for which 'hee hath always been much in their hearts'. Naturally, in return, he demanded the strictest of discipline; numerous English soldiers were executed for plundering.[31] The sick and wounded were now to be shipped off to Berwick, but the cold and the illnesses continued to disturb the army's morale. A council of war finally decided on retirement to Dunbar. In his despatches, Cromwell complained of an 'enemy not willing to engage', but Leslie's Fabian tactics had clearly outfoxed him thus far as a general of manoeuvre.

DUNBAR: 31 AUGUST–3 SEPTEMBER 1650

On 31 August the army marched off towards Dunbar, wary of attacks on its rearguard. In due course skirmishes broke out, but these were soon beaten off. The men tramped miserably into Dunbar on 1 September, while Leslie moved his army on to Doon Hill, overlooking their position. The Scots general then moved to block off any further retreat by placing some of his troops in the pass at Cocksburnpath. With the land route to England now cut off, Cromwell was stalled. Dunbar was, of course, accessible by sea, and safe enough from artillery. It had a stream on either side – Beil Water to the west and Brock's Burn, which ran though a steep small glen, to the south-east. A small cottage lay at the bottom of the glen, and the English swiftly occupied this. The land between Dunbar and Haddington was also rough ground. Near the mouth of the Brockburn lay Broxmouth House, where Cromwell had also placed a garrison. Even so, it was clear that he was in a very difficult position – almost as difficult as the one Essex had experienced at Lostwithiel. One commentator noted that 'they boasted that wee were in Essex his pound ... [and] they were resolved to drive us into the Sea, and drowne us.'[32] Moreover, both Cromwell and his men knew that any reinforcements sent up from Newcastle would have to fight their way through, and, even if he had ships enough to take some of his men off by sea, the others would have to cut their way out. Unless Leslie now sought battle, their surrender, or a prolonged and arduous siege, was entirely probable.

There was only one way that Leslie could attack, if he came down from Doon Hill: he would have to seek battle on the plain to the south-east of the town. The fear of an immediate attack had led Cromwell to distribute his forces outside Dunbar, where they now stood in the increasingly bad weather. The flux was unmistakable amongst them, and the bedraggled redcoats were cold, tired and hungry. As the stormy weather drew in, however, it rained on both sides alike, and the Scots, stood-to on Doon Hill, were rather more exposed to this onslaught of cold and wet. Despite this, Leslie had no real need to give battle, for he held a number of good cards in his hands and only had to wait.

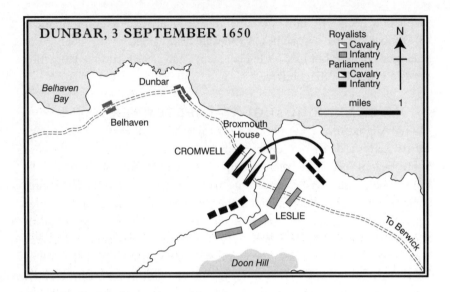

On Monday 2 September the English outposts saw movement on Doon Hill through the drizzle. Leslie, his men suffering from the weather, had also to put up with advice from the committee and Kirkmen present. They had not only merrily continued their purges of his forces, but were now complaining about the general's dilatoriness in destroying the heathen English. With a weariness of lying in fields, they insisted that Leslie remove the army down the hill. As a result, Leslie began to shift some cavalry towards the burn and then to his right, other troops following as the rest of the Scots army moved down, seeking in the process shelter and gentler ground. They were now located at the foot of the hill, and on its lower slopes. Troops were also sent to cover the road to Berwick, with the baggage train placed behind the infantry in the centre. Two troops of Scots lancer cavalry had already clashed with the small English outpost at the bottom of Brock's Glen. Fleetwood and Pride had sent out twenty-four foot and six cavalrymen to hold this position on the Berwick side of the burn. At about four or five o'clock a reconnaissance had led to a sharp fight. The six English horsemen beat a hasty retreat, and lancers mauled the infantry. Three infantrymen were killed and three were captured. One of the prisoners, a one-armed veteran, was dragged before the dour Leslie himself. 'How will you fight when you have shipped half your men and all of your great guns?' the general grimly asked. 'Sir,' replied the redcoat, 'if you please to draw your army to the foot of the hill you shall find both men and great guns also.' For his boldness, the soldier was released, and he went back to the lines; no doubt grumbling at the perversity of generals, he tried Cromwell, who heard his story, admired his pluck and gave him two gold pieces as a reward.

For a time, Leslie still believed that Cromwell was shipping his guns and foot out through Dunbar, although the movement that continued in the afternoon could equally have reassured Cromwell. By four o'clock Leslie had moved the rest of his forces down the hill, the horse moving from the left to the right wing as the centre went on either side of the road to Berwick. The horse on the right could pass the burn if necessary. The English forces, to counter this, swung over to their left and stood to arms near the burn, ready to repel any assault. However, as the day had worn on, Cromwell had been watching the enemy's movements, and the crowding of the Scots on the narrow ground of their left wing. If their right wing were assaulted in the flank, then their left and centre, because of the ground, would have great difficulty in helping them: they 'would be all in confusion, in regard they had not great ground to traverse their regiments between the mountain and the clough [sic] … and the enemy could not wheel about … but must put themselves into disorder.'[33] Artillery could also play on the left wing, to pin them to their ground. In his despatch, Cromwell noted that 'we were in the Mount, and in the Mount the Lord would be seen; and … He would find out a way of deliverance and salvation for us.'[34] However, after a prayer meeting, Cromwell, as he later said, 'felt such an enlargement of heart … and such quiet upon it, that he bade all about him take heart, for God had certainly heard them, and would appear for them.' Walking in the gardens of Broxmouth House, he watched the Scots' movements through a perspective glass and called over John Lambert and 'told him I thought it did give us an opportunity and advantage to attempt upon the enemy, to which he immediately replied, that he had thought to have said the same thing to me.' Others claimed that the general called out, 'God is delivering them into our hands, they are coming down to us.'[35] It now seemed to both men that the Lord had put the idea into each of their hearts, and their resolution was confirmed when George Monck, joining the party, concurred.

That night a council of war was called in Dunbar to persuade the army's colonels of the plan. Some were openly for shipping as many men as possible out through the harbour and letting the cavalry force their way out, but Lambert, speaking for the Lord General, persuaded them that attack was now the best policy and that the Scots' new position could be exploited. Moreover, there was 'no time to ship the foot, for the day would be upon us, and we should lose all our carriages.'[36] 'A drakie nycht full of wind and weit' kept the Scots' heads down as the plan began to unfold. After a couple of false alarms in the wet, many of the Scots officers gave up the night as a bad job and ran for shelter. Some of the horse were also unsaddled. The Scots army began to settle down for the night, and, in order to conserve match, many of the musketeers were ordered to extinguish it; only two matches per company were to be maintained. The bedraggled infantry now huddled under what little shelter they could find as the night wore on.

In the meantime, screened by the foul weather, the English army was on the move. Cromwell, riding about by torchlight on a little Scottish nag, was seen biting his lip until the blood ran, revealing his inner tension. As he moved through his troops, he spoke quietly to his men, encouraging them and attempting to get them quickly into order. Others who saw him later that morning noted that he was 'carried on as with a divine impulse. He did laugh so excessively as if he had been drunk, and his eyes sparkled with spirits.'[37] John Lambert also moved about the army. He was charged with arranging the battle plan, and in the darkness he, Fleetwood and Whalley were to lead six regiments of horse, and Monck a foot brigade of three and a half regiments, in the van of the attack over the burn against the Scots' right wing. Behind them would follow Pride's and Overton's brigades. Cromwell's own regiment and Okey's dragoons were to bring up the rear, guarding the guns to be turned on the Scots' left wing, now hemmed in between the burn and the slope of Doon Hill. The attack was due to go in shortly before sunrise, but the preparations delayed this. John Hodgson, marching with his infantry, stood aside in the damp to hear a young cornet of cavalry preach and pray, and was so inspired by it that he quickly returned to his cold and hungry men and did likewise. There was a spirit of 'so much God in it, as I was satisfied deliverance was at hand.'[38] Stirrings had already begun amongst the Scots, and a trumpet was sounding the stand-to, but at 4 o'clock the signals were finally given and, with the battle-cry 'The Lord of Hosts' in their mouths, the cavalrymen began to splash across the burn below Broxmouth House.

Hurriedly crossing the burn, they soon struck the Scots outposts. These were driven in, and the troops then hit the Scots' right wing. On their right, the English artillery opened up and now the infantry followed the cavalry over the burn to support them. A 'hot dispute' developed between the horse and the English cavalry, who found themselves beginning to be driven back. Monck's infantry were sent in as support, but they also were temporarily repulsed. Under his own direction, Cromwell now sought comfort in a familiar outflanking tactic by ordering his own regiment, as well as Pride and his brigade, to join the fray, but moved them round to the left flank 'to take more ground, to be clear of all bodies' and began 'push at pike and butt end of the musket'.[39] Lambert and Monck took the time given to them to reorganize, and once more they charged forward. Another charge by the English cavalry cut through the Scots infantry and finally made them waver. Then they suddenly broke. Observing this, and the rising of the sun, Hodgson was close by when he heard Cromwell say, 'Now let God arise, and his enemies be scattered.'[40] The Scots horse began to panic, and they fled, many of them riding over their own infantry in order to get clear. Cromwell's loud voice was heard shouting, 'I profess they run!'[41] The now revealed flank of the rest of the Scots infantry in the centre meant that they were unable to deploy properly, and they were next to go. In their confusion, hemmed in and struggling, they smashed into the left wing of Scots army. The English now harried the remaining Scots to 'keep them from bodying; and so the foot threw down their arms and fled.'[42] The Scots army began to disintegrate. Some men died where they stood, cut down by English cavalry sword, pike or musket shot; others fled the field. By this stage the English forces were also somewhat in disorder, so Cromwell, with great presence of mind, halted his cavalry and began loudly to intone Psalm 117 to steady their nerves, as they were re-formed:

'O Praise the LORD, all ye nations; praise him, all ye people.
'For his merciful kindness is great toward us: and the truth of the
    LORD endureth for ever. Praise ye the LORD.'

The horse were then were unleashed in a frenzied pursuit that took them up to Edinburgh.

By nine o'clock it was all over. Leslie had managed to break clear, and he fled into Edinburgh with about 4,000 men. Some 400 of his men were killed on the field and 10,000 made prisoner. The battle had lasted about three hours, and, against all the odds, Cromwell had won his victory. He was more than clear from whence the glory came:

'It is easy to say, the Lord hath done this. It would do you good to see and hear our poor foot go up and down making their boast of God … We that serve you beg you not to own us, but God alone; we pray you own His people more and more, for they are the char-iots and horsemen of Israel.'[43]

STRATEGIC DEADLOCK

There was, of course, much lamenting on the Scots side at Dunbar, but the war was not yet over. Cromwell immediately called for reinforcements since there was still sickness in the ranks of the army, and he sent many of his prisoners south. Lambert and some of his troops were speedily pushed forward to Edinburgh and Leith, and both places surrendered. Cromwell arrived in Edinburgh on 7 September, hoping that the Scots political factions would now disintegrate and that he could exploit the situation. In fact, his subsequent delays allowed the idea of Scottish patriotism, focused around the King, to begin to come into play, although there were still major problems. Parts of the Scots forces were beginning to reassemble at Stirling. Once there, David Leslie found himself blamed for the defeat and was about to resign; public 'invictives' against him were resounding from every pulpit, 'but finding no man tolerablie able to supply his place, and the greatest part of the remaining officers of horse and foot peremptor to lay downe, if he continued not', he was retained.[44] While Leslie's political enemies continued to snipe at him, the Kirk had now lost some of its political control and there were splits in the Scottish forces. The King and the Cavaliers now hoped that they could weld an army together, but the remaining extreme Covenanters were still reluctant to concede control to the King. It was even rumoured that Charles himself had rejoiced at the news of the defeat of Dunbar, given that it raised his own chances to rid him of the Covenanters.

The Scots position was still a strong one around Stirling, and the Lord General now left some men behind to besiege Edinburgh castle, while on 14 September he pushed his forces into West Lothian. Despite the fact that many of the troops now facing him were raw and untrained, Cromwell was to stay his hand before Stirling, still hoping, for political reasons, to come to terms. The politician was now distracting the soldier from his goal, and this hesitation at the council table and in the field was to extend the campaign. Logistically, he may also have been stretched, and the weather, along with the roads, remained poor: rain, wind and mud all hampered operations. He decided to take Linlithgow, within reach of Edinburgh and still close to the Firth of Forth and his shipping. By 17 September he was nearing Stirling. Here, in bad weather, he hesitated yet again. Having been burnt in Ireland, it seems that Cromwell was still reluctant to take a similar action in Scotland and lose the political advantage Dunbar had given by storming the place and failing. Five thousand men now occupied Stirling, and the walls were formidable. However, Cromwell's artillery was inadequate (the two heaviest pieces having had to be sent back, owing to the condition of the roads) and the council of war on 18 September finally decided against an assault. To be more precise, it was decided to contain and hold southern Scotland before the winter came and closed down the campaign completely. On 19 September the army retired. Linlithgow was fortified and occupied, and Cromwell returned to Edinburgh, where the garrison still held out in the castle. While Cromwell busied himself with plans for a renewed campaign, he tried once more to win over Scottish hearts and minds and dabble in Scottish politics.

His other objective clearly had to be Fife, on the other side of the Forth, from where Leslie was receiving his supplies. The natural route to this lay through Stirling, so that was of little use. Boats were therefore commandeered on 27 September and ordered to Leith, and men were embarked before the plan was abandoned, the reason perhaps being the fear that Leslie would attack when they were too distant to defend Edinburgh; furthermore, Edinburgh Castle was of course still holding out. While the reinforced army was maintained under strict discipline, and while some of the troops were occupied with mining and sapping Edinburgh Castle, others were now distributed around the countryside. Cromwell once more turned to politics to try to resolve the war, by addressing various letters to the Scottish Estates and others in order to spread dissension amongst them.

In the enemy camp, the extreme Covenanters, led by Warriston, had now refused to join with the others. David Leslie's position was still a difficult one. He wanted the former Engager officers back in the army, and he had resigned and then rescinded his resignation numerous times in the tortuous politics of the day. The Covenanters were soon beginning to gather a Covenanting army around Glasgow, led by Colonels Strachan and Kerr. Strachan had refused to assist Leslie, and Leslie was more than glad to see him go. The northern Highlanders were also gathering to support the King. The Committee of Estates was attempting to conciliate or alienate both sides, and Charles II himself was trying to unite Engagers and Royalists (distrusting Argyle, who was now barely clinging to power). He was also making demands to be included in debates with all parties. Mistrust was rife, strengthened by Charles II's attempt to escape the clutches of his erstwhile allies after an abortive *coup* was bungled. Even his crowning at Scone on 1 January 1651 merely confused the issue. Charles's strategy had to remain defensive: he needed to unite the nation and Engagers, Royalists as well as moderate Covenanters, in order to raise a reliable army to invade England, and this was proving difficult.

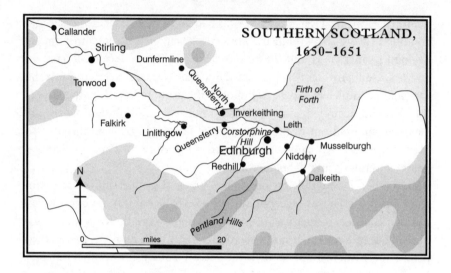

In snow and ice, Cromwell moved towards Glasgow on 11 October with 9,000 men in a show of force meant to exploit the political divisions in the Scots' camp. Negotiation failed, and, while he was not willing to attack the Covenanters who had encouraged his presence in the area, he just as quickly left once more for Edinburgh, on 14 October. He did discover that the Covenanters in the west were unwilling to help Charles II and would remain neutral, an attitude which raised the dislike of both Cromwell and the Estates. The latter eventually ordered some of the army against the Western forces, only to find that Cromwell had already marched against them. Yet again Cromwell hesitated, only to be handed a victory by the more energetic Lambert. Kerr and Strachan were taken prisoner, and Scotland south of the Clyde and Forth was now in English hands, albeit with a few problems around the border with moss-troopers. Edinburgh Castle finally fell on 24 December 1650.

Charles II, now desperate, was willing to submit to any ordeal to gain some form of power. In fact, the situation began to change for the King. A Parliament began the raising of further troops, and, as Argyll's influence waned, the King's began to grow. Charles was finally crowned in January 1651, and the repeal of the Act of Classes that month at long last left him to fill his army in June 1651 with those men he so desired, mostly free of qualification – although the military initiative still lay with Cromwell.

Cromwell, who had attempted to re-launch a campaign in the terrible weather of February, had by this point fallen seriously ill, hampering subsequent operations. He was to remain sick until June 1651, and only with the recovery of his health was the army able to be made ready for the new campaign. In England a Royalist plot had failed, and June finally brought the Scots out towards Torwood, where they stood in a defensive position. The next two weeks were spent in trying to engage them in battle, but once more the plan failed. With Leslie advising, Charles managed his forces well, and a fruitless war of manoeuvre around Falkirk was the result. Cromwell probed and sought a battle, and the Scots took to pounding his lines, but they refused his invitation to fight. Skirmishes followed, and the King was seen scurrying about, evidently at some risk to his person. Intelligence came to the general from the enemy camp, where his spies had been operating, that the Scots would not move. A council of war followed, and it was decided to withdraw. It may be that Cromwell yet again hoped to draw out the Scots after him, but they once more demurred. The army marched towards Linlithgow, and on 5 July it moved south again towards Glasgow. Cromwell seems to have been at a loss after 'waiting upon the Lord, and not knowing what course to take, for indeed we know nothing but what God pleaseth to teach us of His great mercy'.[45]

Yet he had fixed the main Scots army at Stirling and Torwood. Surely this could be exploited? Cromwell's next strategy was to think of moving west in order to try to outflank the forces facing him. A party was sent out to reconnoitre the route, but the idea was eventually rejected and the army retired towards Edinburgh on 12 July. As yet, Cromwell was unwilling to uncover the route into England. Scots patrols were now ranging far and wide, however, and one of them fired on the Lord General as he and Lambert were making their way back to camp. In revenge, Callander House, a strongpoint close by Falkirk and held by the Scots, was chosen as an example. It was decided to storm this garrison, thus removing one problem and once again giving the enemy provocation. Guns were placed and a heavy barrage was laid down on the walls.

By evening the walls had been breached, but, although some negotiations about surrender took place, the delay was too much for Cromwell and the place was stormed in full view of the Scots army. The Governor and sixty-one men of the garrison were killed, and thirteen men were allowed to surrender. Still the Scots refused to respond: Dunbar had made Leslie still more cautious, and their position was too strong to attack. An alternative now loomed. This was to cut the Scots from their supplies by moving into Fife. To do so, Cromwell would have to return to the risky strategy of crossing the Forth and attacking Perth, thus severing the Scots lines. If effective, Charles and Leslie would either be forced to battle or into a march south, out of their lines. This was a daring manoeuvre, as it would divide the Cromwellian army in front of the Scots and place the Forth between them. Certainly, Thomas Harrison was on his way north with 4,000 reinforcements, but, if the strategy went wrong, Cromwell could be defeated in detail. His eagerness to come to some resolution, however, seems to have made Cromwell less cautious, and the manoeuvre was cleverly managed.

Watched by Scots spies, part of Colonel Daniel's regiment, which had been garrisoning Leith, was sent out on 17 July as though moving on the main army, and four companies of foot and four troops of horse under Colonel Overton joined them. Instead of moving into Cromwell's camp, however, they crossed the Forth in already prepared flatboats and landed at North Queensferry. They quickly sought to hold the position. Harrison's troops were not yet with the army, but were close to hand, and on 19 July, Overton having secured the crossing, John Lambert and his forces (two regiments of horse and two of foot), with some difficulty, crossed the Forth. Lambert now had some 5,000 men on the other side of the Forth, while Cromwell and the rest of the army sat and covered the main Scots forces. Leslie had now to counter this outflanking move. He ordered a force of 4,000 men under Sir John Brown into Fife, towards the landing place. On 20 July 1651, John Lambert smashed into these Scots forces at Inverkeithing in a very smart action. He took the fight to the enemy and charged up hill, routing their forces. The troops killed many of the enemy, and also captured Brown and 1,500 prisoners.

This was the defining moment of the campaign. Cromwell had risked defeat in detail, and the manoeuvre, cleverly disguised at first, had come off, but Lambert had provided the much-needed victory. He had been in the forefront of the action, and later found three musket balls lodged between his cuirass and jacket. Cromwell noted of the victory: 'This is an unspeakable mercy ... We can truly say, we were gone as far as we could in our counsel and action, and we did say to one another, we knew not what to do.'[46] Naturally, it was the Lord's doing. Leslie's army, watched by the English, was now forced to abandon the strong position at Torwood, leaving behind their sick, as well as some supplies, in order to support the remnants of his forces and perhaps try to crush Lambert. Cromwell now moved forward after him, hoping for action, but, fearing being caught between two forces, Leslie retired once more. Cromwell had reached the old field of Bannockburn, but the Scots refused him battle once again. They returned to Stirling, and Cromwell to Linlithgow, but the impasse had been broken.

Cromwell now resolved to exploit Lambert's success. He would carry most of the army across the Forth and assault Perth. This would naturally uncover the road into England. Whether Cromwell had calculatingly intended to allow an invasion so that he could seek the battle of annihilation he so desired, and thus end the war, is a moot point. The general plan was to force the Scots to fight, and if Providence furnished an invasion, then Cromwell would act upon it. It is often difficult to discern the calculation in his actions, mixed as it was with his Providential outlook.

On 23 July his forces began to cross the Forth, leaving behind four regiments of horse and four of foot as guards. As a confident Cromwell, with some 14,000 men, pushed through Fife towards Perth, he kept a strict discipline (he hanged two soldiers for straggling and looting). Perth surrendered on 2 August, and his manoeuvre now left Charles II and his generals to decide what to do next. Many of the Scots in the army had begun to desert. Cromwell was certainly clear in his strategic aims at this point, for he wrote to Bradshaw:

'The enemy is at his old lock, and lieth in and near Stirling, where we cannot come to fight him, except he please, or we go upon too-too manifest hazards; he having strongly laid himself, and having a very great advantage there … It is our business still to wait upon God, to show us our way how to deal with this subtle enemy; which I hope He will.'[47]

He then demanded more men and supplies, sought to consolidate his position and waited for the next move of Charles and Leslie's army. Perth's fall would cut the Royal army's supply route. Therefore the King must stay where he was and starve, or break up his forces, or retreat into the Highlands, or even gamble on an invasion of England. This last was what he decided to do. On 29 July Cromwell wrote, 'The enemy's affairs are in some discomposure, as we hear.'[48] News soon came in that they had taken the bait and were moving off towards the border.

THE RACE TO WORCESTER

With Charles II and the Royalist army now marching south, Cromwell had already begun his preparations to follow. Having finally forced the King's hand, he sent Thomas Harrison south with 3,000 horse to Berwick to shadow the Royal army and, if necessary, to impede their advance by action. A body of horse under Colonel Rich was advancing to join him.

Meanwhile Cromwell took the surrender of Perth on 2 August 1651. Once he had accomplished this, he then left George Monck with 5,000–6,000 men to besiege Stirling Castle. The rest of the army began its move south in pursuit of the King. Cromwell also took time at Leith to reassure his political masters in London that he knew what he was about:

> 'I do apprehend that if he goes for England, being some few days march before us, it will trouble some men's thoughts, and may occasion some inconveniences; of which I hope we are as deeply sensible, and have, and I trust shall be, as diligent to prevent as any; and indeed this is our comfort, that in simplicity of heart as to God, we have done to the best of our judgments, knowing that if some issue were not put to this business, it would occasion another winter's war, to the ruin of your soldiery, for whom the Scots are too hard in respect of enduring the winter difficulties of this country, and been under the endless expense of the treasure of England in prosecuting this war. It may be supposed we might have kept the enemy from this, by interposing between him and England; which truly I believe we might; but how to remove him out of this place, without doing what we have done, unless we had had a commanding army on both sides of the river of Forth, is not clear to us; or how to answer the inconveniences aforementioned, we under stand not.'[49]

So endless war and treasure, he claimed, could only be the result, had he not moved as he had. Citing the victory at Preston, he ended with the words 'This is not out of choice on our part, but by some kind of necessity; and it's to be hoped, will have the like issue.'[50] God had shown the route he must follow, and he now adapted his plans accordingly. Lambert, with 3,000 more horse, was now sent off to skirmish at the rear of the enemy, while Cromwell with the rest of the troops followed up behind. In the meantime, Charles, with an army of some 20,000 men, was moving south with some difficulty. Near Carlisle on 6 August 1651, the King issued a declaration promising a pardon to those who would join his forces. It was received with little enthusiasm. Lancashire, the next destination, offered more hope, but even here few troops were raised, and many of the men Charles had already recruited now deserted his cause. The Scots troops also began to pillage the countryside and continued to desert, weakening the Royal army still further.

By 9 August Lambert reached Penrith in the rear of the Royal army and Harrison, pausing at Newcastle on 5 August, had marched on to Ripon. Charles had already reached Preston when the two republican generals finally joined forces. In the south, the Council of State had also begun to raise its defences, calling out the militia and other forces. Desborough joined with 2,000 foot at Reading, while another 8,000 infantry and 2,000 cavalry rendezvoused at Barnet. By 15 August, Lambert and Harrison were at Bolton and by 16 August had joined the militia at Warrington. There they skirmished with the Royalists, but soon broke off awaiting the coming of Cromwell. The latter was now advancing south on a track parallel to that of the Royal army. His troops were marching at a rate of over twenty miles a day, and it was so hot that Cromwell allowed his men to march in their shirt-sleeves, though many of them still fell out through sheer exhaustion. Catterick on 16 August, then Ripon, were his targets. Supplies were ordered at Doncaster.

Charles was at Stoke, while Lambert and Harrison harried his forces. On 19 August Lambert and Harrison were at Uttoxeter and Charles was at Market Drayton. Meanwhile the Council of State acted to defend the capital. Charles Fleetwood was sent out and John Desborough was at Reading. Charles II now retired into the city of Worcester, which he reached by 22 August 1651. By this time, Cromwell had left Ripon, nearing Ferrybridge on 19 August. At Newburn, Colonel Lilburne was detached to hinder the potential retreat of the Royal army. He also skirmished with the opposition on 22 August, taking on Lord Derby at Wigan in difficult circumstances. Nevertheless Lilburne was victorious and smashed the mostly English Royalist enemy on 25 August in a clash at Wigan. No further help for the King would emerge from Lancashire. Fleetwood and his men now lay at Banbury, while Lord Grey was moving on Worcester with 1,100 cavalry. Cromwell had reached Mansfield on 22 August and then sent off his own regiment of infantry to join Lilburne. By 23 August he was at Leicester, and then he turned west, the next day running into Warwick, where his officers awaited him.[51]

WORCESTER: 3 SEPTEMBER 1651

By Wednesday 27 August 1651, an army of 28,000 men had converged at Evesham, with 5,000 militia located in Coventry. It was decided to advance on Worcester in two columns: Fleetwood and Lambert were to lead some 11,000 men towards Upton to capture the bridge there, thus giving the Republican troops access to the western bank of the Severn. In the meantime, the rest of the army under Cromwell was to advance up the eastern bank, reaching strong positions to block any further advance towards London. Supplementary troops were sent north to prevent the Royalist army's retreat. It was apparent that the Royal army was in the process of entrenching at Worcester, since the suburbs of the city were soon burning to clear the field of fire. The Lord General, although he was prepared for a siege, still wanted a battle of annihilation – if he could obtain it.

While the main army advanced from the east towards Worcester, the eager John Lambert marched towards the bridge at Upton on the Severn. Here Lambert found the crossing broken down, with the arches reduced to rubble and only planks placed across them. However, the remains of the bridge were lightly guarded and the Major-General, in his usual style, acted decisively to seize them. In the early morning of 28 August, some eighteen of his dragoons bravely scrambled across the planks and pushed forward into a nearby churchyard. A fierce attack now developed and the dragoons retired into the church, barricading the doors and windows. The forces located in Upton were under the command of Lieutenant-General

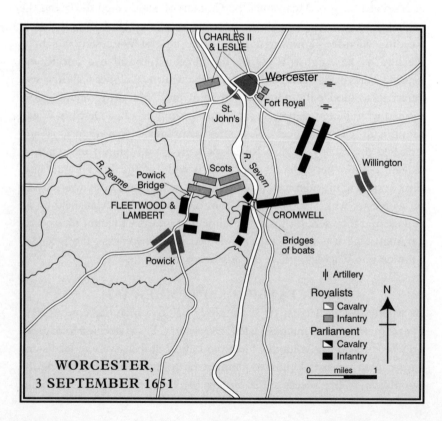

WORCESTER,
3 SEPTEMBER 1651

Edward Massey and were mostly Scots. They had been placed there to defend the broken crossing, but Massey's negligence had given Lambert the initiative. Massey's troops now milled around the building, pushing musket and sword blades through the windows, but they were beaten off.

Lambert risked sending a group of cavalry across the river, as he had been informed that it was fordable. They splashed across, formed up on the western bank, and charged the Scots. More troops now waded across to join them. They finally drove the Scots off. About forty carbines were trained on Massey, and his horse was shot from under him. He had also been hit in the arms and legs, and, injured, he limped off to safety. With men now pouring over the river, the Scots were beaten out of their position and scurried off back towards Worcester. Lambert then coolly halted and ordered up further forces, even placing some of his infantry on horseback to bring them up as swiftly as possible. Troops were allocated to repair the bridge, and the rest of the force then passed over, and, with this side of the Severn now secure, they and some 11,000 men could continue the advance. Cromwell came down to pay them a visit and was 'entertained with abundance of joy, by extraordinary shouting of each regiment, troop and company, as he went to salute them.'[52]

Pleased, he soon retired back to the other column, now marching further up-river, some two miles from the city of Worcester. He covered the road to London by placing his men on some hills on the eastern side of the city, while Fleetwood and Lambert possessed the southern routes. Other forces were converging and probing the defences, intent upon blocking any retreat into Scotland: either Charles would come out or if 'they avoid fighting, and lead us a jaunt, we shall do as God shall direct.'[53] Still Cromwell had superior numbers of troops, and, the initiative now firmly in his hands, a council of war took place on 29 August. Cromwell and his generals saw that the city had been fortified, that the suburbs were still burning and that an outwork to the east of the city, Fort Royal, had been repaired and garrisoned. A plan was devised that would involve the army in a frontal assault over two rivers (the Teme and the Severn), in an attempt to storm the city from the south. Although he had some 30,000 men, the danger still lay in dividing the army. Cromwell intended to leave a force on the eastern side of the city and send in his main attack from the south. This would cut the Royal force off from any retreat towards Wales, while forces already coming in from the north would prevent any retreat to Scotland. To assist in his aim, Cromwell now ordered the construction of two pontoon bridges, using boats taken locally, to connect both banks

at the confluence of the Severn and Teme. Troops under Deane were also
to storm Powick Bridge, broken, as had been the bridge at Upton, by the
defenders. The assault was to be one of Cromwell's most daring operations, for the pontoon bridges would be thrown up in face of the enemy
and then his men would race across. Eleven thousand men were placed
under the command of Fleetwood and Lambert below the Teme for the
attack. Cromwell held some of his veteran troops in reserve, the rest of the
army being held on the eastern banks.

Meanwhile all was not well in the Royal camp. Here the choices came
down to marching out and fighting, or laying in provisions for a siege, or
trying to find another way to London, or retreating into Wales. Leslie
remained disgruntled by the whole business and kept first giving and then
rescinding orders; the arrogant Duke of Buckingham, with no military
skills to speak of, was huffy, believing that he should be commanding the
army; and the wounded Derby had arrived on 31 August, with the remains
of his forces and with news of his defeat. The army itself had become sickly
and mutinous, and the population of Worcester was beginning to suffer.
The infantry were then very upset to discover a plan for the cavalry to
break away and abandon them, and it took the King and his officers a long
time to placate them. Yet the position between the two rivers was potentially a strong one. Charles had control of the interior lines and a good
vantage point from the Cathedral tower to watch over the battle, and a
more able general could have concentrated his forces against different
parts of his opponent's divided army when they attacked. However, one
attempt to disrupt the English lines on 29 August had led to a repulse with
heavy losses, and as a result morale sank even further. Many close to the
King now wished that he were far away from Worcester's streets. Nothing
daunted, however, Charles bustled about trying to bring some order.

By the afternoon of Cromwell's lucky day – 3 September – all was
ready. The weather was fine and clear, and the battle sign was given out to
the army. It was to be that which the men had used on that very day a year
before, in the fields outside Dunbar – 'The Lord of Hosts'. With the Scots
wearing white as their field signs, the Cromwellian troops were ordered to
eschew any form of white cloth so as to distinguish them. Cromwell had
mixed his veterans with the more inexperienced militia, who had flooded
to the cause of repelling the Scots invasion. Holding a reserve of veterans
to himself between the Teme and Severn, and letting the guns on the
eastern side of the city play on the walls and Fort Royal so as to give the
impression of an attack there, Cromwell ordered the southern echelons to

prepare to go in across the Teme. Fleetwood's men had taken most of the day to march up from Upton. They gradually forced back the Scots, who had left a rearguard under Colonel Keith near the church on the ridge at Powick. A spattering of fire, using the Church as a target, had led the stubborn Scots to begin a withdrawal towards the partly demolished Powick Bridge and across the Teme. Fierce fighting now broke out at the bridge.

In the meantime, the two bridges of boats had been dragged and hammered into place, one over the Severn and the other over the Teme, about fifty yards apart. It was around two o'clock in the afternoon, and a screen of musketeers was thrown out on the other side to protect the work. The right wing of the southern force reached the bridges while the Scots dithered and did nothing to prevent the task being completed, and the Republican troops now raced across the wooden structures over the Teme. There they struck at the Scots lining the numerous hedges and a sharp firefight and push of pike ensued. At around three o'clock, elements of the reserve – Hacker's cavalry regiment and the infantry of Ingoldsby and Fairfax, as well as Cromwell's horse and part of the lifeguard – were hurried across the bridge over the Severn by Cromwell to support Deane and Goffe's regiment of foot, who had seized the bridgeheads and struck at Pitscottie's highlanders. They briefly gave way, then resisted.

A full-blown combat now began in the narrow ground, which was also cluttered with many defensible hedges. Disdaining the role of executive general once more, Cromwell personally led his men over the bridge of boats on the Severn. They also struck at the Highlanders. Still the stiff resistance continued. By Powick Bridge, Deane and his men again tried to storm the bridge, meeting stout resistance and furious hand-to-hand fighting and push of pike. Men waded across under fire, and a 'hot dispute' broke out as the Scots, under Montgomery, and Keith's men pushed back throughout the day. Numerous bodies began to litter the landscape as the mêlée continued. The action proved difficult for the cavalry, but this was to be no Second Newbury, for some of them managed to splash across a ford a mile further upstream from Powick. Now, under this intense pressure, the Scots gradually began to crumble and fall back into Worcester, whereupon more Cromwellian infantry and cavalry began to pour over the bridges.[54]

Charles II, following an early and rigorous inspection of his lines, had been observing the actions from the cathedral tower. He now raced to Powick to support his troops, ordering them to hold the bridge there. He then passed his reserve at St John's and returned to his observation post at the cathedral. At around four o'clock in the afternoon Charles decided upon an attack of his own, and personally launched two columns out of Sidbury Gate from Worcester on to the eastern bank. Royalist horse and infantry came out of St Martin's and Sidbury Gates towards the command of Lambert and Harrison. The Scots cavalry under Leslie demurred from entering the fight, but the advancing infantry, 'giving our men a very hot salute', struck the newly raised, trained bands of Cheshire and Essex. They shuddered, took serious casualties and began to fall back. Messengers were immediately sent south to inform Cromwell, and he hastened north with his cavalry and some infantry in order to rally his men. His arrival on the King's right flank now turned the tide, and the Royalists and Scots began fall back towards the city. Desperate hand-to-hand fighting with sword and pike forced the enemy back into Worcester. 'It was', noted Cromwell, 'a stiff business.'[55] Lambert, ever at the forefront of the action, had yet another horse shot from under him, while Cromwell took to riding up and down the enemy line, offering quarter and oblivious to the returning shots. The position at Fort Royal and its guns now fell to the Essex militia as the Cromwellian line advanced, the militiamen breaking into the fort and slaughtering the garrison. They then turned the captured guns on the fleeing Scots. The King and Hamilton's men were driven into the streets of Worcester

Charles II's army now began to disintegrate. The Cromwellian forces finally broke the opposition in front of them and poured into the city through Sidbury Gate. Fleetwood's men had by now also managed to break through in the west, and they began to enter the city. In the wreck of his army, Charles, who had led numerous gallant charges and risked his life, was able to escape, while the fighting began to spread from street-to-street and house-to-house, the dead bodies of men and horses of the enemy littering the roadways.[56] While some of his cavalry fled, the rest of the King's army was now completely routed. Nearly 10,000 of his troops surrendered and some 2,000 died. This was Cromwell's last battle. It was a massive final victory, a 'crowning mercy' indeed, that had ended his military career in the field on a glorious note. One veteran afterwards wrote: 'In all the engagements that ever hath beene, I think we have not seen a more immediate hand of God appearing than in this.'[57]

In fact, while ably managed, Worcester had been one of his easier victories. Given superior numbers, he had been able to divide his army, sending his veteran troops over the Severn and Teme to tackle the Scots there and driving them into the suburbs of St John's, while the militia and other units masked the city on the east bank. Despite the need to attack over a river crossing, which resulted in some fierce fighting, the strategy proved a sound one. The King's attack on the eastern side led to further fighting, and was at first an opportune move that could have caused problems for his opponents, but the units there held on until Cromwell came to succour them. Their revenge was to drive into the city itself, leaving Worcester a mass of dead and dying men as the fighting took them into the streets and alleys. It fell to Harrison to remark that the city was left 'such a nastiness, that a man could hardly abide the town.'[58]

The Cromwellians eventually rounded up the numerous prisoners and pushed them into the cathedral. On their side, it was said that as few as 200 Republican troops had lost their lives. An intelligent strategy from beginning to end had been Cromwell's aim. Even though heavily outnumbered, Charles and his disgruntled army had still put up a desperate resistance. The end game of 1651 was a gamble from the moment that Lambert broke the Scots at Inverkeithing. The King had performed valiantly, but Charles felt betrayed by his Scots allies. Leslie did little in the course of the battle. The next weeks were to be spent by Charles attempting to escape capture – a capture that would almost certainly have cost him his life had it occurred. When he did finally escape, the erstwhile King was forced to spend the next nine years in exile.

WESTMINSTER: 12 SEPTEMBER 1651

On a bright sunny day in September 1651, Oliver Cromwell met the Speaker of the Parliament and Lord President of the Council on a green between Aston and London. Great shouts of joy and salutes greeted the victorious general, who had been met with great solemnity:

'All the Fields were thronged with innumerable Flocks of people that came to see him, and many thousands of Quality on Horse-Back. There was also the Lord Mayor, Aldermen, Sheriff, and Militia of London, with Guards of soldiers both Horse and Foot; who all testified their joy in his victorious return, by loud volleys and Acclamations.'[59]

While Cromwell left in a rich, caparisoned coach of state within the hour, the next day thousands of weary and ragged Scots prisoners trooped over the same ground. They were heading for Tothill Fields, after having first been conducted through the city to 'shew the Cavaliers a true copy of their King's countenance'. So it was that the Lord General, Oliver Cromwell, finally returned home from the wars with many victories on his brow, a long way from the colonel who had won his first real skirmish on that balmy evening outside Grantham in 1643. His military struggles might well be over, but whether he, and his army, could now win the peace proposed by politicians remained to be seen.[60]

CONCLUSION:
A GENIUS FOR WAR?

THE WARRIOR

Given the above history of his campaigns, how does Oliver Cromwell fit into what Carl von Clausewitz was later to call the general's 'genius for war'? From the beginning, we must understand that Cromwell made war in an era when the idea of the heroic general was still at its height. In effect, this idea often overrode any technical ability a general may have had in the modern sense. Instead, he was to be a figure of glory and honour, seeing and doing in the 'school of Mars' rather than acting as a mere mechanic of war. More often than not, such men had gained their authority by virtue of their rank and aristocratic status – by having, or at least claiming to possess, the innate characteristics of a gentleman. Consequently, Civil War generals, like their counterparts in Europe, tended to be men who, once the battle began, swiftly abandoned the actual role of commander in order to lead by example – to fight in the front line. There they acted with bold deeds and bold words, and demonstrated their heroic virtue to their troops in a manner a world away from the professional functionaries of modern warfare.

We can see this tendency amongst the generals of the Civil Wars. Men such as Prince Rupert and George Goring never lost their taste for leading a charge. Rupert was tactically impetuous, bold and daring, and with a heroic ability to launch apparently decisive attacks, but he was unable to restrain his men. Goring was ambitious, brave and skilful, and only his personal failings finally let him down: he was far too fond of arguments, of women and of the bottle. Both men were larger-than-life characters of the heroic mould. Essex and Waller were more sober, but equally keen to become involved in hand-to-hand combat when it was demanded of them. Waller was energetic and had good tactical skills. One opponent said that he was the best 'shifter and chooser of ground … I ever saw.'[1] Essex had fewer successful attributes as a general, but he was a solid administrator. However, despite his failings, men would follow him, both because of who he was and because of his heroism in action. The mild-mannered Sir Thomas Fairfax, often thought of by historians as the best general to come out of the wars, only seems to have come alive when he fought face to face with the enemy. However, his strategic skills were high and his men loved him. In this sense, Oliver Cromwell was no different from these men. Although he was a late-comer to war, the urge to combat was deeply embedded in his military career. It enabled him to express in his own way the custom for generals of the day: bravery and heroic deeds were to be his forte. This was a convention that had been to the forefront since at least the time of the Ancient World, and those who did not take part in it, or refused to do so, were no generals.

In any event, early seventeenth-century warfare was naturally full of conventions and limitations. It was limited rather than total warfare; strategy contained numerous gaps, because of which men would wait upon their opponent's moves, or for the Lord to show them the way. When forces did engage in battle, generals would invariably position their cavalry upon the left and right of the line, with infantry located in the centre; the artillery, by and large, played a minor part. The guns were clumsy and often immobile, and, while they might bombard the opposition, the heroic general had little time for them outside the siege. While the infantry lines moved forward to fight, the cavalry on either flank was there to engage with their opposite numbers and, having done so, swing round to crush the centre of the enemy line of infantry. With few reserves available and a generally limited grand tactical vision, most early seventeenth-century combat, as we have seen, tended at this point to disintegrate into poorly co-ordinated, although often deadly, fighting between more or less disciplined blocks of men, who, once engaged with one another, habitually took part in a struggle of attrition along the whole of the battle line. Quite often there was little real co-ordination between the forces ostensibly controlled by their commander. While the Early Modern general sought to bring as many of his forces to the field of combat as possible, and, once there, to assemble them for the fight as best he could, after this the vital motivational element of combat often lay in his personality and presence and with the regimental officers and the troops themselves rather than with any 'great' generalship.

When all is said and done, the Early Modern general's real role in combat was to act heroically. In this role he persistently sought to show his personal and physical bravery in battle and to act as an example for his troops. If he achieved this, he could gain glory, honour and respect, if not victory. The idea of the general as a battlefield co-ordinator was an element that only really emerged through the continued use of professional and experienced troops and subordinate officers. In the Civil Wars, this element came rather late in the day. In this sense, as in many others, Early Modern warfare was in transition. It looked back to the Ancient World and, to some extent, forward to the modern. From the outset of his career as a soldier, Oliver Cromwell undoubtedly fell into the manner of a heroic front-line warrior rather than a modern chief executive of war; indeed, for most of his military career he literally led from the front line. There he was able to use his undoubted personal qualities of inspiration and physical courage, take the same risks as his men and be well regarded for his deeds by others. In so doing, he was merely following some universal precepts of war in his day, and, as one military historian has noted, 'Officers in every armed force must find ways of inducing their men to fight and risk their lives – a most unnatural activity ... they must be pulled by the prestige of their immediate leader ... the personal qualities of authority are important, but so is an evident willingness to share in the ... deadly risks of war.'[2] As another American analysis put it, 'You can't direct them – you have to lead them.'[3]

'Château generalship' had little place in Early Modern warfare, and Cromwell, until perhaps he became Head of State, would not be an advocate of it. Yet the transition from bold hero to practical general was beginning to emerge in the wars of the day. Some thought that there was more to generalship than strutting heroically around on the field of battle. We can discern elements of this move in the career of Cromwell, for he soon realised, consciously or unconsciously, that mere heroism was not going to be enough to win the war. To assist in heroic actions in the field there must be training. There must be the installation of a good *esprit de corps*, and there must be severe discipline. These were to become Cromwell's hallmarks on the field of battle. He would choose his men well, he would seek to train his men hard, in order to maintain their formations in combat, and he would seek to instil obedience, reducing the individual as far as possible into a body of cohesive identity. In effect, Cromwell began to search for the creation of a godly community at arms, much as later, when, as Lord Protector, he sought to bring England together as a godly community at peace.

In other senses, the idea of the hero and war leader naturally gave legitimacy to the Early Modern general's role. It was, as John Keegan has noted, something created and 'sustained by a readiness to go to the battlefield and fight with courage once there'.[4] At the end of the day, the general had to persuade his men to go into combat and face death. How could he do this? We can, in fact, outline certain elements in Early Modern gener-alship that allowed the general to function as he did – the dramatisation of his role, the psychology of language, the selection of subordinates, the use of sanctions or rewards, and the use of action and example.

Early Modern generals always tended to dramatise their roles as means of creating authority. The Press, of course, realised this very early on, and produced numerous illustrations and engravings that became archetypes for what the warrior general should be. He is nearly always depicted on a stallion, stern yet noble, with battle behind him and a list of his famous deeds around him. The references to the Ancient World are also obvious. It was part of what Michel Foucault has called the 'bodily rhetoric of honour'. In the real world of human interaction, generals were able to use the tools of social choreography in order to continue to drama-tise their roles. They were much concerned, either consciously or uncon-sciously, with covert and overt 'presentation of the self' to their troops. Public performance and ritual were, in any case, deeply embedded into the Early Modern world. Men and women expected to see their leaders engaging in performance on a day-to-day basis. Politics was, in many senses, all about performance, whether in the church, the palace, the city, or the village. Early Modern relationships were governed by the social choreography of the day: status, rank, body, ritual and costume were mutually supportive and often predetermined roles. 'Group life in general,' notes Chandra Mukerji, 'emerges from mutually choreographed performances', it is dictated by face-to-face performance, and an army, more than most organisations, functions as a mutually choreographed drama.[5] Training, rank and hierarchy sustain it, impose order, determine power, and allow soldiers to see themselves, their officers and their generals in particular roles, to acquire and give reputation and respect, whether as heroes, as tough disciplinarians, as fighters or, on occasion, as cowards. Naturally, access to their superiors by the ordinary soldiers of the day tended to be limited by distance and rank, but it was nearly always observable through public deeds. Men became especially aware of it in that most extreme of all human situations, battle – which is, after all, the ultimate purpose of any army. So we find generals in the midst of the charge, or in the breach at the cannon's mouth, fighting alongside their men or, where necessary, dying gloriously on the field of battle. This was their role, their function, and their purpose.

Naturally, the Early Modern general tried to select his subordinates from amongst those who would carry out his orders and reflect his values. Such men were not hard to find, for most officers shared the view of war as a glorious experience. Together they sought to instil these values into the common soldier. In addition, in Early Modern warfare, the general was still able to speak directly to the troops, since war was still by and large a small-scale affair. The general could talk to his men, often through the pre-campaign or pre-battle speech, or in some cases by actual face-to-face contact. At the regimental or company level, this could also be achieved by the choice of images and symbols for his flag. Such techniques allowed the force of the commander's personality to emerge, and also allowed the soldiers to learn to 'know' the mind of their commander. A commander could, in effect, give 'an impression of himself to his troops'.[6] This was not necessarily the real impression, nor even a true one, but it was one that would serve the purpose of battle. Speeches could be made to encourage the men, to flatter them, and, occasionally, to bargain with them. Promotion or even medals could sanction rewards for bravery. Conversely, the Early Modern commander had many other, rather more brutal sanctions available, including death and a multitude of lesser military punishments. These were used in order to discipline and chastise his troops, to keep them in order. At times the troops had to know fear, not only from the enemy but also from their general.

The Early Modern general also had to be capable of action, of knowing the enemy, and of going into the field to see the enemy's movements where he could. He had to be prepared to take risks to enable him to gain 'real time intelligence'.[7] This also allowed him to be seen to share the risks of his soldiers, to bond with them in adversity and join the band of brothers that was military honour. This was something all commanders had to face. Military honour had obligations on both sides: they would fight for him, but he should be careful of them and their lives. Thus Early Modern commanders were to some extent forced into the role of hero by the values of the day. The 'hero' ethic demanded that they fight in the front line and be seen to be fighting; thereby they could legitimatise their rule.

Naturally, the numerous Cromwellian leadership qualities in war and in battle fitted into this contemporary image. Unquestionably supreme was Cromwell's hard-won and strongly held faith in himself and his God. This faith was initiated by his fundamental religious beliefs and sustained by its focus on himself as the chosen instrument of God in a Providential universe. Indeed, Cromwell and his relationship to his God have a unique role to play in this particular soldier's story. As we have seen, it was not by any means a simple tale of a military professional rising to high rank (as happened with many of his contemporaries), but rather the story of a godly soldier. We have earlier examined his religious ideology in some detail: this may be said to have been the core of his motivation as a commander, and any glory he acquired was acquired in order that he might praise God for its coming.

Cromwell's uncompromising and aggressive nature as a soldier is one of the most prominent features of his style of warfare. On the surface at least, this may appear to be unusual for the times. Although trained to be heroic soldiers, many of Cromwell's contemporary generals in the seventeenth century were also habitually locked into fruitless wars of manoeuvre, and it was often the successful siege and seizure of territory, rather than the battle, that showed their true artistry. Cromwell was different in this respect. In fact, the rather atypical Cromwellian aggression in war made him a hasty and distinctive, if sometimes unsubtle, soldier in the field. Although Cromwell never really reached the heights of a master of the strategic manoeuvre (he was no Napoleon), he did become a very sound and capable tactician. He was the first to admit that 'I must acknowledge myself guilty of oversights ... [as] they can rarely be avoided in military matters.'[8] His later campaigns in Ireland and Scotland, and that in England in 1651 – the real measure of his generalship alongside the Preston campaign of 1648 – were based on sound planning, intelligence and sharp manoeuvres. This planning was not so rigid that he could not adapt, but it usually found its focus in what Delbruck has called campaigns of annihilation – the destruction of the enemy's field army. Wars of attrition tended to frustrate Cromwell: exhausting the enemy's will to fight by manoeuvre and siege was not usually his chosen method. Instead, he saw war and politics as complementary matters. 'Pax Quaeritur Bello' (Let peace be sought through war), was his motto. Above all, in the field, Oliver Cromwell was a general who tried to dominate the enemies he faced, and the men he commanded, by sheer force of will; he seems to have been instinctively aware of the later Napoleonic dictum that, in war, moral forces can far outweigh the physical. It is arguable that it is this element that gives Cromwell his distinctiveness in his era. In his day, he became the moral commander *par excellence*, dependent on his own self-assurance and religious certainty to bring him through the chaos of the conflicts of that period.

The combined result of Cromwell's military career was more or less continual victory from 1642 to 1651. It is remarkable to note that this emerged by way of a man who had never been trained from his youth in the art of war, unlike most of the military gentlemen of his era. His soldiering did not commence until his forty-third year, and in this sense he never became a fully professional soldier. However, if Cromwell came late to war, he also left early. His career as a soldier spans a mere ten years, in comparison to his twenty-eight years as a politician on the local, national and international scene. Yet military success unquestionably gave his whole career momentum. While he was certainly not the new Gustavus Adolphus of Sweden that many flattering newsletter writers (and some subsequent historians) tried to make him out to be, military success gave him public stature. Cromwell was, as we have noted, well aware of the continued need to make political capital out of his campaigns and victories in order to assist his cause, but he never once fought outside the British Isles, he commanded relatively small forces, and we have no real external measure of him as soldier, at least, in the great European conflicts of the day.

In truth, Oliver Cromwell's background until 1642 had, on the surface, been relatively unexciting. Education, marriage, some financial and personal troubles, membership of the House of Commons – these were experiences shared by many of his contemporaries in the gentry class to which he belonged. In 1642 he became eager to resolve the political conflict of the day through war, mainly because God seemed to point in that direction. The fact that Cromwell had never seen the field of battle prior to 1642, and that what he found there at first seems to have disappointed and even dismayed him, is significant. The self-belief and self-righteousness of his new cause met the reality of battle, and he discovered that others did not seem to share his directness about the great business in which all were now engaged. This at least motivated him to seek a different route through the field of war. He now saw that the men he had to lead in this conflict ought to be highly disciplined and godly soldiers – honest men; men who fought for a cause; men, as he argued, like himself. It is this belief, as much as anything else, that was to make his military reputation.

We should also recall that Cromwell's reputation in the Civil Wars took a little time to be made. As we have seen, in 1642 he was unknown as a soldier, and not much more prominent as politician. His first real military role was as a vigorous raiser of men for the Parliamentary cause. Indeed, he won no reputation at all at Edgehill, although he seems to have learnt much by the experience. By 1643, his part in some local victories at Grantham, Gainsborough and Winceby, in an otherwise poor year for the Parliamentarian side, had sufficiently raised his profile in the Press of the day to begin to give him some repute: here were Colonel Cromwell and his men fighting for the cause. This was a medium that Cromwell and his friends knew how to exploit, and it was partly as result of the reporting of his adventures in the Press that in 1644 his military reputation really begin to take off, first at Marston Moor, where we now know he had a good (if somewhat contested) claim to be the architect of that victory, and later that same year in the important political conflict that erupted following the Second Battle of Newbury – a battle in which, as we have seen, he singularly failed to distinguish himself. The year 1645 was to add a more lustrous reputation, and the years that followed saw him lauded and at the height of his eminence as a soldier – a maker and breaker of governments and men.

In a military sense, Cromwell's initial lack of experience of soldiering at least gave him some flexibility, for he did not know, or did not at first subscribe to, all the current military doctrines that every officer of his day was supposed to know. Instead, he seems to have replaced them with his own particular brand of personal leadership and understanding as a gentleman who was used to some authority, and who could use this to encourage discipline in his troops, and with an astute common sense regarding men and horses. He learnt the technicalities of war by reading and, in a more practical form on actual campaign, by observation and trial. On another level, his lack of knowledge was of course eventually to restrict his development as a soldier, particularly regarding that most important measure of the general's art in the seventeenth century – the siege. In the end, as Joshua Sprigge generally said of the New Model officers (and it was true of Oliver Cromwell more than most), they 'were [men who were] better Christians than soldiers, and wiser in faith than fighting.'[9] Yet they, and Cromwell, were open enough to learn their trade in a school of very hard knocks, and the experience of battle, if one survived it, was to prove an excellent training ground.

Cromwell's resolution in the face of the inevitable difficulties brought about by war was another of the outstanding characteristics of his generalship. Still more significant was his 'energy in action'. The means by which a leader sought to direct his forces to achieve victory were generally limited by their own energy. Cromwell's energy was exceptional, and when mixed with certain decisive leadership qualities it enabled him to exploit the moral and psychological factors within his own forces and those of the enemy. However, in critically examining his career as soldier it can also be argued that, in the end, there is really no rising profile in Cromwellian warfare: it could be said that Oliver Cromwell, as a commander, peaked at some point around 1644–45. By this stage he had learned all he needed to know of the technical side of soldiering for the purpose of the Civil Wars, and the rest of his career was merely using the pattern of his experience by adapting the methods of a very good cavalry officer to the wider sphere of generalship. Thereafter, as a soldier he rested on a level developmental plateau. The ideas of the captain and colonel of horse in 1644–45 were in some ways the same ideas that he tried to exploit in 1648, 1649, 1650 and 1651 – fast, mobile, dynamic and very aggressive warfare in campaigns of annihilation. In point of fact, his statement after Preston in 1648 sums up the general Cromwellian strategic imperative very well: 'It was thought that to engage the enemy to fight was our business.' Cromwell's strategic vision throughout his military career was clearly to fight and to win – and to win as quickly as possible. This imperative could have led him to as many disasters as victories, and, arguably, in Ireland and Scotland it very nearly did, for here his aggression simply played him false. In Ireland he became bogged down in a bloody war of attrition, and his aggressive tendencies were also, at least initially, foiled in 1650 by the skilful manoeuvring of David Leslie in the lowlands of Scotland, it being only Leslie's mistake (and Cromwell's tactical opportunism) at Dunbar that rescued him from disaster. Moreover, his view of the Scots as merely misguided and his guilt over fighting fellow Protestants were matched with unhealthiness in body and led him into errors.

This is not to say that Cromwell did not have some moments of inspiration. His strength of mind to shift his forces across the Firth and allow the Scots invasion of England in 1651 is a notable point in his career. He did have others, although, again, he invariably put these down to God's Providence. So, for the most part Cromwell remained an impulsive and heroic commander, who led from the front, and was relatively non-reflective (except in the sense of his continual searching for God's grace) and a tactical specialist in cavalry warfare. Above all things, Cromwell was a soldier with a cause to fight for – God's cause.

From the very beginning of his wars, combat to Cromwell was not going to be a stately dance between professionals, but a bloody resolution of the nation's political and religious problems on the Providential field of battle. His campaigns were, in many senses, 'holy wars'. Warfare and battle were meant to be means to an end – peace – and not an end in themselves. His supposed speech to those he raised as his first troop of horse in Huntingdon set out his observations at the beginning of his military career in this respect. On this occasion Cromwell was claimed to have had said that

> '... he would not deceive nor cozen them by the perplexed and involved expression in his commission to fight for "King and Parliament", and therefore that if the King chanced to be in the body of the enemy that he was to charge, he would discharge his pistol upon him as at any other private person, and if their conscience would not permit them to do the like, he advised them not to list themselves in his troop or under his command.'[10]

Another witness to this speech claimed that Cromwell also said that he 'sought ... our welfare, and to stand with us for the liberty of the gospel and the laws of the land'.[11] Glory and honour might come his way, but a just peace and a righteous religious settlement were his principal aims.

Of course the 'genius for war', as Clausewitz noted, needs other attributes – courage, both moral and physical, an ability to deal with physical exertion and suffering through the inner strength of body and mind, and an indifference, if not selfishness, to others' needs. Cromwell certainly had all these elements in his character. In the province of friction and uncertainty that is war, he eventually revealed a good tactical ability to read a battle, and he acquired the necessary *coup d'oeil* – a swiftness to see and to seize the main chance in combat. These were virtues that were noted by one nineteenth-century commentator on cavalry tactics as the 'qualities requisite for a good cavalry leader ... a good eye for the country, and a quick one for the enemy's movements, great energy, courageous decision, and rapid execution'.[12]

It must be said that many opportunities eluded Cromwell from 1642 until 1648, since in this phase of his career he was nearly always the subordinate of other men. This doubtless frustrated him, especially since many of his superiors were not as driven as he was. Only in the Second Civil War, the Irish Campaign of 1649 and the Scottish war of 1650–51 was he finally to emerge as a general of armies. As a subordinate, he remained satisfactory, with certain caveats: although he was impatient, he tended to obey orders and was keen to do his duty. William Waller noted that Cromwell, under his command in April 1645, 'had never shown extraordinary parts, nor do I think that he did himself believe that he had them. For although he was blunt, he did not bear himself with pride or disdain. As an officer he was obedient and did never dispute my orders nor argue upon them.'[13] When he rose to the rank of lieutenant-general, he was focused on cavalry generalship as well as, by 1644, the wider political frustrations of fighting a war that many of his superiors were still reluctant to win. Of course, by this stage he had become a prominent politician, and battles lost or won in the field could be, and often were, re-fought once more in the House of Commons. Where he could, however, Cromwell sought to exploit the result of battles in the field and was always willing to use his men sensibly to gain victory. He also had the moral courage to take tough decisions.

Cromwell's military legacy is more difficult to assess. While he certainly made his mark on his own times, and the reputation of his soldiers in the 1640s and 1650s was high, he arguably had a restricted impact on the art of war. Moreover, the army he left behind him virtually disappeared in 1660. His own person and reputation were regarded as particularly repugnant following the Restoration in 1660, and Cromwell was rather a figure to be vilified by Royalist propaganda as the bloody regicide and not an able soldier whose military career had something to teach others, although his reputation, once the follies of the Restoration regime were revealed, did, it seems, have some closet supporters. Even so, Cromwell was arguably a limited innovator, tending to operate inside the boundaries of what was possible in the conflict of his day. This is because, as we have seen, as a field commander Cromwell was operating in the heroic mould of leadership that had been around in warfare since at least the time of Alexander the Great – as of course were all of his contemporaries.

HERO OF BATTLE

In combat we can see another side to Cromwell – that explosion of energy visible under the surface in him that sometimes bordered on madness. It was something John Aubrey called 'afflatus'. There is little doubt that a pent-up energy, even anger, existed for most of his life in Oliver Cromwell. It often seems that, for him, English society of the day was constricting at the best of times – structured and hierarchical, with a series of tensions at its heart over the family, Church and State. All of these increased the pressure upon him, and this pressure gained its greatest release in combat. Cool and clinical warfare driven by logic and reason were not really his forte. Time and again we hear of pent-up energy revealing itself in his continual prayer, his restlessness and tension before combat, his nervous actions such as wild laughing, the biting of his bottom lip until the blood flowed, his intoning of psalms and his exhortations, and an anticipation that was released in actual combat with exultation and a perceived sparkling of his eyes and face with joy.

Cromwell knew the thrill of combat, and it may be that engaging in combat was one of the few activities in his life when he actually felt free of the restraints of the day. He often seems to have seen in it something truly divine – a true explanation of God's Providential plan in the world around him, and his part in that plan. During one battle he enquired, 'to see this is it not to see the face of God?' This view makes his battlefield reports, if not difficult to follow, then certainly imbued with an air of Cromwellian obscurity. It is arguable that, as with his other experiences in life, in his battlefield experience he sought the 'face of God', so that the technical side of his capacity as commander was more often than not subsumed into a Providential spectacle or theatre. When things went wrong, such as at Newbury or Clonmel, his silence is very noticeable. On these occasions, Providence and God had spoken against him, and there was little else to do but accept God's judgement and try harder.

The practical result of Cromwell's joining in actual combat was that it would have been difficult for him to see very much at all of the wider picture in the first place, as he was very often too close to the action, and to his opponents trying to kill him. Yet this was, after all, the style of heroic and brave leadership of his day, a style followed by nearly all of his contemporaries. We can see him at Worcester in 1651 still much as he had been at Grantham in 1643, 'riding up and down in the midst of the shot and riding himself in person to the Enemies foot, offering them quarter, whereto they returned no answer but shot',[14] or in the midst of the earlier actions at Winceby, Marston Moor or Naseby, fighting alongside his troops. Only occasionally, for example at Preston and Dunbar, was Cromwell able to restrain himself sufficiently to assist his generalship, but, as we have seen, the nature of Early Modern battle meant that he remained close to the front line, an immediate viewer of the action, involved in actual combat more often than not or, at the least, riding up and down the line and ordering his men into the fighting. This would, and did, enable him to exploit the disorganisation of the enemy swiftly and to assess the morale of his own troops, as well as to give orders face to face with his subordinates. In this sense, he would be able to 'read' the battle. It would also, naturally, place him in danger.

It is clear that Oliver Cromwell, imbued with a Calvinist sense of his own destiny, was not overly fearful of wounds or death in battle. Long before 1642, his religious conversion had placed his life in God's hands. In fact, he was lucky in combat. The number of injuries he sustained was quite low, given the great number of actions in which he was involved, the numerous shots fired at him, either in battle or when viewing the enemy's dispositions, and the sword-cuts made when in the midst of mêlées. A pragmatist, he would have seen these deliverances as a significant part of God's plan. He did have numerous horses shot from under him in combat and suffered heavy falls as a result, most notably at Winceby in 1643 when, as he was riding in the front line, his horse was killed and fell on him. On rising he was again knocked down, but he was eventually able to remount. At Marston Moor he was wounded in the neck. He was forced from the fighting, but the wound was then dressed and he returned to the action and his courage was not in doubt.

At other times, it was rather the dangers of disease that left him prostrate. Early Modern military camps were not healthy places at the best of times, and, as a result, Cromwell suffered from a variety of ailments, many of which seem to have been brought on by his own periods of depression (as in 1647) and the general tiredness a man of his age living such a life would experience. He was certainly subject to bouts of low fever brought on by 'tertian ague', or malaria. This had been picked up either in his native Fen country, or in Ireland in 1649, where it was rife amongst the troops. It seems to have recurred in February 1651, when a serious attack, probably the result of exposure in the bad Scottish weather, prostrated him completely and made others fear for his life. He had, however, already written to his wife, after the battle of Dunbar in September 1650, that 'I have been in my inward man marvellously supported; though I assure thee, I grow an old man, and feel infirmities of age marvellously stealing upon me.'[15] He was, by this stage, fifty-one years of age, and he continued to push his body in the field, but it undoubtedly began to limit his capacity for making war. His ailments did not improve his temper, and he seems to have been a poor patient. He also suffered from an attack of the stone – a problem that may have eventually killed him in 1658.

Otherwise, Cromwell's temperament was often clouded in the field, and his anger could be intense. He was described more than once as being 'choleric', and not averse to giving 'blows' against those who crossed him. Edward Sexby, who later turned violently against him, noted 'his Highness is naturally choleric and must call men rogues, and go to cuffs.'[16] This could be reflected on the battlefield. On the other hand, Cromwell seems to have had a certain blunt charm and presence, and was able to use his personality to persuade. He could lead both his men and his superiors where he wished at times, and in so doing he was more than willing to appear sincere if necessary, allegedly telling one person that it is 'lawful to play the knave with a knave'.[17] Waller noted that 'He did ... seem to have great cunning, and whilst he was cautious of his own words, not putting forth too many lest they should betray his thoughts, he made others talk, until he had as it were sifted them, and known their inmost designs.'[18] If necessity had no law, then lying or exaggerating was also presumably part of his art of man-management. 'Spongy eyes and a supple conscience', as Edward Sexby called it, were also part of his repertoire.[19] More than once, he resorted to tearful exhortations to try to get his own way. He remained an emotional man throughout his life, and, as H. N. Brailsford has pertinently noted, 'one should [always] try to discover rather what he felt than what he thought.'[20]

Cromwell's routine prior to battle seems to have been fairly typical of the day. A preliminary reconnaissance in the saddle was carried out in the days and hours preceding combat. Where possible, he tried to see things with his own eyes, and he often wandered quite close to the enemy to gather 'real-time' intelligence. At the least, he often got close enough to exchange words with the enemy, and for the latter to take shots at him. In Scotland in 1650, he sarcastically berated some of the Scottish infantry who had fired at him and missed. He was not a general averse to receiving the salutes of his soldiers prior to battle, and many were the shouts of 'A Cromwell! A Cromwell!' that greeted him in the field. In this he was unlike, for example, the later Duke of Wellington, who hated such displays. In the manner of most heroic generals of the day, Cromwell ultimately knew he had a public role to play for his men, and he encouraged their praises. However, while he genuinely cared for his men, he is likely to have viewed this appreciation with as much of a jaundiced eye as he did those of the civilians at Northampton: when met by a large and enthusiastic crowd there, he observed to John Lambert and Richard Ingoldsby, 'Do not trust to that, for these very persons would shout as much as if you and I were going to be hanged.'[21] Being a godly man on a godly cause, he encouraged the men to sing psalms as part of their preparation for combat, and probably as a way of dispelling their nervousness. He was also nearly always willing to hear them preach. Prayer and fasting were, in truth, ritual components of his pre-combat activities. Hugh Peters, the notorious Parliamentarian chaplain, noted Cromwell's night of prayer prior to the storming of Basing House in 1645, and this was not at all an unusual activity for the general. After the battle, whatever his actions in it, he was usually very self-effacing in his reports, and, in England at least, kind to the wounded of both sides, claiming that any success was entirely a result of God's will rather than his own efforts. This might have been, as some of his enemies claimed, religious posturing, but it is more likely, given his character, that he really believed the sentiments he expressed.

Otherwise, Cromwell had little enough time for battlefield ceremony and theatre beyond the needs of the day. Certainly, as a civilian he had been a plain-dressing and plain-spoken man, and as a soldier he was apparently just the same. His unsophisticated style in speech and dress meant simplicity and honesty – a route to becoming godlier. It appealed to the men he led. One contemporary noted that he was 'plain in his Apparel and rather negligent than not' in his dress.[22] Apparently indifferent to the outward man (although his enemies again said that this was deliberately cultivated), he maintained this attitude throughout his career. A later observer noted that he was confident 'that his Highness [Cromwell was by this stage Lord Protector] is pleased with those phylacteries and fringes of state (if pleased with them at all) because he must. And that his Highness knows that there is no more in harmless ceremonies of state only than common and weak eyes discern, or have any wise cause to be offended at.'[23] Plain, black clothes became the norm, and his dress in war was not generally affected by richness, as was Prince Rupert's, but more likely to be a buff coat, cuirass, helmet and relatively unembellished gear.

Consultation with senior officers was also part of Cromwell's method of war. Cromwell was usually lucky in his subordinates, and he also had the knack of making a good choice of men. While he increasingly relied upon his own judgement as a general over the years, he was a man who took advice. The consultation with Lambert and Monck before Dunbar is a case in point. The result was not necessarily a war by debate, although in Early Modern warfare there was always room for the council. In this, Cromwell shared the ideas of his age. Sir Thomas Fairfax, for example, used the council of war as a means of debate and engaging men with his ideas, although in the end the decision was his.

Cromwell did likewise. He was a great believer in the power of persuasion, particularly his own, throughout his life. Once convinced of the righteousness of his action, through frequent prayer, he would try to convince others. In this council of war both the general staff and the commanders of regiments could have voice in free discussion. Prayer and fasting were used as part of this debate, and with more indecisive men they could be persuaded thereby to do things their instinct told them not to do. Nevertheless, Cromwell also used the council of war to convince and explain his strategy much as Fairfax had done before him. In terms of his inferior officers, for example Michael Jones in 1649 and John Lambert in 1648–51, Cromwell was fortunate in finding loyal subordinates who, like himself under Fairfax, were not afraid of speaking their minds but would nevertheless do their duty. Such persuasive techniques were, in any case, a feature of the politician's art in Cromwell.

While we should not, as so many have, place him in the ranks of hypocrites for using these tactics, there is little doubt that at times he could be both devious and subtle. One critic even claimed that Cromwell thought dissimulation and double dealing to be no vices, and even lying could in necessity be tolerable. Certainly, many agreed that he had 'great command over all his Passions and affections; could weep when he saw his Friend in tears and laugh as he saw occasion.'[24] If these really were the politician's arts, then they transferred well enough into his military career. However, we should not doubt his sincerity at the actual time he said things, for he often appears as a man who impulsively believed in what he said at the time he said it. This could, of course, lead to contradictions, but the virtue of the cause he followed drove him on, alongside a Providential world view. His religion, like that of many another convert, had not only rescued him from severe mental distress but shown him the righteousness of his path. Why not use the ideas in his mind to persuade and dominate others, if it were for the greatest of all causes? By so doing he was able to 'manage' the Earl of Manchester for a good while, and these techniques had a similar effect on Sir Thomas Fairfax and Sir William Waller. His men, on the other hand, may have found his views and oddities obscure, as we do today, but at least Cromwell generally brought them victory and cared for their welfare, and in time of war that in the end was enough for any soldier.

Although we hear little about Cromwell's inspiring speeches to his men or the other ostentatious techniques of the general's art, they did exist. Ironically, given his long-windedness in Parliament, his speeches seem to have been simple, short and to the point. They tended to be extemporary, and akin to the preacher's style of the day. He took his men at their worth and was tender of their consciences, loving them as 'honest men', but he was also a severe disciplinarian, swearing, drunkenness, mutiny and looting all being sternly punished. His argument about their religion with Major-General Crawford in 1644, however, was blunt and to the point: 'Sir, the state, in choosing men to serve them, takes no notice of their opinions, if they be willing faithfully to serve them, that satisfies', or, as he later put it, 'If I were to choose the meanest officer in the Army ... I would choose a godly man that hath principles; especially where a trust is to be committed, because I know where to have a man that hath principles.'[25] The objective of his leadership was victory, and the men chosen were 'godly, honest men' whom he could lead to destroy the enemy forces in the field. Nevertheless, if he sought particular men to lead, sectaries by preference, he was also willing openly to oust others in the name of unity if both he (and God) saw fit to do so. Ultimately, Cromwell as soldier remains as much a man of contradictions as Cromwell as a politician and as a man – on the one hand apparently open and frank, deeply religious and sincere, but on the other capable of great shrewdness and cunning.

CAVALRY TACTICIAN

In the field of grand tactics, Cromwell appears to have learnt their use while on campaign. Just occasionally, as at Preston against Langdale, he was flexible and cautiously experimental, but, in general, his tactical view of the use of cavalry, the primary arm with which he was involved, seems to have developed in his mind gradually, as a result of both experience and observation. Initially he was a hesitant soldier, for example at Grantham in 1643, and, like much of the Parliamentary cavalry of the early days of the war, his tactics were prone to use shot rather than the mass weight of a cavalry charge to make his point. On the other hand, the caracole, that fancy use of shot and horsemanship in the so-called 'Dutch style', never seems to have been employed by Cromwell's troops. Instead, the troopers were gradually taught to rely on shock and cold steel. At first they also used firepower at the last moment, from pistols, to disrupt the opposition before charging home in their three ranks. Indeed, there is evidence that, once fired, the pistols or carbines would be thrown at the faces of the opponent. This necessitated riding up close to the opponent, almost to 'their horses' noses' in the front rank.[26] Later, as Cromwell's experience grew, he began to take more tactical initiatives. At this point, we find the use of weight of men and horse ever more essential to his methods.

These were methods undoubtedly adopted from the original Swedish practice, as well as from observation, reading and a consideration of the tactics used by that doyen of all cavalrymen in the war, Prince Rupert of the Rhine. Hence the use of cavalry became an action carried out in close order and reserving fire. On charging home, Vernon noted that 'In grosse bodies, if you have field room enough, all the troops are to be drawn up into battalions, each being not above three deepe; likewise each troop must be a least a hundred paces distance from each other for the better avoiding of disorder.'[28] Three deep had been Gustavus Adolphus's ideal for the Swedish cavalry, and this was adopted by Rupert and exploited by him in England. Sir Richard Bulstrode noted Rupert's instructions to his cavalry prior their engaging at Edgehill in 1642. The cavalry should go forward 'Sword in hand, to receive the Enemy's shot, without firing either carbine or Pistol, till we broke in amongst the Enemy, and then make use of our Fire-Arms as need should require.'[29] It was also a technique used by Cromwell and by most of his contemporaries. General George Monck refined it by suggesting that the first two of the three sub-divisions of a cavalry brigade should be moving at an easy trot while the other moved at a walking pace. Once the first two groups made contact, the latter could be used as a reserve, or sent into immediate action to bolster the forward lines. John Vernon goes on to give a clear view of the internal movements needed in such action as the troops went forward into battle:

'... those troops that are to give the first charge being drawn up in battail as before, are to be at their close order, every left hand man's right knee must be close locked under his right hand man's left ham ... In this order they are to advance toward the enemy with an easie pace, firing their carbines at a convenient distance, always aiming at their enemies breast or lower, because that powder is of an elevating nature.'[30]

One of the pistols was to be drawn by the right hand, the other left in the holster but 'charged, spann'd and primed ... in case of retreat'. Having fired, the troops were to charge 'at full career, but in good order with their swords fastned with a riband or the like unto their wrists, for fear of losing out of their hand if they should miss their blow.' At this point the enemy would open ranks, voluntarily, deliberately or because they had fallen by shot, or be bowled over (unlikely) or retire in some disorder (more likely). This was the objective of a charge – to 'break through and disorder the enemy's array, then make use of the sword to complete his discomfiture.'[31] It was also at this point that most cavalry became disorganised in action; and it is here that we find Cromwell's greatest tactical innovation. This was the inculcation of sufficient discipline in his men to hold them in check and recover them after the first charge. It was invariably difficult for officers to keep their troopers and themselves under control once the action had begun, and, ironically, 'the charge and mêlée do not last long enough to inflict or sustain a heavy loss in men and horses.'[32] It was the pursuit that did the most damage, and this was the action most difficult to halt once started, as Prince Rupert was to find out. Nolan later explained: '… it is difficult to recall the men: they are maddened with the excitement of the fight, and intent only on cutting down the unfortunate fugitives in front of them.'[33]

Cromwell, on the other hand, discovered the tactical keys necessary for victory. First, there was 'solidarity and weight', rather than outright pace, in attack; he seems to have sent his men in on a 'pretty round trot'. Again, Nolan later suggested 'a trot to within one hundred and fifty yards, then sound the gallop, and immediately afterwards the charge; thus brought up close to the enemy fresh and well in hand you hurl them upon him in close array with irresistible speed.'[34] Importantly, Cromwell was also able to rally his men, and on occasion hold back a reserve. Clarendon put it more forcefully: 'Cromwell's troops if they were prevailed, or though they were beaten and routed, presently rallied again, and stood in good order till they received new orders.'[35] He also seems to have favoured, where he could achieve it, the attack in the flank, rolling up an already occupied enemy by detaching some of his troops to charge their front. Secondly, Cromwell's choice of men and his care for their arms, horses and morale assisted his battlefield control. Morale he tried to keep up through the cause, regular pay and the prevention of plunder and indiscipline. He insisted that the horses be well cared for and well chosen. He kept an iron discipline on and off the field,[36] one contemporary news writer of Cromwell's regiment of horse noting that

'No man swears but he pays his twelve pence; if he be drunk he is set in the stocks or worse, if one calls the other "Roundhead" he is cashiered; insomuch that the countries when they come leap for joy of them, and come in and join with them. How happy were it if all the forces were thus disciplined.'[37]

So what were the duties of the officers of the troop in the tactical charge? Lord Orrery later suggested the senior officer should not lead the charge above 'the length of his [horse's] head beyond the front rank of troopers',[38] the reason being that they would be exposed to fire and that the shot of their own men would be hindered; indeed, their own men could kill them. Some claimed that it animated the men to see their officers heroically out in front. Orrery disagreed, as 'good soldiers need not such airy animations', and the officer would be unable to retreat into the first rank, they being 'well wedged up'.[39] Yet Cromwell himself, when engaging in tactical warfare on the battlefield, seems regularly to have chosen to lead by example, from the front rank.

SIEGE WARFARE

One of the crucial tests of the Early Modern general's art was that of siege warfare. Cromwell had been engaged in this form of combat since at least 1643, and, as in battle, he was not favourably disposed towards the contemporary elaborate blockade and timely gaining of advantages over besieged towns or castles by the use of sap and parallel. Instead, for him, especially in his Irish campaign of 1649, if a place needed to be captured, then the act should be undertaken as swiftly as possible. Siege warfare to Cromwell was perhaps as much a political act as a military problem. Although he was willing to offer terms if he could, he took little responsibility for the fate of the garrison if it went against what he saw as the will of God in such matters. Consequently, his siege warfare tended to be a blunt instrument. In it we may see actions at Basing House in 1645 and at Drogheda and Wexford in 1649, but also the failures at Kilkenny and Clonmel. Accordingly, when campaigning in Scotland in 1650 he largely tried to avoid it, or left it to others such as Monck while he went off in search of battle.

LOGISTICS

Logistics in Early Modern warfare was not yet the refined art it was to become. At times, both men and beasts suffered feast or famine owing to the inadequacies of providing the materials of war. The heroic commander was forced to deal with the more substantial needs of his men, but often did so reluctantly. In this particular capacity, however, Oliver Cromwell has often been underestimated: he, at least, was well aware of the importance of logistics. It was essential for Cromwell to get his men their daily rations of cheese, bread, biscuit and beer and the supply of fodder for the horses. Clothing, footwear and shelter were often more problematic, but still necessary. His frequent and noisy cries throughout his military career for supplies and money show that he always had an eye for the logistical side of war; for example, his care on the march to Preston in 1648 to obtain ample numbers of shoes for the infantry is noticeable. His concern not only gave the soldiers an important boost to their morale, but also, just as vitally, enabled them to continue their punishing march north.

Cromwell's main aims in his logistical warfare were to sustain morale and discipline. He needed adequate supplies to prevent his men from breaking away and plundering the countryside. Looting would inevitably lead to indiscipline and the breakdown of authority. All seventeenth-century armies were prone to this, but Cromwell fought hard to prevent it and punished the culprits accordingly. Only occasionally did he let his men off the leash, and then the devastating results must have shocked even him. To Cromwell, good supply would also enable his forces to be concentrated in readiness for battle, rather than dispersed and searching for the basic necessities of life.

The essential *matériel* of any Early Modern campaign lay in supplies of food, replacement horses for cavalry troops or transport purposes, general equipment, munitions, actual reinforcements in the shape of recruits, and lastly finance to pay for all of this. In his later campaigns in Ireland and Scotland, we see Cromwell at his most successful as a logistician. Significantly, he recognised the value of sea power in these campaigns in underpinning the army's logistical demands in areas of poor resources. Ships could be used to bring in tons of clothing, munitions and supplies at set points, or to sail up and down the coasts and reach the army at its established bases. They could be used to transport his heavy artillery, and to bring in the constant supply of recruits he demanded of central government. They were also used to evacuate wounded and sick men. In poor places such as Ireland, devastated by war for some years before the army arrived in 1649, and Scotland, poor in local resources and deliberately denuded of supplies and population by the enemy, this use of logistical support by sea was vital to the eventual success of the campaign. Cromwell was well aware of the magnitude of logistics, having had ample experience of poor supplies and finances in the First Civil War. Even here, and later during the Preston campaign, however, his insistence on swift supplies and money as the 'sinews of war' marks him out from many of his contemporaries, who were sometimes swamped by haphazard logistical support.

Above all, he saw money as vital. It was needed to pay his troops and preserve the local population. By it men were kept together and justly rewarded for their service, and the population was spared the ravages of war. His insistence on having substantial funds to campaign in both Ireland and Scotland is noticeable; it doubtless stemmed from his first experiences in war with the Eastern Association. Many were the pleas from the newly established Colonel Oliver Cromwell to the local and central authorities for pay and monies for his troops. In these he was generally successful, although even he sometimes despaired of the hesitant country committees. Nevertheless, his troops were always noted as not being akin to the ravening hordes that early seventeenth-century armies always threatened to become. This was also a practical tactic, for by it he could win over local hearts and minds by getting his troops to pay the locals for their supplies. In short, this logistical element to his skills as a soldier was the vital bedrock of his notable military successes.[40]

INTELLIGENCE

Intelligence-gathering in both the tactical and strategic sense was naturally an important part of the heroic general's art. Clarendon, for one, was rather scornful of the intelligence work in the Civil Wars, claiming, for example, that, prior to Edgehill, neither side had any idea of the whereabouts of the other, and that the fact that each met the other in the field was a miracle. Correspondence and published newsletters were extensive on both sides of the political divide, and they could reveal much about the plans of opposing generals, although, equally, such material could contain many rumours and some barefaced lies. For more specific military intelligence, the main responsibility in the armies for gathering such material fell to the scoutmaster.[41]

Most armies had a scoutmaster to undertake the co-ordination of intelligence operations, and his position, apparently peculiar to the English military world, was an important one in the forces of the day. Some proved to be very good at intelligence-gathering, while others, such as the Royalist Scoutmaster Ruce prior to Naseby in 1645, were very poor indeed. The post allowed one individual to be tasked with the duty of sending out scouts into the local areas before the army, in order to reconnoitre the ground ahead. However, this military function soon expanded into more general espionage activity, with the scoutmaster interrogating locals, or captured prisoners, who could provide information. He also acted to intercept couriers and despatches, as well as sending out spies. Many men and women were sent on secret missions behind the lines to spy out the enemy's plans. The essential information desired would be that relating to numbers of troops, orders of battle and other general intelligence regarding the quality of the opponents and their whereabouts when they were in the field. In an era of poor-quality maps and a somewhat naive attitude to time (watches, if not rare, were often unreliable) and distance, good intelligence could be vital in making military decisions.

Sir Samuel Luke had served well enough as the Earl of Essex's scoutmaster, while Lionel Watson, who also held the rank of major, served as scoutmaster in both Manchester's army and the New Model, where Cromwell will have undoubtedly come across him. Sprigge noted that Watson's continued diligence in getting timely intelligence of the enemy's movements then and always 'redounded not a little to the enablement of the army'.[42] Later, the civilian Henry Jones, Bishop of Clogher, fulfilled the same function in Ireland, while the notorious Sir George Downing served the army as its scoutmaster in Scotland in the 1650s. The scoutmaster was well paid and needed to be, for he had to be able, as often as not, to reward his agents and buy intelligence. Imprisonment or execution often awaited those who were caught in such activities. In the field, cavalry were used to gather operational information ahead of the army. Patrols and sentries were used to observe the opponent, and, closer to the battle, the good general would always try to scout ahead and see for himself, as well as listen to the news of others.

Cromwell's capacity for intelligence work always seems to have been a sound part of his soldiering. He took care to observe the enemy in the field from the shortest possible distance, often, as we have seen, placing himself in some danger as consequence, but he also took advice from his scoutmasters and personally interrogated agents and local civilians. Later, when he was Lord Protector, he was renowned, alongside his secretary John Thurloe, for placing much value on the gathering of good intelligence on former friends and old enemies alike, and for paying well to obtain it. He is likely to have learned the value of such secret matters in the field.

GRAND STRATEGY

If logistics and intelligence were difficult conundrums for any early seventeenth-century general, then strategy in the Civil Wars was even more problematic. How did Cromwell fit into this picture? After Edge-hill, the strategy for both sides in England developed into a localised affair, dictated as much by the needs of supply as by local and central politics. Peace parties, neutrals and extremists on the Parliamentary side fought over what to do with the new armies once they were formed. Indeed, after the first shock at Edgehill and the discovery that the war was not going to be such a short affair after all, both sides were eager to seize as much territory as possible, whether castles, towns or fortified houses, in order to maintain garrisons to control the disputed areas of the country. Troops in garrisons would additionally give access to the materials of their hinterland, although they generally had to be drawn from the field armies. Consequently battles, where they occurred, tended to be untidy affairs and to have localised consequences, reflecting the ideas of both sides that minimal risk was perhaps the best policy.

Many in Parliament thought that this territorial struggle would eventually bring accommodation and negotiation – a stalemate of peace – by which the rightful rulers of the state, the King on one side and Parliament's aristocratic generals and politicians on the other, could reach agreement. The Earl of Manchester, for example, 'was of the opinion that this war would not be ended by the sword ... but it would be better for the kingdom if it were ended by an accommodation.'[43] Consequently, the years 1642–44 became years of battle and skirmish, of the seizure of territory and of manoeuvring for the best position. It was thought by some, including Oliver Cromwell, that this was not necessarily the best way to resolve the nation's problems.

The military structures that evolved in the first years of the war also tended to aid this strategy by being localised and parochial in their outlook. Militias and recruits alike often proved reluctant to move outside of their county or association borders, and central control on both sides was far too lax; a general war-winning strategy was, as a consequence, difficult to create. Eventually, the absence of this type of strategy would lead to severe arguments and dissension. The famous quarrel between Manchester and Cromwell in 1644 exemplified the strategic dilemma. By 1644 Charles I did not seem to be able to win the war outright, and some of the Parliamentary generals were apparently not trying to win it at all. Manchester was eventually forced to admit that he was against fighting 'that if we should beat the King never so often yet he would be King still and his posterity, but if he should beat us but once we must be hanged and our posterity undone', to which Cromwell angrily replied that 'if this principle was true it condemned all our former fighting as foolish, and was an argument against fighting in the future, and a ground for making peace how dishonourable soever'.[44]

From this crisis would emerge a second strategy – that of a winnable war. In this, it was argued, Parliament needed to turn to a war of annihilation, thereby destroying the King's field army, and then seize territory. One side – that is, Parliament – had to win, in order to secure the peace. It would mean a move away from localised forces to create a professional standing army, willing to move wherever Parliament ordered it, and win the victories necessary to achieve peace. As Sir William Waller wrote, following his difficulties with the London Trained Bands in 1644, 'I write these particulars to let you know that an army compounded of these men will never go through with your service, and till you have an army merely your own, that you may command, it is in a manner impossible to do anything of importance.'[45] This would inevitably have political consequences. Cromwell saw this, and the political struggle to establish the New Model would also carry with it the logic of a new strategy to seek out the King's main army and crush it in battle. Cromwell was even willing to give up his command if this strategy could be achieved. It was; he took his part; and in doing so the strategy altered the face of the conflict.

Cromwell's later campaigns in Ireland and Scotland were other matters. Strategically, victory in Ireland was thought by Cromwell to be only really possible through a re-conquest and a complete resolution of the religious and political problems of that state by Parliamentary intervention. Here, the soldiers were working towards a greater political end – the security of the newly established English republic. The strategy used, therefore, was as much political as military: crush the Irish and their armies and impose a peace on that nation. Cromwell still sought his battle, but he was eventually forced into a war of attrition by the nature of the conflict. When he left in May 1650, the campaign was incomplete.

At first Cromwell regarded Scotland as a useful ally in the war with the King, although he soon grew hostile to the religious overtones of the Solemn League and Covenant. Later still he viewed the Scots, unlike the Irish, as capable of persuasion, if only they would listen to the voice of God as seen in himself and the army he commanded. Military victory and godly persuasion were indeed to be the two points of Cromwellian strategy in his dealings with the Scots in the 1650s. Only when the latter took a naturally divergent view and introduced Charles II did Scotland have to be brought to submission by outright military victory. Once again, Cromwell's attempts to bring the Scots to battle only resulted in a war of attrition. Yet while, in the end, he achieved his victory, the war continued. It was only the calculated move over the Forth or God's Providence that created the invasion of England in 1651 and brought his desired result in the fields outside Worcester.

THE SHADOWS OF WAR

Early in the year 1642, the shadows of civil war had begun to creep over the Cromwell household, as they did over many another household in England. For most of the men and women of the day, war was a reluctant last choice in a period of often agonising choices. For some, however, civil war was, if not looked for, then taken as part of God's divine plan for England, and subject to what John Milton later called 'eternal providence'. We must always keep this in mind when we explore any of Oliver Cromwell's subsequent actions, for, as we have seen, everything Cromwell did had to him a purpose, and his military life was at one with his life in general, which was merely part of God's greater plan.

Nevertheless, in early 1640 Oliver Cromwell had been merely an obscure forty-one-year-old Cambridge farmer with, as far as we know, few if any military ambitions. In a speech in 1653, he was to comment upon God's raising up 'a poor and contemptible company of men', amongst whom he counted himself: 'neither versed in military affairs, nor having much natural propensity to them, even through the owning of a principle of godliness – of Religion.'[46] In fact, following various social and financial misfortunes in the late 1620s and the early 1630s, Cromwell in 1640 was much more concerned with his family and estate than with soldiering. The Cromwell of the 1640s was a good family man and neighbour, with a very keen sense of his religious duty; he also acted as a not very successful (indeed, rather over-enthusiastic) Member of Parliament. He was a man on the fringes of power and, to those who held it, arguably of little real consequence – a backwoods Member of Parliament, useful to launch against opponents, but with none of the subtlety of some of his kin, such as John Hampden and Oliver St John; as a general, a military man, his vision did not as yet go so far, or, if it did, he kept quiet about it (although it was transfixed by the fortunes of the great Protestant hero of Europe, Gustavus Adolphus). Yet, in war, Cromwell would find a resolution of both the country's political ills and his own personal agonies over matters of conscience, and within a mere ten years outstrip all his rivals and come to dominate the political and military scene of his country.

NOTES

Introduction

1. R. Burton, *The History of Oliver Cromwell, Lord Protector &c* (1698), i.
2. T. S. Baldock, *Cromwell as a Soldier* (1899). A notable exception to this is A. Woolrych, 'Cromwell as a Soldier' in J. Morrill (ed.), *Oliver Cromwell and the English Revolution* (1990), 93–118. See also J. C. Davis, *Oliver Cromwell* (2001); P. A. Charrier, 'Cromwell as a Soldier', *Journal of the Royal United Services Institution*, L (1906), 1347–72. This book was written and in the hands of the publisher before I was aware of S. Robbins, *God's General* (2003). As such I have been unable to take its findings into account.
3. J. C. Davis, *Oliver Cromwell*, 88. Cromwell biographies and references are naturally legion; essential reading, however, exists in the works cited above and in B. Coward, *Oliver Cromwell* (1991); W. S. Abbott, *The Writings and Speeches of Oliver Cromwell* (4 vols, Cambridge, Mass., 1939–47; hereinafter cited as *Writings*); C. H. Firth, *Oliver Cromwell and the Rule of the Puritans* (Oxford, 1900); R. S. Paul, *The Lord Protector: Religion and Politics in the Life of Oliver Cromwell* (1955); C. Hill, *God's Englishman* (1970); A. Fraser, *Cromwell, Our Chief of Men* (1973); I. Roots, *The Speeches of Oliver Cromwell* (1989; hereinafter cited as *Speeches*) C. H. Firth, *Cromwell's Army: A History of the English Soldier During the Civil Wars, the Commonwealth and the Protectorate* (1902, reprinted 1967); C. H. Firth, and G. Davies, *The Regimental History of Cromwell's Army* (2 vols, Oxford, 1940); and S. R. Gardiner, *History of the Great Civil War* (4 vols, 1893, reprinted Windrush Press 1987).
4. For all his self-effacement, Cromwell certainly knew how to use the Press: see A. N. B. Cotton, 'John Dillingham, Journalist of the Middle Group', *English Historical Review*, XCIII (1978), 817–34. As an example of the popular art, see *A Perfect List of all the Victories obtained by the Lord General Cromwell* (1650).

Chapter 1

1. The history of the Cromwell family is given in M. Noble, *Memoirs of the Protectoral House of Cromwell* (2 vols, Birmingham, 1784). The early history of Cromwell is to be found in the important essay by J. Morrill, 'The Making of Oliver Cromwell' in J. Morrill (ed.), *Oliver Cromwell and the English Revolution* (1990), 19–48; and in S. J. Weyman, 'Oliver Cromwell's Kinsfolk', *English Historical Review*, VI (1891), 48–60.
2. *Speeches*, 42.
3. *Writings*, I, 29.
4. A. Fraser, *Our Chief of Men*, 5–6, 20–1.
5. *Writings*, I, 69.
6. J. Sharpe, *Early Modern England: A Social History, 1550–1760* (1987), 166–7.
7. J. Morrill, 'The Making of Oliver Cromwell', 24.
8. *Writings*, I, 262.
9. *Speeches*, 134.
10. *Writings*, I, 96–7.
11. R. Burton, *The History of Oliver Cromwell, Lord Protector &c* (1698), Cromwell, 2.
12. J. Hodgson, *Autobiography of Captain John Hodgson* (Brighouse, 1882), 37.
13. R. Burton, *op. cit.*, 171.
14. *Writings*, I, 121.
15. R. S. Paul, *The Lord Protector: Religion and Politics in the Life of Oliver Cromwell* (1955), 48.
16. J. Raymond, 'An Eye-witness to King Cromwell', *History Today*, XLVII (1997), 38.
17. *Ibid.*
18. L. L. Knoppers, *Constructing Cromwell: Ceremony, Portrait and Print, 1645–1661* (Cambridge, 2000), 11.
19. J. Raymond, *op. cit.*, 39.
20. D. Underdown, *Prides Purge: Politics in the English Revolution* (1985), 8; R. F. Horton, *Oliver Cromwell: A Study in Personal Religion* (1897); B. Worden, 'Oliver Cromwell and the Sin of Achan', in D. Beales, G. Best (eds), *History, Society and the Churches: Essays in Honour of Owen Chadwick* (Cambridge, 1985), 125–45; P. Miller, *The New England Mind: The Seventeenth Century* (Boston, 1961), 14–15.
21. N. H. Keeble (ed.), *The Autobiography of Richard Baxter* (1974), 56–7; R. S. Paul, *The Lord Protector: Religion and Politics in the Life of Oliver Cromwell* (1955); J. C. Davis, *Oliver Cromwell* (2001), 112–37.

22. C. Hill, *The English Bible in the Seventeenth Century Revolution* (Harmondsworth, 1994), 35–6.

23. *Ibid.*, 36.

24. R. J. Acheson, *Radical Puritans in England, 1550–1660* (1990), 1.

25. Quoted in N. Tyacke, *Anti-Calvinists, The Rise of English Arminianism, c. 1590–1649* (Oxford, 1990), 2.

26. *Ibid.*, 6.

27. *Writings*, I, 64.

28. *Ibid.*, 65.

29. *Ibid.*, 65

30. *Ibid.*, 96–7.

31. M. A. G. Haykin, *To Honour God: The Spirituality of Oliver Cromwell* (Ontario, 1999), 27.

32. *Speeches*, 72.

33. J. Sproxton, 'From Calvin to Cromwell through Beard', *Journal of European Studies*, XXV (1995), 27; B. Worden, 'Providence and Politics in Cromwellian England', *Past and Present*, CIX (1985), 55–99.

34. M. A. G. Haykin, *op. cit.*, 23–4.

35. *Writings*, I, 696–9. See also Paul's Letter to the Romans, for Biblical parallels.

36. K. Thomas, *Religion and the Decline of Magic Studies in Popular Beliefs in 16th and 17th Century England* (Harmondsworth, 1999 ed.), 137.

37. *Ibid.*

38. Richard Bernard, *The Bible-Battells, or the Sacred Art Military* (1629), 1.

39. *Ibid.*, vii.

40. See J. Morrill, 'King-Killing No Murder: Cromwell in 1648', *Cromwelliana* (1998), 12–21.

41. Carrington, quoted in R. S. Paul, *op. cit.*, 300–1.

42. Psalm 71:7.

43. Psalm 46:9–11.

44. Fraser, *op. cit.*, 371.

45. Psalm 68:1.

46. Carlyle, *On Heroes* (1895), 352.

47. R. F. Horton, *Oliver Cromwell: A Study in Personal Religion* (1897), 25–6.

48. Arrowsmith and Marshall, quoted in S. P. Revard, *The War in Heaven: Paradise Lost and the Tradition of Satan's Rebellion* (1980), 117–18.

49. S. R. Gardiner, *Oliver Cromwell* (1901), 30.

50. *Speeches*, 9–10.

51. J. F. C. Fuller, *The Generalship of Ulysses S. Grant* (1991), 13.

52. *Speeches*, 73. See also G. Drake, 'The Ideology of Oliver Cromwell', *Church History*, XXV (1966), 295–72.

53. J. Heath, *Flagellum or the life ... of Oliver Cromwell* (1663), 16–17.

54. M. Roberts, *Swedish diplomats at Cromwell's court* (Camden Society, 4th series XXXVI, 1988), 83–4.

55. *Writings*, II, 103.

56. B. Donagan, 'Halcyon Days and the Literature of War: England's Military Education before 1642', *Past and Present*, CXLVII (1995), 78.

Chapter 2

1. Hobbes, *Leviathan* (Oxford, 1996), 222. Work on the Civil Wars of the Three Kingdoms is legion. One should begin with C. Russell, *The Fall of the British Monarchies, 1637–1642* (Oxford, 1991), C. Russell, *The Causes of the English Civil War* (1990), and K. Sharpe, *The Personal Rule of Charles I* (Yale, 1992). Still essential is S. R. Gardiner, *History of England* (10 vols, 1900).

2. C. Carlton, *Charles I: The Personal Monarch* (1984 ed) remains the most sensible of biographies. See also C. Russell, *The Causes of the English Civil War* (1990), 185–212.

3. K. Sharpe, *The Personal Rule of Charles I*, 180.

4. *Ibid.*

5. See the essays in J. Morrill, *Oliver Cromwell and the English Revolution* (1990).

6. S. R. Gardiner, *op. cit.*; M. Perceval-Maxwell, *The Outbreak of the Irish Rebellion of 1641* (Dublin, 1998); B. Fitzpatrick, *Seventeenth Century Ireland: The Wars of Religion* (Dublin, 1988); B. Mac Cuarta (ed.), *Ulster 1641: Aspects of the Rising* (Belfast, 1993).

7. See B. Mac Cuarta, *op. cit.*, 5.

8. Clarendon, quoted by K. J. Lindley, 'The Impact of the 1641 rebellion upon England and Wales 1641–5', *Irish Historical Review*, XVIII (1972), 151.

9. S. R. Gardiner, *op. cit.* X.

10. S. R. Gardiner, *Puritan Revolution 1603–1660* (1920), 127. See also G. Seel, 'Cromwell's trailblazer? Re-Interpreting the Earl of Essex', *History Today*, XLV (1995), 22–8; and V. F. Snow, *Essex the Rebel: The Life of Robert Devereux, the Third Earl of Essex, 1591–1646* (Lincoln, Nebraska, 1970).

Chapter 3

1. Joseph Hill, quoted in S. L. Revard, *The War in Heaven: Paradise Lost and the tradition of Satan's Rebellion* (1980), 131. See also A. Cunningham and O. Grell, *The Four Horsemen of the Apocalypse: Religion, War, Famine and Death in Reformation Europe* (Cambridge, 2000).

2. See P. Contamine, *War in the Middle Ages* (1984), 219; and C. Oman, *The Art of War in the Middle Ages* (2 vols, 1991 edn).

3. See P. Contamine, *op. cit.*, 229.

4. W. N. Archer, *The Double-Armed Man* (1625).

5. See C. Oman, *The Art of War in the Sixteenth Century* (1937), 63–73.

6. J. R. Hale, *War and Society in Renaissance Europe, 1450–1620* (1985), 46. The discussion on the military revolution can be followed in M. Roberts, *Essays in Swedish History* (1967); G. Parker, *The Military Revolution, 1500–1800: Military Innovation and the Rise of the West* (Cambridge, 1988); J. Black, *A Military Revolution? Military Change and European Society 1550–1800* (1991); J. Childs, *Warfare in the Seventeenth Century* (2003); and T. M. Barker, J. Black and W. F. Cook, 'Geoffrey Parker's Military Revolution: Three reviews of the Second Edition', *The Journal of Military History*, LXI (1997), 347–54. On the strategy and tactics of the era, see *The Rudiments of Militarie Discipline* (Edinburgh, 1638); *The English Military Discipline* (1672); G. Monck, Duke of Albemarle, *Observations upon Militarily and Political Affairs* (1671); D. Parrott, 'Strategy and Tactics in the Thirty Years' War', *Militargeschichtliche Mitteilungen*, II (1985), 7–25; and C. Duffy, *Siege Warfare: The Fortress in the Early Modern World, 1494–1660* (1979).

7. Onasander, quoted in A. Goldsworthy, *In the Name of Rome: The Men who won the Roman Empire* (2003), 12.

8. J. Childs, *The Nine Years' War and the British Army, 1688–1697* (Manchester, 1991), 91.

9. See M. C. Fissel, *English Warfare, 1511–1642* (2001)

10. *Ibid.*, 255.

11. See G. Davies, 'The Parliamentary Army under the Earl of Essex, 1642–5', *English Historical Review*, XLIX (1934), 32–53. See also N. Wharton, 'Letters from a Subaltern Officer of the Earl of Essex's Army', *Archeologia*, XXXV (1853).

12. N. Wharton, *op. cit.*, (1853), 313.

13. *Ibid.*, 317

14. *Ibid.*, 321.

15. *Ibid.*, 322.

16. *Ibid.*, 325.

17. See W. P. Guthrie, *Battles of the Thirty Years' War from White Mountain to Nordlingen, 1618–1635* (2002), 3.

18. S. Bull and M. Seed, *Bloody Preston: The Battle of Preston, 1648* (1998), 8

19. *The Rudiments of Militarie Discipline* (Edinburgh, 1638), 6.

20. W. P. Guthrie, *op. cit.*, 4.

21. B. P. Hughes, *Firepower: Weapons Effectiveness on the Battlefield, 1630–1850* (1974), 27; J.

Tucker and L. S. W. Linstock (eds), *The English Civil War: A Military Handbook* (1972).

22. R. Ward, *Animadversions of Warre* (1639), Bk. II, 61; *The Military Garden or Instructions for all Young Soldiers* (1629).

23. See F. Jones, 'The role and effectiveness of cavalry in the English Civil War, 1642–1645' (unpublished M.Phil, Wolverhampton, 2000), 4.

24. J. Cruso, *Militarie Instructions for the Cavalrie* (Cambridge 1632; reprinted edn New York, 1968), 88, 95–6.

25. J. Keegan, *The Face of Battle* (1978), 148.

26. L. E. Nolan, *Cavalry: Its History and Tactics* (1853 ed), 228

27. A. du Picq, *Battle Studies: Roots of Strategy*, vol. 2 (Mechanicsburg, 1987), 210.

28. J. Cruso, *op. cit.*, 88–9.

29. W. Barriffe, *Militarie Discipline or the Young Artilleryman* (1661), 26.

30. Montecuccoli, quoted in F. Tallett, *War and Society in Early Modern Europe, 1495–1715* (1997), 30.

31. Bulstrode, quoted in P. Young, *Edgehill 1642: The Campaign and the Battle* (1998 ed), 259. The sources for Edgehill are reasonably accessible, the majority being printed in Young's volume. Where necessary they have been checked against the original Thomason and other tracts in the British Library. See also *A Relation of the Battaile lately Fought Between Keynton and Edghill* (Oxford, 1642); A. H. Burne and P. Young, *The Great Civil War: A Military History of the First Civil War, 1642–1646* (Gloucester, 1998), 17–3; and G. Davies, ' The Battle of Edgehill', *English Historical Review*, XXXVI (1921), 30–44.

32. Bulstrode, quoted in Young, *op. cit.*, 258.

33. *Ibid.*, 255.

34. S. R. Gardiner, *Oliver Cromwell* (1901), 29.

35. S. Peachey and A. Turton, *Old Robin's Foot: The Equipping and Campaigns of Essex's Infantry 1642–1645* (1987), 22–3.

36. R. Codrington, 'Life and Death of the Illustrious Robert, Earl of Essex' (1646), *Harleian Miscellany*, (10 vols, 1808–13), I, 223.

37. C. H. Firth (ed.), *Memoirs of Edmund Ludlow* (Oxford, 2 vols, 1894), I, 38.

38. *Writings*, I, 199.

39. S. R. Gardiner, *History of the Great Civil War*, I, 31.

40. N. H. Keeble (ed.), *The Autobiography of Richard Baxter* (1974), 40–1.

41. Bulstrode, quoted in Young, *op. cit.*, 255.

42. *Ibid.*

43. Parliamentary Account, quoted in Young, *Edgehill*, 291.

44. *Ibid.*

45. James II, quoted in *Edgehill*, 263.

46. Young, *Edgehill*, 93.

47. Clarendon, quoted in C. Carlton, *Charles I: The Personal Monarch* (1984 edn), 260.

48. N. Wharton, 'Letters from a Subaltern Officer of the Earl of Essex's Army', *Archeologia*, XXXV (1853), 322. For Rupert see A. H. Burne, 'Generalship in the First Civil War, 1642–1644', *History Today*, I, (1951), 63–9; and M. Ashley, *Rupert of the Rhine* (1976).

49. W. D. Macray (ed.), *Clarendon, History of the Rebellion*, (6 vols, Oxford 1888, 1959 edn), II, 358

50. R. Wiseman, *Chirurgicall Treatises* (1676), 348–9.

51. Warwick, Young, *Edgehill*, 271.

52. Davies, *Edgehill*, 35.

53. Warwick, Young, *op. cit.*, 271. See also S. R. Gardiner, *Civil War*, I, 44.

54. Bulstrode, quoted in Davies, *Edgehill*, 32.

55. Clarendon, quoted in Davies, *Edgehill*, 32.

56. Barriffe, quoted in *op. cit.*, 11.

57. Keegan, *op. cit.*, 163.

58. Bifield, quoted in Young, *Edgehill*, 301.

59. Wharton, quoted in *op. cit.*, 316

60. J. Shay, *Achilles in Vietnam: Combat Trauma and the Undoing of Character* (1994), 10. See also S. Stouffer, *The American Soldier: Combat and its Aftermath* (Studies in Psychology in World War II, 4 vols, Princeton, 1949), II, 76–7, 82–3, 125; V. D. Hanson, *The Western Way of War: Infantry Battle in Classical Greece* (2nd edn, 2000); I. Gentles, 'Why Men fought in the British Civil Wars, 1639–1652', *History Teacher*, XXVI (1993), 407–18; A. Kellett, *Combat Motivation: The Behaviour of Soldiers in Battle* (Boston, 1982).

61. R. Wiseman, *Chirurgicall Treatises* (1676); J. Woodall, *The Surgeon's Mate or Military and Domestic Surgery* (1655 edn); and C. Carlton, *Going to the Wars: The Experience of the British Civil Wars, 1638–1651* (1992), 223–6.

62. James II, quoted in Young, *Edgehill*, 264.

63. H. J. C. von Grimmelhausen, *Simplicius Simplicissimus* (1669), trans. H. Weisenborn and L. Macdonald (1964), 148–9.

64. Firth, *Ludlow*, I, 42.

65. James II, quoted in Young, *op. cit.*, 266.

66. Holles, Young, *Edgehill*, 276.

67. Firth, *op. cit.* I, 45.

68. Parliamentarian Account, quoted in Young, *Edgehill*, 293.

69. Knightley, quoted in Young, *Edgehill*, 302. Richard Baxter visited the field the day after the battle and found 'about a thousand dead bodies in the field ... (and I suppose many were buried before)' See N. H. Keeble (ed.), *The Autobiography of Richard Baxter* (1974), 42.

70. Knightley, quoted in Young, *op. cit.*, 302.

71. Knightley, quoted in Young, *op. cit.*, 302.

72. I. Roots (ed.), *Speeches*, 134.

Chapter 4

1. J. H. Hexter, *Reign of King Pym* (Harvard, 1979 edn), 4; M. A. G. Wanklyn, 'Royalist Strategy in the South of England, 1642–1644', *Southern History*, III (1981), 54–79.

2. For Waller see J. Adair, *Roundhead General: A Military Biography of Sir William Waller* (1969).

3. C. V. Wedgwood, *The King's War, 1641–1647* (1977 edn), 207–8.

4. See C. H. Firth (ed.), *Duchess of Newcastle: The life of William Cavendish, Duke of Newcastle* (1886). For the war in Lincolnshire see C. Holmes, *Seventeenth Century Lincolnshire* (Lincoln, 1980), 158–176. For Nottinghamshire see A. C. Wood, *Nottinghamshire in the Civil War* (Oxford, 1937), 29–93.

5. For Sir Thomas Fairfax see A. H. Burne, 'Generalship in the First Civil War, 1642–1644', *History Today*, I (1951), 63–9; and C. R. Markham, *The Life of the Great Lord Fairfax* (1870).

6. *Writings*, I, 208; C. H. Firth, 'The Raising of the Ironsides', *Transactions of the Royal Historical Society*, N.S. XIII (1899), 17–73; C. H. Firth, *Cromwell's Army: A History of the English Soldier During the Civil War, the Commonwealth and the Protectorate* (Oxford, 1902, 1967 edn); C. Holmes, *The Eastern Association in the English Civil War* (Cambridge, 1974).

7. *Writings*, I, 216.

8. C. H. Firth and G. Davies, *The Regimental History of Cromwell's Army* (2 vols, 1940), I, 4.

9. *Ibid.*, I, 15; N. H. Keeble (ed.), *The Autobiography of Richard Baxter* (1974), 42.

10. M. Stace (ed.), *Cromwelliana – A Chronological detail of events in which Oliver Cromwell was engaged, from 1642 to his death in 1658: with a continuation of other transactions to the Restoration* (1810), 4, 11. Hereinafter *Cromwelliana* (1810)

11. *Writings*, I, 216.

12. R. S. Paul, *The Lord Protector: Religion and Politics in the Life of Oliver Cromwell* (1955), 65; *Writings*, I, 277.

13. For more on Sexby's career see A. Marshall, 'Killing No Murder', *History Today*, LIII (2003), 20–5.

14. Sexby in A. S. P. Woodhouse, *Puritanism and Liberty* (1986 edn), 1–2.

15. *Writings*, I, 248.

16. *Ibid.*
17. F. A. Inderwick, *The Interregnum* (1891), 28; *Writings*, I, 231.
18. Paul, *op. cit.*, 67.
19. *Writings*, I, 264.
20. *Ibid.*, I, 260.
21. *Ibid.*, I, 262.
22. J. Berry and S. G. Lee, *A Cromwellian Major-General: The Career of Col. James Berry* (Oxford, 1938), 8.
23. J. Vernon, *The Young Horseman or the Honest Plain Dealing Cavalier* (1644; 1993 edn), 34.
24. C. Chenevix Trench, 'Horsemanship in History', *History Today*, XX (1970), 772.
25. Vernon, *op. cit.*, 43.
26. Cavalry Officer, *Cavalry Tactics* (1897), 74.
27. Vernon, *op. cit.*, 44. See also Ward, *Animadversions*, Bk I, 283–9.
28. S. Angelo, *Martial Arts of Renaissance Europe* (Yale, 2000), 256. See also J. Tincey, *Ironsides: English Cavalry, 1588–1688* (2002).
29. J. Cruso, *Militarie Instructions for the Cavalrie* (Cambridge 1632; reprinted edn New York, 1968), 42.
30. La Touche, quoted in Angelo, *op. cit.*, 269.
31. A. du Picq, *Battle Studies: Roots of Strategy*, vol. 2 (Mechanicsburg, 1987), 214.
32. *Cavalry Tactics*, 79; Firth, *Cromwell's Army*, 144.
33. *Cromwelliana* (1810), 4; T. Bevis, 'The Siege of Crowland', *Lincolnshire Life*, XXXVI (1997), 53.
34. *Cromwelliana* (1810), 4.
35. *Writings*, I, 230. *Cromwelliana* (1810), 6–7; A. C. Welby, 'Belton Fight: Cromwell's Victory Near Grantham, 15 May 1643', *Lincolnshire Notes and Queries*, XV (1915), 38–47.
36. *Writings*, I, 230.
37. *Ibid.*, 245; J. West, *Oliver Cromwell and the Battle of Gainsborough* (1992); P. Gaunt, 'The Battle of Gainsborough', *Cromwelliana* (1998), 8–11.
38. *Writings*, I, 243.
39. *Ibid.*, 245.
40. *Ibid.*, 246; *The Copy of a Letter Written by Colonel Cromwell to the Committee at Cambridge* (1643).
41. *A true relation of the late fight* (1643), 5; *Cromwelliana* (1810), 7–8; B. Brammer, *Winceby and the Battle* (Boston, 1994).
42. *A true relation of the Great Victories* (1643), 4.
43. *A true relation of the late fight* (1643), 6.
44. *A true relation of the late fight* (1643), 5.
45. *A true relation of the Great Victories* (1643), 3.
46. *A true relation of the late fight* (1643), 6–7.
47. *A true relation of the late fight* (1643), 6–7.
48. *A true relation of the Great Victories* (1643), 3.
49. *A true relation of the Great Victories* (1643), 4.
50. *Writings*, I, 340.
51. J. Morrill, 'King-Killing No Murder: Cromwell in 1648', *Cromwelliana* (1998), 15.

Chapter 5

1. C. V. Wedgwood, 'The Covenanters in the First Civil War', *Scottish Historical Review*, XXXIX (1960), 1–15.
2. D. Laing (ed.), *Letters and Journal of Robert Baillie*, (3 vols, Bannatyne Club Edinburgh, 1842), I, 213.
3. C. S. Terry (ed.), *Papers relating to the Army of the Solemn League and Covenant 1643–1647* (Scottish History Society, XVI–XVII, 1917), lxxxii; C. S. Terry, *The Life and Campaigns of Alexander Leslie, First Earl of Leven* (1899); P. Dukas, 'The Leslie family in the Swedish Period (1630–5) of the Thirty Years' War', *European Studies Review*, XII (1982), 401–24. C. S. Terry, 'The Scottish Campaign in Northumberland and Durham', *Archaeologia Aeliana*, N.S. XXI (1899), 171–3.
4. P. Young, *Marston Moor: The Campaign and the Battle* (1997 edn), 194. Most of the sources for the battle are now in print. These have been checked against the original Thomason and other tracts in the British Library. See also *Cromwelliana* (1810), 9–11. Of the other works on the battle, the most significant recent undertaking has been P. R. Newman and P. R. Roberts, *Marston Moor: The Battle of the Five Armies* (Pickering, 2003). See also C. H. Firth, 'Marston Moor', *Transactions of the Royal Historical Society*, N.S., XII (1898), 17–79; A. Woolrych, *Battles of the English Civil War* (1961); P. R. Newman, *Marston Moor, July 2nd 1644: The Sources and the Site*, Borthwick Institute of Historical Research No 13, (York, 1978); C. S. Terry, *The Life and Campaigns of Alexander Leslie, First Earl of Leven* (1899); P. A. Charrier, 'Cavalry in Battle', *Cavalry Journal*, I (1906), 185–90; Sir H. Cholmeley, 'Memorials touching the Battle of York', *English Historical Review*, V (1890), 347–52; and Sir T. Fairfax, 'A Short Memorial of the Northern Actions', *Yorkshire Archaeological Journal*, VIII (1884), 220–2.
5. L. Watson, Young, *Marston*, 208. This is the best of the contemporary accounts, and Watson had the benefit for us of being with Cromwell's command.
6. Fairfax, quoted in Young, *Marston*, 219.
7. Newman and Roberts, *op. cit.*, 51; *Writings*, I, 217–18.
8. Slingsby, quoted in Young, *Marston*, 200.
9. Duchess of Newcastle, quoted in Young, *Marston*, 204.
10. Firth, *Marston Moor*, 31.

11. Newcastle, quoted in Young, *op. cit.*, 204.
12. Trevor, quoted in Young, *Marston*, 206.
13. Monckton, quoted in Young, *Marston*, 206.
14. Watson, quoted in Young, *op. cit.*, 211
15. *Writings*, I, 217–18.
16. Ogden, quoted in Young, *Marston*, 202.
17. Watson, quoted in Young, *op. cit.*, 211.
18. P. R. Newman and P. R. Roberts, *op. cit.*, 83; Young, *op. cit.*, 112.
19. Watson, quoted in Young, *op. cit.*, 212.
20. Holles, quoted in Young, *Marston*, 116. Controversy over the exact nature of Cromwell's wound continues, although he himself does not mention it in any correspondence.
21. Watson, quoted in Young, *op. cit.*, 211.
22. Ogden, quoted in Young, *op. cit.*, 202.
23. Firth, *op. cit.*, 40.
24. Slingsby, quoted in Young, *op. cit.*, 200.
25. Prince Rupert's Diary, quoted in Young, *Marston*, 198.
26. D. Laing (ed.), *Letters and Journal of Robert Baillie*, (3 vols, Bannatyne Club, Edinburgh, 1842), II, 209.
27. *Writings*, I, 287.
28. 'The Diary of Mr Robert Douglas' in C. S. Terry, *Life and Campaigns of Alexander Leslie, First Earl of Leven* (1899), 282.
29. *Writings*, I, 289.
30. J. Bruce and D. Masson (eds.), *The Quarrel Between the Earl of Manchester and Oliver Cromwell* (Camden Society, N.S. XII, 1875).
31. *The Parliament Scout*, 17 October–24 October 1644, 562; J. Rushworth, *Historical Collections of Private Passages of State* (8 vols, 1721–1722), V, 720–6.
32. *Mercurius Civicus*, 24–31 October 1644, 697; *The Scottish Dove*, 18–25 October 1644; *A Diary or an Exact Journal* (1644), 185–6.
33. *The True Informer*, 26 October–2 November 1644, 387.
34. J. Bruce (ed.), *Calendar of State Papers: Domestic series of the Reign of Charles I*, (23 vols, 1858–97), 1644–5, 152; Bruce and Masson, *op. cit.*
35. S. R. Gardiner, *History of the Great Civil War* (4 vols, 1987 edn), II, 48. Second Newbury and Cromwell's part in the battle have been strangely neglected, given their political importance. Gardiner has one of the few accounts of Second Newbury, and this is somewhat dated. The other main work on the battle is W. Money, *The First and Second Battles of Newbury and the Siege of Donnington Castle* (2nd edn, 1884).
36. *A Letter Sent to the Honourable William Lenthall* (1644), 4.
37. *The True Informer*, 26 October–November 1644, 386.

38. *Mercurius Civicus*, 24–31 October 1644, 697.
39. W. Money, *op. cit.*, 179.
40. *The Parliament Scout*, 24–31 October 1644, 571; Bruce and Masson, *op. cit.*, 78–9.
41. *The Parliament Scout*, 24–31 October 1644, 571. Bruce and Masson, *op. cit.*, 78–9; S. Ash, *A True Relation of the Most Chief Occurrences at, and Since the Late Battle of Newbury* (1644). See also A. H. Burne, *The Battlefields of England* (1950), 230–8; and M. Bennet, *Traveller's Guide to the Battlefields of the English Civil War* (1990), 140–9.
42. *Mercurius Civicus*, 24–31 October 1644, 697.
43. CSPD, 1644–5, 151.
44. *Ibid.*

Chapter 6

1. The squabbles of the winter of 1644–5 are covered in M. Kishlansky, *The Rise of the New Model Army* (Cambridge, 1983) and S. R. Gardiner, *History of the Great Civil War*, II.
2. C. Carlton, *Charles I*, 280.
3. I. Gentles, *The New Model Army in England, Ireland and Scotland, 1645–1653* (1992), Ch. 2. See also I. Gentles ' The choosing of the Officers for the New Model Army', *Historical Research*, LXVII (1994), 264–85; I. Gentles, 'The New Model Officer Corps in 1647: A Collective Portrait', *Social History*, XXII (1997), 127–44; and M. Kishlansky, *op. cit.*
4. *Writings*, I, 314.
5. *Ibid.*, I, 315.
6. *Ibid.*, I, 316.
7. D. Laing (ed.), *Letters and Journal of Robert Baillie*, (3 vols, Bannatyne Club, Edinburgh, 1842), II, 247.
8. See R. Hutton, *The Royalist War Effort* (2nd edn, 1999).
9. *Writings*, I, 340; *An Abstract of a Letter from Lieutent General Crumwell to Sir Thomas Fairfax* (1645)
10. *Writings*, I, 342.
11. *Ibid.*, 340
12. *Ibid.*
13. Brief Memorials, P. Young, *Naseby* (1985) 313. For the Naseby battle – a well-researched battle in general – most of the original accounts are in print. Where the accounts are in print they have been checked against the original Thomason and other tracts in the British Library. Still useful are J. Sprigge, *Anglia Redivia* (Oxford, 1854); *Three Letters* (1645); *A True Relation of a Great Victory* (1645); and *Cromwelliana* (1810), 18–19. The best modern account is G. Foard, *Naseby: The Decisive Campaign* (Whitstable, 1995). See also M. M. Evans, P. Burton and M. Westway, *Naseby, June 1645* (2002) for evidence relating to the

field archaeology; I. Gentles, *The New Model Army in England, Ireland and Scotland, 1645–1653* (1992), 55–60; A. Woolrych, *Battles of the English Civil War* (1961), 111–38; S. R. Gardiner, *History of the Great Civil War*, II, 242–5; and A. H. Burne, *Battlefields of England* (1950), 239–55.

14. Brief Relation, quoted in Young, *Naseby*, 315.
15. *Writings*, I, 365; N. H. Keeble (ed.), *The Autobiography of Richard Baxter* (1974), 46–8.
16. R. P. Stearns, *The Strenuous Puritan: Hugh Peter, 1598–1660* (Urbana, Illinois, 1954), 249.
17. G. Bishop, quoted in Foard, *Naseby*, 408.
18. N. Burt, *Militarie Instructions* (1644). For Okey and his account, see H. G. Tibbutt, *Colonel John Okey, 1606–1662*, Publications of the Bedfordshire Historical Record Society, XXXV (Streatley, 1955), 10–11.
19. Rushworth, quoted in Foard, *Naseby*, 403.
20. Young, quoted in *Naseby*, 249.
21. Okey, quoted in Young, *Naseby*, 339.
22. Slingsby, quoted in Young, *Naseby*, 311.
23. Brief Relation, quoted in Young, *Naseby*, 318.
24. Rushworth, quoted in Foard, *op. cit.*, 430.
25. Slingsby, quoted in Young, *op. cit.*, 311.
26. Rushworth, quoted in Foard, 404.
27. Bishop, quoted in Foard, *op. cit.*, 407.
28. *Ibid.*
29. Young, *op. cit.*, 270.
30. Slingsby, quoted in Young, *op. cit.*, 312.
31. Okey, quoted in Young, *op. cit.*, 339.
32. Burt, *op. cit.*
33. Brief Relation, quoted in Young, *op. cit.*, 319.
34. Bishop, quoted in Foard, *op. cit.*, 408.
35. *Writings*, I, 360.
36. *Ibid.*, 365.
37. A true relation, quoted in Young, *Naseby*, 373.
38. *Writings*, I, 365. For Langport see J. Sprigge, *op. cit.*, 68–73; *A More Full Relation of the Great Battel fought between Sir Tho: Fairfax, and Goring* (1645); *A True relation of a Victory … Langport* (1645). *Cromwelliana* (1810), 20; Keeble, *op. cit.*, 49–50; and A. H. Burne, *More Battlefields of England* (1952), 192–202.
39. *Writings*, I, 364. For Bridgwater see Sprigge, *op. cit.*, 74–83; *A Brief relation of the Taking of Brigewater by the Parliament's forces* (1645); and *Cromwelliana* (1810), 20.
40. *Writings*, I, 369. For the Clubmen of the South West, see Sprigge, *op. cit.*, 83–90; *Cromwelliana* (1810), 20–1; and *Two Great Victories* (1645)
41. *Writings*, I, 375. For the siege of Bristol see Sprigge, *op. cit.*, 97–128; *Cromwelliana* (1810), 22–4; and *A True Relation of the Storming of Bristol* (1645).
42. *Writings*, I, 377.

43. *Ibid.*, 377–8.
44. See A. Marshall, *Fierce and Bloody: The Trial of Thomas Harrison, 1660*, unpublished paper (2003), and C. H. Simpkinson, *Thomas Harrison, Regicide and Major-General* (1905). For the siege of Basing House see *Cromwelliana* (1810), 26–8; *Lieutenant-General Cromwell's Letter sent to the Honourable William Lenthall Esq … Concerning the Storming and taking of Basing House* (1645); *A Looking Glasse for the Popish Garrisons* (1645). Sprigge, *op. cit.*, 148–53; H. Peters, *The Full and Last Relation of All Things Concerning Basing House* (1645). J. Adair, *They Saw It Happen: Contemporary accounts of the Siege of Basing House* (Hampshire, 1983); and Stearns, *op. cit.*, 259–61.

Chapter 7

1. D. Underdown, *Pride's Purge: Politics in the Puritan Revolution* (1985), 44–75; R. Ashton, *Counter-Revolution: The Second Civil War and its Origins, 1646–8* (1994)
2. Underdown, *op. cit.*, 69–70.
3. *Writings*, I, 410. However, Hoover shows Cromwell had in reality retained his commission with the 'tacit allowance of parliament' and by the simple expedient of not rendering up his commission. C. Hoover, 'Cromwell's Status and Pay in 1646–7', *Historical Journal*, XXIII (1980), 703–15.
4. *Writings*, I, 416.
5. There is a wealth of literature on the Leveller movement. A. S. P. Woodhouse (ed.), *Puritanism and Liberty* (1986), gives the text of the Putney and other debates, while H. N. Brailsford, *The Levellers and the English Revolution* (1983 ed), is old, radical (no bad thing) and still a sound beginning for understanding the movement. M. Mendle (ed.), *The Putney Debates of 1647: The Army, the Levellers and the English State* (Cambridge, 2001), is an outstanding collection of essays. See also C. H. Firth (ed.), *The Clarke Papers* (4 vols, Camden Society, XLIX, LIV, LXI, LXII, 1891–1901); and P. Gregg, *Freeborn John: A Biography of John Lilburne* (1986 edn). A. Woolrych, *Soldiers and Statesmen, The General Council of the Army and its Debates, 1647–1648* (Oxford, 1987), covers the influence of the Levellers on the army and much else besides.
6. 'Apology of the Soldiers to their officers' (1647), in Woodhouse, *op. cit.*
7. Brailsford, *op. cit.*, 218.
8. *Writings*, I, 446; N. H. Keeble (ed.), *The Autobiography of Richard Baxter* (1974), 49–50.
9. Woodhouse, *op. cit.*, gives the text of the

Putney and other debates involving Ireton and Cromwell.

10. *Writings*, I, 606, 619. For Cromwell on the campaign, see also *A Great and Bloody fight at Pembrook Castle* (1648); H. G. Tibbutt, *Colonel John Okey, 1606–1662*, Publications of the Bedfordshire Historical Record Society, XXXV (Streatley, 1955), 28–30, 31–2. and *Cromwelliana* (1810), 39. It was also reported that Cromwell was 'ill of an extreme lameness in one of his legs'.

11. For the Scots army see R. M. Furgol, 'Scotland Turned Sweden: The Scottish Covenanters and the Military Revolution, 1638–1651' in J. Morrill (ed.), *The Scottish National Covenant in its British Context* (Edinburgh, 1990), 134–54; S. Reid and G. Turner, *The Scots Armies of the English Civil Wars* (1999); S. Bull and M. Seed, *Bloody Preston: The Battle of Preston 1648* (1998); R. Holmes, *Preston, 1648* (Market Drayton, 1985); D. Laing (ed.), *Letters and Journal of Robert Baillie* (3 vols, Bannatyne Club, Edinburgh, 1842), II; H. L. Rubinstein, *Captain Luckless: James, First Duke of Hamilton 1606–1649* (Edinburgh, 1975); C. H. Firth (ed.), 'Narratives Illustrating the Duke of Hamilton's Expedition to England in 1648', *Miscellany of the Scottish History Society* (Scottish History Society, 1904, No 44), II; and *Clarendon, History*, V.

12. J. Turner, *Memoirs of His Own Life and Times (1632–70)* (Bannatyne Club, 1829) 62.

13. S. Birch in *Historical Manuscripts Commission*, 14th Report, App. II, Portland MSS (10 vols, 1891–1931), III (1894), 174.

14. Turner, *op. cit.*, 59.

15. W. Beamont (ed.), *A Discourse of the Warr in Lancashire* (Chetham Society, LXII, 1864), 68.

16. *The Moderate Intelligencer*, 10–17 August 1648.

17. *Ibid.*, 3–10 August 1648; E. Broxop, *The Great Civil War in Lancashire* (Manchester, 1910), 159–72.

18. S. Birch in *HMC*, Portland, III (1894), 174

19. *The Moderate*, 1–18 August 1648.

20. Turner, *op. cit.*, 62.

21. *Ibid.*

22. *Ibid.*

23. J. Hodgson, *Autobiography of Captain John Hodgson* (Brighouse, 1882), 30. Hodgson provides one of the few soldier's-eye views of Preston. See also D. Farr, 'John Hodgson, Soldier, Surgeon, Agitator and Quaker?', *Journal of the Friends' Historical Society*, LVIII (1999), 220–34.

24. Hodgson, *op. cit.*, 32; *A Copy of Lieutenant-*

General Cromwell's Letter (1648); *The Bloody Battel at Preston in Lancashire* (1648); Sir M. Langdale, *An Impartiall Relation of the late Fight at Preston* (1648); *Lieut-General Cromwell's Letter to the Honourable William Lenthal Esq.* (1648); *A Full Relation of the Great Victory* (1648); *The Moderate Intelligencer*, 3–10 August 1648; *ibid.*, 10–17 August 1648; *ibid.*, 17–24 August 1648; *The Red Horse or the Bloodiness of War* (1648); *Packets of Letters From Scotland, and the North Parts of England to the Members of the House of Commons* (1648); *The Moderate*, 1–8 August 1648; *The Overthrow of the Scots Army* (1648); *Cromwelliana* (1810), 44–6; Bull and Seed, *op. cit.*; Holmes, *op. cit.*

25. W. Beamont (ed.), *A Discourse of the Warr in Lancashire* (Chetham Society, LXII, 1864), 65.

26. Hodgson, *op. cit.*, 33.

27. Beamont, *op. cit.*, 65

28. S. Birch in *HMC*, Portland, III (1897), 175.

29. *Writings*, I, 636.

30. Turner, *op. cit.*, 68.

31. *Writings*, I, 639

32. Reade's Relation, C. H. Firth (ed.), 'Narratives Illustrating the Duke of Hamilton's Expedition to England in 1648', *Miscellany of the Scottish History Society* (Scottish History Society, 1904, No 44), II, 300.

33. Hodgson, *op. cit.*, 31.

34. Hodgson, *op. cit.*, 33.

35. *Writings*, I, 638.

36. D. Iagomarsino and C. J. Wood (eds), *The Trial of Charles I: A Documentary History* (1989); S. R. Gardiner, *History of the Great Civil War*, IV, 254–330; D. Underdown, *op. cit.*; B. Worden, *The Rump Parliament* (Cambridge, 1973). T. Barnard, *The English Republic, 1649–60* (2nd edn, Harlow, 1997).

Chapter 8

1. *Writings*, II, 204–5.

2. J. McCavitt, 'The Political Background to the Ulster Plantation, 1607–1620', B. Mac Cuarta (ed.), *Ulster 1641:Aspects of the Rising* (Belfast, 1993), 7.

3. Clarendon, quoted by K. Lindley, 'The Impact of the 1641 Rebellion Upon England and Wales 1641–5', *Irish Historical Review*, XVIII (1972), 151.

4. J. C. Beckett, 'The Confederation of Kilkenny Reviewed', *Historical Studies*, II (1959), 30; P. Lenihan, 'Confederate Military Strategy', M. Ò. Sichrú (ed.), *Kingdom in Crisis Ireland in the 1640s* (Dublin, 2001).

5. J. T. Gilbert (ed.), *Contemporary History of Affairs in Ireland from 1641–1652*, (6 vols, 1879–80), II, 55.

6. B. Fitzpatrick, *Seventeenth Century Ireland: The Wars of Religion* (Dublin, 1988), 187–194; C. V. Wedgwood, *The King's War, 1641–1647* (1977 edn.), 498–9; T. W. Moody, F. X. Martin and F. J. Byrne (eds), *A New History of Ireland: iii, Early Modern Ireland, 1534–1691* (Oxford, 1976), 314

7. John Denham, quoted in A. Brooke-Tyrrell, 'Michael Jones Governor of Dublin', *Dublin Historical Record*, (1970, Dec.), 160.

8. K. Ferguson, 'Contemporary Accounts of the Battle of Rathmines 1649', *Irish Sword*, XXI (1999), 21, 86, 381; T. Carte (ed.), *The Life of James, Duke of Ormonde* (6 vols, 1851), III, 467–75.

9. K. Ferguson, 'Contemporary Accounts', 381.

10. *Ibid.*, 384.

11. *Ibid.*, 366.

12. *Ibid.*, 374.

13. *A Grand Victory obtained by Colonel Jones and the Parliament Forces at Dublin in Ireland* (1649); *Lieut. General Jones's Letter to the Councel of State* (1649); *Ormonde's Breakfast or a True Relation* (1649); G. Wither, *Carmen Eucharisticon: A Private Thank Oblation* (1649); Ferguson, *op. cit.*, 366.

14. Ferguson, *op. cit.*, 366.

15. *Ibid.*, 364.

16. *Ibid.*, 371.

17. Gilbert, *op. cit.*, II, 46.

18. Ferguson, *op. cit.*, 379.

19. *Ibid.*, 379–80.

20. S. R. Gardiner, *History of the Commonwealth and Protectorate* (4 vols, 1988 edn), II, 108.

21. *Writings*, II, 104. See also D. Murphy, *Cromwell in Ireland: A History of Cromwell's Irish Campaign* (Boston, 1893); J. S. Wheeler, *Cromwell in Ireland* (Dublin, 1999); J. Burke, 'The New Model Army and the Problems of Siege Warfare, 1648–51', *Irish Historical Review*, XXVII (1990–1), 1–29; HMC Leyborne Popham (1899), 14, 15, 21, 26, 35.

22. Quoted in Brailsford, *The Levellers and the English Revolution*, 509. See also C. Durston, '"Let Ireland Be Quiet": Opposition in England to the Cromwellian Conquest of Ireland', *History Workshop Journal*, XXI (1986), 105–16.

23. *Writings*, II, 104.

24. *Ibid.*, 107.

25. *The Moderate Intelligencer*, August 1649, 22–37.

26. *The Swedish Intelligencer* (3 vols 1632–3), III, 188.

27. *Two Letters from Dublin* (1649), 4.

28. M. Corcoran, 'The Streets and Lanes of Drogheda', *The Old Drogheda Society*, III (1978–9), 27–39.

29. G. Bate, *Elenchus motuum nuperorum in Anglia: The History of the Rise and Progress of the Civil Wars in England from the Years 1625 to 1660* (2nd edn, 1688–9), 26; E. Borlase, *The History of the Execrable Insurrection* (1680); J. D'Alton, *The History of Drogheda and its Environs* (2 vols, Dublin, 1844), II, 278–9.

30. Gilbert, *op. cit.*, II, 235–6, 241.

31. *Ibid.*, 249

32. *Ibid.*, 250.

33. *The Last Great and Bloody Fight in Ireland* (1649), 2.

34. C. H. Firth, *Cromwell's Army*, 169; *The Impartiall Intelligencer* (1649), 222; H. O'Sullivan, 'Military Operations in County Louth in the Run up to Cromwell's Storming of Drogheda', *County Louth Archeological and Historical Journal*, XXII (1990), 187–208.

35. *A Modest Narrative of Intelligence, 15 September–22 September* (1649), 195–6, 200; *The Last Great Bloody fight In Ireland* (1649), 2.

36. Gilbert, *op. cit.*, 253; *The Impartiall Intelligencer*, 13–20 September 1649, 224.

37. *The Impartiall Intelligencer*, 13–20 September 1649, 223.

38. Gilbert, *op. cit.*, 253.

39. *Ibid.*, 259.

40. *Writings*, II, 125.

41. *Writings*, II, 126.

42. Gilbert, *op. cit.*, 259.

43. *The Kingdome's Weekly Intelligencer*, 25 September–2 October 1649, 1520; *The Moderate Intelligencer*, 27 September–4 October 1649; *Two Great Fights in Ireland* (1649); B. Whitelocke, *Memorials of English Affairs* (4 vols, 1853), III, 111–14: D'Alton, *op. cit.*, II, 278–9; *Mercurius Elencteus*, 5–15 October 1649, 87; E. H. *The History of the War of Ireland from 1641 to 1653 by a British Officer of the Regiment of Sir John Clotworthy* (Dublin, 1873), 87–91.

44. Gilbert, *op. cit.*, 270; *The Kingdome's Weekly Intelligencer*, 2–9 October 1649.

45. J. Keegan, *The Face of Battle* (1978), 47; *Two Letters, One from Dublin in Ireland and the Other From Liverpoole of a Bloody Fight in Ireland, at the Taking of Drogheda* (1649); Carte (ed.), *op. cit.*, III, 481. See also T. Reilly, *Cromwell, An Honourable Enemy* (2000).

46. Ferguson, *op. cit.*, 377.

47. Borlase, *op. cit.*, 223; C. H. Firth and G. Davies, *The Regimental History of Cromwell's Army*, II, 666.

48. See *The Man in the Moon: Discovering a World of Knavery under the Sunne* (1649), 213.

49. *Writings*, II, 131.

50. *A Briefe Relation* (1649), 3; *The Perfect Weekly*

NOTES

Account, 26 September–3 October (1649), 622; *The Kingdome's Weekly Intelligencer* (1649), 1513.

51. Gilbert, *op. cit.*, 466.
52. *A Perfect and Particular Relation of the Severall Marches and Proceedings of the Armie in Ireland* (1649), 7. *A Briefe Relation*, 9 October 1649.
53. R. L., *The Taking of Wexford: A Letter from an Eminent Officer in the Army* (1649), 3–4; *A Perfect and Particular Relation of the Severall Marches and Proceedings of the Armie in Ireland* (1649); *A Letter from the Attorney of Ireland, Concerning the Taking of the Towne of Wexford by Storme* (1649); *A Letter from the Lord Lieutenant of Ireland, to the Honourable William Lenthall* (1649).
54. Sinnott, quoted in P. H. Hore (ed.), *History of the Town and County of Wexford* (6 vols, 1900–11), V, 279.
55. *Ibid.*, 281.
56. *A Perfect and Particular Relation of the Severall Marches and Proceedings of the Armie in Ireland* (1649), 7.
57. *Ibid.*
58. *Writings*, II, 142.
59. *A Very Full and Particular Relation of the great progresse and happy proceeding of the Army* (1649), 53.
60. *A Perfect and Particular Relation of the Severall Marches and Proceedings of the Armie in Ireland* (1649), 8.
61. *A Briefe Relation* (1649), 45.
62. *Ibid.*, 85.
63. Hore, *op. cit.*, V 303; *A Perfect and Particular Relation of the Severall Marches and Proceedings of the Armie in Ireland* (1649), 7–8; *Collections of Letters from Several Parts concerning the Affairs of the Armies* (1649), 3; *A Briefe Relation*, 13–20 November 1649, 54–5; *ibid.*, 30 October 1649, 68.
64. *Writings*, II, 144. J. B. Williams, 'Cromwell's Massacre at Wexford', *Irish Ecclesiastical Review*, 1913, Series 5, II, 561–78; *Historical Manuscript Commission*, Leybourne Popham (1899), 44.
65. Gilbert, *op. cit.*, 465.
66. *A Breife Relation*, 3–10 October 1649, 632; *ibid.*, 6–13 November 1649, 83; J. G. Simms, 'Cromwell's Siege of Waterford 1649', J. G. Simms, *War and Politics in Ireland, 1649–1730* (1980), 11–19
67. S. R. Gardiner, *History of the Commonwealth*, I, 141–2.
68. For Jones's death see A. Brooke-Tyrrell, 'Michael Jones, Governor of Dublin', *Dublin Historical Record* (1970), 159. Jones probably died of cholera.
69. T. J. Clohosey, 'Cromwell's Siege of

Kilkenny', *Old Kilkenny Review*, VIII, (1955), 836–46.
70. Good articles on the siege are P. F. Dineen, 'The Siege of Clonmel', and P. Lyons, 'The Cromwellian Assault on Clonmel' in P. O'Connell and W. C. Darmody, *Siege of Clonmel Commemoration: Tercentenary Souvenir Record* (Clonmel, 1950), 6–18. W. P. Burke, *History of Clonmel* (Waterford, 1907), 42–79.
71. S. R. Gardiner, *op. cit.*, I, 155–9. Cromwell's relatively short period in Ireland still has its political reverberations today. See R. C. Richardson (ed.), *Images of Oliver Cromwell: Essays by and for Roger Howell* (Manchester, 1993).
72. M. Lenihan, *Limerick: Its History and Antiquities* (1866, 1967 ed), 148–84.

Chapter 9

1. O. Airy (ed.), *G. Burnet: History of My Own Time* (2 vols, 1897), II, 93–4. For the background to the Scottish War see S. R. Gardiner, *History of the Commonwealth and Protectorate* (4 vols, 1988), I, II; W. S. Douglas, *Cromwell's Scotch Campaigns, 1650–51* (1898); J. D. Grainger, *The Last Anglo-Scottish War 1650–1652* (East Linton, 1997); and D. Stevenson, *Revolution and Counter Revolution in Scotland 1644–1651* (1977).
2. For the discussions with Fairfax on the morality of the invasion see B. Whitelocke, *Memorials of English Affairs* (4 vols, 1853), III, 206–11.
3. J. Hodgson, *Autobiography of Captain John Hodgson* (Brighouse, 1882), 36, 41.
4. D. H. Fleming (ed.), *The Diary of Sir Archibald Johnston of Wariston* (Scottish Historical Society, 2nd Series, 1919), II, 5.
5. Hodgson, *op. cit.*, 37; *Cromwelliana* (1810), 82–8.
6. Whitelocke, *op. cit.*, 223.
7. *Ibid.*, 223–4.
8. *Ibid.*, 225; *A Large Relation of the Fight at Leith Neere Edenburgh* (1650).
9. Hodgson, *op. cit.*, 37–8.
10. S. R. Gardiner (ed.), *Letters and Papers illustrating the relations between Charles II and Scotland in 1650* (Scottish Record Society, 1894), 135.
11. *Ibid.*, 136, 139; *A True Relation of the Proceedings and transactions of the English Army in Scotland* (1650).
12. Fleming, *op. cit.*, II, 9.
13. *Ibid.*, 5.
14. *Writings*, II, 300; *A True Relation of the Proceedings and transactions of the English Army in Scotland* (1650).

15. C. H. Firth and G. Davies, *The Regimental History of Cromwell's Army*, I, 67–8.
16. Whitelock, *op. cit.*, 226. *A True Relation of the Proceedings and transactions of the English Army in Scotland* (1650).
17. *Writings*, II, 300; *Cromwelliana* (1810), 88–91; H. G. Tibbutt, *Colonel John Okey, 1606–1662* (Publications of the Bedfordshire Historical Society, XXXV, Streatley, 1955), 38–9.
18. Fleming, *op. cit.*, 6.
19. *Mercurius Politicus*, No 13, August–September 1650, 202.
20. Hodgson, *op. cit.*, 39.
21. Fleming, *op. cit.*, 10.
22. *Mercurius Politicus*, No 13, 196.
23. *Ibid.*, 206
24. *Several Letters from Scotland* (1650), 3.
25. *Ibid.*, 5.
26. *Ibid.*, 5
27. *Ibid.*, 6.
28. *A Brief Relation of Some Affairs* (1650), 811.
29. Hodgson, *op. cit.*, 43.
30. *Several Letters from Scotland* (1650), 6.
31. *A Brief Relation of Some Affairs* (1650), 812. See also *A True Relation of the Daily Proceedings and Transactions of the English Army in Scotland* (1650).
32. *Mercurius Politicus*, 12–19 September 1650, 227; C. H. Firth, 'The Battle of Dunbar', *Transactions of the Royal Historical Society*, XIV, 2nd Series (1900), 19–52.
33. Hodgson, *op. cit.*,, 44; *Emanuel, or, God with Us* (1650); O. Airy, (ed.), *op. cit.*, 95–6; J. Nicholl, *A Diary of Public Transactions and other Occurrences chiefly in Scotland from January 1650 to June 1667* (Bannatyne Club, LII, 1836), 26, 28, 31; *A Brief Relation* (1650).
34. *Writings*, II, 323.
35. O. Airy, *op. cit.*, 95; *A True Relation of the Routing of the Scottish Army near Dunbar* (1650); *Writings*, II, 323; C. H. Firth (ed.), *Memoirs of Edmund Ludlow* (Oxford, 2 vols, 1894), I, 252–4.
36. Hodgson, *op. cit.*, 44.
37. Aubrey, *Miscellanies upon Various Subjects* (5th edn, 1890), 143.
38. Hodgson, *op. cit.*, 44.
39. *Ibid.*
40. *Ibid.*, 45; the opening verse of Psalm 68 – Biblical references were never far from Cromwell's mind.
41. Hodgson, *op. cit.*, 45.
42. *Ibid.*
43. *Writings*, II, 325.
44. D. Laing (ed.), *Letters and Journal of Robert Baillie* (3 vols, Bannatyne Club, Edinburgh, 1842), III, 111.
45. *Writings*, II, 432.
46. *Ibid.*, 433; Hodgson, *op. cit.*, 46–7; Whitelocke, *op. cit.*, III, 321–4.
47. *Writings*, II, 436; Hodgson, *op. cit.*, 46; Whitelocke, *op. cit.*, 325.
48. *Writings*, II, 439; Whitelocke, *op. cit.*, 327.
49. *Writings*, II, 444; Hodgson, *op. cit.*, 46–7; Whitelocke, *op. cit.*, 328–9.
50. *Writings*, II, 444.
51. Whitelocke, *op. cit.*, 335, 338–9.
52. *Ibid.*, 341.
53. *Writings*, II, 455. For Worcester see *An Exact and Perfect Relation of Every Particular of the Fight at Worcester* (1651), 1–3 ; *Cromwelliana* (1810), 109–16; *Mercurius Politicus*, 28 August–4 September 1651; *ibid.*, 4–11 September 1651; Whitelocke, *op. cit.*, 345–7; *Writings*, II, 461–2; *CSPD* (1651), 436–7; W. D. Macray (ed.), *Clarendon: History of the Rebellion* (6 vols, Oxford, 1888), V, 187–92; S. R. Gardiner, *History of the Commonwealth and Protectorate*, II, 42–8; M. Atkin, *The Battle of Worcester, 1651* (Tiddington, 2001); M. Atkin, *Cromwell's Crowning Mercy: The Battle of Worcester, 1651* (Stroud, 1998); J. W. Willis Bund, *The Civil War in Worcestershire* (1905); R. Ollard, *The Escape of Charles II* (1996).
54. Whitelocke, *op. cit.*, 345–7; *Writings*, II, 461–2.
55. *Writings*, II, 462.
56. Whitelocke, *op. cit.*, 346, 348.
57. *An Exact and Perfect relation of Every Particular of the Fight at Worcester* (1651), 2.
58. Whitelocke, *op. cit.*, 348.
59. *Mercurius Politicus*, 11–18 September 1651, 1071.
60. For what happened after Worcester see B. Worden, *The Rump Parliament* (Cambridge 1973); A. Woolrych, *From Commonwealth to Protectorate* (Oxford, 1982); and B. Coward, *The Cromwellian Protectorate* (Manchester, 2002).

Conclusion

1. Slingsby, quoted in A. H. Burne and P. Young, *The Great Civil War: A Military History of the First Civil War, 1642–1646* (1998 edn), 66.
2. E. Luttwack in J. Shay, *Achilles in Vietnam: Combat Trauma and the Undoing of Character* (1994), 10.
3. V. D. Hanson, *The Western Way of War: Infantry Battle in Classical Greece* (2nd edn, 2000), 109
4. J. Keegan, *The Mask of Command* (1988), 312.
5. M. Foucault, *Discipline and Punish: The Birth of the Prison* (1991), 135; C. Mukerji, *Territorial Ambitions and the Gardens of Versailles* (Cambridge, 1997), 224.

6. Keegan, *op. cit.*, 319.

7. *Ibid.*, 326.

8. *Writings*, I, 314.

9. C. H. Firth, *Cromwell's Army: A History of the English Soldier During the Civil Wars, the Commonwealth and the Protectorate* (1902, reprinted 1967), 47.

10. *Writings*, I, 191–2.

11. *Ibid.*

12. L. E. Nolan, *Cavalry: Its History and Tactics* (1853 edn), 61.

13. J. Adair, *By the Sword Divided: Eyewitness Accounts of the English Civil War* (Stroud, 1998), 162.

14. *Writings*, II, 460.

15. *Ibid.*, II, 329. See also W. White Cooper, 'Historical Notes Concerning Certain Illnesses, the Death and Disinterment of Oliver Cromwell', *Dublin Quarterly Journal of Medical Science*, V (1848), 339–70; C. H. Davidson, 'The Diagnosis of Oliver Cromwell's Fatal Illness', *Cromwelliana* (1993), 27–32.

16. E. Sexby, 'Killing No Murder' (1657), in D. Wootton, *Divine Right and Democracy: An Anthology of Political Writing in Stuart England* (1988), 370.

17. H. N. Brailsford, *The Levellers and the English Revolution* (1983), 155.

18. J. Adair, *By the Sword Divided: Eyewitness Accounts of the English Civil War* (Stroud, 1998), 162.

19. Sexby, *op. cit.*, 368. See also Sir John Reresby, who wrote of Cromwell: 'Tears he had at will', M. K. Geiter and W. A. Speck (eds), *Memoirs of Sir John Reresby* (2nd edn, 1991) 22–3.

20. Brailsford, *op. cit.*, 157.

21. *Writings*, II, 281.

22. Geiter and Speck, *op. cit.*, 22–3.

23. R. Sherwood, *The Court of Oliver Cromwell* (1977), 73; L. L. Knoppers, 'The Politics of Portraiture: Oliver Cromwell and the Plain Style', *Renaissance Quarterly*, LI (1998), 1283–1319.

24. R. Burton, *The History of Oliver Cromwell, Lord Protector &c* (1698), 171.

25. *Speeches*, 25.

26. J. Vernon, *The Young Horseman or the Honest Plain Dealing Cavalier* (1644; 1993 ed), 21.

27. *Ibid.*, 86.

28. *Ibid.*

29. Bulstrode, quoted in P. Young, *Edgehill 1642: The Campaign and the Battle* (1998 edn), 258.

30. Vernon, *op. cit.*, 86.

31. L. E. Nolan, *Cavalry: Its History and Tactics* (1853 edn), 279. See also *Cavalry Tactics* (1897); G. T. Denison, *A History of Cavalry from Earliest Times with Lessons for the Future* (1877); and H. Belloc, *The Tactics and Strategy of the Great Duke of Marlborough* (1933).

32. Nolan, *op. cit.*, 282.

33. *Ibid.*

34. *Ibid.*, 280.

35. Clarendon, quoted in Firth, *Cromwell's Army*, 91.

36. Firth, *op. cit.*, 144.

37. *Writings*, I, 231.

38. Orrery 'Art of War', 198–9, in Firth, *op. cit.*, 392

39. *Ibid.*, 392–3.

40. See J. S. Wheeler, 'The Logistics of the Cromwellian Conquest of Scotland, 1650–51', *War and Society*, X (1992), 1–18; J. S. Wheeler, 'Logistics and Supply in The Cromwellian Conquest of Ireland', M. Fissel (ed.), *War and Government in Britain 1598–1650* (Manchester, 1991), 38–56; P. R. Edwards ' The Supply of Horses to the Parliamentarian and Royalist Armies in the English Civil War', *Historical Research*, 68 (1995), 49–66; A. Nusbacher, 'Civil Supply in the Civil War: Supply of Victuals to the New Model Army on the Naseby Campaign, 1–14 June 1645', *English Historical Review*, CXV (200), 145–60.

41. See A. Marshall, *Intelligence and Espionage in the Reign of Charles II* (1994), 18, 264.

42. J. Sprigge, *Anglia Rediviva* (Oxford, 1854), 35

43. *CSPD*, 1644–5, 152.

44. *Ibid.*, 151.

45. S. R. Gardiner, *History of the Great Civil War*, II, 5.

46. *Speeches*, 10.

BIBLIOGRAPHY

Printed Primary Sources

Abbott, W. S. *The Writings and Speeches of Oliver Cromwell.* 4 vols., Cambridge, Mass., 1939–47

An Abstract of a Letter from Lieutenant General Crumwell to Sir Thomas Fairfax. 1645

Akerman, J. Y. ed. *Letters from Roundhead Officers written from Scotland and chiefly addressed to Captain Adam Baynes. July MDCL–MDCLX.* Bannatyne Club, 1856

Birch, T. ed. *A Collection of the State Papers of John Thurloe.* 7 vols. 1742

Airey, O. ed. *G. Burnet, History of My Own Time.* 2 vols., Oxford, 1897

Archer, W. N. *The Double-Armed Man.* 1625

Ash, S. *A True Relation of the Most Chief Occurrences at, and Since the Late Battle of Newbury.* 1644

Aubrey, J. *Miscellanies upon Various Subjects.* 5th ed., 1890

Barriffe, W. *Militarie Discipline, or the Young Artilleryman.* 1661

Barton, W. *Halleujah, or certain Hymns composed out of Scripture ... Upon Occasion of those two glorious and most remarkable appearances of God for them, at Dunbar and Worcester.* 1651

Bate, G. *Elenchus motuum nuperorum in Anglia: The History of the Rise and Progress of the Civil wars in England from the Years 1625 to 1660.* 2nd ed., 1688–9

Beamont, W. ed. *A Discourse of the Warr in Lancashire.* Chetham Society, LXII, 1864

Bernard, N. *The Whole proceedings of the Siege of Drogheda in Ireland.* 1642

Bernard, R. *The Bible-Battells, or the Sacred Art Military.* 1629

The Bloody Battel at Preston in Lancashire. 1648

Borlase, E. *The History of the Execrable Insurrection.* 1680

A Brief Relation. 1650

A Briefe Relation 1649–50

A Brief Narrative of the Great Victorie, which it hath Pleased God to give to the Armie of this Commonwealth against the Scots Armie, Near Dunbar ... the third of this instant September, related to the Council of State &c. 1650

A Brief Relation of Some Affairs. 1650

A Brief Relation of the Taking of Bridgewater by the Parliament's forces. 1645

Bruce, J. ed. *Calendar of State Papers, Domestic Series of the Reign of Charles I.* 23 vols., 1858–97

— and Masson, D. eds. *The Quarrel Between the Earl of Manchester and Oliver Cromwell.* Camden Society, NS XII, 1875

Burt, N. *Militarie Instructions, or the souldier tried for the use of the Dragon &c.* 1644

Burton, R. *The History of Oliver Cromwell.* 1698

Carte, T. ed. *The Life of James, Duke of Ormonde.* 6 vols., 1851

Carey, H. *Memorials of the Great Civil War in England from 1642–1652.* 2 vols. 1842

Codrington, R. 'Life and Death of the Illustrious Robert, Earl of Essex, 1646.' *Harleian Miscellany*, 10 vols., 1808–13

Collections of Letters from Several parts concerning the affairs of the armies. 1649

The Copy of a Letter Written by Colonel Cromwell to the Committee at Cambridge. 1643

A Copy of Lieutenant-General Cromwell's Letter. 1648

Cruso, J. *Militarie Instructions for the Cavalrie.* Cambridge, 1632, reprinted ed., New York, 1968

A Diary or an Exact Journal. 1644

E. H. *The History of the War of Ireland from 1641 to 1653 by a British Officer of the Regiment of Sir John Clotworthy.* Dublin, 1873

Emanuel, or, God with us. 1650

The English Military Discipline. 1672

Evats, W. *The Most excellent Hugo Grotius his three books treating of the rights of War and Peace.* 1682

— *An Exact and perfect Relation of Every Particular of the Fight at Worcester.* 1651

Fairfax, Sir T. 'A Short Memorial of the Northern Actions', *Yorkshire Archaeological Journal,* VIII, 1884, 220–2

Firth, C. H. and Rait, R. S. eds. *Acts and Ordnances of the Interregnum, 1642–1660.* 3 vols., 1911

Firth, C. H., ed. *The Clarke Papers.* 4 vols., Camden Society, XLIX, LIV, LXI, LXII, 1891–1901

— Duchess of Newcastle, *The life of William Cavendish, Duke of Newcastle.* 1886

— *Memoirs of Edmund Ludlow.* 2 vols., Oxford, 1894

— 'Narratives Illustrating the Duke of Hamilton's Expedition to England in 1648'. *Miscellany of the Scottish History Society.* Scottish History Society, II, 1904

Fleming, D. H. (ed.). *The Diary of Sir Archibald Johnston of Wariston.* Scottish Historical Society, 2nd series, 1919

A Full Relation of the Great Victory. 1648

Gardiner, S. R. ed. *Letters and papers illustrating the relations between Charles II and Scotland in 1650.* Scottish Record Society, 1894

Geiter, M. K. and Speck, W. A. eds. *Memoirs of Sir John Reresby.* 2nd ed. 1991

Gilbert, J. T. *Contemporary History of Affairs in Ireland from 1641–1652.* 6 vols., 1879–80

Great Britaines Paine-full Messenger. 1649

Green, M. A. E., ed. *Calendar of State Papers, Domestic Series 169–1660.* 13 vols., 1965 ed.

A Grand Victory obtained by Colonel Jones and the Parliament Forces at Dublin in Ireland. 1649

A Great and Bloody fight near Drogheda in Ireland, on Sept. 6, 1649. 1649

A Great and Bloody fight at Pembrook Castle. 1648

Grimmelhausen, H. J. C. von. (trans. by Weisenborn, H.). *Simplicius Simplicissimus.* 1669, Macdonald 1964

Heath, J. *Flagellum or the life … of Oliver Cromwell.* 1663

Historical Manuscripts Commission. Leybourne Popham, 1899

— 14th Report, Appendix VII, Ormonde MSS, 8 vols., 1899–1920

— 14th Report, Appendix II, Portland MSS, 10 vols., 1891–1931

Hobbes, Thomas. *Leviathan: or the Matter, Forme and Power of a Commonwealth Ecclesiastical and Civil.* 1651. Oxford, 1996 ed.

Hodgson, J. *Autobiography of Captain John Hodgson.* Brighouse, 1882

The Honour of the English Soldiers, illustrated by way of parallel betwixt them, and those of other nations. 1651

The Impartiall Intelligencer. 1649

Keeble, N. H. ed. *The Autobiography of Richard Baxter.* 1974

The Kingdome's Weekly Intelligencer. 1649

Laing, D. ed. *Letters and Journal of Robert Baillie.* 3 vols., Bannatyne Club, Edinburgh, 1842

Langdale, Sir M. *An Impartiall Relation of the late Fight at Preston.* 1648

A Large Relation of the Fight at Leith Neere Edenburgh. 1650

The last great and bloody fight in Ireland. 1649

A Letter from the Attorney of Ireland, Concerning the Taking of the Towne of Wexford by Storme. 1649

A Letter from the Lord Lieutenant of Ireland, to the Honourable William Lenthall. 1649

A Letter sent to the Honourable William Lenthall. 1644

Letters from the Head Quarters of our Army in Scotland, being a Diary of all Proceedings in the Army to October 30, 1650. 1650

Letters from Ireland relating the several great successes it hath pleased God to give unto the Parliament's forces there. 1649

Lieut-General Cromwell's Letter to the Honourable William Lenthal Esq. 1648

Lieutenant-General Cromwell's Letter sent to the Honourable William Lenthall Esq … Concerning the Storming and taking of Basing House. 1645

Lieut. General Jones's Letter to the councel of State. 1649

Lomas, S. C. ed. T. Carlyle, *The Letters and Speeches of Oliver Cromwell.* 3 vols., 1904

A Looking Glasse for the Popish Garrisons. 1645

Macray, W. D. ed. Clarendon, *History of the Rebellion.* 6 vols, Oxford, 1888, 1959 ed.

The Man in the Moon Discovering a World of Knavery under the Sunne. 1649

Massey, E. *The Declaration of Major Gen. Massey upon his death-bed at Leicester.* 1651

Mercurius Civicus. 1644–5

Mercurius Elenctcus. 1647–9

Mercurius Hybernicus. 1649

Mercurius Politicus. 1650–5

Mercurius Republicus. 1649

The Military Garden or Instructions for all Young Soldiers. 1629

The Moderate. 1648–9

A Moderate Intelligence. 1648–9

The Moderate Intelligencer. 1648–9

A Modest Narrative of Intelligence. 1649

Monck, G., Duke of Albemarle. *Observations upon Military and Political Affairs.*1671

A More Full Relation of the Great Battel fought between Sir Tho: Fairfax, and Goring. 1645

A More Full Relation of the Great victory obtained by our Forces near Worcester. 1651

Nicholl, J. *A Diary of Public Transactions and other Occurrences chiefly in Scotland from January 1650 to June 1667.* Bannatyne Club, 1836

Original Memoirs, Written During the Great Civil War. Edinburgh, 1806

Ormonde's Breakfast or a True relation. 1649

The Overthrow of the Scots Army. 1648

Packets of letters From Scotland and the North parts of England to the Members of the House of Commons. 1648

The Parliament Scout. 1643–5

A Perfect List of all the Victories obtained by the Lord General Cromwell. 1650

A Perfect and Particular relation. 1649

A Perfect and Particular Relation of the Severall Marches and Proceedings of the Armie in Ireland. 1649

A Perfect Table of one hundred forty and five victories obtained by the Lord Lieutenant of Ireland. 1650

The Perfect Politician or a Full View of the Life and Actions (Military and Civil) of O. Cromwell. 1659

The Perfect Weekly Account. 1649

Peters, H. *The Full and Last Relation of All Things Concerning Basing House.* 1645

The Red Horse or the Bloodiness of War. 1648

A Relation of the Battaile lately Fought Between Keynton and Edghill. Oxford, 1642

R.F. *A Great Victorie in the North.* 1648

R.L. *The Taking of Wexford, A letter from an Eminent Officer in the Army.* 1649

Roberts, M., ed. *Swedish diplomats at Cromwell's Court.* Camden Society 4th Series, XXXVI, 1988

Roots, Ivan. *The Speeches of Oliver Cromwell.* 1989

The Rudiments of Militarie Discipline. Edinburgh, 1638

Rushworth, J. *Historical Collections of Private Passages of State.* 8 vols., 1721–2

The Scottish Dove. 1644–6

Several Letters from Scotland. 1650

Sexby, E. 'Killing No Murder' in Wootton, D. ed. *Divine Right and Democracy: An Anthology of Political Writing in Stuart England.* 1988

Sprigge, J. *Anglia Redivia.* Oxford, 1854 ed.

Stace, M., ed. *Cromwelliana. A chronological detail of events in which Oliver Cromwell was engaged, from 1642 to his death in 1658: with a continuation of other transactions to the Restoration.* 1810

The Swedish Intelligencer. 3 vols., 1632–3

Terry, C. S., ed. *Papers relating to the Army of the Solemn League and Covenant, 1643–7.* Scottish History Society, 16–17, 1917

Three Letters. 1645

The True Informer. 1644

True Intelligence from the Head Quarters of the Daily Motives ... of the Parliament's Army under the Lord general Cromwell, since they entered Scotland, 23–30 July, 1650. 1650

A True Relation of the daily proceedings and transactions of the English Army in Scotland. 1650

A True relation of the Great Victories. 1643

A True Relation of a Great Victory. 1645

A True Relation of the Late Fight. 1643

A True Relation of the Proceedings of the English Army. 1650

A True Relation of the Routing of the Scottish Army near Dunbar. 1650

A True Relation of the Storming of Bristol. 1645

A True Relation of a Victory ... Langport. 1645

Turner, Sir J. *Memoirs of his own Life and Times 1632–70.* Bannatyne Club, 1829

Two Great Fights in Ireland. 1649

Two Great Victories. 1645

Two Letters from Dublin. 1649

Two Letters, One from Dublin in Ireland and the other from Liverpoole of a Bloody Fight in Ireland, at the Taking of Drogheda. 1649

Vernon, J. *The Young Horseman or the Honest Plain Dealing Cavalier.* 1644, reprinted 1993

Ward, R. *Animadversions of Warre.* 1639

Wharton, N. 'Letters from a Subaltern Officer of the Earl of Essex's Army'. *Archaeologia,* XXXV, 1853

Whitelocke, B. *Memorials of English Affairs.* 4 vols., 1853

Wiseman, R. *Chirurgicall Treatises.* 1676

Wither, G. *Carmen Eucharisticon: A Private Thank Oblation.* 1649

Woodall, J. *The Surgeon's Mate or Military and Domestic Surgery.* 1655 ed.

Woodhouse, A. S. P. *Puritanism and Liberty.* 1986 ed.

Young, P. and Tucker N. eds. *Military Memoirs, The Civil War.* 1967

Secondary Sources

Abbott, W. C. *A Bibliography of Oliver Cromwell.* Harvard, 1929

Acheson, R. J. *Radical Puritans in England, 1550–1660.* 1990

Adair, J. *By the Sword Divided, Eyewitness Accounts of the English Civil War.* Stroud, 1998

— *Roundhead General: A Military Biography of Sir William Waller.* 1969

— *They Saw It Happen, Contemporary Accounts of the Siege of Basing House.* Hampshire, 1983

Angelo, S. *Martial Arts of Renaissance Europe.* Yale, 2000

Ashley, M. *General Monck.* 1977

— *Rupert of the Rhine.* 1976

Ashton, R. *Counter-Revolution, The Second Civil War and its Origins, 1646–8.* 1994

Atkin, M. *The Battle of Worcester, 1651.* Tiddington, 2001

— *Cromwell's Crowning Mercy, The Battle of Worcester, 1651.* Stroud, 1998

Aylmer, G. 'Was Cromwell a Member of the Army in 1646–7 or not?' *History,* LVI, 1971

Baker, A. *A Battlefield Atlas of the English Civil War.* 1986

Baldock, T. S. *Cromwell as a Soldier.* 1899

Barker, T. M., Black, J. and Cook W. F. 'Geoffrey Parker's Military Revolution: Three reviews of the Second Edition,' *The Journal of Military History,* LXI, 1997

Barnard, T. *Cromwellian Ireland, English Government and Reform in Ireland 1649–1660.* Oxford, 2000 ed.

— *The English Republic, 1649–60.* 2nd ed., Harlow, 1997

Beckett, J. C. 'The Confederation of Kilkenny Reviewed'. *Historical Studies* II. 1959

Belloc, H. *The Tactics and Strategy of the Great Duke of Marlborough.* 1933.

Bennett, M. *The Traveller's Guide to the Battlefields of the English Civil War.* 1990

Bevis, T. 'The Siege of Crowland'. *Lincolnshire Life,* XXXVI, 1997

Berry J. and Lee, S. G. *A Cromwellian Major-General: the Career of Col. James Berry.* Oxford, 1938

Black, J. *A Military Revolution? Military Change and European Society 1550–1800.* 1991

Blackmore, D. *Arms and Armour of the English Civil Wars.* 1990

Bourke, J. *An Intimate History of Killing, Face-to-Face Killing in Twentieth century Warfare.* 1999

Brailsford, H. N. *The Levellers and the English Revolution.* 1983

Brammer, B. *Winceby and the Battle.* Boston, 1994

Brooke-Tyrrell, A. 'Michael Jones Governor of Dublin'. *Dublin Historical Record,* Dec. 1970

Broxop, E. *The Great Civil War in Lancashire.* Manchester, 1910

Buchan, J. *Montrose.* 1996 ed.

— *Oliver Cromwell.* 1941 ed.

Bull, S. and Seed , M. *Bloody Preston: The Battle of Preston, 1648.* 1998

Burke, J. 'The New Model Army and the Problems of Siege Warfare, 1648–51'. *Irish Historical Review,* XXVII, 1990–1

Burke, W. P. *History of Clonmel.* Waterford, 1907

Burne, A. H. *The Battlefields of England.* 1950

— 'Generalship in the First Civil War, 1642–1644'. *History Today,* I, 1951

— *More Battlefields of England.* 1952

— and Young P. *The Great Civil War, A Military History of the First Civil War, 1642–1646.* 1998 ed.

Capp, B. *Cromwell's Navy: The Fleet and the English Revolution, 1648–1660.* Oxford, 1989

Carlton, C. *Charles I, The Personal Monarch.* 1984 ed.
— *Going to the Wars: The Experience of the British Civil Wars, 1638–1651.* 1992
Carlyle, T. *On Heroes.* 1895
Cavalry Officer. *Cavalry Tactics.* 1897
Chandler, D. *Atlas of Military Strategy: the Art, Theory and Practice of War, 1618–1878.* 1980
— *The Campaigns of Napoleon.* 1966, 1978 ed.
Charrier, P. A. 'Cavalry in Battle'. *Cavalry Journal*, I, 1906
— 'Cromwell as a Soldier'. *Journal of the Royal United Services Institution.* L, 1906
Chenevix Trench, C. 'Horsemanship in History'. *History Today*, XX, 1970
Childs, J. *The Nine Years' War and the British Army, 1688–1697.* Manchester, 1991
—*Warfare in the Seventeenth Century.* 2003
Cholmeley, Sir H. 'Memorials touching the Battle of York'. *English Historical Review*, V, 1890
Clarke, A. *The Old English in Ireland, 1625–42.* Dublin, 2000
Clohosey, T. J. 'Cromwell's Siege of Kilkenny'. *Old Kilkenny Review*, VIII, 1955
Collinson, P. *English Puritanism.* 1983
Contamine, P. *War in the Middle Ages.* 1984
Corcoran, M. 'The Streets and Lanes of Drogheda'. *The Old Drogheda Society*, III, 1978–9
Cotton, A. N. B. 'Cromwell and the self-denying Ordinance'. *History*, LXII, 1977
— 'John Dillingham, Journalist of the Middle Group'. *English Historical Review*, XCIII, 1978
Coward, B. *The Cromwellian Protectorate.* Manchester, 2002
— *Oliver Cromwell.* 1991
Croxton, D. '"The Prosperity of Arms is Never Continual": Military Intelligence, Surprise and Diplomacy in 1640s Germany', *The Journal of Military History*, LXIV, 2000
Cunningham, A. and Grell, O. *The Four Horsemen of the Apocalypse, Religion, War, Famine and Death in Reformation Europe.* Cambridge, 2000
Creveld, M. von. *Supplying War: Logistics from Wallenstein to Patton.* Cambridge, 1977

Cruickshank, C. G. *Elizabeth's Army.* 2nd ed., Oxford 1966
D'Alton, J. *The History of Drogheda and its Environs.* 2 vols., Dublin, 1844
Davidson, C. H. 'The Diagnosis of Oliver Cromwell's Fatal Illness'. *Cromwelliana*, 1993
Davies, G. 'The Battle of Edgehill'. *English Historical Review.* XXXVI, 1921
— 'The Parliamentary Army under the Earl of Essex, 1642–5'. *English Historical Review*, XLIX, 1934
Davis, J. C. *Oliver Cromwell.* 2001
Dawson, W. H. *Cromwell's Understudy.* 1938
Denison, G. T. *A History of Cavalry from Earliest Times with Lessons for the Future.* 1877
Denton, B. *Vermuyden and Cromwell, Regimental Histories of the New Model Army.* 1990
Dineen, P. F. 'The Siege of Clonmel' in O'Connell, P. and Darmody, W. C. *Siege of Clonmel Commemoration: Tercentenary Souvenir Record.* Clonmel 1950
Donagan, B. 'Atrocity, War Crime, and Treason in the English Civil War'. *American Historical Review*, XCIX, 1994
— 'Codes and Conduct in the English Civil War'. *Past and Present*, CXVIII, 1988
— 'Halcyon Days and the Literature of War: England's Military Education before 1642'. *Past and Present*, CXLVII, 1995
— 'Prisoners in the English Civil War'. *History Today*, XLI, 1991
— 'The Web of Honour: Soldiers, Christians, and Gentlemen in the English Civil War'. *Historical Journal*, XLIV, 2001
Douglas, W. S. *Cromwell's Scotch Campaigns, 1650–51.* 1898
Dow, F. D. *Cromwellian Scotland, 1651–1660.* Edinburgh, 1971
— *Radicalism in the English Revolution, 1640–1660.* Oxford, 1985
Drake, G. 'The Ideology of Oliver Cromwell'. *Church History*, XXV, 1966
Duffy, C. *Siege Warfare, The Fortress in the Early Modern World, 1494–1660.* 1979
Dukas, P. 'The Leslie family in the Swedish Period (1630–5) of the Thirty Years' War'. *European Studies Review*, XII, 1982
Du Picq, A. 'Battle Studies'. *Roots of Strategy.* Vol. 2, Mechanicsburg, 1987

Durston, C. '"Let Ireland Be Quiet": Opposition in England to the Cromwellian Conquest of Ireland'. *History Workshop Journal*, XXI, 1986

Ede-Borrett, S. 'The Royalist Army at the Second Battle of Newbury: 27 October 1644'. *Journal of the Society for Army Historical Research*, LXXVII, 1999

Edwards, P. R. 'The Supply of Horses to the Parliamentarian and Royalist Armies in the English Civil War'. *Historical Research*, LXVIII, 1995

Engstrom, H. R. 'Sir Arthur Hesilrige: The Forgotten Knight of the Long Parliament'. *Albion*, VIII, 1976

Evans, M. M., Burton, P. and Westway, M. *Naseby, June 1645*. 2002

Farr, D. 'John Hodgson, Soldier, Surgeon, Agitator and Quaker?' *Journal of the Friends Historical Society*, LVIII, 1999

— *John Lambert, Parliamentary Soldier and Cromwellian Major-General, 1619–1684*. 2003

Feinberg, B. S. 'The Political Thought of Oliver Cromwell: Revolutionary or Conservative?' *Social Research*, XXXV, 1968

Ferguson, K. 'Contemporary Accounts of the Battle of Rathmines 1649'. *Irish Sword*, XXI, 1999

Firth, C. H. 'The Battle of Dunbar'. *Transactions of the Royal Historical Society*, XIV, 2nd Series, 1900

— *Cromwell's Army: A History of the English Soldier During the Civil Wars, the Commonwealth and the Protectorate*. 1902, reprinted 1967

—'The Later History of the Ironsides'. *Transactions of the Royal Historical Society*, N.S. XV, 1901

—'Marston Moor'. *Transactions of the Royal Historical Society*, N.S. XII, 1898

— *Oliver Cromwell and the Rule of the Puritans*. Oxford, 1900

— 'The Raising of the Ironsides'. *Transactions of the Royal Historical Society*, N.S. XIII, 1899

— and Davies G. *The Regimental History of Cromwell's Army*. 2 vols., Oxford, 1940

Fissel, M. C. *The Bishops' War, Charles I's Campaigns Against Scotland, 1638–1640*. Cambridge, 1994

— *English Warfare, 1511–1642*. 2001

— ed. *War and Government in Britain, 1598–1650*. Manchester, 1991

Fitzpatrick, B. *Seventeenth Century Ireland: The Wars of Religion*. Dublin 1988

Fletcher, A. *The Outbreak of the English Civil War*. 1989 ed.

Foard, G. *Naseby, the Decisive Campaign*. Whitstable, 1995

Foucault, M. *Discipline and Punish, The Birth of the Prison*. 1991

Fraser, A. *Cromwell, Our Chief of Men*. 1973

Fuller, J. F. C. *The Generalship of Alexander the Great*. 1998 ed.

— *The Generalship of Ulysses S. Grant*. 1991

— *Julius Caesar: Man, Soldier and Tyrant*. 1998 ed.

Furgol, R. M. 'Scotland turned Sweden: The Scottish Covenanters and the Military Revolution, 1638–1651' in Morrill, J. ed. *The Scottish National Covenant in its British Context*. Edinburgh, 1990

Gardiner, S. R. *History of the Commonwealth and Protectorate*. 4 vols., 1988 ed.

— *History of England*. 10 vols., 1900

— *History of the Great Civil War*. 4 vols., 1987 ed.

— *Oliver Cromwell*. 1901

— *Puritan Revolution, 1603–1660*. 1920

Gaunt, P. 'The Battle of Gainsborough'. *Cromwelliana*, 1998

— ed. *Cromwell 400*. 1999

— *The Cromwellian Gazetteer*. Stroud, 1987

— ed. *The English Civil War*. Oxford, 2000

— *Oliver Cromwell*. 1996

Gentles, Ian. 'The choosing of the Officers for the New Model Army'. *Historical Research*, LXVII, 1994, pp 264–285

—*The New Model Army in England, Ireland and Scotland, 1645–1653*. 1992

—'The New Model Officer Corps in 1647 A Collective Portrait'. *Social History*, XXII, 1997

— 'Why Men fought in the British Civil Wars, 1639–1652'. *History Teacher*, XXVI, 1993

— Morrill, J. and Worden, B. eds. *Soldiers, Writers and Statesmen of the English Revolution*. Cambridge, 1998

Goldsworthy, A. *In the Name of Rome, the Men who won the Roman Empire*. 2003

Grainger, J. D. *The Last Anglo-Scottish War 1650–1652*. East Linton, 1997

Green, H. *The Battlefields of Britain and*

Ireland. 1983 ed.

Gregg, P. *Freeborn John: A Biography of John Lilburne.* 1986 ed.

Griffith, P. *Battle Tactics of the American Civil War.* Marlborough, 2001

Guthrie, W. P. *Battles of the Thirty Years' War from White Mountain to Nordlingen, 1618–1635.* 2002

— *The Later Thirty Years' War from the Battle of Wittstock to the treaty of Westphalia.* 2003

Hale, J. R. *War and Society in Renaissance Europe, 1450–1620.* 1985

Hall, B. S. *Weapons and Warfare in Renaissance Europe, Gunpowder, Technology and Tactics.* Baltimore, 1997

Haller, W. 'The Word of God in the New Model Army'. *Church History,* XIX, 1950

Hamilton, R. 'The Mind of Cromwell'. *Pax: review of the Benedictines of New Caldey Abbey.* XL, 1950

Hanlon, G. *The Twilight of a Military Tradition: Italian Aristocrats and European Conflicts, 1560–1800.* 1998

Hanson, V. D. *The Western Way of War: Infantry Battle in Classical Greece.* 2nd ed., 2000

Haykin, M. A. G. *To Honour God, The Spirituality of Oliver Cromwell.* Ontario, 1999

Hexter, J. H. *Reign of King Pym.* Harvard, 1979 ed.

Hill, C. *The English Bible in the Seventeenth Century Revolution.* Harmondsworth, 1994

— *God's Englishman.* 1970

Holmes, C. *The Eastern Association in the English Civil War.* Cambridge, 1974

— *Seventeenth Century Lincolnshire.* Lincoln, 1980

Holmes, R. *Preston, 1648.* Market Drayton, 1985

Hoover, C. 'Cromwell's Status and Pay in 1646–47'. *Historical Journal,* XXIII, 1980

Hore, P. H. ed. *History of the Town and County of Wexford.* 6 vols., 1900–11

Horton, R. F. *Oliver Cromwell: A Study in Personal Religion.* 1897

Houston, S. J. *James I.* 2nd ed., 1995

Hughes, B. P. *Firepower: Weapons Effectiveness on the Battlefield, 1630–1850.* 1974

Hutton, R. *Charles II, King of England, Scotland and Ireland.* Oxford, 1989

— *The Royalist War Effort.* 2nd ed., 1999

Iagomarsino, D. and Wood C. J. eds. *The Trial of Charles I, A Documentary History.* 1989

Inderwick, F. A. *The Interregnum.* 1891

Jones, J. R. *Charles II, Royal Politician.* 1987

Keegan, J. *The Face of Battle.* 1978

— *The Mask of Command.* 1988

Kellett, A. *Combat Motivation, the Behaviour of Soldiers in Battle.* Boston, 1982

Kenyon, J. *The Civil Wars of England.* 1989

— and Ohlmeyer, J. eds. *The Civil Wars: A Military History of England, Scotland and Ireland, 1638–1660.* Oxford, 2002 ed.

Kerr, A. W. M. *An Ironside of Ireland, the Remarkable Career of Lieut-General Michael Jones.* 1923

King, D. W. 'The Establishments and Personnel of the Cromwellian Train of Artillery in Ireland, 1649–1660'. *Journal of the Society for Army Historical Research,* LIII, 1975

— 'Ralph Margery, Cromwell's Plain Russet Coated Captain'. *Journal of the Society for Army Historical Research,* LVIII, 1980

Kishlansky, M. *The Rise of the New Model Army.* Cambridge, 1983

— 'What Happened at Ware?' *Historical Journal,* XXV, 1982

Knoppers, L. L. *Constructing Cromwell, Ceremony, Portrait and Print, 1645–1661.* Cambridge, 2000

— 'The Politics of Portraiture: Oliver Cromwell and the Plain Style'. *Renaissance Quarterly,* LI, 1998

Leinhan, P. *Confederate Catholics at War, 1641–49.* Cork, 2001

— 'Confederate Military Strategy' in Ó Sichrú, M. ed. *Kingdom in Crisis: Ireland in the 1640s.* Dublin, 2001

Lenihan, M. *Limerick, Its History and Antiquities.* 1866, 1967 ed.

Liddell Hart, B. H. *Great Captains Unveiled: From Genghis Khan to General Wolfe.* 1989

— *The Strategy of the Indirect Approach.* 1946

Lindley, K. J. 'The Impact of the 1641 Rebellion upon England and Wales 1641–5'. *Irish Historical Review,* XVIII, 1972

Lowe, J. 'Some Aspects of the Wars in Ireland, 1641–1649'. *Irish Sword*, IV, 1960

Lucas Philips, C. E. *Cromwell's Captains*. 1938

Lynn, J. *Giant of the Grand Siecle: The French Army 1610–1715*. Cambridge, 1997

Lyons, P. 'The Cromwellian Assault on Clonmel' in O'Connell, P. and Darmody, W. C. *Siege of Clonmel Commemoration; Tercentenary Souvenir Record*. Clonmel, 1950

MacCormack, J. R. *Revolutionary Politics in the Long Parliament*. Cambridge, Mass., 1973

Mac Cuarta, B. ed. *Ulster 1641, Aspects of the Rising*. Belfast, 1993

Markham, C. R. *The Life of the Great Lord Fairfax*. 1870

Marshall, A. *Intelligence and Espionage in the Reign of Charles II*. 1994

— 'Killing No Murder'. *History Today*, LIII, 2003

Marshall, S. L. A. *Men Against Fire: The Problem of Battle Command*. Norman, Oklahoma, 2000 ed.

Masson, D. *The Life of John Milton and History of his Time*. 7 vols., 1859–94

Mendle, M. ed. *The Putney Debates of 1647: the Army, the Levellers and the English State*. Cambridge, 2001

Miller, P. *The New England Mind: The Seventeenth Century*. Boston, 1961

Money, W. *The First and Second Battles of Newbury and the Siege of Donnington Castle*. 2nd ed., 1884

Morrill, J. 'King Killing No Murder: Cromwell in 1648'. *Cromwelliana*, 1998

— 'The Making of Oliver Cromwell' in Morrill, J. ed. *Oliver Cromwell and the English Revolution*. 1990

— 'Textualising and Contextualising Oliver Cromwell'. *Historical Journal*, XXXIII, 1990

Mukerji, C. *Territorial Ambitions and the Gardens of Versailles*. Cambridge, 1997

Murphey, R. *Ottoman Warfare, 1500–1700*. 1990

Murphy, D. *Cromwell in Ireland. A History of Cromwell's Irish Campaign*. Boston, 1893

New, J. F. H. 'Cromwell and the Paradoxes of Puritanism'. *Journal of British Studies*, V, 1965

Newman, P. R. *Marston Moor July 2nd 1644 – The Sources and the Site*. Borthwick Institute of Historical Research No. 13, York, 1978

— and Roberts, P. R. *Marston Moor, The Battle of the Five Armies*. Pickering, 2003

Noble, M. *Memoirs of the Protectoral House of Cromwell*. 2 vols., Birmingham, 1784

Nolan, L. E. *Cavalry: Its History and Tactics*. 1853 ed.

Nusbacher, A. 'Civil Supply in the Civil War: Supply of Victuals to the New Model Army on the Naseby Campaign, 1–14 June 1645. *English Historical Review*, CXV, 2000

Ohlmeyer, J. H. 'A Failed Revolution? The Irish Confederate War in its European Context'. *History Ireland*, III, 1995

— *Ireland from Independence to Occupation, 1641–1660*. Cambridge, 1995

— 'Irish privateers during the Civil War, 1642–50' *Mariner's Mirror*, LXXVI, 1990

Ollard, R. *The Escape of Charles II*. 1996

Oman, C. *The Art of War in the Middle Ages*. 2 vols., 1991 ed.

— *The Art of War in the Sixteenth Century*. 1937

O'Sullivan, H. 'Military Operations in County Louth in the Run up to Cromwell's Storming of Drogheda'. *County Louth Archaeological and Historical Journal*, XXII, 1990

Palmer, W. G. 'Oliver St John and the Middle Group in the Long Parliament, 1643–1645: A Reappraisal'. *Albion*, XIV, 1982

Parker, G. *The Military Revolution, 1500–1800, Military Innovation and the Rise of the West*. Cambridge, 1988

— *The Thirty Years' War*. 1987 ed.

Parrott, D. *Richelieu's army: War, Government and Society in France, 1624–1642*. Cambridge, 2001

— 'Strategy and Tactics in the Thirty Years War'. *Militargeschichtliche Mitteilungen*, II, 1985

Paul, R. S. *The Lord Protector: Religion and Politics in the Life of Oliver Cromwell*. 1955

Peacey, J. T. ed. *The Regicides and the Execution of Charles I*. Basingstoke, 2001

Peachey, S. and Turton, A. *Old Robin's Foot,*

The Equipping and Campaigns of Essex's Infantry, 1642–1645. 1987

Perceval-Maxwell, M. *The Outbreak of the Irish Rebellion of 1641.* Dublin, 1998

Piper, D. 'The Contemporary Portrait of Oliver Cromwell'. Walpole Society, XXXIV, 1958

Quintrell, B. W. *Charles I, 1625–1640.* 1993

— 'Oliver Cromwell and Distraint of Knighthood'. *Bulletin of the Institute of Historical Research,* LVII, 1984

Raymond, J. 'An Eye-Witness to King Cromwell'. *History Today,* XLVII, 1997

Reid, S. *All the King's Armies: A Military History of the English Civil War 1642–1651.* Staplehurst, 1998

— *The Campaigns of Montrose, A Military History of the Civil War in Scotland 1639–1646.* Edinburgh, 1990

— *The Scots Armies of the English Civil Wars.* 1999

Reilly, T. *Cromwell, An Honourable Enemy.* 1999

Revard, S. P. *The War in Heaven, Paradise Lost and the Tradition of Satan's Rebellion.* 1980

Richardson, R. C. ed. *Images of Oliver Cromwell; Essays by and for Roger Howell.* Manchester, 1993

Roberts, M. *Essays in Swedish History.* 1967

— *Gustavus Adolphus: A History of Sweden 1611–1632.* 2 vols., 1953, 1958

— *Gustavus Adolphus and the Rise of Sweden.* 1973

Ross, W. G. 'Military Engineering during the Great Civil War, 1642–9'. *Professional Papers of the Corps of Royal Engineers,* XIII. 1888

Rubinstein, H. L. *Captain Luckless: James, First Duke of Hamilton 1606–1649.* Edinburgh, 1975

Russell, C. *The Causes of the English Civil War.* 1990

— *The Fall of the British Monarchies, 1637–1642.* Oxford, 1991

Seel, G. 'Cromwell's Trailblazer? Re-Interpreting the Earl of Essex'. *History Today,* XLV. 1995

Sharpe, J. *Early Modern England, A Social History, 1550–1760.* 1987

Sharpe, K. *The Personal Rule of Charles I.* Yale, 1992

Shaw, H. *The Levellers.* 1968

Shay, J. *Achilles in Vietnam: Combat Trauma and the Undoing of Character.* 1994

Sherwood, R. *The Court of Oliver Cromwell.* 1977

Simms, J. G. 'Cromwell's Siege of Waterford 1649'. *War and Politics in Ireland, 1649–1730.* 1980

Smith, A. 'The Image of Cromwell in Folklore and Tradition'. *Folk-Lore,* LXXIX, 1968

Snow, V. F. *Essex the Rebel, The Life of Robert Devereux, the Third Earl of Essex, 1591–1646.* Lincoln, Nebraska, 1970

Sproxton, J. 'From Calvin to Cromwell through Beard'. *Journal of European Studies,* XXV. 1995

Stearns, R. P. *The Strenuous Puritan, Hugh Peter, 1598–1660.* Urbana, Illinois, 1954

Stevenson, D. *Revolution and Counter Revolution in Scotland, 1644–1651.* 1977

Stouffer, S. 'The American Soldier: Combat and its Aftermath'. *Studies in Psychology in World War II,* 4 vols., Princeton, 1949

Tallett, F. *War and Society in Early Modern Europe, 1495–1715.* 1997

Taylor, F. L. *The Art of War in Italy, 1494–1529.* Westport, Conn., 1973 ed.

Taylor, S. A. G. *The Western Design, An Account of Cromwell's Expedition to the Caribbean.* 1969

Temple, R. K. G. 'The Original Officer List of the New Model Army'. *Bulletin of the Institute of Historical Research,* LIX, 1986

Terry, C. S. *The Life and Campaigns of Alexander Leslie, First Earl of Leven.* 1899

— 'The Scottish campaign in Northumberland and Durham'. *Archaeologia Aeliana,* NS XXI. 1899

Thomas, K. *Religion and the Decline of Magic: Studies in Popular Beliefs in 16th and 17th century England.* Harmondsworth, 1999 ed.

Tibbutt, H. G. *Colonel John Okey, 1606–1662.* Publications of the Bedfordshire Historical Record Society, XXXV. Streatley, 1955

Tincey, J. *Ironsides, English Cavalry, 1588–1688.* 2002

— *Soldiers of the English Civil War (2) Cavalry.* 2003

Tucker, J. and Linstock, L. S. W. eds. *The English Civil War, A Military Handbook.* 1972

Turton, A. *The Chief Strength of the Army: Essex's Horse (1642–1645)*. No date

Tyacke, N. *Anti-Calvinists, The Rise of English Arminianism, c. 1590–1649*. Oxford, 1990

Underdown, D. *Pride's Purge: Politics in the English Revolution*. 1985

Wanklyn, M. A. G. 'Royalist Strategy in the South of England, 1642–1644'. *Southern History*, III, 1981

Watts, M. *The Dissenters from the Reformation to the French Revolution*. Oxford, 1985 ed.

Wedgwood, C. V. 'The Covenanters in the First Civil War'. *Scottish Historical Review*, XXXIX, 1960

— *The King's War, 1641–1647*. 1977 ed.

— *The Trial of Charles I*. 1967 ed.

Welby, A. C. 'Belton Fight, Cromwell's Victory Near Grantham, 15 May 1643'. *Lincolnshire Notes and Queries*, XV, 1915

West, J. *Oliver Cromwell and the Battle of Gainsborough*. 1992

Weyman, S. J. 'Oliver Cromwell's Kinsfolk'. *English Historical Review*, VI, 1891

Wheeler, J. S. *Cromwell in Ireland*. Dublin 1999

— *The Irish and British Wars, 1637–1654, Triumph, Tragedy and Failure*. 2002

— 'The Logistics of the Cromwellian Conquest of Scotland, 1650–51'. *War and Society*, X, 1992

— 'Logistics and Supply in The Cromwellian Conquest of Ireland', Fissel, M. ed., *War and Government in Britain 1598–1650*. Manchester, 1991

White Cooper, W. 'Historical Notes Concerning Certain Illnesses, the Death and Disinterment of Oliver Cromwell'. *Dublin Quarterly Journal of Medical Science*, V, 1848

Willis Bund, J. W. *The Civil Wars in Worcestershire*. 1905

Williams, J. B. 'Cromwell's Massacre at Wexford'. *Irish Ecclesiastical Review*, II, 1913

Wilson, J. *Fairfax*. 1985

Wood, C. *Nottinghamshire in the Civil War*. Oxford, 1937

Woolrych, A. *Battles of the English Civil War*. 1961

— 'Cromwell as a Soldier' in Morrill, J. ed. *Oliver Cromwell and the English Revolution*. 1990

— *From Commonwealth to Protectorate*. Oxford, 1982

— *Soldiers and Statesmen, The General Council of the Army and its Debates, 1647–1648*. Oxford, 1987

Worden, B. 'Oliver Cromwell and the Sin of Achan', Beales, D. and Best, D. eds., *History, Society and the Churches: Essays in Honour of Owen Chadwick*. Cambridge, 1985

— 'Providence and Politics in Cromwellian England'. *Past and Present*, CIX, 1985

— *Roundhead Reputations, the English Civil War and the Passions of Posterity*. 2001

— *The Rump Parliament*. Cambridge, 1973

Young, P. *Edgehill, The Campaign and the Battle*. Gloucestershire, 1998 ed.

— *Marston Moor: The Campaign and the Battle*. 1997 ed.

— *Naseby*. 1985

— and Emberton, W. *Sieges of the Great Civil War, 1642–1646*. 1978

— and Holmes, R. *The English Civil War, A Military History of the Three Civil Wars 1642–1651*. 1974 ed.

Zagorin, P. 'The Political Beliefs of John Pym to 1629'. *English Historical Review*, CIX, 1994

Unpublished works

Jones, F. *The Role and Effectiveness of Cavalry in the English Civil War, 1642–1645*. Unpublished M.Phil, Wolverhampton, 2000

Marshall, A. *Fierce and Bloody: The Trial of Thomas Harrison, 1660*. Unpublished paper, 2003

INDEX